COIN

1992 YEAR BOOK
compiled by the staff of
COIN MONTHLY

contents

Editor .... MARION HORNETT
Assistant Editor ⎫
Data Collator   ⎬ .... PHILI IPA HUNT
Editorial Assistant .... JAN MIDDLETON

Advertisement Manager
.... KAREN SULLIVAN-PAIN
Advertisement Executives .... SUE BRETT
.... PAM BAILEY

Publisher .... PETER WILLIAMS

PUBLISHED BY: Numismatic Publishing Co.
Sovereign House, Brentwood, Essex CM14 4SE, England
(0277) 219876.

PRINTED: in Great Britain

NEWS TRADE SALES BY: SM Distribution,
6 Leigham Court Rd, Streatham, London SW16 2PG.
081-677 8111.

BOOK TRADE SALES BY: Argus Books Ltd,
Boundary Way, Hemel Hempstead, Hertfordshire. HP2
7ST. (0442) 66551

Coin Year Book - 1992
1. Numismatics — Collectors and collecting — Periodicals
I. Title
737'.05 CJ1

ISBN 0 901265 27 6

© Copyright 1991
NUMISMATIC
PUBLISHING
COMPANY

COIN 1992 YEAR BOOK

Welcome to this the 25th edition of the *Coin Year Book*. Most of the regular authors of *Coin Monthly* have contributed to the new editorial features in the 1992 edition.

There have been several important changes to numismatics since Peter Williams published the first edition in 1967 – the most dramatic being the change-over to decimal coinage in 1971. Our lead article this year is by James Mackay and he examines the rebirth of 'the écu'. One wonders if the editor of the 50th edition of the *Year Book* will be looking back on the écu as our common currency!

The 'Notes to Note' feature, by Alistair Gibb, portrays an update on the latest designs and specifications of UK banknotes and includes the controversial new £5 note. Mr Gibb also advises us on investment and coin care.

C W Hill writes about a 'Silver Celebration', and 'Numismatists' Library', another of his features, incorporates several new titles. This feature is always updated as much as possible, but we do stress that prices fluctuate and that books can be out of print, so you may have to shop around for some of the titles. Look out for C W Hill's 'Collectors' Bookshelf' which appears every month in *Coin Monthly*.

John Anthony, another regular author to *Coin Monthly* who provides us with an endless collection of interesting tales for his 'Among the Ancients' feature, has written a 'Guide to Tokens and Allied Coins' in this *Year Book* publication. This appears together with his regular 'Collecting Roman' article. In his spare time, John Anthony kindly replies to your numerous questions in his regular Q&A section.

From the other side of the Atlantic, Timothy Benford writes an interesting feature on the 'US Constitution Medals and their Designers', and also included in this edition is Dennis G Blair's new guide, explaining medal terms, symbols and valuation factors.

The *Year Book* has to include some repeated articles, such as 'Coin Grading', 'Numismatic Dictionary' and 'UK Currency', as it is a complete reference work on all aspects of coin collecting – however, Peter Walker regularly updates 'Collecting and the Law', to warn us of any new unknown pitfalls.

A great deal of work goes into compiling the updated prices for the 'blue' market movement pages and for the directory section. It never ceases to amaze me that so many cards are 'mislaid' or 'lost in the post' each year, despite them being meticulously dispatched in mid-January. Come on, chaps, try to complete your cards on time next year, after all it is a free service and it would save us a great deal of hassle! Please remember to forward your latest lists and diary dates for your fairs, auctions and club activities to *Coin Monthly* – again, this is a free service.

1991 has seen some splendid auctions, culminating in the successful Sotheby's Bunker-Hunt sale – these are reported in the 'Auction News' column of the monthly magazine.

It was heartening to learn that the Royal Numismatic Society is encouraging our young collectors. It has offered six bursaries of £200.00 each to enable students in full-time education to attend the International Numismatic Congress in Brussels, on 8-12 September 1991.

To end on a non-numismatic note, a new hobby has recently evolved – fusilately – the collecting of telephone cards. It falls somewhere between numismatics and philately, and has quite a following of collectors. Yves Arden wrote a three-part article on the subject in the February, March and May 1991 issues of *Coin Monthly* – I understand that even our local football team has recently issued colourful cards depicting the team and bearing the club's crest. I wonder if they will increase in value should the team be elevated to Division 1? However, I can't quite imagine anyone discovering a hoard of telephone cards in years to come!

I hope you will continue to enjoy your profitable hobby – ed.

THE RISE, FALL AND REBIRTH OF THE ECU

by James Mackay

A common currency

One of the long-standing aims of the European Community has been the establishment of a common currency. In the 1970s the hypothetical unit was referred to as the Eurodollar, for want of a better or more acceptable term. This avoided national susceptibilities; the Germans might have objected to a Eurofranc, while the French would certainly have repudiated the Euromark, and only the British and Irish would have been happy with the Europound. In the 1980s, however, a new expression gradually won acceptance. This was the rather prosaic and cumbersome European Currency Unit. Inevitably it was soon known simply by its initials – ECU.

It was regarded, for the time being, as a purely notional unit, convertible into the various real currencies of the EC countries, but it was not long before attempts were made to give it real substance.

This began in Belgium, appropriately

The 1991 20 ECU coin recently issued by the Belgian Royal Mint to celebrate the 40th anniversary of King Baudouin's reign

enough, as Brussels is the headquarters of the Community. The paying of a restaurant bill by means of a cheque made out in ECU can only be regarded as a stunt, but the striking of coins denominated in ECU had to be taken more seriously. These gold and silver coins, struck in 1987, portrayed the Emperor Charles V (1500-58).

The choice was an excellent one, for in his person he embodied the spirit of Europe. He was born in Ghent in what is now Belgium, the son of Philip of Burgundy and Joanna of Castile. In 1506 Philip died, so Charles became Count of Burgundy. In 1516 his grandfather, Ferdinand of Aragon, died and two years later Charles was proclaimed King of Spain.

Shortly afterwards his paternal grandfather Maximilian died, and Charles now inherited the vast Habsburg dominions as well as the duchy of Wurttemberg. By the time he was twenty he ruled over Spain, Belgium, the Netherlands, Luxembourg, Austria and a very large part of what is now Germany. His dominions included Navarre and Franche Comte in what is now France, and the kingdoms of Naples, Sicily and Sardinia. On 23 October 1520 he was crowned Holy Roman Emperor at Aachen. Thus he was the ruler over a very substantial part of Europe, incorporating many of the countries which now form the EC. It might be added that he also drove the Turks out of central Europe (1532), conquered Tunisia (1535) and completed the Spanish conquest of Latin America, the Indies and the Philippines.

These Belgian coins were not intended for general circulation, and the precise status of some of the other ECU issues of more recent times has also been questioned. In 1990, for example, gold pieces denominated 100 and 50 ECU were produced in Ireland and very handsome they are too, with their harp and stag motifs; but a claim that they were legal tender was immediately repudiated by the Irish government.

In 1990 the Netherlands issued a crown-sized silver coin denominated 10 ECU, and subsequently France issued gold, platinum and silver coins. The latter mark an important breakthrough, being denominated in both national and European currencies. The obverse of the gold and platinum coins bears the value of 500 francs, whereas the value on the reverse is given as 70 ECU.

Curiously enough, the 100 franc silver coin is tariffed at 15 ECU; on that basis one would have expected the gold and platinum coins to be tariffed at 75 ECU. The common reverse of these coins bears a stylised portrait of the Emperor Charlemagne (742-814).

In some respects Charlemagne's life and career paralleled those of Charles V. He began as ruler of the Franks but later became King of the Lombards and then acquired the Greek provinces of Venetia, Istria and Dalmatia. He conquered the Saxons and the Bavarians and in 796 subjugated the Avars of Hungary. He then turned his attention to Spain and campaigned against the Moors. In 800 he was crowned emperor at Rome, but till his death in 814 he preferred to govern his vast dominions from his palace in Aachen which became effectively the nerve centre of the Holy Roman Empire.

Another point about these French coins is the manner in which the value was expressed on the reverse, eg 70 ECUS. This shows how what had started as a set of initials had developed into an acronym – 'Ecu' – hence the plural form. In effect, however, it signalises what the French regard as something of a national triumph, for the initials ECU actually spell out the French word for 'shield', and this was, in fact, used as the name of the principal coinage unit for many centuries.

Introduced by King Louis IX

The écu was introduced by King Louis IX in 1266 in an attempt to reinstitute gold coinage in France. Officially this handsome gold coin was called the *denier d'or à l'écu* (literally the gold penny of the shield) from its principal motif showing a shield bearing the lilies of France. It contained 4.2g of pure gold, 58.3 being struck from a fine mark of Paris measure. It was the same weight as the silver gros tournois which Louis had previously introduced, but had ten times its value. This gave a gold-silver ratio of 10:1 which seriously undervalued the écu and explains why it failed to get into general circulation. Very few examples are now extant and even references to it in contemporary literature are rare. When Philip III succeeded Louis in 1270 the écu was quietly dropped.

After more than half a century in limbo it was revived in January 1337 when Philip VI ordained a new issue of the écu. These were slightly heavier than before, being coined at the rate of 54 to the Paris mark, but were more sensibly tariffed at 20 sols tournois, twice the previous value.

The name of the earlier gold coin may have been revived, but not its motifs, for the new écu had as its obverse a full-length seated portrait of the king holding an

A Philip VI 1337 écu d'or

1338 lion d'or

1339 pavillon d'or

1340 couronne d'or

heraldic shield in his left hand. The reverse had a very elaborate cross in a quatrefoil. This was, in fact, the design used for the more aptly named *chaise d'or* (from the elaborate gothic throne) which had been introduced in 1303, but when Philip VI re-issued it in 1337 as a much lighter coin he deliberately revived the name of the écu to distinguish it.

This ruse was unsuccessful and on 31 October 1338 the écu was replaced by the *lion d'or*. Superficially the design was much the same, but the heraldic crown was dropped, and the King's feet rested on a lion. It was followed in short order by the *pavillon d'or* (showing the king seated in a tent (1339) and the *couronne d'or* (1340) showing a crown on a ground of fleur de lis. Other exotically named gold pieces ensued before the gold franc brought order out of chaos in 1360.

The écu á la couronne

In 1385 the council of regency for the infant Charles VI replaced the gold franc with a new coin known as the *écu à la couronne* (the shield of the crown), from the large crown surmounting the shield on the obverse. The reverse bore a large quatrefoil containing a cruciform arrangement of lilies, with a star at the centre. This was to be the standard gold coin for the next 200 years, providing a stabilising influence in a period of great economic and monetary upheaval. Its weight was gradually reduced, but its nominal value increased more sharply during the Hundred Years War.

After the disastrous defeat at Agincourt (1415) the écu, now debased and much lighter in weight, was raised in value to 30 sols tournois.

The Dauphin Charles struck similar but even more debased écus at the mints south of the Loire. In Normandy Henry V of England struck his own version of the écu. This was the *salut d'or*, which took its name from the salutation or greeting extended by the Archangel Gabriel to the Virgin Mary, depicted in the upper part of the obverse.

The lower portion, however, showed two shields side by side, bearing the arms of France and England.   •

FIJIAN GOLD

NEW MINT... NEW COINS

In the remote and exotic South Pacific Islands of Fiji they mine a very special kind of Gold. From deep in the heart of an extinct volcano a peculiar alloy of gold and silver is used in its rich, raw condition to make the Fijian national gold coinage.

The new **"Pacific Sovereign Mint"** has been constructed at the mine head and very individual techniques employed to create the stunning coins of this mould breaking issue. Hammer struck on random buttons of gold, the forms are reminiscent of the coinage of ancient Greece. Each coin is edge numbered, photographically recorded and certified as being of a minimum eighteen carat fineness. Each coin is manually overstruck with a mintmark and datemark.

In Fiji, they make coins that reflect the warm hearts and welcoming smiles of a relaxed and fun loving nation.

All this combines to make every coin unique, the only legal tender issue in the world to abandon an obsession with sameness and revel in the inidividuality of each coin.

| ONE OUNCE TABUA | QUARTER OUNCE BURE KALOU | HALF OUNCE BATI |

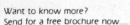

Want to know more?
Send for a free brochure now.....

Send to Pacific Sovereign Mint
at one of the addresses
listed quoting dept. **CYB**

Marketing Office
Ermington Mill, Ivybridge,
South Devon UK Pl 21 9NT
Telephone: 0548 830071
Fax: 0548 830046

US Office
Suite 236, 830 N Tejon Street,
Colorado Springs, CO 80903 USA
Telephone: 719 475 7979

Pacific Sovereign Mint
Vatukoula, Fiji.

This theme was repeated under Henry VI, who also introduced a silver (or rather debased billon) version known as the *grand blanc aux écus*, from the twin shields on the obverse, with the King's name, slightly abbreviated, inscribed above them. The *angelot d'or*, introduced in 1427 in the English dominions in France, had an angel displaying the twin shields.

The design of the écu itself remained unchanged till 1475 when Louis XI added the sun emblem and for this reason the coin came to be known as the *écu au soleil*. By 1515 the écu was tariffed at 36.75 sols. Under Francis I it was lightened and debased in 1519 but continued for a while at the same value. By the time of his death in 1547 it had risen to 45 sols, a depreciation of 28% in the course of this reign.

In 1541 Francis introduced the *écu d'or à la croisette*. The obverse continued to bear a crowned heraldic shield but the reverse now showed a small plain cross in the centre. The écus and demi-écus struck for circulation in Dauphiné were similar, but in the shield the arms of France (lilies) and Dauphiné (a dolphin) appeared in alternate quarters. Under his successor Henry II (1547-59) the *écu à la croisette* was minted at first, but in 1552 it was followed by the *écu aux croissants*, so-called because the shield was now flanked by two crescents.

Henry also introduced a parallel series in 1549, consisting of the *henri d'or* with its multiple and sub-division. His portrait graced the obverse, while the heraldic shield was transferred to the reverse.

In 1577 the traditional method of accounting using the £sd (livres, sols, deniers) tournois system was abolished. The opportunity was taken to stabilise the value of the écu at 3 livres tournois and the new monetary system was to be based upon it, with all prices henceforth quoted in écus. This was an important and radical change, as it now meant that the coinage and the currency were one and the same. As part of this policy two new silver coins were introduced – the franc, tariffed at one livre tournois, and the quarter-écu (which was therefore ¾ of a franc). The latter coin retained the crowned shield of its gold counterpart.

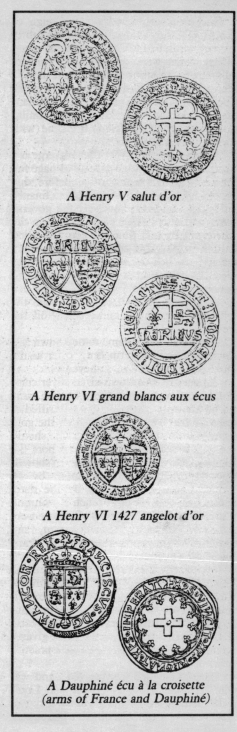

A Henry V salut d'or

A Henry VI grand blancs aux écus

A Henry VI 1427 angelot d'or

A Dauphiné écu à la croisette
(arms of France and Dauphiné)

Gold écus continued till the reign of Louis XIV and changed their motifs subtly as they continued to rise in nominal value. These coins were given exotic epithets alluding to the subtle changes made in their design. Thus we find the écu au porc épic (porcupine), écu à la salamandre (salamander, in this case an heraldic creature similar to a dragon) and the écu de Bretagne (with the Breton ermine tail emblem).

The 17th century saw France emerge as a world power. Paradoxically its coinage fell into even greater disorder than before, due to the incompetence of successive finance ministers. In 1640, however, the government of Louis XIII decided to reform the currency. By that time the écu was being struck in 23 carat gold, but its nominal value had risen to over five livres. It was decided to restrike it in 22 carat gold and tariff it at five livres exactly. The new écu bore a portrait of Louis XIII on the obverse, with the heraldic shield on the reverse.

For this reason it came to be known as a louis d'or and the term écu, so far as the gold coin went, fell into abeyance.

Conversely, the crown-sized silver coin, introduced as the louis d'argent, soon came to be known as the écu. It was tariffed at three livres, the original value of the gold écu, so it was logical that the name should be transferred to it. The obverse bore the bust of Louis XIII, but the reverse showed the heraldic shield surmounted by an ornate crown and flanked by the date. From this time till the French Revolution the crown-sized silver coins of France were officially known as écu d'argent, and unofficially the name stuck to the 5 franc piece till the end of the 19th century.

Technically speaking, the silver écu was interesting as its issue coincided with the re-activation of coining machinery at the Paris Mint. In conjunction with milling machinery, new dies were engraved by Jean Varin for the purpose and the coins were given a grained edge to prevent the age-old practice of clipping.

Louis XIII died in May 1643 and was succeeded by his five-year-old son Louis XIV. During his long reign of seventy-two years his portrait changed at frequent intervals. Many of these portrait changes were reflected in the names of the coins. Thus the earliest coins were known as écus à la mèche courte (short locks of hair), while the best-known of the later coins was the écu à la perrugue, from the full-bottomed wig which the bald Sun King sported from 1686 onwards.

Louis XIV's réformations

Three years later, when an expansionist France was embroiled in war with its neighbours, a series of desperate measures was adopted. All plate in private hands was ordered to be brought in for minting. At the same time, Louis XIV introduced what he was pleased to call his réformations. These were a series of currency reforms designed to raise revenue at the expense of the long-suffering public. The government would announce that on a certain date all major coins in circulation would be withdrawn and demonetised. Écus brought to the mint in good time, however, would be credited at 62 sols – a small premium on the official rate of 60 sols – and other coins correspondingly tariffed. They would then be struck with a new design and re-issued at 66 sols, thus giving Louis a profit of 4 sols, less minting expenses.

In practice the cost of restriking was kept to the bare minimum by not melting the obsolete coins down. Instead they were merely restruck, so that the original design tended to show through. After re-issue, the 66 sol écus would gradually be reduced to 60 sols by a series of edicts. Once they reached that level, the whole shabby process would begin all over again.

This ploy took place no fewer than five times between 1689 and 1715, then once more in the early years of Louis XV when the ministry of the Vicomte de Noailles taxed the public a swingeing 20% at one stroke. The coins of the réformation period were likewise known by the salient feature that marked the change. Thus the écu aux huit LL took its name from the eight crowned monograms of the king on the reverse. It was superseded by the écu aux palmes whose reverse had the three fleur de lis in a circle, surmounted by a crown and flanked by palm fronds. In 1726 a variation on this theme produced the *écu aux lauriers*. The reverse had the lilies in an upright crowned oval, surrounded by two sprigs of laurel. This remained the standard reverse type till 1791, but there were several changes in the obverse busts of Louis XV and Louis XVI.

John Law

As if the wretched *réformations* were not enough, the French had to endure the monetary chicanery of John Law, the Scottish adventurer.

One of his more zany notions was to abolish coinage altogether and use paper for all transactions. He did not quite succeed in this respect, as two minor subsidiary coins continued to circulate during the period when he was in power.

Law's experiments collapsed in utter disorder, causing complete financial chaos. Six years elapsed before the ministry of Cardinal Fleury was able to restore sound money, and introduce the *écu aux lauriers*. Even so, the silver écu was now tariffed at 5 livres – almost as much as the old gold écu of the previous century.

Inflation ravaged the economy

The inflation which ravaged the economy in the latter years of Louis XV and throughout the reign of his unfortunate successor was reflected in the écu which was devalued by 20% in 1740. Thereafter the écu held its value and by the outbreak of the Revolution in 1789 it was tariffed at 120 sols or six livres. Up to and including 1791 the obverse bore a bust of the king with the abbreviated Latin legend LUD. XVI D.G. FR ET NA. REX (Louis XVI, by the Grace of God, King of France and Navarre). The reverse bore the Latin motto BENEDICTUM SIT NOMEN DOMINI (Blessed be the Name of the Lord).

Following the flight of the Royal family to Varennes, their arrest and forcible return to Paris, Louis was compelled to accept the new constitution, and on 13 September 1791 he took the oath. As a constitutional monarch he was no longer King of France but King of the French, and this subtle change was reflected in the legend on the coins.

Louis XIII 1643 silver ecú d'argent

Louis XIV 1686 ecú used in Flanders

Louis XV 1715 ecú à la mêche courte

Louis XV 1725 ecú aux huit LL

On the écu the legends now appeared in French and Louis was styled ROI DES FRANCOIS. The reverse, however, was even more radically altered. In place of the crowned lilies there now appeared the winged Genius of the Revolution inscribing a tablet with the new constitution, flanked by the Gallic cock and the fasces emblem topped by the Phrygian cap of liberty. Instead of the pious invocation the motto was REGNE DE LA LOI (Rule of Law). The date according to the Christian calendar appeared below the truncation of the bust, but on the reverse a second date was inscribed in the exergue L'AN 4 DE LA LIBERTE (Year 4 of Liberty).

The designs were selected by the celebrated artist, Jean-Louis David and engraved by Augustin Dupre.

The *écu constitutionel*, as it was known, was the last in the long line of écus. In 1793 the monarchy was abolished, the King and Queen went to the guillotine and the écu, as a symbol of the *ancien régime*, was replaced by a silver coin of the same size and weight but now known more simply as the 6 livres.

The Genius of the Constitution was promoted to the obverse while the reverse was inscribed SIX LIVRES within a circular wreath surrounded by the legend REPUBLIQUE FRANCAISE, with the revolutionary year at the foot. At first the date 1793 appeared in the exergue on the obverse, but subsequently this was erased and only the revolutionary date on the reverse was shown. Confusingly this changed from Arabic to Roman numerals and while the last of the écus dated 1793 had borne the year 5, the republican six livre coins bore the year II (ie second year of the republic).

The écu has re-emerged

In 1794 even the six livres, along with the last vestiges of the old currency, was swept away and replaced by a decimal system based on the franc of one livre. Even at the height of the Revolution, however, the innate traditionalism of France asserted itself; but the écu had gone. Now it has re-emerged, albeit in the disguise of the European Currency Unit. *Plus ça change, plus c'est la même chose.*

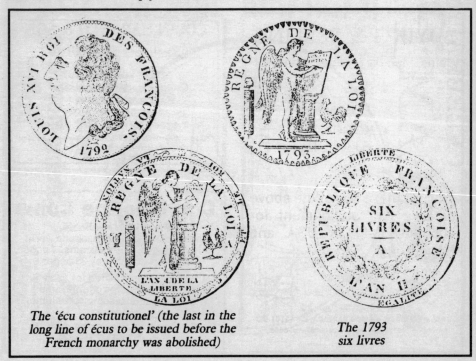

The '*écu constitutionel*' (the last in the long line of écus to be issued before the French monarchy was abolished)

The 1793 six livres

COIN
MONTHLY

BRITAIN'S BEST SELLING COIN MAGAZINE

ON SALE SECOND THURSDAY OF EACH MONTH

LATEST NEW RELEASES

BOOK REVIEWS

QUESTIONS & ANSWERS

UP-TO-DATE COIN PRICES
NEWS ROUND-UP

Interesting and Informative Features
on Coins, Tokens, Medals, Paper Money . . .

Notes to ~Note~

By Alistair Gibb

The big news on the banknote front in 1990 was, of course, the launch of the Stephenson fiver by the Bank of England.

It was brought about by the Bank's decision to shrink the sizes of the notes of all denominations – perhaps, who knows, to make room for the introduction of a £100 denomination in the not too distant future.

The new £5 note is thus the first of a whole new series which will culminate on the 300th anniversary of the founding of the Bank (1994) with a new £50 note, depicting the first Governor.

Full details of the series can be found in the August 1990 edition of *Coin Monthly*.

The launch of the first of these 'E' series notes as they are technically called, was the occasion of unprecedented publicity. The Bank even made up first and last sets of the old and new notes with the serials SE90 and A01 for sale.

This change of attitude reflected the Bank's conversion to the view that one of the best safeguards against counterfeiting is a public who take an interest in their paper money and are therefore that much more likely to be able to spot an unusual piece in circulation. The highlight of the Bank's publicity campaign was undoubtedly an 'Horizon' programme on BBC devoted entirely to the birth of the new note. The full transcript of this programme, which featured interviews with the Governor, Roger Withington, the designer, Malcolm Gill, the signatory and many others was published by the 'BBC's Broadcasting Support Services'. Those few who were lucky enough to get a copy before they ran out will be able to savour Malcolm Gill's reaction to the suggestion of his signature being printed with blue ink – *'A blue signature! It's a bit radical isn't it?'*

For collectors, the decision to change the size of the Bank's notes will bring a bonanza. All the other issuing banks will have to follow suit and downsize their notes to match.

But it also brought some bad news. The Bank of England, one must assume deliberately, has made the new dimensions of its £5 very similar to the old £1 size which is a denomination still in use in some parts of the UK. Pound notes, although popular with the general public, are expensive to maintain in circulation, not least because they have a very short average life.

That being so, it was not really surprising that some of the banks who still issued £1 notes decided to use the excuse to stop doing so.

A Bank of Scotland £1 banknote
'Unlucky for collectors – the very last Bank of Scotland
£1 notes bore the prefix E/13'

SCOTLAND

Bank of Scotland

The Bank of Scotland was the first to stop production. After 200 years of producing pound notes, the series ended with the appropriate serial of E/13.

In fact, the E serial Bank of Scotland £1 notes are of great interest to the collector. The E/1 prefix is split between two signature combinations. It starts with Risk/Pattullo and changes to Risk/Burt at E/1 0650001. (The Bank is unusual in that it does not use the first of the seven digits in this serial sequence.) The very last Bank of Scotland pound note bore the serial E/13 0650000. But don't bother hunting for it: it can be seen in the Bank's museum at The Mound in Edinburgh. The new smaller Bank of Scotland £5 notes started at EA 000001 and incorporate a number of minor design changes, including, curiously, the addition of the word 'sterling' to the promise to pay. One can only wonder if anyone asked to be paid in anything else!

For the record, the new signature combination started on the £10s at CX 600001 and on the £100s at A 225001. The starting serial for the £20 denomination is not yet known but they will be dated 1 July 1991.

Clydesdale Bank

The Clydesdale Bank also took the opportunity to withdraw its pound notes and their issue ceased at D/DW 1000000 which was dated 9 November 1988. The D series £5 ceased at D/LU 2000000 dated 28 June 1989 and was followed by the first of the small £5s dated 2 April 1990 and bearing the serial E/AA 000001. This note carries a reworked portrait of Robert Burns.

The new design (but still in the larger size) of Clydesdale £10 note was dated 7 May 1988 as this was the 150th anniversary of the first day of business of the original company. Since a smaller note will come into issue in due course, the new design ran on in serial numbers and starts at D/SW 025001.

The details of the smaller £20 note are, as I write, still confidential but the note will be available by the time this contribution appears. It will fulfil the promise made at the time of the withdrawal of the £1 note, and carry a new design featuring Robert the Bruce.

Collectors may not be aware that the Clydesdale is the only Scottish bank issuing a £50 denomination and this too will be reduced in size in due course, although there are currently no plans to reduce the £100 note.

Royal Bank of Scotland

Alone amongst the Scottish banks, the Royal has decided to retain, for the present at least, its one pound note issue. This gives it an advantage over its rivals who can now only issue pound coins to their customers and they are not liked north of the border. The smaller version of the Lord Ilay one pound design commences at prefix A/41.

The smaller £5 issue commences at A/55 and I understand the next reduced note will be its £20 denomination, which is due to appear in the autumn.

Isle of Man Government

The Manx Treasury withdrew the last of the ten shilling notes circulating in the British Isles in November 1989 at which time there were a mere 375,000 outstanding. They had of course long since changed to 50p notes, but they were an important link with the past nevertheless.

The new smaller Manx pound was announced in March 1990 and the issue commenced in the middle of the R prefix at R 500001. The opportunity was taken to rework the design with a broad white panel to the left which allows the watermark to show through more easily. While Her Majesty, known locally as the Lord of Man, has not visibly aged, provision has been made for the visually impaired in that a single raised dot has been incorporated into the bottom left of the reverse design.

The new smaller £5 was issued from 1 February 1991 with two such raised dots and a host of improved security features. The £20 appeared in April this year (1991) and the £10 will appear in April 1992 and the £50 in the spring of 1994.

Northern Bank

The Northern Bank took the opportunity of combining the change of size with the introduction of a new series of notes featuring inventors connected with Northern Ireland, including Harry Ferguson who did so much to mechanise small farms and James Martin whose aircraft ejection seats are in use all over the world. These new smaller notes first appeared in December 1988 in denominations of £5, £10 and £20 but dated 24 August 1988. They are signed by the bank's Chief Executive, S H Torrens and the series has recently been completed by the addition of the £50 and £100 denominations.

Ulster Bank

The Ulster Bank has so far only issued a £5 denomination in the new sizes, starting at prefix D, and none of the others will appear until next year.

The new smaller Jersey £1 banknote with the Hepple portrait of the Queen. (Reduced in size.)

Bank of Ireland

There is more good news for collectors from the Bank of Ireland. Their new £5 note is the first of a completely new series which will be introduced over the next two years and culminate in what is described as a 'commemorative' £50 denomination. The series re-introduces the practice of dating notes; the £5 starts at A000000 and is dated 28 August 1990. To preserve the proprieties, the notes are signed by the bank's Belfast manager, Denis Harrison, as this is a Dublin based institution.

The £5 was issued in special collector packs, both mounted and unmounted, and purchasers are given the opportunity to obtain the higher values with the same serial number. Any profit from the issue of these collector specials will be donated to charity. A splendid precedent for other issuers to follow!

CHANNEL ISLANDS

Jersey

The States of Jersey introduced their smaller notes in September 1989. The £1,

£5, £10, £20 and £50 denominations all bore the initial series AC 000001 and are known as the 'C' series. It has already been announced that the present signatory, Mr Leslie May, will be succeeded by Mr George Baird.

In the future, Jersey will also be introducing a new aid to the partially sighted by redesigning the upper right serial in solid form. This new feature will appear first on the £5 note, although no date has yet been announced.

Guernsey

The States of Guernsey too have a new signatory. Mr Brown has succeeded Mr Bull in that capacity and made his debut on the H prefix £1, splitting the letter with his predecessor. The first of his £5s appear to be the G prefix but I await confirmation that this is indeed the changeover point.

Acknowledgements: This article would not have been possible without the co-operation of our note-issuing authorities and banks. The reader will be able to infer which of them were particularly helpful.

Dates on Coins

Nearly all coins bear the date in a prominent position on one or other of their sides. With the European, part of the African, and the majority of the American countries, no problem of reading the date is experienced, since all these places use an identical dating system and the same numbers. However, in Arabic countries, and some countries of the Near and Middle East, the European alphabet and numbering system is not used, but a peculiar design of wavy lines and loops instead. This, believe it or not, tells the local population the date and usual information contained on a coin.

As we are most interested in the dates and not in a complete translation of the legends on these coins, we have included a table (on the opposite page) which gives the equivalent characters in the most widely-used foreign scripts to our European numerals. Before you start sorting through that box of unidentifiable coins, however, a word of warning. Not only do these coins use non-European characters, they use different points in time on which to base their dating systems. This is because they are not Christian countries – our dating system, which is based on the birth of Christ, would not seem logical to an ardent Mohammedan!

Here are the main dating systems in use in the world, and the methods for converting them to the Christian system of dating.

Arabic countries

The AH (after Hegira, or since the flight of Mohammed in 622 AD from Mecca to Medina) system is rather complicated, as at times the countries which use the system have used the lunar year of 354 days, about 3% fewer than our normal year of 365 days.

Let us suppose that you have an Arabic coin bearing the AH date of 1320.

3% of 1320 = 39.60,40 being the nearest whole number.

1320−40 = 1280

1280+622 = 1902 AD

Thus the equivalent date of this coin is 1902. It must be noted that some countries using western numerals also use the AH dating system.

Siam

There are three dating systems in use on these coins: (1) The 'Buddhist' era (BE). This dates from 543 BC. To convert these dates to AD subtract 543. Four numerals are found on modern issues. (2) The 'Bangkok' or 'Ratanakosinel-sok' era (RS). This dates from 1781 AD and to convert RS to AD, add 1781. These coins have a three-numeral date. (3) The 'Little' or 'Chula-Sakarat' era (CS). This dates from AD 638 – to convert these to AD add 638.

India

There are two main eras from which coin dates are calculated for this country. (1) The 'Saka' era. This originated in the southwest corner of Northern India, and starts at 78 AD. To convert a Saka date to an AD date, add 78. (2) The 'Vikrama' era. This is the minor of the two Indian systems, and has its initial point at 57 BC. To convert Vikrama (also called Samvat) dates to the AD system subtract 57.

China

Dates on Chinese coins should be read from right to left, and as the dating system is based on a most peculiar sixty year cycle, it is usually easier to trace a coin by leafing through a catalogue than to attempt to compute its true date!

foreign numeral translation

	1	2	3	4	5	6	7	8	9	0	10	100	1000
ARABIC-TURKISH	١	٢	٣	٤	٥	٦	٧	٨	٩	٠	١٠	١٠٠	١٠٠٠
MALAY PERSIAN	١	٢	٣	۴	۵	٦	٧	٨	٩	٠			
CHINESE, JAPANESE, KOREAN, ANNAMESE (Ordinary)	一	二	三	四	五	六	七	八	九		十	百	千
CHINESE, JAPANESE, KOREAN, ANNAMESE (Officia)	壹	貳	叁	肆	伍	陸	柒	捌	玖		拾	(半=½)	
INDIAN	१	२	३	४	५	६	७	८	९	०			
SIAMESE	๑	๒	๓	๔	๕	๖	๗	๘	๙	๐	๑๐	๑๐๐	
BURMESE	၁	၂	၃	၄	၅	၆	၇	၈	၉	၀			

This chart shows the characters equivalent to our numerals used to date foreign coins

THE TRIAL OF THE PYX

*A trial plate of 1279 – once believed to be the oldest
example (Modern day scholars have challenged its authenticity
and suggest it could merely be an ingot)*

COURTESY OF THE ROYAL MINT

There are those among us who cannot remember the time when the coins in current circulation contained precious metals. However, for those who can, regard with new eyes the decimal coinage which now passes through your hands. No matter how inferior you may think modern money is, look upon it kindly, for it too may have suffered the trauma of trial!

The trauma of trial!

The Trial has taken place in some form since Saxon times, though it may pre-date this period to the Roman occupation of Britain.

During the reign of Henry II (1154-1189) the Trial was being carried out at regular intervals, and by the 13th century it could be recognisable as the one used today.

In 1248 Henry III issued a writ which set the precedent for selection of jurors. He declared that the Mayor and citizens of London were . . .

'to select twelve of the more discreet and lawful men of our city of London and join with them twelve good goldsmiths of the same city, making twenty-four discreet men in all, who shall go before the Barons of our Exchequer at Westminster and examine, upon oath, together with the Barons, both the old and new money of our land, and make provision how it may be bettered; and that it be made of good silver, and that it be lawful and for the good of the realm.'

Ceremonial trial

The 'Trial of the Pyx' is a ceremony after which coins are tested for accuracy of composition and weight. Although the majority of our coinage no longer contains precious metals, the ceremony is nevertheless carried out with the same diligence as if gold and silver coins were still our everyday legal tender.

Early regulations stated that a penny should be taken from each ten-pound of coinage minted and put into a Pyx to await weighing and assaying. Today, things remain much the same, with the Mint foremen setting aside one coin, selected at random, from each batch minted.

'Pyx' is generally described as being a small box. So, not only is it acknowledged as a mint box, but one in which the consecrated host, used during Holy Communion, was placed for safe-keeping and transportation to the sick.

The 1870 'Trial of the Pyx' – (COURTESY OF THE MANSELL COLLECTION)

An early example of a Pyx, which dates back to around 1300 AD, can be found at the Public Records Office. This is a large oak box measuring about 99 x 166 x 76cm. It was formerly housed at Westminster Abbey, and was inscribed at one time with the words TRYAL PIECES.

The box was kept in the Pyx Chapel, where the sovereign's treasure chest was also put for safe-keeping. The door had seven locks which could not be opened unless the seven separate people entrusted with keys were all present at one time.

During the history of the Trial, it is rare that the reigning monarch was present, however, records have shown that King James I and King Charles I attended as observers.

Change of venue

Early Trials of the Pyx were held at Westminster Hall, the Star Chamber and, in later years, in the Exchequer at Westminster. It was not until the Coinage Act of 1870 that the Goldsmiths' Hall became the regular venue. The same Act declared the Trial was to be presided over by the Queen's Remembrancer (taking the place of the Lord Chancellor).

The Jury are seated at a table and members of the Mint take their places beside the Pyx boxes lining the walls of the Court Room. A cry of *'Pray silence for the Queen's Remembrancer'* heralds his arrival and subsequent opening address. Each juror is named and takes an oath. Their foreman is then elected and the Trial begins.

The Trial proceeds

Before each jury member there is a pair of scissors, two bowls, one of copper and one of wood and sealed bags, each containing fifty coins. The juror proceeds by cutting the seal and selecting one coin which is then placed in the copper bowl. The remaining forty-nine coins are counted and placed in the wooden bowl. The contents of the two bowls are then removed. The seal on the next bag is broken, and the process is repeated. It is the coins removed from the copper bowl which are weighed and then taken to the Assay Office.

Modern Innovation

In recent years a modern apparatus has been introduced in the form of a coin-counting machine. Approximately half the coins brought to Goldsmiths' Hall are handled by the machine, thereby speeding up the process considerably. The other half are treated in the traditional way.

In 1537 Thomas Cromwell, who was at that time the Chancellor of the Exchequer, called a 'Trial of the Coinage' from the Episcopal Mint at Canterbury. For reasons known to himself, Goldsmiths' Hall was chosen as the venue, instead of Westminster. One can only hope the coinage conformed to standard. If the coins were found lacking, at best the minter lost his job, or at worst a hand was chopped off!

At one time, the all-important trial plates were kept at the Pyx Chapel in Westminster Abbey and later in the Royal Mint. Today, they are presented for Trial by the Standards Department of the Board of Trade, though portions of the gold, silver and cupro-nickel are held by the Royal Mint, the Treasury and the Goldsmiths' Company.

Earliest trial plates

Until quite recently the example of 1279 illustrated on our introductory page was thought to be the oldest surviving silver trial plate. Modern day scholars have challenged its use as a trial plate, feeling that this is merely an ingot. Therefore, the gold and silver examples of 1477, also possessed by the Royal Mint, are acknowledged to be the earliest surviving examples.

The gold example illustrated overleaf shows the impression of an angel of Edward IV bearing the cinquefoil pierced mint-mark. The silver trial plate (not illustrated) bears the impression of a groat and has been double-struck.

The earliest trial plate in the possession of the Goldsmiths' Company dates to 1688, earlier specimens having been destroyed in a fire which razed the Assay Office to the ground.

Although there have been very few occasions when the Trial has not proceeded smoothly, one such occasion was in 1710.

Sir Isaac Newton was at that time Master of the Mint and was very distressed to learn the jury had come to the conclusion that the coins which had been brought before them fell below standard. It transpired that the trial plate being used was, in fact, of a better quality gold than the represented coins!

Delay before verdict

Although the first part of the Trial takes place during February each year, it is not

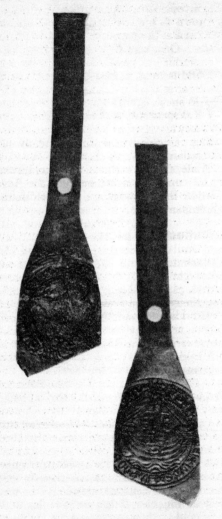

*A 1477 gold trial plate of
King Edward IV*
(COURTESY OF THE ROYAL MINT)

until May that it is reconvened for the verdict. In the intervening period the selected coins are weighed and taken along to the Assay Office for the final testing of the metals in the furnace.

On his return to Goldsmiths' Hall, the Queen's Remembrancer requests to hear the verdict of the jury. If everything is in order, the proceedings take but a short time and the jury and guests prepare for lunch.

The Pyx luncheon is normally held in the Livery Hall where, amongst the chosen guests and dignitaries, the principal speaker is the Chancellor of the Exchequer in his role as Master of the Mint.

Meanwhile, back at the Royal Mint, the boxes will again be slowly refilling. One coin selected from every freshly minted batch – one coin in every fifty standing the 'Trial of the Pyx'.

The 1991 trial

In 1990, under the 'Coinage Act of 1971', a proportion of the 1.4 million UK coins then minted were 'sent to trial'.

Included among the 1991 'Trial' coins were the new 5p pieces, Maundy money and the Queen Mother's 90th birthday £5 crown. Also in 1991, in addition to the requirement to test the UK coinage, the New Zealand Government requested that the Goldsmiths' Company test the New Zealand coins produced at the Royal Mint, in Llantrisant. Although this was not a new procedure, it did include the testing for the first time of 1 and 2 dollar New Zealand aluminium bronze-alloy coins. The High Commissioner for New Zealand was present at the proceedings.

The Trial was presided over in 1991, for the first time, by Master Topley, the Queen's Remembrancer and Senior Judge at the Strand Law Courts.

The jury's verdict was delivered on 3 May 1991 to the Chancellor of the Exchequer, Mr Norman Lamont, who is also Master of the Mint.

An article written by Lori O'Malia on the history of the 'Trial', was originally published in the July 1990 edition of *Coin Monthly*.

COLLECTING AND THE LAW

BY PETER WALKER

Coin dealers and collectors are not expected to be fully conversant with all facets of the law. Nonetheless, they are advised to make themselves aware of those provisions which may, directly or indirectly, affect their business or hobby.

Because our legislation is constantly changing, it is difficult to keep abreast of the law and even more difficult to assimilate every detail. Even so, a general knowledge of the prevailing rules and regulations is advised, and the following article purports to provide the basis of this.

The information which follows is **for guidance only** and should not be regarded as an authoritative account. Dealers and collectors with specific queries or problems should seek professional advice.

VAT registration

It is not only professional dealers and collectors who may be liable to register for Value Added Tax. It could apply to part-timers too.

The general rule is that anyone who is conducting a business, whether full-time or part-time with an annual turnover of more than £35,000, must register with HM Customs and Excise for the payment of Value Added Tax (VAT). The person to be registered can be a sole proprietor, a partnership (including a husband and wife), a limited company, a club or association, or even a charity.

Anyone of these with an annual turnover of less than the prevailing limit does not need to register, although they can make application if they feel it is advantageous.

The figure of £35,000 previously quoted was specified in the March 1991 budget, and was a 40% increase on the previous threshold. The VAT rate was also increased from 15% to 17.5%. These figures are always liable to change and dealers should remain alert to any such alterations.

HM Customs and Excise (whose address is in your local telephone directory) has a range of leaflets to guide you through the VAT complexities and if you wonder whether or not you should register, you are advised to obtain a copy of **Should I be Registered for VAT** – Leaflet No 700/1/90, which was revised in May 1990.

Once registered, there are leaflets which explain the technical aspects of trading. For example, supplies of coins, when sold as collectors' items, or for investment purposes or for other numismatic interests, are taxable at the standard rate of VAT on the full sterling price. If they are more than 100 years old, however, **and if certain conditions are met,** they may be classified as antiques, in which case a special scheme applies. If you are registered for VAT, you must normally charge VAT on any second-hand goods in exactly the same way as for new goods. But in the case of antiques or collectors' items, the scheme reduces the amount of VAT payable by making it taxable only on the margin by which the selling price exceeds the purchase price.

The full details of this scheme are contained in HM Customs and Excise Notice No 712, revised in May 1990, which is available free of charge from HM Customs and Excise offices.

For dealers in gold, or gold coins, there is a special VAT leaflet No 701/21/87, dated 1 July 1987, which outlines specific matters relating to gold and gold coins. It explains the VAT liability of transactions in gold and gold coins under the Value Added Tax Act 1983.

The general situation is that supplies and importations of gold and gold coins are standard-rated, but some transactions are specifically zero-rated and others are outside the scope of UK VAT. It contains good advice for gold dealers, pointing out that gold smuggled into the country can be forfeited. **This applies whether or not the gold is found in the possession of an innocent purchaser** and HM Customs and Excise stress that when buying gold, it is important to safeguard your own position so far as the source of the gold is concerned. You should ask where it has come from and establish its other credentials before agreeing to the deal, otherwise you could lose the lot.

Dealers and collectors who intend to use computers for their business records and accounts should seek advice on VAT accounting systems before committing themselves to a particular programme. Your VAT office will provide the necessary information.

Exportation of coins

The Export Licensing Unit of the Department of Trade and Industry deals with export enquiries and licences. A new Export of Goods (Control) Order was published on 14 February 1990 and on 1 December 1990, a new Open General Export Licence was issued. The following coins remain under control:-

Any coin, or matching set of coins, United Kingdom or foreign, which is more than fifty years old at the date of exportation and which is valued at more than £30,000 per coin or matching set.

Enquiries about the up-to-date rules on the exportation of coins should be addressed to The Department of Trade and Industry, Export Licensing Unit, Kingsgate House, 66-74 Victoria Street, London SW1E 6SW. Your contacts are Mr F J O'Byrne, Room 529 (071-215 8106) and Mr K N Harper, Room 530 (071-251 8138).

Importation of coins

The restrictions governing the importation of coins were repealed in 1979, and coins are now admissible under Open General Import Licence from any country. An individual licence is not required. Information about any duty to which the coins may be liable can be obtained from HM Customs and Excise, King's Beam House, Mark Lane, London E3 or any local Customs and Excise office. The only coins which are prohibited are Krugerrands from South Africa, and this prohibition is now on a European footing by EEC Council Regulation No 3302/86.

Thus gold coins minted in, or after, 1961 originating in the Republic of South Africa may not be imported into the UK under the Open General Import Licence unless they are in free circulation within the European community.

Further information on importing can be obtained from the Department of Trade and Industry, Import Licensing Branch, Queensway House, West Precinct, Billingham, Cleveland TS23 2NF Telephone: 0642 553671.

Coins from overseas

Before ordering coins from overseas, it is wise to first write and ask for details of the coins available, at the same time seeking advice on the mode of delivery and the required method of payment. There may be special order forms and for a reply to your postal query, you are advised to send International Reply Coupons. These are available from your post office to cover the cost of the return letter.

Check with the post office about the restrictions involved in sending coins overseas. Coins and banknotes may **not** be sent overseas as a remittance of payment, except via authorised banks, and cheques drawn on British banks should not be used. A bank will advise on the most suitable method of payment and will notify you of any regulations currently in force.

The Giro system can be used to send money overseas and details can be obtained from any post office. Full details of the prevailing conditions for sending money overseas or transferring it to a foreign land, and lists of countries that will accept money orders or Giro transfers, can be obtained from any post office. The information is also detailed in the **Post Office Guide**.

Insurance

Every coin dealer and collector must consider suitable insurance against all risks of fire, damage, burglary, theft or loss in transit, and even loss about their own premises.

The problem of the difference between the face value of a coin and its retail value must be explained to the insurance company, and there are specialist companies who offer cover of this kind.

Business names

The present rules governing business names came into effect on 1 July 1985 and replaced the provisions of 1982. The relevant legislation is The Business Names Act, 1985 and one of the main effects is that there is now no requirement for the owners of businesses to register their business names. There are, however, certain restrictions on the use of names for business purposes.

The basic rule is that any business of whatever size which is carried on under a name **other** than that of the owner or owners, must disclose the name of the owner or owners and the business address. This can be achieved very simply by placing them on business letters, written orders for goods or services, invoices and receipts issued in the course of the business, and on written demands for payment of business debts.

Another rule is that the names of the owner or owners and the business address must be displayed prominently upon the premises. This must be done so that customers and suppliers can easily read them; furthermore, these names and addresses must be disclosed in writing upon request by anyone who has done or discussed matters relating to that business. Failure to comply with these requirements is a criminal offence.

There are no formal requirements for the size and design of those details, other than they must be legible. Clearly, a large organisation which has lots of customers will require a larger sign on its premises than will a small coin dealer's shop. If the business has more than twenty partners, however, it is not necessary to list them all on business documents, although it should be stated that a full list is available for inspection at the business premises. One important aspect is that the omission of some partners' names is not permitted; they must all be listed, or none.

In some cases, the choice of a business name may require the written approval of the Secretary of State. Generally, this would occur if the name itself, or if certain words or expressions contained within it, implied that the business was in some way associated with Her Majesty's Government or a local authority, or that it had a pre-eminence or status which was not true, or if it implied specific objects or functions.

Examples of such words include: International, National, European, British, English, Scottish, Welsh, Irish, Board, Authority, Council, Association, Federation, Society, Institute, Foundation, Benevolent, Trust, Insurer, Group and so forth. Names incorporating words like Royal, Prince, Queen, Royalty, Majesty, etc, also require approval, as do those which suggest professional qualifications such as Nurse, Breeder, Apothecary, Pharmacist and so forth.

The use of a business name is the responsibility of the proprietor; he or she must ensure that it conforms with the prevailing regulations.

One area to avoid is a name which sounds or looks too like that of another company, for example Eye-See-Eye, Prodential, Arrods or Marcs and Spencer. With millions of names in use, however, there is bound to be some which are identical. Neither the Business Names Act nor the Companies Act restricts this, but if someone did call his company Marcs and Spencer, then Marks and Spencer plc, if they felt justified, could take out an injunction to restrict or prohibit its use.

The following are examples of some basic conditions: if Mr W Jones, a coin dealer, wants to name his business, he will have to bear in mind the notes mentioned above. If he calls his business 'W J Coins', for example, he will have to make sure that name is on his premises and stationery, etc. This does not apply if he uses his own true name, for example, if he calls his business W Jones or perhaps William Jones.

If two people, P Brown and J Smith become partners in a coin dealing business called Penny Wise or Brown Smith Enterprises, then they must follow these rules. If they called themselves P Brown and J Smith, then they would not have to comply with the new rules.

Clearly, business names which do not contain the owners' names must comply with these simple rules; examples might include Coinerama, Coins 'n' Things, etc.

It is wise for a potential coin dealer to consult a solicitor before settling the business, but free leaflets are readily available from the Registrar of Companies, Companies House, Crown Way, Maindy, Cardiff CF4 3UZ, telephone: 0222-380801, or in the case of Scottish dealers, from the Registrar of Companies, Companies Registration Office, 102 George Street, Edinburgh EH2 3DJ, telephone: 031-225 5774.

If your business is a success, you may decide to form a company and this could be either a private company or a public one. In this case, the company would have to comply with the provisions of the Companies Act 1985, further details of which can be obtained from either of the two addresses given above.

A valuable feature of Companies House is that its offices are available for a public search of their records for a small charge and this could be particularly useful if a dealer wants to avoid a name which is already in use. Microfiche files can be inspected at the addresses given, and also at Companies House, 55-71 City Road, London EC17 1BB, telephone: 071-253 9393. There are also facilities for a postal search at a small cost for those who are unable to make a personal visit. Furthermore, visitors are welcome at Companies House, Maindy, Cardiff where, by arrangement, a talk on the work will be given.

Other matters
Finding coins in public places
Coins can be acquired simply by finding them, either in the street or elsewhere like a beach, building site, on private land, modes of transport, or in public places like parks, sports stadiums and racecourses. Unfortunately, the old saying 'finders keepers' is not strictly true because if someone does find a coin, whatever its value, **in a public place**, the finder has a statutory duty to take reasonable steps to locate the owner. Anyone who keeps it without making a reasonable effort to find the owner, could be prosecuted for theft.

The simplest way to fulfil one's legal obligations when finding any property in a **public place** is to report the matter to the police. If the property is not claimed within a reasonable time, it may be restored to the person who found it, although it must be remembered that the true owner always keeps a claim to the goods.

There are, however, special rules governing the finding of treasure trove (see the following page).
Finding coins on private premises
A different situation prevails for coins and other property found on private premises and this does not generally concern the police, unless there is a suggestion that the found object was the proceeds of a crime or if there is a possibility that it is treasure trove.

Many private organisations such as large stores, business premises, hotels, hospitals, factories, British Rail, various transport organisations, airlines and other such places, have their own rules for dealing with property found on their premises or in their vehicles. In each case, the appropriate official must be informed of the discovery and local internal procedures will then be followed.

The finder does not necessarily retain any rights on such property, and each organisation will have its own rules for subsequent disposal of any finds. For example, British Rail and bus operators are bound by regulations which state that any objects found on their vehicles or premises belong to the organisation if not claimed.

Treasure trove

The law on treasure trove is among the most ancient in our country, but for the past few years it has been undergoing an extensive review. It is vital that coin collectors, especially those who use metal detectors, keep themselves abreast of the new treasure trove laws if and when they are implemented because the legislation might include items of historic value.

At the time of going to press, the treasure trove law of England and Wales applies **ONLY to objects made of, or containing, gold or silver, whether in the form of plate, coin or bullion, which have been deliberately hidden and where the owner cannot be readily found.** No other valuables, whether jewels, metal or glass are yet included within the procedures for treasure trove, nor are bronze or copper coins, however old, valuable or interesting. The other items beyond the reach of this law include items of archaeological interest, precious stones, objects of historical interest and so on.

The prevailing law on treasure trove applies only to gold or silver but the review is considering whether these provisions should be extended to include other objects, such as those of historic or archaeological interest.

In Scotland, the rules do apply to all objects found in the manner of treasure trove if they are considered to be of antiquarian interest (*bona vacantia*). Such finds must be reported to the Procurator Fiscal.

In England and Wales, a find of gold or silver coins, bullion or plate which was concealed in the soil or hidden within a building, must be notified to the coroner. This is done by informing the police and the task of the coroner is to decide whether or not the objects found are treasure trove. Today, lots of interesting treasure is being unearthed due to the increasing use of metal detectors, but also through new building work, road construction and land clearance schemes.

If gold or silver is found, therefore, there are many points to satisfy before it is declared treasure trove. First, it must be shown that it is either gold or silver, or that it has gold or silver content. Secondly, it must be shown that the object was hidden and not merely lost or abandoned, and thirdly, it must be shown that the owner cannot be found.

The purpose of the coroner's inquest is to determine these points and the found objects will be placed in his custody until his decision is reached. If the coroner decides that the gold or silver object had been lost or abandoned (such as a gold coin being found beneath a woodland footpath), he will declare it not to be treasure trove. In this case, it could therefore belong to the finder, or to the owner, or even the tenant of the land or building in which it was found.

It is not the coroner's duty to determine ownership – if the individuals cannot agree, it might be necessary to take the matter to a civil court. In the case of treasure hunters going on land to seek coins or precious metal with a metal detector, it is very wise to make a legal agreement with the landowner or occupier, and indeed with any partners involved in the search, to determine the disposal or share-out of any finds or their proceeds – **and do so before the finds are made.**

If the inquest decides that the found objects were deliberately concealed, the coroner will declare them treasure trove.

This means they belong to the State, but the find will be considered by the Treasure Trove Reviewing Committee of the Treasury, and they may award the finder with today's full cash value of their discovery. The discovery will be lodged in the British Museum, and this is a clear example of honesty being the best policy.

If someone finds gold or silver which may be treasure trove and fails to declare it, that person can be charged with theft and the valuables confiscated. Any reward that might have been paid to the finder will be lost.

Metal detectors

If metal detectors are used on private land, permission to do so must first be sought, otherwise there can be allegations of trespass. Furthermore, it is recommended that users make a binding agreement with the landowner or occupier about the disposal of any finds.

A similar agreement should be reached among any partners involved in the search – this should be determined before the hunting begins. It may be wise to compile a form of written contract or agreement, with the aid of a solicitor, which all parties sign before any exploration begins.

Metal detectors no longer require a licence under the Wireless Telegraphy Act of 1949, but the Home Office does advise users to check on local by-laws before operating them.

Auctions

The main message for anyone buying anything at auction, especially coins, is **Buyer Beware**. In legal jargon, this is known as *caveat emptor* from the Latin phrase *caveat emptor, quia ignorare non debuit quod ius alienum emit* which means 'Let a purchaser beware, for he ought not to be ignorant of the nature of the property which he is buying from another party'.

This is particularly apt at auctions because any mistake, however innocently made, cannot afterwards be rectified. For this reason, buyers of small objects like coins or medals, should carefully inspect the goods which are for sale before committing themselves to a purchase. This opportunity is given before a sale begins.

One problem with tiny objects is that mistakes can be made both by the auctioneer and by the purchaser. An auctioneer could be handed the wrong one, or he could wrongly describe it, even by accident, but if the mistake is made by the auctioneer there is just a possibility that it could be rectified.

This is by no means guaranteed, however, because the onus rests firmly upon the purchaser. It is assumed he or she knows what is being bought. Only if the sale is fraudulent is the buyer protected because the contract becomes void. Proving a sale is fraudulent is not the easiest of tasks, but at least this provision does remain.

A bid made at an auction constitutes an offer and the fall of the hammer signifies acceptance of that offer. Thus a binding contract is made and legally enforceable contracts do not have to be in writing. Verbal contracts are just as enforceable as written ones, which means that a dispute between an auctioneer and a purchaser could terminate in legal proceedings.

One point to be considered is the reputation of the auctioneer. All auctioneers should have, on the premises where they operate, a ticket or board giving their name and address. If there does not appear to be one, caution is advised, even to the point of suspecting a fraudulent operation!

At auctions, it all adds up to that famous advice – **BUYER BEWARE!**

A SILVER CELEBRATION

—————— BY C W HILL ——————

*The reverse of the 1967 sixpence issued twenty-five years ago
and depicted on the cover of the Coin 1992 Year Book.
Designed by Cecil Thomas and Edgar Fuller, the reverse
features an interlaced rose, thistle, shamrock and leek
representative of England, Scotland, Ireland and Wales*

(PHOTOGRAPH BY COURTESY OF THE ROYAL MINT)

The publication of this, the 25th edition of the *Coin Year Book*, seems an appropriate moment to take a glance at the state of the hobby when the first edition appeared.

One of the most striking changes since then has been the removal of the official restrictions on coin collecting which were in force twenty-four years ago.

Following the return of Harold Wilson's Labour government with an increased majority in March 1966, strenuous efforts were made to curb inflation and to improve Britain's balance of payments. The following month, in pursuit of this policy, Parliament passed the 'Exchange Control Act' making it necessary for anyone wishing to purchase one or more post-1837 gold coins to obtain a licence from the Bank of England.

Exchange Control Act

The purpose of this control was to prevent the hoarding of gold coins or bullion by speculators, while providing for genuine numismatists to add to their collections. As a guarantee of the authenticity of his or her claim to be a genuine collector, a detailed list of every post-1837 gold coin in the applicant's collection had to accompany the application form. For silver and base metal coins only their quantity and estimated value were required. The decision of the Bank of England was final and if refused the applicant was legally bound to sell all but four of his post-1837 gold coins. Even with a licence, the collector was allowed to own only two examples of each post-1837 gold coin, though examples differing in date or mint-mark could be regarded as different coins.

The 1887 Victorian double-florin

To these stringent controls of gold coins was added in June 1968 the requirement of an export licence for the dispatch abroad of pre-1947 silver, or silver alloy coins, in quantities of more than ten. This control, intended to prevent the export of silver coins for melting down, did not apply to coins more than 100 years old, which were already covered by the long-standing control on the export of antiques. While rejoicing at the demise of these austerity measures and the removal of such controls from coin collecting, it must be remembered that less than six weeks after the election of Mrs Margaret Thatcher's government in May 1979 the rate of VAT was almost doubled, from 8% to 15%.

Happier times are recalled by a study of the prices prevailing during the late 1960s, especially if the inflation of the intervening years is cheerfully ignored. The 1902 Edward VII Proof crown and the 1927 George V Proof crown, both with mintages of a little over 15,000, were generally available in 1968 for about £35.00 each. Today's price is around the £100.00 mark. The 1887 Victorian double-florin, both the Roman and the Arabic numeral types, could be bought in Uncirculated condition for about £18.00, against today's price of around £30.00 and £35.00 respectively. More elusive and valuable coins have generally shown more spectacular gains, emphasising once again the validity of the customary investment advice: *'rare coins in first class condition bring investors better results than coins in the lower classes of scarcity and condition'*.

In view of the fluctuating fortunes of the hobby during the past quarter-century it is surprising to note that the number of numismatic societies and of dealers has remained fairly constant over the years. In the early editions of the *Coin Year Book* about seventy societies and 170 dealers were listed in their respective directories. Approximately the same number of societies can be found in recent editions, but the number of dealers has risen towards the 300 mark, though these include a few more companies offering accessories rather than coins and medals. With an average of eighty more pages, more features, more comprehensive Blue Pages and more advertisements, recent editions of the *Coin Year Book* offer greater help to collectors and dealers than their pioneer predecessors.

In the wider world 1967-68 cast its shadow well before it. With the US becoming ever more deeply involved in the war in Vietnam, the North Vietnamese launched the Tet offensive on some thirty South Vietnamese cities, shattering American hopes of a quick and easy end to the conflict. The Middle East was, as ever, in turmoil; Martin Luther King and Senator Robert Kennedy were assassinated; and during the summer there were violent riots by students in Paris. From the scientific front there came better news. In South Africa Dr Christiaan Barnard performed the first successful heart transplant operation, his patient surviving for nineteen months. Three American doctors shared a Nobel Prize for 'breaking the genetic code' and the Bell Laboratories produced a pocket-sized laser capable of carrying hundreds of thousands of TV signals, telephone calls and other communications. The *Coin Year Book* was certainly born at a turbulent and exciting time.

INVESTING
IN
COINS

by Alistair Gibb

'*That*' as Millicent Martin used to sing so mellifluously, '*was the year, that was. It's over, let it go.*' Such were the sentiments of most investors as far as 1990 was concerned.

The year began by being oversold as the start of a new decade (actually, it wasn't: it was the final year of the old decade because the first year was year 1, not year 0) and it ended with the world waiting for war.

It was a year when the chickens came home to roost by the barnful.

High interest rates not only cut into the profits of heavily borrowed companies, they also forced their customers to rein in their spending so that they could meet their mortgage commitments. Those who found the burden too much, discovered that property prices were wilting under the weight of forced sales. Just as inflation seemed to have peaked, unemployment started to rise again and as their confidence fell, the public started to save more. That cut discretionary spending even further and as the profit forecasts of our leading companies were revised downwards, share prices came under pressure too.

It was, in short, a year when it paid to keep one's head below the financial parapet.

Feet of clay

Exposure to fashion was expensive. One after another, the financial favourites of the 1980s proved to have feet of clay. Polly Peck, Docklands property, impressionist paintings (indeed almost anything Alan Bond touched), Saatchi & Saatchi, exotic cars, Coloroll and Harris Queensway all fell out of bed, and even the redoubtable George Walker was on his knees to his bankers.

But, as usual, the headlines only told part of the story. Collapses of confidence are good news for the papers. The steady trickle of good news from the coin auction rooms rarely made the national press. Yet anyone who follows the regular 'Auction News' feature in *Coin Monthly* will know that there were some very good realisations last year.

Perhaps the most spectacular of the recent offerings was the sale by Glendining's of only the second known specimen of a Scottish silver crown ryal, struck during the short marriage of Mary Queen of Scots to the wimpish Lord Darnley.

Expected to realise around £20,000, bidding started at £15,000, soared through the estimate and eventually reached £48,000 before the hammer finally fell – a world record price for a British silver coin. (See illustration overleaf.)

Sotheby's sold a St Nazaire raid VC group for £55,000 in the summer and their Battle of Britain Medal sale saw Ginger Lacey's DFM and bar group fall for £30,800, around double the estimate.

The 1565 Celebrated Marriage Ryal of
Mary, Queen of Scots and Henry Stewart, Lord Darnley.
(£48,000 was realised for this coin in December 1990 in a Glendining auction)

Christie's sold a million pound 'Treasury Note' for £21,000 during the clutch of paper money sales held in October. One might almost have thought it was business as usual in the numismatic market.

1991 began with the start of the Gulf War and was followed by more doom and gloom as the unemployment figures rose with a worrying rapidity.

Surprisingly perhaps, given the deterioration in the British economy, the pound rose to two dollars on the foreign exchange market. These were all bad bits of news for the coin market.

The Gulf War stopped people travelling. Fewer visitors mean lower sales for the dealers who are already cutting back on their purchases. The rise of the pound makes British prices seem dearer to foreign buyers so that even postal sales will be hit. Most of the dealers I contacted recently in the course of a straw poll were gloomier than I had ever known them.

A real stinker

All in all it seems that the coming year could be a real stinker as far as the coin market is concerned.

But, to turn the well-known saying on its head, one man's poison is another man's meat. To be sure, this is not the time to be selling one's collection. Anyone who has been thinking of doing so would be well advised to postpone the parting until better times return. The truly dedicated collector will probably keep buying anyway. But those of us who have the ultimate resale price of a collection in mind will need some reassurance about what we are doing with our money.

It seems to me that there are two possible reactions to the current situation. Either one can bury one's head in the sand and wait for it all to end, or one can take the long term view and plan on the basis that the market will recover in time. We may not know when, but the chances are that it will recover. After all, the best known **Financial Times'** share index reached its all-time low in 1940. Buying shares in those black days was probably reason enough to be certified – but it would have brought considerable wealth too!

Long term objective

For the bulk of us who are trying to add to our collections, there could be some real opportunities about. The investment aspect of coin collecting should always be regarded as a long term objective. There are rarely opportunities to make a quick killing in the coin market. Slow and steady buying enables one to take advantage of price fluctuations. We can afford to buy more coins when prices fall, even if we have to rein in on the acquisitions when they are buoyant. Over a reasonable period this will mean that our collection has cost less than the average prices ruling during the period when it was being formed. This is the 'pound-cost' averaging effect, so beloved by unit trust salesmen, but it is a remarkably persuasive argument for steady buying over a number of years. Anyone who doubts its truth is welcome to get out the pencil and paper and do some sums for themselves.

A few simple rules

As well as keeping up the purchases in bad times as well as good – indeed *especially* in bad times – one should bear a few other simple rules in mind.

It is not an accident that the pieces which are still selling well are the better ones. The auctioned coins previously mentioned are, it is true, the more spectacular examples, but an analysis of the realisations at all price levels tells the same story. Buying quality coins is one of the best ways of protecting their value against short-term fluctuations in the market. Unusual pieces in the better conditions will always be desired. Poorer specimens may be sought after when the market is strong and there are many buyers about. Some will, no doubt, settle for second best. But when the market is depressed, buyers can afford to be choosy. The prudent investor who has bought quality items will then be able to reap his just reward.

Keeping in the mainstream

Another means of protecting oneself against a depressed market is to concentrate on 'mainstream' fields. Classic coins, British Hammered pieces for instance, never seem to go out of fashion. Other collecting interests may come and go but they just go on for ever it seems. Avoid fashion like the plague, however tempting it may be. I have no doubt that those who put down a deposit on a Docklands flat hoping to sell it in a matter of months at a higher price thought they were taking very little risk. No doubt Terence Conran did too. But with the benefit of hindsight we can see they were the victims of a fashion bandwagon. It happens in the coin field too. I remember when people were trading sealed bags of mint £sd coins in the run up to decimalisation. The bottom fell out of that market too.

Collect what interests you

I am sometimes asked by a new collector what type of coins he should collect. Investors ask the same question although not, perhaps, frequently enough. Since one hopes that they will, in time, become dedicated to their collection, the answer must lie with the asker. Collect, I reply, what interests you. Collectors and investors alike make better buyers when they know more about their subject. This is something which can only come with time, experience and patient study and study will come much more easily when there is a genuine interest to support it. Provided they are inclined or intending to concentrate on a classic or mainstream area of numismatics they do so with my blessing, whatever their choice might be.

Bullion coins

An ever growing list of countries is marketing bullion coins to the collecting public. This is a field which was pioneered by the South Africans with their krugerrand which gave the collector an ounce of fine gold. To this basic concept, a number of variants have appeared on the market: fractional coins, platinum equivalents, Proof varieties and designs changing every year.

To a purist, a true numismatist, they have little to offer but to an investor they are a simple and straightforward way of investing in coins. The most important point to bear in mind when buying these pieces is the VAT regulations. It is payable on purchases in the UK but not recoverable on sales. The only way to avoid this is to hold the coins offshore which a number of banks will do for a small fee.

Since they are a convenient means of buying pure bullion the investor should concentrate on those which trade nearest to their bullion content. This means sticking to the full ounce pieces and may mean buying krugers which some do not favour for non-numismatic reasons.

Those attracted to the potential profits of dabbling in the bullion markets should be warned that the price of gold can be very volatile and that it went over 800 dollars over a decade ago. In theory, it should go up when economies (and therefore currencies) are in trouble, or when people see their world collapsing around them, in times of war for instance.

One of the surprising features of the bullion markets last year was the stability of the price of gold. It oscillated around 400 dollars and even the outbreak of the Gulf War caused little more than a ripple in the markets. It seems there has been a fundamental change in the way the mines do business.

When gold falls below 350 dollars an ounce, marginal mines slip into losses and stop producing. The consequent reduction in supply forces the prices back up. When it rises significantly above 400 dollars, they sell future production on the gold futures market and so guarantee their predicted profits. This struggle by the mining companies, especially those in South Africa, to stay afloat explains why the price of gold has moved within this narrow price range throughout the last year.

Before 'Glasnost' one might have expected the Russians to upset the apple-cart, but given their preoccupation with their own internal struggles, they are probably as glad as the South African and other producers to see some stability in the price level.

If this analysis is correct, it means that the gold market has lost much of its ability to protect holders against economic disruption. And it may be a less exciting place for investors too.

COLLECTING ROMAN

BY JOHN ANTHONY

Sestertius of Nero
(54-68 AD)

A Brief Guide to Eight Centuries of Coinage

Roman coins are conventionally divided into three groups:

Republican (c 290-49 BC): The Republic was governed by the Senate and elected officials – consuls, tribunes, quaestors etc – and among the junior appointments were three moneyers, elected annually. From about 206 BC onwards, these moneyers authorised issues of coins that conferred prestige on their families. The designs, which were frequently changed, alluded to the family gods, ancestors' exploits on the battlefields, benefits conferred on the city and so on. Silver denarii are the Republican coins most likely to be encountered by collectors, although there are earlier 'anonymous' issues and bronzes.

Imperatorial (c 49-27 BC): An unstable period, when the Republican institutions were collapsing and ambitious politicians fought each other for supreme power. Though short, this period has been well researched, documented, dramatised and filmed. Famous personalities such as Pompey, and Julius Caesar, Brutus, Cassius, Mark Antony and Octavian (later called Augustus) minted silver, along with some gold and bronze. Their portraits are keenly sought after.

Imperial (27 BC - 476 AD): Five centuries in which power rested with the emperors, though the Senate survived. The coinage underwent many changes and it is still so plentiful that most collections consist mainly of 'Imperial' coins, so the remainder of our guide relates to them.

The emperors and their titles

Every emperor claimed legitimate power by asserting that he had the support of the Senate; was the adoptive heir of the first supreme ruler; had been elected to the highest offices, or had led his country to victory.

Care was taken to provide the reigning emperor, and often members of his family, with well-executed coin portraits surrounded by appropriate titles such as:

Imperator – Commander in Chief.

Augustus – The approximate equivalent of Highness or Excellency, implying adoptive descent from Octavian, who had been granted that title and had founded the Empire.

Caesar – His family name and also that of 'the greatest Roman of them all'.

Pontifex Maximus – High Priest, the principal figure at state ceremonies.

Consul (COS) – Head of State in Republican times.

TRP (Tribunicia Potestas) – Having the powers and authority of the elected representatives of the common people (tribunes).

DN (Dominus Noster) – Our Lord.

Divus or Diva – The deified one (on posthumous coins).

Coins may be dated by means of titles that record how many times the Senate had honoured the emperor by re-conferring powers upon him, eg COS III TRP VIII indicates a third consulship and an eighth tribunate.

*Republican denarius
(c66 BC)*

*Aureus
Tiberius (14-37 AD)*

*Solidus
Magnus Maximus (383-388 AD)*

*Imperatorial denarius
Mark Antony and Octavian*

Denominations

Denominations changed over the years and coins that had originally been silver, progressively became debased because of financial crises.

Gold remained at a high standard of fineness, though weights were decreased. Several attempts were made to reform the coinage and the most successful was Diocletian's at the end of the 3rd century. (Diocletian's reign 284-304 AD)

Gold, silver and bronze

Principal denominations with diameters in millimetres and dates of introduction are as follows:

Gold
  Aureus (18) 43 BC
  Solidus (18) 310 AD
Silver
  Denarius (18-20) 211 BC
  Antoninianus (22 or less) 214 AD
  (Debased in later years so that it
  resembled bronze).
  Argentius (18) c290.
  Siliqua (18) c320.
  Miliareuse (25) c320.
Bronze (Imperial Period)
  As (30) c18 BC.
  Dupondius (30) c18 BC.
  Sestertius (35) c18 BC.
  Follis (25) c290.
  Centenionalis (22) c348.

All base-metal coins are catalogued as bronze (AE), though they may be copper, brass (orichalcum), or some other alloy. 4th century bronzes are referred to as AE1-AE4 in descending order of size.

Reverses

The reverses of coins were used to publicise the benefits brought by the reigning emperor – victories, diplomatic coups, construction of public buildings, the protection brought by his personal gods, his virtues and so on. He might also commemorate anniversaries, public games, state visits and, eventually, deification.

Identification

Some reverses name the deity or virtue depicted; others carry the Imperial titles and leave identification to depend upon the attributes, ie the things that the personage carries. For example, Hercules has a club and lion skin, and Pax (peace) carries an olive branch and a sceptre. (Further details can be found in earlier editions of the *Coin Year Book*.)

The wide variety of reverse designs is one of the principal attractions of Roman coinage.

Mints

Although it is often possible to assign earlier coins to particular mints, identification of mint-cities became easy after Diocletian's reforms. He standardised the coinage, insisting that each mint identify its products by putting letters in the exergue (the bottom of the reverse design). Preceding these letters were P (Pecunia), SM (Sacra Moneta) or M, all of which mean 'money'. Thus we have PLN for London, or SMAL for Alexandria. Any other letters refer to the workshops within the mints and served as additional quality controls.

Byzantine

There were also many cities that had the right to produce a bronze coinage for local use. Most were in the Greek-speaking part of the Empire and this complex subject is, nowadays, treated separately as the 'Greek Imperial' coinage.

After the European part of the Roman Empire (with its capital at Rome) collapsed, the mints there ceased to operate. In the East, where the capital was Byzantium (Istanbul) coinage continued for about a thousand years. We describe these issues as 'Byzantine', though the emperors still used the title 'King of the Romans'.

Some collecting tips

• **Decide on a theme:** No-one can hope to cover the whole field of Roman coins. Choose your own speciality – portraiture, deities, buildings, women, the army, or whatever else appeals to you.

• **Condition and value:** Like all types of coins, value depends on the state of preservation. **Seaby's** prices are for GVF or VF specimens and prices fall off sharply for lower-grade material. As always, buy the best you can afford.

• **What to avoid:** Illegible coins, examples with missing letters, off-centre strikings, bad cracks (slight splitting around the edge is acceptable), roughly cleaned coins. The ideal is an EF coin that has the patina of age.

• **Fakes and forgeries:** The most likely to trouble collectors are imitation sestertii and counterfeit late gold. Beware of casting marks, filing scratches, 'tooling' (the enhancing of worn details by means of a sharp point), signs of mechanical production (too round, too perfect) and coins of the wrong weight.

If you buy from reputable sources, you should have no problems and will enjoy collecting these fascinating coins.

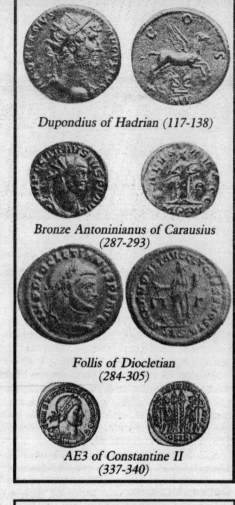

Dupondius of Hadrian (117-138)

Bronze Antoninianus of Carausius (287-293)

Follis of Diocletian (284-305)

AE3 of Constantine II (337-340)

Essential Reference

Roman Coins & Their Values by David R Sear, published by B A Seaby, is the basic guide for all collectors.

As experience and the desire for further information develop, consult **Seaby's Roman Silver Coins** (4 vols) and **Late Roman Bronze Coinage** by R A Carson. The definitive works, often referred to in price catalogues, are the multi-volume **Roman Imperial Coins** (RIC) and the **British Museum Catalogues** (BMC). Well-illustrated auction catalogues are very useful and much cheaper.

US CONSTITUTION MEDALS

by Timothy Benford

You don't have to be an American to have been aware of the excitement generated by the 200th anniversary of the most crucial document of United States government history, the Constitution.

Gaining this significant step in the country's independence was originally a two-step process, with the signing of the document in 1787, and its ratification by the required number of individual States being completed in 1788.

The first of two medals issued by The United States Capitol Historical Society honouring the signing, was a 1987 medal struck in bronze, silver and gold. It was designed by sculptor Marcel Jovine and struck by the Medallic Art Company of Connecticut in six different sizes. Prices ranged from $8 for one of the 2,500 1½in diameter antique bronze strikes, to $575 for one of the fifty 1⁵⁄₁₆in diameter, 18-carat gold medals. The Medallic Art Company's other credits include the striking of official inaugural medals for ten US Presidents, the Pulitzer Prize Medal and the National Medal for Science.

The Society's 1988 medal, designed by Eugene Daub, is also produced by Medallic Art and honours the Ratification. It was offered in five sizes at prices ranging from

$9 for a 1½in diameter bronze, to $675 for the 1⁵⁄₁₆in diameter medal in 18-carat gold. It is the eleventh medal in the Society's medal series.

Marcel Jovine

The 1987 medal was created by sculptor Marcel Jovine and depicts both the scene of the signing of the Constitution by the thirty-nine signatories and the tripartite Federal Government created by the instrument itself.

The obverse features an adaptation of the famous painting by Howard Chandler Christy of the scene at the signing of the Constitution on 17 September 1787, with George Washington himself presiding as one of the central figures shown. The painting, which hangs in the House of Representatives' wing of the nation's capitol, shows just over forty of the signatories of the Constitution. Mr Jovine decided to concentrate on George Washington, James Madison, Alexander Hamilton and Benjamin Franklin, and in his rendering he depicts these four prominent men surrounded by a handful of other members of the Continental Congress. The inscription around the relief reads THE COMMISSION ON THE BICENTENNIAL OF THE

UNITED STATES CONSTITUTION 1787-1987.

The reverse combines creative artistry with historical authenticity of the Constitution. The great structural achievement of the creation of a national government, consisting of three branches, is the theme. These are portrayed by symbols representing each branch; legislative (the two houses of Congress); executive (the Presidency); and judicial (the court system headed by the Supreme Court). To add to the historical meaning, above each symbol are the actual words from Articles I, II and III of the Constitution. It was one of several reverse designs submitted by Mr Jovine to the Society.

Articles of Confederation

For those unfamiliar with their US history this is easily explained in that, prior to the Ratification of the Constitution, the thirteen former British colonies functioned as thirteen individual States under the original 'Articles of Confederation'. In fact, they were quite independent of each other. The Constitution united them in a common, national interest. Thus it was with the Ratification of this document in 1788, not the Declaration of Independence in 1776, that the United States was officially born.

Marcel Jovine is a renowned sculptor whose steadily rising career has been marked by many awards and honours. As an immigrant to the United States during World War II, he took particular interest in creating the 1987 medal honouring the formation of the national government, his adopted country.

In his native Italy, Mr Jovine attended the University of Naples and after coming to the United States he became quite well-known for his sculptures and medallic renditions of many of the great thoroughbred racehorses. At the 1983 Exhibition of the National Sculpture Society his bronze of the horse **Spectacular Bid** was awarded the M H Lamston prize for meritorious sculpture.

Left: Marcel Jovine working on the plaster for the 1987 medal commemorating the signing of the Constitution in 1787

In the field of medallic art, Marcel Jovine created numerous medals for the same Medallic Art Company that produced both his 1987 and Eugene Daub's 1988 medals for the Society. In 1985 he accepted the coveted American Numismatic Society's 'J Sanford Saltus Award' and joined an elite list of world-famous sculptors, which now numbers approximately forty recipients. He lives and works in his studio home in Closter, New Jersey.

It is worth noting an interesting aside here: a month after the United States Capitol Historical Society announced that Mr Jovine's design had been accepted for its 1987 medal, he was one of eleven American artists, three women and eight men, invited by the US Treasury Department to submit designs for the 1987 gold and silver Constitution coins.

Mr Jovine's bold eagle and script WE THE PEOPLE, with quill, were selected as the obverse and reverse designs for the US $5 coin.

Eugene Daub

On the obverse of the 1988 medal, Mr Daub features three portraitures of the authors of the famed Federalist Papers: Alexander Hamilton, James Madison and John Jay. The individual portraits are strong and presented in such a way that each man is facing in a different direction. Surrounding the portraits are the words from the preamble of the 'Constitution' – IN ORDER TO PRESERVE A MORE PERFECT UNION . . .

The Federalist Papers, a series of eighty-five letters, were sent to newspapers in the various States urging ratification of the Constitution. Hamilton, the first Treasurer of The United States, Madison, the country's fourth President, and Jay, the first Chief Justice of the Supreme Court, published the collection in book form.

The reverse centres on the 'Act of Ratification' by the nine States required for ratification and by the original thirteen States. The historic date of Ratification by each State is shown. In the centre of the medal is one word RATIFICATION, against the background of a quill pen flowing from the bottom to the top of the medal. It

Marcel Jovine's 1987 medal depicting the scene of the signing of the Constitution

symbolises the signing by the conventions of the several States.

Medals Advisory Committee

When the 1988 medal was formally presented to the public the Society's president, Mr Fred Schwengel, called attention to the Society's nine-member Medals Advisory Committee, five of whom are widely considered a virtual **Who's Who** in US medallic and numismatic art: Katherine D Ortega, The Treasurer of the United States; Elvira Stefanelli, Executive Director of the Smithsonian Institution's Numismatic Collection; Melvin M Payne, Chairman of the Board Emeritus of the National Geographic Society; J Carter Brown and Charles Atherton, Chairman and Secretary, respectively, of the Commis-

sion of Fine Arts. It was the advisory committee which offered advice on the theme for the 1988 medal and its design elements.

Following his selection as sculptor of the 1988 medal, Eugene Daub was among a select handful of artists invited to submit sketches for the US Olympic commemorative coins by the Treasury Department.

Mr Daub left the commercial art field to pursue the broader and higher pursuits of art. His works range from a series of 3in Presidential busts, to a 6ft statue of **Christ The Healer**. In 1986 Mr Daub was commissioned to sculpt one of the pieces celebrating immigrant groups in the New World for the Statue of Liberty/Ellis Island Foundation. His 'lady liberty headmedal' was chosen by the American

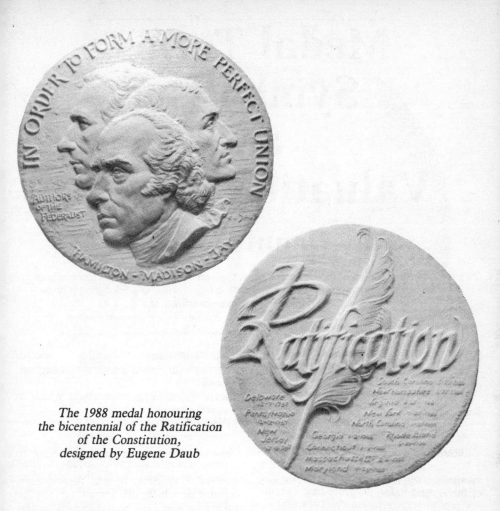

*The 1988 medal honouring
the bicentennial of the Ratification
of the Constitution,
designed by Eugene Daub*

Numismatic Society as its commemorative piece for the 100th anniversary of the Statue of Liberty.

Christie McAuliffe Memorial

Mr Daub recently completed the Christie McAuliffe Children's Memorial Bass Relief, for the American Federation of Teachers in Washington, DC (Mrs McAuliffe was the civilian teacher selected as a mission specialist who perished along with six other crew members in the space shuttle **Challenger's** disaster on 28 January 1986).

In 1991 Eugene Daub also received the 'J Sanford Saltus Award' for his 1988 design

honouring the 'Ratification', and thus joined Marcel Jovine and the elite group of sculptors and designers.

The US Capitol Historical Society was founded in 1962 and was authorised by congressional charter in 1978 to produce historically significant medallic art. Its charter ordains its mission to be one of research and to publish information about the Capitol and the Congress in order to instil patriotism throughout the nation, by dispensing such information.

Further details are available from The United States Capitol Historical Society, 200 Maryland Avenue, NE, Washington, DC 20002, USA.

Medal Terms, Symbolism and Valuation Factors

by Dennis G Blair

To aid the understanding of medal descriptions as given in catalogues and reference books, together with general appreciation and valuation factors, this article addresses these considerations under three headings of:
Medallic Glossary, Symbolism on British Medals and Valuation Factors.

Medallic Glossary

This section covers terms used in the description of medals and their condition.

Bar: Sometimes referred to as a clasp, an attachment indicating a) re campaigns – place, action or date. b) re service – duration or type. c) re gallantry/decorations – a subsequent deed meriting second recognition. Attached to the medal suspender or preceding bar, or direct to ribbon, as on the 1914 Star.

Beading: String of embossed dots, usually lining the rim, as on the 1818-55 Arctic Medal.

Boxed: Within the original box of issue.

Brooch: Fastening for affixing a medal to clothing, sometimes integral with a bar.

Brooched: Refers to a medal spoilt by possessing evidence of having had a fixing secured to its flan.

Campaign Award: Medal for participants in a campaign or battle.

Carriage: Back plate of a bar, to contain the ribbon.

Cartouche: Ornamental plaque containing the inscription (eg, as within the 1900 Ashanti Medal reverse design).

Cast: Technique of forming a medal through the use of a mould and molten metal.

Centre Stem: The pivot about which a swivel suspender turns.

Citation: Description of action accompanying an award for bravery.

Clasp: Term to describe the bottom straight ribbon support, used in conjunction with certain awards that have ring attachments, eg the Victoria Cross (see bar).

Claw: Ornate connection between medal flan and suspender.

Clip: Plain link crimped on to a medal rim to which a ring suspender connects, eg the Waterloo Medal.

Coat of Arms: Heraldic shield design, eg reverse of the 1880-97 Cape General Service Medal.

Coinage Head: Monarch's portrait as occurring on respective contemporary coins, eg the 1914-19 Mercantile Marine Medal obverse design.

Conjoined: Description of two overlapping busts as on the obverse of the 1935 Jubilee Medal (sometimes termed jugate, or cojoined).

Commemorative: In honour of an occasion or person, eg the 1900 Visit To Ireland Medal.

Contact Mark: Impact scar of the flan.

Converted: Having a pin or clip added to provide direct brooch fixing (suspender usually removed too).

Copy: Reproduction replica.

Cross: Cruciform or pattée shaped award, eg the 1940 George Cross and Victoria Cross, respectively.

Crowned Effigy: Portrait of the monarch wearing a crown, as occurring on most British medal obverse designs.

Decoration: Award for meritorious, or gallant conduct, eg Distinguished Service Order.

Defective: Not in original state, ie incomplete, renamed, damaged or spoilt.

Device: Emblematic design motif, eg reverse of the 1882-89 Egypt Medal.

Documented: Formally recorded with details.

Duplicate: Official replacement for a lost medal.

Ears: Lugs at the ends of bars to receive any subsequent bar.

Edge: The outer circumference of the flan, usually bearing recipient's details.

Edge Knock: Impact scar on the edge.

Emblem: Attachment to the suspension ribbon to indicate class, or other distinguishment, eg Oak Leaf, denoting mention in dispatches.

Embossed: With raised inscription/design.

Engraved: With an incuse inscription added.

Erased: Indicates that edge naming or other details have been abraded away intentionally.

Exergue: Segment below the reverse design often containing dates as on the 1857-58 Indian Mutiny Medal.

Field: Background area of the flan possessing no design.

Fishtail Bar: Description given to the fishtail shaped bars of the 2nd China and Indian Mutiny Medals.

Flan: Whole body of a medal.

Flaw: Defect in manufacture.

Forgery: A copy made to deceive as being original or having falsified details, eg incorrect naming.

Frosted: Matt finish, often used to contrast with polished highlighting.

Gallantry Award: For bravery, eg Military Medal.

Gazetted: Publicised in the **London Gazette**, ie the citation announcement.

Ghost Dates: Where dates have been officially removed but are still discernable, as on certain early issues of the Queen's South African Medal.

Grade: The condition in respect of wear, symbols used are the same as those used for coin grading, eg EF, VF etc (see Valuation Factors section).

Group: A number of medals awarded to one person.

Impressed: Indented details applied.

Incuse: Legend or design formed by indentation.

Inscription: Wording occurring as part of the design or wording added.

Jugate: Another term for conjoined.

K I A: Abbreviation indicating that the recipient was 'Killed in Action'.

Lacquered: Having a coating of clear lacquer.

Late Issue: Deferred award (often due to delayed claim) may consequently not possess the original style of naming used.

Laureated: With laurel leaves design, eg as on the 1845-66 New Zealand Medals.

Legend: Wording inscribed radial with the rim, eg as on the reverse of the 1848-49 Punjab Medal TO THE ARMY OF THE PUNJAB.

Long Service Award: For a period of unbroken service, often coupled with the requirement of Good Conduct in continuity.

Loop: Ring form affixed to the rim for ribbon or cord attachment, eg as on the 1837 Coorg Medal.

Lunette Contained: Within a watch style casing.

Medalet: Refers to pieces measuring 25mm in diameter, or less.

Medallion: Piece not intended to be worn, often a prize or commemorative.

Mentioned in Dispatches: Recorded conduct from the theatre of war.

Miniature Medal: Piece reproduced at approximately half of the full size, often worn when full dress is inappropriate.

Moiré: Description given to watered silk ribbon, as used with the South Atlantic Medal.

Motto: An inscribed maxim as on the Royal Humane Society Medal for life-saving.

Mounting: Method of wearing medals in order of precedence. May be 'standard', whereby medals hang freely, or 'royal style', whereby medals are sewn to a background piece arranged.

Named: Having the recipient's name etc (usually edge impressed or engraved).

Native Award: Issued to a native, as against a member of home forces.

Oak Leaf: Emblem affixed to the ribbon, to indicate 'mentioned in dispatches'.

Obverse: The side on display when being worn.

Officially Corrected: When the name or other details have been amended by the issuing body.

Order: Insignia of certain revered brotherhoods, eg Most Honourable Order of the Bath.

Ornament: Added embellishment to provide design balance, as below the cartouche on the 1896-97 Queen's Sudan Medal.

Pair: Two medals awarded to one person.

Patinated: Oxidation coating formed on the surface of bronze and copper medals in particular.

Pierced: With a hole drilled through, usually for unofficial suspension fitting.

Pitted: Surface spoiling by minute holes, caused by chemical attack or contact from another medal.

Plated: With a thin coating of metal applied, usually silver or gold.

Plugged: Having a hole made good by filling.

Polished: Excessively shined-up, resulting in loss of highlight detail.

Privately Engraved: Engraved subsequent to issue by the recipient.

Regimental (Named): Engraved or impressed after issue through the recipient's regiment.

Relief: Raised design or legend/inscription.

Renamed: When original naming has been removed and other naming substituted.

Researched: Checked out against roll and records.

Restored: When a defective medal has been fully repaired or any missing parts replaced.

Restrike: Copy produced from original dies subsequent to original issue.

Reverse: The back of a medal not seen when being worn.

Riband Bar: Strip (100mm deep) faced with medal ribbons worn to show medals awarded.

Ribbon: Strip of fabric for suspender attachment and of respective colour/s to suit each particular medal.

Ribbon Roller: The rod of a suspender over which the ribbon passes.

Rim: Raised outer ring to a medal's edge.

Rimless: When the edge is on the same plane as the field, eg the Victory Medal of World War I.

Roll: Official list of those to whom a medal/bar has been awarded.

Roses: Ornamental florets on certain bars serving to conceal rivet fixings, as on the Indian General Service Medals.

Rosette: Rose emblem attached to medal ribbons to indicate distinguishing factors, as on the South Atlantic Medal denoting close action involvement.

Set: A complete assembly of a collecting theme, eg all combinations of bars issued for one campaign.

Shaded Ribbon: Description of the colours merging as against positive stripes, eg the 1843 Scinde Campaign Medals.

Skeletal: Of open design as on the Territorial Decoration.

Specimen: Medal struck at the same time as the original manufacture, but not intended for issue.

Stain: Localised permanent surface discolouration.

Star: Stellar shaped award, eg the 1899-1900 Kimberley Star.

Struck: Technique of medal manufacture by stamping the blank piece between two dies.

Suspender: Means by which a medal is attached to its ribbon, it may be swivel or fixed, straight, horn or scroll shaped, floreate or otherwise ornate.

Tailor's Copy: A fair reproduction made up as a dress piece, also referred to as jeweller's copy.

Toning: The natural darkening of silver occurring with age and exposure.

Tooled: Touch-up work effected with a chasing tool.

Tressure: An ornamental border following the rim as on the reverse of the George V Coronation Medals.

Trio: Three medals awarded to the one person, usually refers to World War I medals.

Trophy of Arms: Design showing an assembly of armaments representative of the defeated enemies' weaponry, as included on the reverse of the Victorian China medals.

Uniface: With design on one side only.

Un-named: Issue without indication of the recipient's name.

Verdigris: Damaging greenish deposit which forms particularly on copper, brass or bronze.

Verified: Particulars of a recipient checked against a medal roll and found to be correct.

WWI/WWII: Abbreviations for the First and Second World War.

Wreath: Representation of a ring of foliage, eg as on the reverse of the 1914-19 Territorial Force War Medal.

Obverse of the South Atlantic Medal with straight suspender and shaded moiré ribbon fitted with rosette emblem (True size 37mm in diameter)

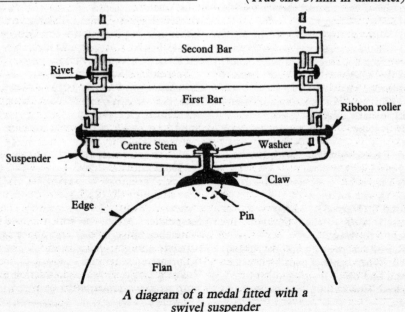

A diagram of a medal fitted with a swivel suspender

Left: Reverse of the
2nd China War Medal with horn
suspender and fishtail bars.
The design comprises a Trophy of Arms
with the legend above and exergue below
(True size 36mm in diameter)

*Obverse of the 1937 Coronation Medal
with ring suspender.
The crowned and robed portraits
are conjoined on a rimless flan
(Reproduced at the true size)*

*Obverse of the Royal Humane Society
Medal with scroll suspender and buckle
brooch. The 'boy' forms the central device,
above which is the legend and below,
the exergue containing the inscription
(True size 38mm in diameter)*

Symbolism on British Medals

In the design of medals, particularly Victorian awards, symbols by way of emblems, personifications etc, are often used to express a medal's concept. The interpretation of these symbols is not always obvious so the following glossary, which includes reference to examples, sets out to clarify understanding.

Anchor: Representative of hope, as on many religious medals in particular.

Anchor with Crown: Insignia of the Royal Navy, as on the first issue Naval Long Service and Good Conduct award.

Britannia: Female personification, often with helmet, shield and trident (or spear), representative of Great Britain.

Clasped Hands: Symbolic of fellowship and solidarity, frequently used on Temperance Medals.

Cornucopia: Expresses plentitude (the fruits of industry) as used notably on school prize medals.

Crown: Emblem of monarchy and royal patronage, as on the 1896 Ashanti Star Medal.

Dove: Expressive of peace, .as used on many unofficial Victory medals.

Dragon/Serpent: Representative of the enemy, as on the 1939-45 War Medal.

Eagle: Insignia of the Royal Air Force, featured on the RAF Long Service and Good Conduct Medals.

Fame: Classical male figure personification of renown, as represented on the Army Best Shot Medal.

Fern: National plant emblem of New Zealand, incorporated into the design of the suspender of the 1845 New Zealand Medal.

Hermes: Classical messenger of God used in the design of the Air Force Cross and other Royal Air Force awards.

Hercules: Classical hero of strength shown restraining the serpent Hydra on the 1950-53 Korea Medal.

Hibernia: Personification female figure representative of Ireland, as used on the 1900 Visit to Ireland Medal.

Justice: Personification female classical figure usually portrayed carrying scales, as Exemplary Police Service Medal.

Laurel Foliage: Symbolic of victory and associated with excellence, often used in wreath form on academic as well as war medals.

Lion: Emblematic animal representation of Great Britain, as used in many medal designs, notably the 1890-97 British South Africa Company Medal.

Lotus Blossom: National flower emblem of India, as used to embellish the Indian Army Long Service Award.

Maple Leaf: The national plant which is the emblem of Canada. It was integrated into the design of the 1885 North West Canada Medal.

Natalia: Female personification figure representative of Natal, as depicted on the 1906 Natal Medal.

Neptune: God of the sea, featured on the Naval Good Shooting award.

Oak Leaves: Symbolic of distinction, frequently used in wreath form in respective appreciation, as on the Royal Humane Society Medal.

Olive Sprig: Representative of peace, much used on Victory medals.

Palm Frond: Symbolic of triumph and achievement, used on academic as well as Victory medals.

Pax: Classical personification of peace, as portrayed on the 1798 Davison's Nile Medal.

Sphinx: Fabulous creature with a lion's body and man's head adopted to represent Egypt as on the 1882-89 Egypt Medal.

St George: Patron Saint of England, but adopted as symbolic of goodness too, appears on many civilian medals.

Tiger: Representative of India as used on the 1936-39 Indian General Service Medal.

Trophy of Arms: Composition of captured arms denoting military success, as used on the three Victorian China War Medals.

Victory: Classical winged female personification, frequently occurring on campaign awards, as on the 1896-98 Queen's Sudan Medal.

Warrior: Single soldier figure adopted to represent the British Army, as on the 1854-56 Crimea Medal.

The obverse of Davison's Nile Medal of 1798.
This conveys peace achieved through Lord Nelson, by featuring the figure of 'Pax' holding a sprig of laurel, together with a shield bearing the portrait of the Admiral. 'Pax' is shown standing firmly on a rock refuge, upon which there is also an anchor and beyond, the sea is seen extending to the horizon.
Designer C H Küchler. (True size 45mm in diameter)

The large Naval Gold Medal of 1794-1806
employs symbolism in both its obverse and reverse designs. The obverse depicts the triumph of Great Britain by showing the figure of 'Victory' placing a laurel wreath upon the proud head of Britannia, whilst the reverse, which provides for the recipient's name to be centrally engraved, has a wreath surround half of laurel (acknowledgement of victory) and half of oak leaves (recognition of distinctive service).
Designer R Wood. (True size 53mm in diameter)

Valuation Factors

Whereas the value of coins is governed by condition, scarcity and demand, the valuations placed upon medals not only include these factors, but are complicated by many other considerations too, as explained in the following review.

Grading The condition of medals is identified by the same system adopted to describe that of coins, but usually together with special notes added in respect of, for example, a defective suspender, missing bars etc, or a particularly bad blemish, such as a deep edge knock.

FDC (Fleur de Coin) Mint, ie never worn and without blemish.

EF (Extremely Fine) With only the slightest of wear.

VF (Very Fine) No significant damage.

F (Fine) Worn or blemished.

Poor Very significantly worn or damaged.

Often descriptions give in-between standards by adding **N** (Nearly) eg NEF – just below **EF** standard or **G** (Good) eg GVF – just above VF standard. **A** is sometimes prefixed to indicate Average, ie the mean standard between obverse and reverse sides where their condition varies, or else each side may be separately graded.

Evidence of wear is considered by some collectors not to necessarily detract from a medal's value, as this is taken as indicative of it having being worn on the uniform of the proud recipient.

Scarcity Medals of which only a comparitive few were issued have understandably an enhanced value. This consideration extends to bar numbers and combinations, issues to particular units, and even to unusual ranks or to women. Strangely, a genuine no bar medal can in fact be rated higher than some multibar examples of the same medal, because of the comparatively few issued, as in the case of the Queen's South Africa award for Boer War Service.

Generally, because of the difficulty in researching records relating to colonial forces, the awards to so called 'natives' are rated lower than those to Imperial forces. There are however exceptions, such as the 1914-19 War Medal, struck in bronze for 'natives', as there were sixty times more medals struck in silver for other recipients.

Ranks The more senior rank held by a medal recipient, the more value is placed on that medal. A rough guide to this is – plus 5% for Junior NCOs, plus 10% for Senior NCOs, plus 25% for Subalterns and up to plus 60% for Field Officers. The particular appeal of officers' medals is because their service records are more readily available for research. Other plus factors include approximately 10% for Guard Regiments, and 20% in respect of Cavalry Regiments.

Groups Groups of named medals can be particularly interesting as they serve to record not only their recipients' service and possibly gallantry, but also career progression by way of promotions. This consideration can add some 15% to the aggregate value of that of respective single awards. Family groups, reflecting for example a father and son's service, or say that of two brothers, also have a special appeal to certain collectors.

Orders and Decorations In the case of Orders, some examples of those of a high class can be rated less in value than those of a lower order. This is because of age enhancement, former owner considerations and the quality of workmanship to the insignia itself, which can vary. However, in the case of gallantry decorations the value of more recent awards can sometimes be rated higher than that of the same award made much earlier. This is because 'associations' often still exist to be 'experienced' (ie places and persons) as against read about, and in the case of the Victoria Cross, the level of valour required in recent times is said to be higher than that formerly demanded in Victorian times. Awards to military personnel are rated higher than those to civilians, which may seem strange as the latter incidence is more infrequent, but this is because of the greater field of interest in servicemen by the majority of collectors.

Supporting Documentation A medal sold with respective papers, such as a discharge certificate or citation, benefits from this value enhancing input, and likewise too, any biographical particulars or the original box containing the medal as issued. Further, the medal of a serviceman who has survived from a sunken ship, or who became a battle casualty, also has a special appeal which is reflected in its value. When a war medal becomes separated from its group companions, with evidence of the other entitled medals, particularly if the group included a gallantry award, this too reflects favourably upon the single medal's value.

It is the case therefore, that indication values published in books only amount to rough guides, for every medal is an individual piece with its own particular associations and interest.

Below: The South Africa Medal with 1879 bar. This medal can vary in value from approximately £120.00 to £4,500, depending upon whether it was awarded for the Defence at Rorke's Drift, or one of the less illustrious engagements during campaigning in 1879. Designers W Wyon & L C Wyon

Above: The Queen's South Africa Medal 1899-1902 was issued with twenty-six different bars (a maximum of nine to any one medal), comprising state bars and date bars besides battle bars, to a wide range of units. This gave rise to over 200 basic combinations and a respective number of guide valuations. Designer G W de Saulles (True size of both these medals is 36mm in diameter)

MEDALS FOR THE ANDES

BY CYRIL BRACEGIRDLE

Two American engineers, Wyman and Harrison, are jointly honoured on this medal for their construction of the Correro de Pasco line

(PHOTOGRAPH COURTESY OF GLENDINING'S)

Richard Trevithick

St Newly East in Cornwall is the home of the 'Lappa Valley Railway Maze'. A layout of brick paths measuring 161ft by 101ft in the shape of the steam locomotive built in 1801 by Richard Trevithick (1771-1833), it is the first of its kind ever to run on rails. The engine was nicknamed 'Puffing Billy', which is why steam trains were known thereafter as 'puffers'.

Many years later on another continent, American engineers blasted away mountain-sides, risking earthquakes and hostile tribes to carve the highest railways in the world across the Andes. Those achievements earned many commemorative medals for the pioneers. However, Richard Trevithick was not awarded a medal, although he certainly deserved one.

Shortly after his success in Cornwall, this man who never made money out of his inventions and was to die in poverty, went to South America taking with him a high pressure steam-engine capable of working at high altitudes. He tried to interest several Spanish governors in the idea of building railways that could transport the gold and silver of the mountain mines to the coast. Simón Bolivar was leading the revolt against the yoke of Spain at the time and the Governors had other problems. Also his engine was not yet powerful enough to conquer the many awesome gradients. Trevithick went home disappointed.

Richard Trevithick's Lappa Valley Railway Maze

Many commemoratives issued

The great age of railway building in South America really began in 1855. For the next few decades medals were issued for every new line opened, every bridge thrown across a ravine, and every tunnel bored through a mountain. In all, several hundred commemorative pieces were struck, some quite spectacular in design. Many of these are now rarities and greatly sought after.

Henry Meiggs

The true king of the South American railways was Henry Meiggs, who knew nothing at all about engineering. Meiggs was an adventurer, wanted by the police in San Francisco for various shady dealings. The ship in which he fled that city was pursued for some miles out of San Francisco Bay by a vessel full of a sheriff's posse, but the lawmen's ship broke down, which was lucky for Meiggs and for the future of railways in the Southern Continent.

The High Andes constitute a great rocky barrier running down the western side of the continent, starting in the north close to where the Isthmus of Panama begins, and stretching down to the Argentine, petering out into Patagonia.

Pizarro Francisco (1478-1541) the Spanish adventurer, had previously climbed that fearsome wall in his armour, to snatch the gold of the Incas which had always barred the way into the interior of South America from the Pacific coast.

The Incas had a road system crossing the barrier and encompassing their entire empire. There were rest houses at intervals for the messengers of the sun god and for the baggage trains of llamas. The Spanish introduced horses and mules, but getting the produce of the mines to the coast was always a great labour.

Henry Meiggs had seen how railways had opened up the North American prairies, and when he landed in Peru, feeling himself far enough away from the San Francisco police to be safe, he realised that the newly independent Spanish colonies were ripe for exploitation. The railway was the answer and by this time the engines were much more powerful than in Trevithick's day.

Meiggs bribed and talked government officials into awarding him a contract to build 115 miles of track between Santiago and Valparaiso. The cost was estimated at six million pesos and the job was to take three years. However, Meiggs knew how to cut corners, and he cannily inserted into the contract a clause to the effect that he would get an extra ten thousand pesos for every month gained. He intended to gain quite a few months.

His first big problem was the reluctance of the native Indians to do a full day's work. Such labour was not in their culture. The Spanish had discovered this long ago and had imported African slaves, but the African physique was unsuitable for work at high altitudes, so Meiggs solved this problem by importing several thousand Chinese labourers. He finished the job in two years.

Meiggs moved on to build a railway from Callao on the coast, to Oroya in the mountains. Tracks had to be slashed along the slopes of almost sheer cliffs and thus the Varrugus viaduct was built to a height of 575ft. To mark this achievement, the Peruvian authorities sent to England for J S and A R Wyon to produce the medal which now bears the head of Meiggs on the obverse and a representation of the viaduct on the reverse. One of these medals, in mint condition, is currently worth approximately £150.00.

Meiggs' next task was to build a line from Puna in the Andes to Arequipa, the second city of Peru, and then on to Mollendo on the coast. He was still discussing the contract when nature hit out by flattening Arequipa with an earthquake. The American promptly gave 50,000 dollars to earthquake relief and obtained the contract. During the two years it took to complete, he employed 12,000 men and killed 2,000 through accidents and illness, the latter being mainly caused by epidemics. Many of the casualties occurred when a train carrying 250 barrels of blasting powder blew up in a station. But these were pretty normal conditions for the Andes.

F-C T Medal

A particularly fine medal was struck for the completion of the FERRO-CARRIL TRASANDINO, showing a train on a viaduct with mountains in the background. An eagle with a female figure – possibly an Inca motif – on its back, is hovering over the train.

Another line built by Meiggs, the Cuzco to Santa Ana, though intended for access to mines, is now used for taking tourists on one of the most spectacular railway journeys in the world, to see the fabulous Inca city of Machu Piccu.

The medal to commemorate the Varrugus viaduct on the
Callao to Oroya line, depicts Henry Meiggs on the obverse.
Designed by JS and AR Wyon
(PHOTOGRAPH COURTESY OF GLENDINING'S)

The Pacific coast littoral region of South America is a geological fantasy land with six great upland basins called altiplanos, all of these being between 7,000 and 13,000ft above sea level, backed by the snowy battlements of the Cordillera. It was on the altiplanos that the Indian civilisations developed.

Henry Meiggs and his competitors had to drive their lines to those dizzy heights through some of the most breathtaking scenery in the world. In the early years mist, frost and thin rain would cause wheel slip on downward runs, and sometimes a train would hurtle down out of control. There were instances of crews throwing themselves out when this happened.

A collection of all the South American railway medals would be quite an acquisition, but many do not seem to have found their way to Europe and remain rarities.

The Ferro-Carril Trasandino medal
(PHOTOGRAPH COURTESY OF GLENDINING'S)

Two other American engineers, Wyman and Harrison, are honoured by a joint medal for the construction of the Correro de Pasco line, which unlocked the vast mineral wealth in that region of the Andes (see illustration on the introductory page).

Although Richard Trevithick had the vision, it was almost entirely Americans who built the Trans-Andean railways. Only one Englishman played a part, Sir John Jackson, who drove a line 285 miles across the mountains from the Chilean coast, to La Paz in the Argentine. This proved to be one of the most vital rail links of all. Most of the lines in Peru and Chile were designed to tap mining areas, but the La Paz line had a different purpose. For decades it had been a long and tiresome business having to haul cargoes by sea around the dangerous Cape where so many ships foundered in the stormy waters. Now, goods from the USA could be shipped down the coast of South America to Valparaiso and then by train across the Andes. Later the line was continued from La Paz right across the continent to Buenos Aires.

This medal was issued in 1910 to celebrate the first South American Congress and is currently worth £70.00
(PHOTOGRAPH COURTESY OF GLENDINING'S)

NUMISMATISTS' LIBRARY

by

C W Hill

This selection of sixty books, including well-known guides published some years ago as well as new publications, covers the main branches of numismatics, so forming the nucleus of a comprehensive library for the numismatist. The prices quoted are **believed to be correct at the time of going to press** but allowances must be made for increases, especially in the prices of books published outside the United Kingdom, which are likely to be affected by changes in the rate of exchange. Some of the older books, included because they are standard works of reference, are now out of print and may cost appreciably more than their original prices. They may be obtainable from second-hand bookshops or on loan from public libraries. The recent publications should be obtainable from one or other of our advertisers but in case of difficulty C W Hill will be pleased to help.

New books of interest to collectors of coins, tokens, medals, medallions, badges and paper money are reviewed by C W Hill in his column 'Collectors' Bookshelf', which appears in every issue of *Coin Monthly*.

Contents

I General Guides

Collecting Coins by P Frank Purvey (pub B A Seaby Ltd), 160 pp, price £7.95. The first part of this book gives an historical account of coinages from the ancient Greek to the contemporary British and American. This is followed by a wide-ranging survey of the hobby, with chapters on forgeries, errors, displaying and caring for coins. Well illustrated and comprehensive.

Dictionary of Coin Names by Adrian Room (pub Routledge and Kegan Paul), 256 pp, price £14.95. A welcome addition to the collector's bookshelf because it includes many of the names given to coins in the countries of Asia and Africa which have become independent during the past forty years. Interesting entries on sterling, the sovereign and the humble joey.

II Ancient Coins

Dictionary of Ancient Greek Coins by John Melville Jones (pub B A Seaby Ltd), 264pp, price £29.50. Arranged alphabetically and includes purely numismatic terms, mythological celebrities and deities, and many of the emblems found on Greek coins. Amply illustrated with coin photographs and has tables showing the various alphabets used on ancient coins in the Western civilisations.

Ancient Greek Coins by G K Jenkins (pub B A Seaby Ltd), 182 pp with eight colour plates, price £35.00. A revised and redesigned edition of the book published in 1972 by Barrie and Jenkins Ltd. As well as a chronological account of the Greek coinage from the archaic period to the Empire of Alexander, the book has chapters on the origins of the coins, the process by which they were made, their weights and denominations, and the various means of dating them. The text is illustrated by 450 photographs in black-and-white and thirty-five in colour, making this a most informative and attractive guide.

Greek Coins and their Values Volume I, Europe by David R Sear, (pub B A Seaby Ltd), 358 pp, price £25.00. A fine catalogue of the coins minted by the ancient Greeks in Europe, including the Celtic coins whose designs are based on Greek originals. About 3,400 coins are listed and priced, with photographs of 1,500 of them from specimens in the British Museum.

Greek Coins and their Values, Volume 2, Asia and Africa by David R Sear, (pub B A Seaby Ltd), 494 pp, price £25.00. The companion to the previous volume, covering coins minted by the ancient Greeks in Asia and Africa. Over 4,500 coins are listed and priced, with photographs of almost 2,000 of them. The two volumes provide the most comprehensive guide to the ancient Greek coinage.

Greek Imperial Coins and their Values: The Local Coinages of the Roman Empire by David R Sear (pub B A Seaby Ltd), 670 pp, price £40.00. The final volume in this author's remarkable survey of the coins of the ancient Greeks and the Romans. Lists the many issues of the Greek cities and colonies which were associated with, or absorbed into, the Roman Empire. Spans three centuries and 600 mints, listing and valuing more than 6,000 coins, of which 1,750 are illustrated with photographs by Frank Purvey.

Dictionary of Ancient Roman Coins compiled by John Melville Jones (pub B A Seaby Ltd), 336 pp, price £29.50. In encyclopedic form this dictionary lists in alphabetical order the denominations, deities, objects and topics associated with, or illustrated on, the Roman coinage, starting with the abacus and ending with the Zodiac. The common abbreviations found on Roman coins are fully explained and many more obscure terms are discussed. Thanks to the compiler's readable style the dictionary is pleasant for browsing, as well as being informative, so that it makes a welcome addition to the library of the collector of Roman coins.

Roman Historical Coins by Colin Foss (pub B A Seaby Ltd), 366 pp, price £29.50. A detailed catalogue of all the Roman coin types that are associated with a specific event, occasion, or subject in Roman history. It is arranged chronologically, beginning with the coins which marked the conquest of southern Gaul in 121 BC and ending with those of the Emperor Basiliscus 475-76 AD. Background historical notes to the various issues and 350 illustrations make this a comprehensive guide to the many coins which feature milestones in the story of ancient Rome.

Roman Coins and their Values by David R Sear (pub B A Seaby Ltd), 388 pp plus twelve plates, price £35.00. Although described as the second edition of the book first published in 1981, this is virtually a new book, with many lists entirely rewritten and expanded. It is the only single-volume guide to the Roman coinage, listing and pricing all the major types of coins issued over a period of about 750 years. More than 4,300 coins are included, with photographs of about 1,000 of them. There are also historical notes on each emperor and empress for whom coins were minted, and over fifty pages devoted to a general survey of the Roman coinage, its denominations, mints and mint-marks.

Roman Silver Coins, Volume I – The Republic to Augustus by H A Seaby (pub B A Seaby Ltd), 176 pp, price £18.50. Revised by David R Sear and Robert Loosley, this edition incorporates the latest researches into the coinage of the Roman republic. All the line drawings have been replaced by approximately 800 photographs.

Roman Silver Coins, Volume II – Tiberius to Commodus by H A Seaby, (pub B A Seaby Ltd), 258 pp, price £18.50. Revised by Robert Loosley, this is the second of the volumes in this standard series on Roman silver coins. Prices have been revised and the illustrations now comprise more than 570 photographs, most of them of specimens in the British Museum.

Roman Silver Coins, Volume III – Pertinax to Balbinus and Pupienus by H A Seaby (pub B A Seaby Ltd), 164 pp, price £18.50. Companion to the previous volume, listing the coins minted between 193 and 238 AD for a succession of little-known emperors and two celebrities, Septimius Severus and Caracalla, both of whom visited Britain.

Roman Silver Coins, Volume IV – Gordian III to Postumus by H A Seaby (pub B A Seaby Ltd), 150 pp, price £18.50. Companion to the previous volumes, cataloguing the coins minted for emperors between 238 and 268 AD, the best known being Gallienus, for whom some 1,400 coins are listed.

Roman Silver Coins, Volume V – Carausius to Romulus Augustus compiled by C E King (pub B A Seaby Ltd), 216 pp, price £18.50. The fifth and final volume in this fine series covering the Roman silver coinage. This volume runs from 286 to 476 AD, the last centuries of the Roman Empire in the west. The coins are priced in two grades of condition and there are photographs of about 300 of them.

Coinage in Roman Britain by Richard Reece (pub B A Seaby Ltd), 152 pp, price £15.95. An account of the Romano-British coinage from the standpoint of the archaeologist rather than the numismatist. The book gives details of hoards found in Britain and interprets their contents in the light of modern research, showing how they illustrate the function of coinage in this outpost of the empire.

Celtic Coinage of Britain by Robert Van Arsdell, (pub Spink and Son Ltd), 600 pp plus fifty-four plates, price £40.00. A detailed account of the use of money in Celtic Britain is accompanied by an illustrated catalogue of some 800 types of Celtic coins found in Britain, either as imports from Gaul or minted by the British tribes themselves. The large number of finds of Celtic coins in recent years, many made by metal-detector enthusiasts, has brought more on to the market and has led to an increased interest in the pre-Roman coinage of Britain. This book will be an essential guide for collectors venturing into a hitherto neglected branch of British numismatics.

Byzantine Coins by P D Whitting (pub Barrie and Jenkins Ltd), 312 pp including seventy-two plates, twenty in colour, price £8.25. A superbly illustrated guide to the coins of the Byzantine Empire, giving information on their general background, the most appropriate methods of collecting them, and the results of modern research into their production.

Byzantine Coins and their Values by David R Sear (pub B A Seaby Ltd), 526 pp, price £49.50. A revised and enlarged edition of the catalogue first published in 1974, with an appendix describing the gold forgeries which have plagued dealers and collectors in recent years. The catalogue covers the period from the reign of Anastasius I (491-518 AD) to the capture of Constantinople by the Turks in 1453. More than 2,600 basic coins are listed with prices in two grades of condition, supplemented by 600 photographs and informative background notes on virtually every aspect of the Byzantine coinage.

III British Coins

The Story of British Coinage by Peter Seaby (pub B A Seaby Ltd), 272 pp, price £15.95. A serious study of the various coinages of the British Isles, Ireland, the Channel Islands and the Isle of Man since Celtic times, supplemented by maps and more than 300 coin illustrations. The account of the new Royal Mint at Llantrisant in Wales, is particularly interesting.

A History of Modern English Coinage, Henry VII to Elizabeth II by James A Mackay (pub Longman Group), 216 pp, card covers, price £5.95. A chronological account of five centuries of the English and British coinage, emphasising the social, economic and political background to the various issues. The publication is informative, entertaining and profusely illustrated.

Standard Catalogue of British Coins, Coins of England and the United Kingdom compiled by Stephen Mitchell and Brian Reeds (pub B A Seaby Ltd), 384pp, price £10.95. This is the 26th edition of the catalogue first published in 1929 and now recognised as the authoritative work of reference on its subject. As well as the comprehensive catalogue, beginning with the Celtic coins brought to southern England by pre-Roman traders and immigrants, there is a useful introduction to coin collecting and appendices adding further information. The valuations, based on Seaby's retail prices, provide a reliable guide to the market in British coins.

Standard Catalogue of British Coins, Volume 2, Coins of Scotland, Ireland and the Islands compiled by Peter Seaby and P Frank Purvey (pub B A Seaby Ltd), 238 pp, price £10.95. A new edition comprising the two previous volumes covering Scotland and Ireland plus the coinages of Jersey, Guernsey, the Isle of Man and Lundy. A useful guide with the usual excellent photographs for which Seaby's catalogues are notable.

A Handbook of Coins of the British Isles by Howard W Bradley (pub Robert Hale Ltd), 220 pp, price £8.95. The second edition of this useful encyclopedia, providing details and accurate information about every aspect of the British coinage. Updated to include coins minted since the 1978 edition.

Scottish Coins by Donald Bateson (pub Shire Publications Ltd), thirty-two pp, card covers, price £1.25. An attractive and informative introduction to the Scottish coinage, beginning with the silver pennies minted for King David II in 1136 and ending with the Queen Anne silver coins minted in Edinburgh in 1709.

Coins and Medals of the English Civil War by Edward Besly (pub B A Seaby Ltd), 128pp, price £18.50. The Great Rebellion, which broke out against King Charles I in 1642 and led to a civil war lasting intermittently until 1660, when his son returned to England to claim this throne, is one of the most interesting periods in British numismatic history. This handsome book, with more than 150 illustrations, including eight colour plates, provides a comprehensive survey of the coins, mints, medals and medallions associated with the war. The Cavalier siege coinages, the Irish emergency money and the coins of the Lord Protector, Oliver Cromwell, are also described and illustrated.

IV World Coins

A) General

The 1988-89 World Coin Catalog, Twentieth Century compiled by Günther Schön (pub Amos Press Inc, USA), 1,632 pp, card covers, price $24.95 or £14.00. This new edition of modern coins of the world covers more than 10,000 issues from about 300 countries, states and territories. Values are given in American dollars for coins in two grades of condition and each country's list is prefaced by brief historical notes.

Coins of the World, 1750 to 1850 by William D Craig (pub Western Publishing Co, USA), 478 pp, price $12.95. An expanded edition of this useful catalogue of world coins. A valuable guide to the period it covers, particularly in the details of the varieties of currencies used in the 18th/19th centuries.

A Catalog of Modern World Coins by R S Yeoman (pub Western Publishing Co, USA), 512 pp, laminated covers, price $6.00. This catalogue covers the period from about 1850 to 1964, a notable feature being the clear photographs of more than 3,000 coins.

Current Coins of the World by R S Yeoman (pub Western Publishing Co, USA), 384 pp, price $5.50. A simplified catalogue of coins issued between about 1950 and 1976, so forming with the two previous volumes a set covering world coins since 1750.

Coins and the Archaeologist edited by John Casey and Richard Reece (pub B A Seaby Ltd), 314 pp, plus eight plates, price £18.50. This scholarly work assembles essays by thirteen authors based on papers presented at a conference held in 1973 at the Institute of Archaeology, London, but is extensively revised and updated in the light of researches and discoveries since then. Roman coins naturally loom large in the story but there are also chapters on Anglo-Saxon and English medieval coins. A number of excellent maps, graphs and diagrams supplement the interesting text.

A Handbook of Islamic Coins by Michael Broome (pub B A Seaby Ltd), 240 pp, price £30.00. A well-researched account showing how the development and expansion of the Islamic faith is illustrated by the coins of the Mohammedan countries of the Near and Middle East. The text is supplemented by excellent photographs of 365 typical coins increased to one and a half times life size.

B) Individual Countries

Coinage in France from the Dark Ages to Napoleon by Nicholas Mayhew (pub B A Seaby Ltd), 172 pp including thirty plates, price £18.50. Beginning with the coins minted by the Merovingian Franks during the early 6th century AD, the story runs through the Carolingian kingdom of Charlemagne, the Capetian, Valois and Bourbon dynasties to end with the issues of the Napoleonic period. Almost 300 coins are illustrated and there are some useful maps and bibliography.

Coin World Guide to United States Coins, Prices and Value Trends compiled by William T Gibbs and Keith M Zaner (pub Amos Press Inc, Sidney, Ohio, USA), 336 pp, card covers, price $4.50 or £2.50. The latest edition of this neat and useful guide to the official American coinage. The emphasis is on the investment angle, with graphs charting the market performances of more than fifty series of coins since 1983. As well as this market analysis there are chapters on such topics as type sets, Proofs and the minting process.

United States Gold Coins: an Illustrated History by Q David Bowers (pub Bowers and Ruddy Galleries, USA), 430 large-format pp plus twenty-four colour plates, price £22.00. Starting with an account of gold prospecting in the United States, the book goes on to describe how American gold coins have been designed and minted, to survey the great American numismatic collections of the past, and to provide a detailed catalogue of the coins themselves. A remarkably fine example of numismatic research.

V Tokens

British Tokens and their Values compiled by Michael Dickinson and P Frank Purvey (pub B A Seaby Ltd), 200 pp, price £7.95. A reprinted and revised edition of the catalogue first published in 1970. A compact guide to the British token coinages of the 17th, 18th and 19th centuries. The comprehensive lists are illustrated by photographs of about 170 typical tokens.

Seventeenth Century Tokens of the British Isles and their Values by Michael Dickinson (pub B A Seaby Ltd), 320 pp including seven plates, price £35.00. This publication is a comprehensive catalogue of some 14,000 tokens with valuations for all but the rarest types and introductory notes on the issues of each county.

Commercial Coins, 1787 to 1804 by R C Bell (pub Corbitt and Hunter), 320 pp, price £2.25. Describes and illustrates only those tokens genuinely issued for commercial purposes during the period concerned, omitting the tokens intended primarily for sale to collectors. This edition acts as a companion to the following five volumes, and together they form the most comprehensive survey of British tokens of the late 18th and early 19th centuries.

Copper Commercial Coins, 1811 to 1819 by R C Bell (pub Corbitt and Hunter), 240 pp, price £2.25. A well illustrated catalogue in large format, with informative background notes on designs, issuers and scarcity.

Special Tokens and those struck for General Circulation, 1784 to 1804 by R C Bell (pub Corbitt and Hunter), 258 pp, price £3.00. Records the tokens intended for sale to collectors or to deceive the unwary, rather than for genuine commercial use by tradesmen and companies. Useful information about the designers and die-engravers.

Tradesmen's Tickets and Private Tokens, 1785 to 1819 by R C Bell (pub Corbitt and Hunter), 316 pp, price £2.25. Records the unofficial pieces, often confused with genuine commercial tokens, which were issued during this period. Well illustrated and with much interesting information on the designs.

The Schwer Price Guide to Unofficial Farthings by Siegfried E Schwer (pub Schwer Coins), 276 pp, card covers, price £9.95. A reprint of the book by R C Bell, **Unofficial Farthings, 1820 to 1870** (pub B A Seaby Ltd), now out of print. This new edition includes all the original text plus a new sixteen-page price guide to the coins listed.

Tokens of Those Trying Times: A Social History of Britain's 19th Century Silver Tokens by James O'Donald Mays (pub New Forest Leaves, Ringwood), 248 pp, price £34.95. A great deal of research, especially among local archives and in the files of old newspapers, has been necessary to unearth the fascinating story of the silver tokens issued in 1811-12 in about a hundred towns and cities in England and Wales by factory-owners and tradesmen. They were desperate for small silver coins to pay their workpeople and to give change to their customers. As the Royal Mint was failing to provide an adequate coinage, private enterprise took on the job. With a wealth of illustration material, this fine book recalls a very lively period in British numismatic history.

The Sovereign Remedy: Touch-pieces and the King's Evil by Noël Woolf (pub The British Association of Numismatic Societies, University of Manchester), 64 pp, card covers, price £7.25. Until the arrival of the Hanoverian King, George I, in 1714, almost every English monarch had, with varying degrees of enthusiasm, attempted to cure people suffering from scrofula by ceremoniously touching their sores with gold or silver coins. The ceremony was accompanied by almsgiving and the coins were known as 'touch-pieces'. This interesting and well illustrated book tells the story of the touch-pieces and their part in the treatment of scrofula, the King's Evil.

VI Medallions, Medals and Militaria

Spink's Catalogue of British Commemorative Medals, 1558 to the Present Day by Daniel Fearon (pub Webb and Bower), 192 pp, price £12.95. A pioneer catalogue of about 1,200 medallions with valuations and useful advice on forming a collection. The arrangement is chronological and there is an index of medallists.

British Commemorative Medals and their Values by Christopher Eimer (pub B A Seaby Ltd), 266 large-format pp plus fifty-two plates, price £35.00. A catalogue of 2,150 medallions arranged in chronological order of the designs, not the date of striking. The first entries cover William the Conqueror and other Norman kings although the medallions concerned were not struck until the 18th century. The listing is supplemented by more than 600 illustrations, by a guide to collecting medallions and by a useful glossary of terms.

Spink's Standard Catalogue of British and Associated Orders, Decorations and Medals compiled by A R Litherland and B T Simpkin (pub Spink and Son Ltd), 224 pp including twenty-four colour plates, price £25.00. This is a revised and considerably extended version of the 1983 edition. The section on the medals awarded for life-saving has now more information on the lesser known awards and the selection of medal ribbons shown in colour has been enlarged. Altogether this is a very handsome production and it is a much more convenient size for the bookshelf. The valuations are based on recent auction realisations, dealers' lists and Spink's own wide knowledge of the market.

An Introduction to Commemorative Medals by Christopher Eimer (pub B A Seaby Ltd), 156 pp plus thirty-six plates, price £12.95. Although offered as an introduction to the subject, this is a remarkably comprehensive view, with a history of medals since their revival in Renaissance Italy, a description of the techniques used in their production, and useful advice on their collection, care and display. More than 300 medals are illustrated, with details of their date of issue, metal, purpose and approximate current market value. Even experienced collectors would find much of interest in this moderately priced introduction and

it is an essential guide for anyone beginning a collection.

Collecting Medals and Decorations by Alec A Purves (pub B A Seaby Ltd), 238 pp plus fifteen plates, price £7.50. An extended edition of this useful guide. The emphasis is on British awards but there is also a chapter on the many foreign awards which may be earned by British subjects.

The Medals, Decorations and Orders of the Great War, 1914-1918 by Alec A Purves (pub J B Hayward and Son), 192 pp, price £16.00. A revised and enlarged edition of the book first published in 1975, with details of obscure foreign awards not previously included. The book covers the awards of some thirty-six countries which participated in the war, or emerged from it as newly independent states. The illustrations include seven colour plates of medal ribbons.

The Medals, Decorations and Orders of World War II, 1939-1945 by Alec A Purves (pub J B Hayward and Son), 176 pp, price £14.00. The companion volume to the previous book, covering the awards made by the forty countries which participated in the conflict. Britain's contribution consisted of twenty awards already existing before the outbreak of war, and a further nineteen awards added during the war years. The illustrations include seven colour plates of medal ribbons and, like its companion, the book is an attractive and informative work of reference.

Military Badge Collecting by John Gaylor (pub Secker and Warburg Ltd), 172 pp plus fifty-six plates, price £11.95. A comprehensive guide, with useful hints on forming a collection and a wealth of information about the designs of British military badges, over 750 of which are illustrated.

Badges of the British Army, 1820 to the Present by F Wilkinson (pub Arms and Armour Press), seventy-two pp, price £6.95. A new edition of this helpful guide, with a supplement giving valuations for the 416 badges which are illustrated by life-size photographs.

Allied Combat Medals of World War 2 by Christopher Ailsby (pub Patrick Stephens Ltd, Wellingborough), 248 pp, price £16.95. A detailed guide for collectors of the medals, badges and other militaria associated with the 1939-1945 conflict. It covers the awards made by Britain, the Commonwealth and five western European countries; Belgium, Denmark, France, Norway and the Netherlands. Individual stories of exploits for which gallantry awards were made and many personal photographs of recipients add interest to the methodical catalogue, which is illustrated in black-and-white and colour.

VII Paper Money

As Good as Gold: 300 Years of British Banknote Design by V H Hewitt and J M Keyworth (pub British Museum Publications), 160 large-format pp, price £15.00. A history of the changing face of paper money in Britain during the last 300 years. The development from elegant calligraphy and heraldic vignettes to allegorical scenes and now to the portraits of celebrities is well illustrated, largely in full colour. A handsome production of considerable interest to collectors of British paper money.

English Paper Money by Vincent Duggleby (pub Spink and Son Ltd), 182 pp, card covers, price £12.50. This is a new edition, the fourth, of the catalogue first published in 1975. Among the new features are the brief biographies, with portraits, of the chief cashiers whose signatures have appeared on Bank of England notes since 1928, when the Bank took over from the Treasury the responsibility for the printing and issue of paper money. As well as the priced catalogue the book has useful hints on forming a collection and on errors, replacement notes, specimens and other facets of collecting.

The Standard Catalogue of Provincial Banks and Banknotes by G L Grant (pub Spink and Son Ltd), 156 pp plus thirty plates, price £9.75. A detailed catalogue of the many notes issued by private and joint stock banks in England and Wales during the late 18th, the 19th and the early 20th centuries. There is an interesting account of the development of banking during this period, and a valuation guide to the various issues.

Scottish Banknotes by James Douglas (pub Stanley Gibbons Ltd), 238 pp, price £5.00. A catalogue, with a valuation guide, of all the Scottish banknotes issued since 1695, a total of more than 800 face-different notes from eighty banks. Much interesting background information not easily obtainable elsewhere, making this a valuable contribution to numismatics and to the economic history of Scotland.

A Collector's Guide to British Cheques by David Shaw (pub Squirrel Publishing Ltd), seventy-two pp, card covers, price £4.95. A pioneer guide to a branch of numismatics that is growing in popularity. The informative text is supplemented by photographs of about 140 cheques, the earliest dating from the second half of the 17th century. Hints on collecting and a bibliography complete this helpful hand-book.

A GUIDE TO

TOKENS AND ALLIED 'COINS'

by John Anthony

Coins and notes in circulation are given status as a country's currency by its government, which makes them 'official', or in Britain's case, 'regal'. In many parts of the world, there have been in circulation substitutes for the government-backed coinage. Since strictly speaking they do not have a value in their own right, but only represent official coins, which for some reason are not readily available, these substitutes are known as 'tokens'. The great majority of them were manufactured privately and were redeemable for 'coin of the realm' if their owners presented them at the issuers' places of business. Tokens circulated in Britain at three distinct periods:-

17th Century Tokens

The Civil War ended the royal monopolies under which certain noblemen had the privilege of providing the country with farthings. Without sufficient small change available, everyday transactions became difficult. The problem was solved by shopkeepers and tradesmen, who had brass farthings and halfpence made with their names on them. Over 10,000 are known to have been manufactured between 1648 and 1672, resulting in new tokens still being discovered to date.

People knew each other in these small towns, where travel was difficult. A reputable businessman's tokens were acceptable only within a narrow radius of his premises (just a few streets in London), as further afield their possessor would not be able to spend them. No one collected tokens at the time, or attempted to keep a systematic record of them, so most of these 17th century tokens are scarce. Few are seen in really good condition and it is no disgrace to have a collection of rough specimens. They were never things of beauty, and modern collectors value them as items of local history, tangible evidence of long-vanished commerce. Tokens were collected thematically, from home-towns or counties, or those issued by particular tradesmen – grocers, bakers, inn-keepers

and so on. They appeal to people who enjoy historical research and, although the number of specialists is quite small, competition between them has made prices surprisingly high.

18th Century Tokens

Britain ran short of ready money once again at the end of the 18th century. The growing army of industrial workers needed their pay and shopkeepers in the much larger towns had to give change. The French Wars were disrupting the economy and the Government had not authorised the minting of large quantities of copper for many years.

Steam-driven machinery was available for striking coins and enterprising businessmen, best known among whom are Boulton and Watt, invited anyone who needed a supply of pence or halfpence to place orders with them. Skilled engravers were paid to cut the dies and they were able to incorporate into the designs whatever the customer required – a view of his shop, or a picture of his product, the arms of his town, allegorical figures, heroes of the past or present, soldiers, ships or any other device that might give a good impression.

When these tokens were issued for genuine commercial reasons, a promise to redeem them was inscribed on them. For

17th century halfpenny issued by Timothy Phelps, landlord of the Eagle and Child, Tooley Street, London

1668 halfpenny used by Samuell Leigh, mercer of Burslem, Staffordshire

18th century penny of the Parys Mine Company, Anglesey

example, the Parys Mine Company on the Isle of Angelsey, where a large work force was situated miles from any big city, used a reverse that had the Company's initials surrounded by WE PROMISE TO PAY THE BEARER ONE PENNY (or HALFPENNY).

A Druid was featured on the obverse, to whom the island would have been sacred. Since the company was producing the raw material, it had no difficulty in making tokens of full weight (an ounce of copper to the penny).

Less fortunate or scrupulous people issued lightweight tokens. This did not matter as long as they were redeemable, but it would make them valueless in the long run if there was no issuer to be called to account. Such was the case with plentiful tokens made 'for general circulation' by businessmen, who had no intention of redeeming them.

It was the age of the gentleman-connoisseur, antiquary and lover of curiosities. In such circles, token collecting became a craze. Realising that they could obtain good prices for rarities, manufacturers deliberately produced varieties, errors, 'mules' (tokens made from dies that were originally not intended to be used together) and edge variations (flans often had the towns where the tokens were valid stamped in the place where milling was more usual).

A considerable number of tokens were intended for the 'cabinet' and never went into circulation. Consequently, both rare and common tokens can be found excellently preserved. Do not buy 18th century tokens in less than GVF condition. The rarities are still expensive, but it is possible to form a collection of genuine commercial tokens for comparatively little.

19th Century Tokens

The 'Cartwheels' issued at the turn of the century superseded the tokens, but a steep rise in metal prices, caused by the Napoleonic War made it profitable to melt down silver and copper with the result that regal coins almost disappeared from circulation. Once again, tokens had to fill the gap.

Whereas the 18th century tokens had been predominantly halfpennies, the 19th century ones were pennies. By and large, they are less fanciful and more workmanlike in design. They seem well suited to a favourite collecting theme, which is the Industrial Revolution – scenes of factories, machinery and even of the Workhouses.

Silver tokens, mainly shillings and sixpences, were available to businessmen. Advertisements make it clear that they were marketed as profitable commodities, because they were very light and cost well under their face value. Though some were redeemable, many had no issuer's name on them and were clearly bogus. None is very plentiful today, so prices are not low. Contemporary collectors preserved enough specimens for us to be able to aim at EF as the average grade for our own purchases.

After the French Wars were over, the Government was able to provide the country with a new coinage and tokens were demonetised. Nevertheless, a great many coin-like pieces were made. These and their forerunners interest people whose collecting is termed as **para-numismatics**. Some of the principal categories are:-

Imitation Regal Halfpence and Farthings:- These lightweight, poorly made pieces appeared in the 18th century before tokens replaced them.

Unofficial Farthings:- The 19th century successors of tokens, used mainly as advertising pieces by shopkeepers.

Pub Tokens:- Hotels and inns used brass counters which were GOOD FOR ONE DRINK, or 'worth a penny or two' at the hostelry. (Their modern counterparts work one-armed bandits.)

Market Checks and Co-op Tokens:- These were small change, valid only in particular stores or stalls.

Hop Tokens:- These represented proof of work done and were presented for payment at the end of the day or week.

Sack Tokens:- These were equivalent to the value of a sack left at the miller's or elsewhere.

Gaming Counters:- Imitations of coins used as 'chips' in card games, roulette etc. Best known are the brass guineas inscribed IN MEMORY OF THE GOOD OLD DAYS.

Medalets:- Small brass coin-size pieces that may have served the same purpose. Most are political (see Cumberland Jack in the Numismatic Dictionary).

Passes:- These were mainly used for theatres, cock-pits, parks etc. They were presented to subscribers or VIPs, and often inscribed with their names.

Comparable items from other countries include:- **American Hard Times** (1830s and 1840s) and **Civil War** (1860s) **Tokens**. **Hacienda Tokens** used on Latin American ranches. **German Spielmarke** (gaming counters) and **Kriegsgeld** (emergency money from WWI). **French Chamber of Commerce** local tokens; these included **Jettons**. These base-metal hammered

counters date from the 13th century and are the subject of scholarly research. This puts them in a class of their own (see Numismatic Dictionary). **Countermarked Coins**. Foreign, or sometimes British, coins stamped with businessmen's names, badges or initials and possibly a new value. They served as tokens or advertisements.

Bibliography

Seaby's Catalogue of **British Tokens & their Values** gives current prices. (The 'classic' works on British Tokens referred to are G C Williamson Tokens, issued in the 17th century.)

18th century halfpenny from Coalbrookdale showing the Iron Bridge and machinery for raising barges

19th century penny from Priestfield Furnaces, Bilston, Staffordshire

1811 shilling from Reess and Morgan, Neath

Mayor and aldermen's pass for the Theatre Royal, Newcastle. Counter-marked coin, 19th century

French 10 centimes advertising Moody's Lodging House, London, 19th century

R Dalton **The Silver Token Coinage 1811-1812.**

R Dalton & S H Hamer **The Provincial Token Coinage of the Eighteenth Century.**

W J Davis **Nineteenth-Century Token Coinage.**

All the aforementioned publications have been reprinted.

Subsequent works on 17th century tokens, especially county studies are listed in **The J L Wetton Library Catalogue** and **The History of Eighteenth and Nineteenth-Century Tokens** is covered by the books of R C Bell. Details of these tokens are to be found in the sales lists from leading numismatic book-dealers.

·COIN CARE·

By
Alistair Gibb

The greening of planet earth is now under way. More effort is currently being put into conserving the environment and more money is being devoted to controlling pollution than ever before. Future generations may well be grateful but, in the meantime, we have to live with the effects of the industrial activity of our forefathers.

For centuries, heavy industry has discharged sulphurous and other gases into the atmosphere and these have combined with water to produce weak acids – hence 'acid rain' when it falls back to earth.

In nature, metals exist as ores; stable compounds which are generally inert. Man extracts these ores and refines them into pure metals. Some, like gold, are stable. Most are not.

Stable skin

Strip a copper wire to fit a plug and the individual strands glisten and shine in the light. Look at an old copper water pipe and it will be dull and, quite possibly, patchily marked. It may even be possible to detect the original fingermarks of the plumber who fitted it. Closer inspection may also reveal some green patches of crumbly material, especially round the joints.

That is what happens to a pure metal in a normal domestic environment. The shining metal of the newly stripped wire becomes the corroded metal of the pipe. Exactly the same sort of processes will occur on the surface of a newly minted coin unless steps are taken to prevent it. The effect may not be so dramatic, but most bare metal surfaces will react with the constituents of the atmosphere to form a stable skin. This skin, or 'patina' as it is called in the context of a coin, can be strikingly beautiful, especially on silver coins and it may even enhance their value. More often than not it disfigures the piece and will detract from its value. Nor are these atmospheric problems the only ones the coin collector has to cope with.

Technological advances have brought many benefits to mankind, but they have also brought us new problems. The older types of paper, which were made from pulped rags, contained nothing but natural products and will last for centuries. Modern paper, which is often made from wood pulp, is certainly cheaper than rag paper but it has had sulphur dioxide added during its manufacture and this results in an acidic end product. Most of the paper we are making today will therefore not last a single century unless it is de-acidified, a laborious and complex process. Even worse, many of these papers will tarnish coins which are stored in them.

Plastics too have brought us cheaper and more convenient products by the thousand. But one of the commonest types of plastic is polyvinyl chloride (PVC) which slowly releases chlorine into its surroundings and this will form another weak acid in the presence of water vapour.

Greasy, green film

PVC can be made into one of the cheapest types of clear film and many envelopes are made from it. These are quite unsuitable for coin storage as they will leave a characteristic greasy, green film on cupronickel coins and will attack all copper compounds such as bronze. Even paper money is unsafe in these PVC clear film types of holders.

Rubber bands contain sulphur from the vulcanising process and I have known them to mark silver coins even through the paper envelopes in which they were individually stored.

The bonding agents used in the manufacture of plywood and similar products are another potential source of trouble to the numismatist. Resinous softwoods sometimes give off volatile reagents which can dull a coin's surface; sunlight will yellow paper money and make it brittle; human skin leaves a mildly acidic deposit on anything it touches. Good news for the detective who is looking for fingerprints, but bad news for the coin collector who is trying to preserve mint lustre.

Saliva is reputed to be the cause of the black spots known as 'carbon spotting' sometimes seen on silver coins, although I must confess to have seen no convincing proof of this.

Enough is enough

The catalogue of potential dangers could be continued but enough is enough! Before the list gets too depressingly long let us turn to solutions.

Coin care is both simple and inexpensive. Most of the problems previously described can be avoided quite easily and some of the remedies are little more than plain common sense.

The key elements of any programme of coin conservation are an awareness of the dangers and an ability to spot deterioration as soon as it starts.

My introductory list should have gone a long way to creating awareness; perhaps even a little apprehension. Apprehension is all the stimulus one should need to take appropriate action.

The ability to spot deterioration as soon as it starts sounds difficult to achieve in practice, but in fact it is not. The problem is that it happens so slowly that many collectors do not realise what is happening to their coins until it has happened. Even those who look at their coins quite often may not spot it. One forms a mental image of a special coin and then adjusts what one actually sees to fit the image. Perhaps it is a trick of the light or a dull day, or we are imagining it. Husbands often do not notice their wives ageing – and, no doubt, vice versa! The same thing happens with anything we think we know well. Then one day one suddenly realises that there has been a change; the coin is not quite as brilliant as it was on the day that it was acquired. By then it is too late to restore it to its former glory.

The answer is to set up a control which can be used as a yardstick. When a batch of coins, especially lustrous ones, are acquired, set aside one of the less valuable ones or, if that is impractical, select another piece of a similar metal in the same condition to act as a checkpiece. Coat it with lacquer, making sure that the protective skin one is applying completely encloses the specimen. The coated coin can then be used as a control and can be compared with the other pieces.

Sensitive test

This is a sensitive test to use and it can also be most instructive. I can think of two collectors in particular who were amazed at what their controls taught them about coin degradation. One lived by the sea and had not realised how corrosive salt-laden air could be, although the state of his aluminium window frames should have served as a warning. The other took a job in the Middle East and only the practice of putting a control in with the coins he took with him alerted him to the dangers of condensation in a climate which alternated between searing daytime heat and surprisingly chilly nights.

The lacquering technique can, of course, be applied to the whole collection. Many museums have adopted it as standard practice because it seals the coins from all atmospheric action and is relatively inexpensive, although somewhat time-consuming. Another advantage of the technique is that it is reversible. The coating can be removed without damaging the coin in any way merely by dipping it in a bath of acetone.

Both cellulose and acrylic lacquers are suitable for use on coins and most hobby shops can supply all the materials one is likely to need. An increasing number of museums are prepared to give advice on conservation and some of them hold 'open days' when members of the public can take along problem pieces for advice, or ask about techniques.

The lacquering and de-lacquering processes involve the use of volatile and inflammable chemicals. They should be carried out in a well-ventilated room and suitable fire precautions taken.

In spite of its advantages, many collectors prefer not to coat their coins. Some argue that the coating prevents one obtaining the 'feel' of a coin and others that some of the detail is lost.

One of the best

For them and, I suspect, for many others, the best answer is silica gel. Most tarnishing action is caused by the presence of water vapour in the atmosphere. Remove the water and the tarnishing processes will be inhibited. Silica gel is one of the most effective water absorbers known. In a closed atmosphere, such as a sealed container, it can keep the atmosphere virtually free of water vapour.

Silica gel is usually supplied in the form of blue crumbs. They turn pink when the gel becomes saturated and that is a sign that it needs to be changed. Fortunately, the gel can be 'recharged' simply by drying it in a gentle heat – perhaps on a dish over a radiator. When the heat has driven off the absorbed water, the crumbs will revert to their original blue colour and they can then be used again.

Probably the most convenient way of using silica gel is to fill a cloth bag with it and put the bag and the coins into an airtight container, such as a tin or snaplock plastic box.

In tropical countries, museums often use hermetically sealed cases to display their coins. These are available but very expensive. The 'silica in a box' method is just as effective and only a fraction of the cost.

Storage

Having protected the collection from atmospheric dangers, one should next consider the storage medium. As previously indicated, many modern papers contain sulphur. In a dry atmosphere this should not be a problem but some collectors prefer not to use them on principle. PVC envelopes are still widely offered. Using them is a false economy as they will degrade the value of the coins by more than the amount saved on their purchase.

Problems with plastics are often caused by the plasticisers (additives used in their manufacture). There is an enormous range of these and so it is particularly difficult to be specific about 'safe' plastics. That said however, polyesters appear to be by far the best. Branded products made from Melinex and Mylar are proving universally acceptable.

For those who prefer to keep their collection in a cabinet, hardwoods such as mahogany and rosewood are best. Resinous softwoods and modern fabricated 'woods' should be avoided.

Handling coins should only be done with cotton gloves. That avoids leaving one's fingerprints on them. I get mine from workwear stores.

Cleaning

It often surprises collectors to learn that even mint coins need cleaning, but modern processes of manufacture can leave contaminants on them and, apart from special issues such as Proofs, there is no guarantee that they have not been handled.

A quick dip in old-fashioned lighter fuel will remove these and any excess liquid will evaporate quickly in the air, leaving a clean, dry specimen. Once again it is a treatment which calls for care and a well-ventilated room.

Circulated coins can be dirty. Since some coinage metals are surprisingly soft, care has to be taken not to scratch the field during cleaning. A dampened wooden cocktail stick gives one a suitably soft but effective tool and, after picking off the dirt, specimens can be washed in soapy water then dried in lighter fuel.

All abrasive and most proprietary cleaners should be avoided. One possible exception is Silver Dip, which is effective in removing unsightly tarnish from silver coins. Experiment before you try it on a valuable coin. Some collectors do not like the slightly too clean appearance of a dipped coin. Only you can decide for your coins.

Some Ancient coins and the finds of treasure hunters need more drastic treatment. Occasionally one meets a coin which has been attacked by verdigris, a green patchy growth often accompanied by pitting on the coin surface. These are all usually jobs for a specialist, so seek expert advice from your local museum or read up the more advanced methods in a standard work such as **The Conservation of Antiquities and Works of Art** by H J Plenderleith. This was originally published by Oxford University Press in 1956, but has gone to several editions and can now be obtained through any public library.

Don't and do's

Most advice on cleaning coins starts with the word 'don't'. Do practise any treatment you propose. Do read the instructions on any chemicals you may use and do take precautions against fire and toxic fumes. Seek advice if you are at all unsure about how to proceed.

Nothing you can do will turn a VF coin into an EF one, so there is no point in trying. Anything you do should be reversible simply because the next owner might not like it. Lacquering is completely reversible in that it can be removed without trace and that is one of its attractions. 'Silver dipping' is not reversible and should therefore only be used on special cases.

And finally, remember the regular 'Questions and Answers' feature in *Coin Monthly*. It is at your service for your queries on coin, medal, token and paper money conservation.

DENOMINATIONS OF THE WORLD

Below is a list of denominations of the world. First we have stated the denomination and then listed the countries from which these coins originate, eg the abassi, first in our list, originates from Afghanistan, Georgia and Persia. This should provide a useful guide to the tracing of world coinage.

Abassi – Afghanistan, Georgia, Persia
Ackey – Gold Coast
Afghani – Afghanistan
Agnel – France
Agora (Agorot) – Israel
Ahmadi – Mysore (India), Yemen
Amani – Afghanistan
Amman Cash – Mewar Udaipur, Pudukota (India Native States)
Angel – England, Scotland, Isle of Man
Angelet – France
Angelot – France
Angster – Luzern (Switzerland)
Anna – Burma, India, Mombasa, Muscat and Oman, Pakistan
Argentino – Argentina
Ariary – Madagascar
Ashrafi – Afghanistan, Awadh, Bahawalpur, Hyderabad (India Native State)
Asper – Algeria, Egypt, Tunisia, Turkey
Att – Thailand (Siam)
Aurar – Iceland
Avo – Macau (Macao), Timor
Baht – Thailand (Siam)
Baiocco – Italy
Baizah – Muscat and Oman ·
Balboa – Panama
Ban (Bani) – Romania
Banica – Yugoslavia
Batzen – German States, Switzerland
Bawbee – Scotland
Belga – Belgium
Besa (Bese) – Ethiopia, Italian Somaliland
Bit – British Guiana, Danish West Indies
Blanc – France
Bodle – Scotland
Bogach – Yemen

Bolivar – Venezuela
Boliviano – Bolivia
Bonnet – Scotland
Broad – England
Bu – Japan
Butut – The Gambia
Candareen – China
Carlino – Italy
Cash – China, Turkestan, Hong Kong, Mysore, Travancore (India Native State)
Cedis – Ghana
Cent – Australia, Bahamas, Belize, Bermuda, Botswana, British Caribbean Territories, British Honduras, British North Borneo, Brunei, Canada, Cayman Islands, Ceylon, China, Curacao, Danish West Indies, East Africa, East Africa and Uganda, Ethiopia, Fiji, Guyana, Haiti, Hawaii, Hong Kong, Jamaica, Kenya, Kiao Chau, Liberia, Malaysia, Malaya, Malaya and British Borneo, Malta, Mauritius, Netherlands, Netherlands Antilles, Netherlands East Indies, Newfoundland, New Zealand, Prince Edward Island, Rhodesia and Nyasaland, Sarawak, Seychelles, Sierra Leone, Singapore, Solomon Islands, South Africa, Straits Settlements, Surinam, Swaziland, Tanzania, Trinidad and Tobago, Tuvalu, Uganda, USA, Virgin Islands, Zanzibar
Centas (Centu, Centai) – Lithuania
Centavo – Angola, Argentina, Bolivia, Brazil, Cape Verde Islands, Chile, Colombia, Costa Rica, Cuba, Dominican Republic, Ecuadore, Guatemala, Honduras, Mexico, Mozambique, Nicaragua, Paraguay, Peru, Philippines, Portugal,

Portuguese Guinea, Portuguese India, Puerto Rico, St Thomas Islands, Prince Islands, Salvador, Timor, Venezuela

Centesimo – Chile, Dominican Republic, Eritrea, Italy, Panama, Paraguay, San Marino, Somalia, Uruguay, Vatican

Centime – Algeria, Belgian Congo, Belgium, Cambodia, Cameroons, Comoro Islands, France, French Cochin China, French Equatorial Africa, French Guiana, French Indo-China, French Oceania, French Polynesia, French Somaliland, French West Africa, Guadeloupe, Guinea, Haiti, Laos, Luxembourg, Madagascar, Martinique, Monaco, Morocco, New Caledonia, Reunion, Switzerland, Tugo, Tunisia, West African States, Westphalia

Centimo – Costa Rica, Paraguay, Peru, Philippines, Spain, Venezuela

Centimo de Escudo – Spain

Centimo de Real – Spain

Chaise – France

Chervonetz – Russia

Chetrum – Bhutan

Chiao – Formosa, Mongolia, Manchukuo

Chon – Korea, North Korea

Chukram – Travancore (India Native State)

Colon (Colones) – Costa Rica, Salvador

Condor – Chile, Colombia, Ecuador

Cordoba – Nicaragua

Corona – Austria-Hungary, Naples

Crown – Australia, Bermuda, Gibraltar, Great Britain, Ireland, Isle of Man, Jamaica, Jersey, Malawi, New Zealand, Rhodesia, Rhodesia & Nyasaland, Scotland, Southern Rhodesia, Turks & Caicos

Crusado – Portugal

Cruzeiro – Brazil

Cuarto – Spain

Daalder – Netherlands

Dak – Nepal

Dalasi – The Gambia

Daler – Danish West Indies, Sweden

Demer – France

Decimo – Argentina, Chile, Colombia, Ecuador

Decimo de Sucre – Ecuador

Demy – Scotland

Denga – Russia

Denier – France

Dime – Canada, Hawaii, United States

Dinar (Dinara) – Afghanistan, Algeria,

Bahrain, Hejaz, Iraq, Kuwait, Morocco, Persia, Saudi-Arabia, Serbia, Tunisia, Turkey, Yugoslavia

Diner – Andorra

Dinero – Peru, Spain

Dirhem – Iraq, Morocco, Qatar and Dubai

Doit – Dutch East Indies, Netherlands

Dokdo – Junagadh, Kutch, Navanger

Dollar – Australia, Bahamas, Bermuda, Canada, Cayman Islands, China, Cook Islands, Fiji, Great Britain, Guyana, Hawaii, Hong Kong, Jamaica, Japan, Liberia, Malaysia, Mauritius, Newfoundland, New Zealand, Scotland, Sierra Leone, Singapore, Solomon Islands, Straits Settlement, Trinidad and Tobago, Tuvalu, USA, Virgin Islands, Western Samoa

Dong – French Indo-China, Vietnam

Double – Guernsey

Drachma (Drachmai) – Crete, Greece

Dub – Hyderabad (India Native State)

Ducat – Austria, Czechoslovakia, Hungary, Italy, Netherlands, Netherlands East Indies, Scotland, Yugoslavia

Ducatoon – Netherlands

Dukat – Germany, Poland, Yugoslavia

Eagle – United States

Ecu – France

Emalangeni – Swaziland

Escudo – Angola, Cape Verde Islands, Chile, Mozambique, Portugal, Portuguese Guinea, Portuguese India, St Thomas & Prince Islands, Spain, Timor

Eyrir (Aurar) – Iceland

Fanam – Travancore (India Native State)

Farthing – Antigua, Ceylon, Great Britain, Ireland, Isle of Man, Jamaica, Malta, Scotland

Fen – Communist China, Manchukuo

Fenig – Poland

Fil – Bahrain, Iraq, Jordan, Kuwait, South Arabia

Filler – Hungary

Fiorino – Italy

Florin – Australia, Austria, East Africa, Fiji, Great Britain, Hungary, Ireland, Malawi, New Zealand, Rhodesia and Nyasaland, South Africa

Forint – Hungary

Franc – Algeria, Belgian Congo, Belgium, Burundi, Cambodia, Cameroons, Central African States, Chad, Comoro Islands, Congo, Danish West Indies, Dominican

Republic, Ecuador, France, French Equatorial Africa, French Indo-China, French Oceania, French Polynesia, French Somaliland, French West Africa, Gabon, Guadeloupe, Guinea, Ivory Coast, Katanga, Luxembourg, Madagascar, Malagasy, Mali, Martinique, Monaco, Morocco, New Caledonia, New Hebrides, Reunion, Ruanda-Urundi, Rwanda, St Pierre & Miquelon, Senegal, Switzerland, Togo, Tunisia, West African States

Francescone – Italy
Franchi – Switzerland
Frank (Franken) – Belgium, Liechtenstein, Saarland, Switzerland, Westphalia
Franks Ari – Albania
Fu – China
Fun – Korea
Gazzetta – Venice
Gersh – Ethiopia
Girsh – Nejd, Hejaz, Saudi Arabia
Golde – Sierra Leone
Gourmier – Morocco
Gourde – Haiti
Grano – Italy, Malta
Groat – Great Britain, Ireland, Scotland
Groschen – Austria, Germany, Poland
Grosso – Italy
Grosz (Grosze, Groszy) – Poland
Guarani – Paraguay
Guerch – Egypt
Guilder (Gulden) – British Guiana, Curacao, Dutch East Indies, Germany, Netherlands, Netherlands Antilles, Surinam
Guinea – Great Britain, Saudi Arabia
Gulden – Austria, Danzig, Surinam
Halala – Saudi Arabia, Yemen
Haler – Bohemia & Moravia, Czechoslovakia
Half-dime – United States
Halfpenny – Australia, Bahamas, Barbados, Bermuda, Great Britain, Ireland, Isle of Man, Jamaica, New Guinea, New Zealand, Nigeria, Rhodesia and Hyasaland, Scotland, South Africa
Haller – Switzerland
Hao – French Indo-China, North Vietnam
Hardhead – Scotland
Hat-piece – Scotland
Heller – Austria-Hungary, German East Africa
Helm – England

Hwan – South Korea
Imadi – Yemen
Imami – Mysore (India Native State)
Imperial – Russia
Johannes – Portugal
Kapang – Sarawak
Keping – Sumatra
Kina – Papua New Guinea
Kip – Laos
Koban – Japan
Kobo – Nigeria
Kopec – Poland
Kopek (Kopeck) – Russia, Tuva
Kori – Kutch (India Native State)
Korona – Bohemia and Moravia, Slovakia, Hungary
Koruna (Koruny, Korun) – Czechoslovakia
Koula – Tonga
Krajczar (Kreuzer) – Hungary
Kran – Persia (Iran)
Kreuzer – Austria, Hungary, Switzerland
Krona (Kronor) – Sweden
Krona (Kronur) – Faroe Islands, Iceland
Krone (Kronen) – Austria-Hungary, Liechtenstein; (Kroner) – Denmark, Greenland, Norway
Kroon (Krooni) – Estonia
Kuna (Kune) – Yugoslavia-Croatia
Kurus – Turkey
Kwacha – Malawi, Zambia
Kyat – Myanmar (Burma)
Lari – Maldive Islands
Lats (Lati) – Latvia
Laurel – England
Lek (Leke) – Albania
Lempira – Honduras
Leone – Sierra Leone
Leopard – England
Lepton – Crete, Greece, Ionian Islands
Leu (Lei) – Romania
Lev (Leva) – Bulgaria
Li – Manchukuo
Liard – France
Libra – Peru
Licenti – Lesotho
Likuta – Congo
Lilangeni – Swaziland
Lion – Scotland
Lira (Lire) – Eritrea, Israel, Italian Somaliland, Italy, San Marino, Syria, Turkey
Litas (Litu, Litai) – Lithuania

Livre – France
Louis d'or – France
Luhlanga – Swaziland
Mace – China, Chinese Turkestan
Macuta – Angola
Makuta – Congo
Maloti – Lesotho
Maravedis (Maravedi) – Spain
Marchetto – Italy
Mariengroschen – Germany
Mark – Denmark, Estonia, Germany, German New Guinea, Livonia, Norway, Sweden
Markka (Markkaa) – Finland
Maton – Ethiopia
Mazuna – Morocco
Merk – Scotland
Mil – Cyprus, Hong Kong, Israel, Palestine
Millieme – Egypt, Lybia, Sudan, UAR
Millime – Tunisia
Milreis (1000 Reis) – Brazil, Portugal
Mohar – Nepal
Mohur – India, Bikanir, Cooch Behar, Gwalior, Hyderabad, Rajkot
Mon – Japan
Mongo – Mongolia
Mun – Korea
Naira – Nigeria
Napoleon – France
Naya Paisa (Naye Paise) – India
Ngwee – Zambia
Nugltrum – Bhutan
Noble – Austria, England, Scotland, Isle of Man
Oban – Japan
Obol (Oboli) – Ionian Islands
Onza – Costa Rica, Spain
Ore – Denmark, Faroes, Greenland, Norway
Ore – Sweden
Orte – Poland
Pa'anga – Tonga
Pagoda – Madras (India Native State)
Pahlevi – Persia
Pai – Hyderabad (India), Thailand
Paisa – Bahawalpur, Bhutan, Rutlam (India Native States), India, Mombasa, Nepal, Pakistan
Paissa – Afghanistan
Para – Hejaz, Moldavia, Montenegro, Serbia, Turkey, Walachia, Yugoslavia
Pardao – Portuguese India

Pataca – Macau, Portugal, Timor
Patrick – Ireland
Pengo – Hungary
Penni (Pennia) – Finland
Penny – Australia, Barbados, British Guiana, British West Africa, Ceylon, Fiji, The Gambia, Ghana, Great Britain, Guernsey, Ireland, Isle of Man, Jamaica, Jersey, Malawi, Mauritius, New Guinea, New Zealand, Nigeria, Rhodesia, Rhodesia and Nyasaland, Scotland, Sierra Leone, South Africa, Southern Rhodesia, Zambia
Perper (Perpera) – Montenegro
Pesa – German East Africa
Peseta – Equatorial Guinea, Peru, Spain, Viscayan Republic
Pesewa – Ghana
Peso – Argentina, Bolivia, Chile, Colombia, Costa Rica, Cuba, Dominican Republic, Guatemala, Honduras, Mexico, Paraguay, Philippines, Puerto Rico, Salvador, Uruguay
Pessa – Zanzibar
Pfennig – German New Guinea, Germany
Piastre – Cambodia, Cyprus, Egypt, French Cochin China, French Indo-China, Italy, Lebanon, Libya, Sudan, Syria, Tonkin, Tunisia, Turkey, United Arab Republic
Pice – Bhutan, East Africa, India, Mombasa, Pakistan
Pie – India, Pakistan
Piso – Philippines
Pistole – Ireland, Scotland
Plack – Scotland
Poisha – Bangladesh
Polushka – Russia
Pond – South African Republic
Pound – Australia, Cyprus, Egypt, Falkland Islands, Ghana, Great Britain, Guernsey, Ireland, Israel, Jamaica, Malta, New Zealand, St Helena, Scotland, South Africa, Sudan, Syria, Turkey, UAR
Pruta – Israel
Puffin – Lundy Island
Pul – Afganistan, Russia
Pula – Botswana
Pya – Myanmar (Burma)
Pysa – Zanzibar
Qindar – Albania
Quart – Gibraltar
Quartillo – Spain
Quarto – Philippines, Spain

Quattrina – Italy
Quetzal – Guatemala
Quiran – Afghanistan
Rand – South Africa, South West Africa, Lesotho, Swaziland
Rappe – Switzerland
Reaal – Curacao, Low Countries
Real (Reales) – Argentina, Bolivia, Chile, Colombia, Costa Rica, Dominican Republic, Ecuador, Guatemala, Honduras, Mexico, Paraguay, Peru, Salvador, Spain, Venezuela
Reichsmark – Germany
Reichspfennig – Germany
Reis – Azores, Brazil, Madeira, Portugal
Rentenpfennig – Germany (Republic)
Rial – Morocco, Muscat and Oman, Persia (Iran), Zanzibar
Rider – Scotland
Riel – Khmer Republic (Cambodia)
Rigsbankdaler – Denmark
Rigsbankskilling – Denmark
Rigsdaler – Denmark, Norway
Rijder – Netherlands
Riksdaler – Sweden
Rin – Japan

Ringgit – Malaysia
Riyal – Iraq
Rouble – Russia, Soviet Central Asia
Rupee – Afghanistan, Bhutan, Burma, Ceylon, East Africa and Uganda, German East Africa, India, Keeling Cocos Islands, Mauritius, Mombasa, Nepal, Pakistan, Saudi Arabia, Seychelles, Tibet
Rupia – Italian Somaliland, Port India
Rupie (Rupien) – German East Africa
Ryal – England, Hejaz, Morocco, Muscat and Oman, Nejd, Persia, Saudi Arabia, Scotland, Yemen, Zanzibar
Santims (Santimi) – Latvia
Sapeque – Annam, French Cochin China, French Indo-China
Satang – Thailand (Siam)
Sceat – Anglo-Saxon England
Schilling – Austria, Germany, Switzerland
Scudo – Bolivia, Chile, Costa Rica, Ecuador, Malta, Italy, Peru
Schwaren – Germany (Bremen, Oldenburg)
Sen – Brunei, Cambodia, China, Indonesia, Japan, Khmer, Malaysia, West Irian
Sene – Western Samoa
Seniti – Tonga
Sent – Estonia
Senti – Tanzania
Sentimo – Philippines
Sesena – Spain
Shahi – Afghanistan, Persia
Shekel – Israel
Shilling – Australia, British West Africa, Cyprus, East Africa, Fiji, The Gambia, Ghana, Great Britain, Guernsey, Ireland, Jamaica, Jersey, Kenya, Malawi, New Guinea, New Zealand, Nigeria, Rhodesia, Rhodesia and Nyasaland, Scotland, South Africa, Southern Rhodesia, Tanzania, Uganda, Zambia
Shillingi – Tanzania
Shokang – Tibet
Silbergroschen – Germany, Luxemburg
Skar – Tibet
Skilling – Denmark, Norway, Sweden
Sol (Soles) – France, Peru
Soldo – Italy
Somalo – Somalia
Sou – France
Sovereign – Australia, Canada, Great Britain, Isle of Man, South Africa

Speciedaler – Denmark, Norway
Srang – Tibet
Stiver – British Guiana, Ceylon, Demerara and Essequibo, Netherlands, Java
Stotinka (Stotinki) – Bulgaria
Stuber – German States
Stuiver – Curacao
Su – French Indo-China, South Vietnam
Sucre – Ecuador
Sueldo – Argentina, Balearic Islands, Bolivia
Sylis – Republic of Guinea
Tackoe – Gold Coast
Tael – China, Chinese Turkestan
Taka – Bangladesh
Tala – Tokelau Islands, West Samoa
Tallero – Eritrea
Talari – Ethiopia
Tanga – Portuguese India, Turkestan
Tangka – Tibet
Taro – Italy, Malta
Tenga – Bukhara (Soviet Central Russia)
Testone – Italy
Testoon – England, Scotland
Thaler (or Taler) – Austria-Hungary, Denmark, Germany, Liechtenstein, Norway, Poland, Sweden, Switzerland

Thebe – Botswana
Tical – Thailand (Siam)
Tien – Annam, Vietnam
Toca – Papua New Guinea
Toman – Persia
Tornese – Italy
Trade Dollar – Great Britain, Japan, United States of America
Tukhrik – Mongolia
Turner – Scotland
Unicorn – Scotland
Unit – Scotland
Unite – England
Venezolano – Venezuela
Vereinsthaler – Austria-Hungary
Vintem – Portugal
Wark – Ethiopia
Warn – Korea
Whan – Korea
Won – South Korea, North Korea
Xu – French Indo-China, Vietnam
Yang – Korea
Yen – Japan
Yuan – China, Communist China
Zaire – Zaire
Zecchino – Italy
Zloty (Zlote, Zlotych) – Poland

Designs and Inscriptions on £1 Coins

Fig 1

Fig 2

Fig 3   Fig 4

Fig 5   Fig 6

The first £1 coins were issued in 1983, almost a decade ago. However, if asked, only a small number of readers could immediately quote the Latin/Welsh inscriptions around the milled edges, let alone decipher the interpretations, especially of the Welsh coin!

Therefore, by courtesy of The Royal Mint, we list the complete issue together with illustrations of the various designs.

The obverses of the 1983 and 1984 coins were designed by Arnold Machin, however, from the 1985 issue, the new portrait of Her Majesty Queen Elizabeth II was designed by Raphael Maklouf.

The composition of the £1 coins is nickel-brass (70% copper, 5.5% nickel and 24.5% zinc). The 22.5mm rounded coins weigh 9.5g, with a 3.1mm milled edge thickness.

A Royal Proclamation describes the designs as follows:

United Kingdom (1983)
— 'the Ensigns Armorial of Our United Kingdom of Great Britain and Northern Ireland'.
The edge inscription reads DECUS ET TUTAMEN. (An ornament and a safeguard.) – **Fig 1**

Scotland (1984 and 1989)
— 'a Thistle eradicated enfiling a representation of Our Royal Diadem'.

The edge inscription reads NEMO ME IMPUNE LACESSIT. (No-one provokes me with impunity.) – **Fig 2**

Wales (1985 and 1990)
— 'a Leek eradicated enfiling a representation of Our Royal Diadem'.
The edge inscription reads PLEIDIOL WYF I'M GWLAD. (True am I to my country.) – **Fig 3**

Northern Ireland (1986)
— 'a Flax Plant eradicated enfiling a representation of Our Royal Diadem'.
The edge inscription reads DECUS ET TUTAMEN. – **Fig 4**

England (1987)
— 'an Oak Tree enfiling a representation of Our Royal Diadem'.
The edge inscription reads DECUS ET TUTAMEN. – **Fig 5**

United Kingdom (1988)
— 'a Shield of Our Royal Arms ensigned by a representation of the Royal Crown'.
The edge inscription reads DECUS ET TUTAMEN. – **Fig 6**

The Royal Mint has chosen the Northern Ireland £1 coin for the 1991 issue. The coin, which depicts the flax plant was designed by Leslie Durbin and originally issued in 1986.

Gibraltar Issues Ecu

A new circulating Gibraltar coin was struck in May 1991 with its value expressed in two currency systems – British pounds sterling and in Ecus.
The 70 ECUS/50 POUNDS 50% gold coin, weighs 3.1103g and measures 22.0mm.
The first of these unique coins was personally struck by the Chief Minister of the Gibraltar Government, Mr Joe Bossano. The Chairman of Pobjoy Mint, Mr Derek C Pobjoy presented the coin to Mr Bossano for placement in the Gibraltar Museum.

Major Varieties on British Coins

by C W Hill

'*Variety's the very spice of life!*' wrote William Cowper in a poem which nobody now reads. His aphorism nevertheless applies to many human activities. Collecting coins is certainly among them. Although the collector who assembles a complete run of Uncirculated British shillings minted from 1954 to 1966 may be proud of his or her achievement, it is the difference between the English and Scottish versions that is most likely to catch the eye of a discerning friend. A row of twenty-six identical obverses does little to quicken the appetite but the two different reverses for each date provide a pinch of spice for an otherwise unappetising dish.

Three categories

The search for variety may, of course, become too much of an obsession, even in coin collecting. Despite the use of modern technology in their production, no two coins are precisely identical in strictly scientific terms. The differences between them may be measurable only by applying advanced techniques far beyond the capacity of the ordinary collector but the differences do exist and earnest devotees of variety are happy to pursue them down to the last hundredth of a millimetre or thousandth of an inch.

For most of us there is satisfaction in discovering the varieties which are visible to the naked eye, complemented perhaps by a magnifying glass, a small pair of scales and a wooden ruler. These varieties may be divided into three main categories – those due to a change in the metal or alloy from which the coins have been minted; those due to major or minor differences in the dies used for minting the coins; and those produced by a malfunction of the minting machinery.

A change in the basic metal is generally easy to discern. Most collectors can distinguish silver from copper and gold from either. Minor changes in an alloy can be more puzzling and for these the collector may need to consult a good reference book or catalogue. The *Coin Year Book,* for example, gives details of the alloys used for British coins since 1797, together with their weights and diameters.

Major changes in the dies, and therefore in the designs of the coins produced from those dies, are normally easily recognised, though some details may be difficult to see on worn specimens. A magnifying glass will usually pick out the die numbers, the designer's initials and the mint-marks on Victorian and other coins.

Freak coins

Most easily recognisable are the freak coins produced in error. These include coins struck on planchets, or blanks, intended for a different issue; genuinely double-sided coins; brockages, on which the coin has the normal design on one side but an incuse or hollowed impression of the same design on the other side; mules, which have the obverse of one coin but the reverse design of a different issue; and coins with defects such as mis-struck letters or figures, or doubled or off-centre impressions.

Personal choice

The extent to which the collector delves into these many variations is a matter of personal choice. As a first step towards a study of the varieties to be found on British coins, this check-list gives details of those which may be identified without any aids other than patience and a magnifying-glass. The list omits freak coins, Patterns and Proofs, nor does it include mis-struck coins or those varieties produced by minor variations in the minting dies. Intended only as a general guide, the list covers base-metal and silver coins minted between 1816, when the British coinage was extensively re-designed, and 1967, when the last of the pre-decimal coins for circulation were produced.

Third-farthings

Victoria
1844
(a) REG on reverse
(b) RE on reverse
1866
Bronze, Bun Head portrait

Half-farthings

George IV
1828
(a) Trident prongs above base of letters
(b) Trident prongs touching base
1830
(a) Trident prongs above base of letters
(b) Trident prongs touching base
(c) Large date
(d) Small date

Victoria
1839
Straight ornament below date
1842
Larger, curved ornament below date
1844
E of REGINA over N

Farthings

George IV
1821
G of GRATIA over O
1823
I for 1 in date
1825
D of DEI over U
1826
(a) Portrait by Benedetto Pistrucci, thick neck
(b) R of GRATIA over E
(c) Re-designed portrait by William Wyon
(d) I for 1 in date

Victoria
1843
I for 1 in date
1851
D of DEI over horizontal D
1853
(a) Designer's initials, WW (William Wyon), raised
(b) WW incuse
1855
(a) WW raised
(b) WW incuse
1856
R of VICTORIA over E
1860
(a) Bronze, Bun Head portrait, outer circle composed of rounded beads
(b) Outer circle composed of toothed or elongated beads
(c) Mule—toothed obverse with beaded reverse
1865
(a) 5 over 2 in date
(b) Large 8 in date
(c) Small 8 in date
1874
(a) More matronly portrait, thicker neck and heavier cheek, Ralph Heaton & Sons mint-mark, H, below date
(b) G of D G and REG both over horizontal G
1875
(a) Pre-1874 portrait, large date
(b) Pre-1874 portrait, small date
(c) 1874 portrait, small date
(d) Pre-1874 portrait, Heaton mint-mark below date
(e) 1874 portrait, Heaton mint-mark below date
1880
(a) Four berries in wreath on Queen's head
(b) Three berries in wreath
1881
(a) Heaton mint-mark below date
(b) Mint-mark doubled
1895
(a) 1860-type portrait, as altered to show ageing

(b) Veiled Head portrait
1897
(a) Brilliant finish, as for previous issues
(b) New black finish, to prevent confusion with half-sovereign

Edward VII
1903
Reverse of 1901 (Victoria) with slightly lower horizon (low tide)

George V
1926
Modified Head portrait introduced

George VI
1949
IND IMP omitted

Elizabeth II
1953
(a) Outline of portrait in low relief
(b) Recut dies, outline of portrait sharper
1954
BRITT OMN omitted

Halfpennies

George IV
1826
6 over 5 in date

Victoria
1848
8 over 7 in date
1851
Dots above shield
1852
Dots above shield
1853
3 over 2 in date
1857
Dots above shield
1858
(a) Normal date
(b) Small date
(c) 8 over 6 in date
(d) 8 over 7 in date
1859
9 over 8 in date
1860
(a) Bronze, Bun Head portrait, outer circle composed of rounded beads

(b) Outer circle composed of toothed or elongated beads
1861
(a) Designer's initials, LCW (Leonard Charles Wyon), on rock
(b) No initials
(c) F of HALF over P
1865
5 over 3 in date
1874
(a) 1860 portrait
(b) More matronly portrait, thicker neck and heavier cheek
(c) Ralph Heaton & Sons mint-mark, H, below date
1875
Heaton mint-mark below date
1881
Heaton mint-mark below date
1889
9 over 8 in date
1895
Veiled Head portrait introduced

Edward VII
1902
(a) Reverse of 1901 (Victoria) with low horizon (low tide)
(b) New reverse with higher horizon (high tide)

George V
1925
(a) 1911 portrait, designer's initials, BM (Bertram Mackennal), above M of IMP
(b) Modified Head portrait, BM above I of IMP
1928
Smaller Head portrait introduced

George VI
1949
IND IMP omitted

Elizabeth II
1953
(a) Outline of portrait in low relief
(b) Recut dies, outline of portrait sharper
1954
BRITT OMN omitted

Pennies

William IV
1831
(a) Designer's initials, ww (William Wyon), on truncation
(b) No initials

Victoria
1841
(a) Colon after REG
(b) No colon after REG
1843
(a) Colon after REG
(b) No colon after REG
1846
(a) Space between DEF and colon
(b) Colon near to DEF
1847
(a) Space between DEF and colon
(b) Colon near to DEF
1848
(a) 8 over 6 in date
(b) 8 over 7 in date
1851
(a) Space between DEF and colon
(b) Colon near to DEF
1853-57
(a) Space between DEF and colon, ornamental trident
(b) Colon near to DEF, plain trident
1854
4 over 3 in date
1857
Small date
1858
(a) 8 over 3 in date
(b) 8 over 6 in date
(c) 8 over 7 in date
(d) Small date
(e) Designer's initials, ww (William Wyon), on truncation
(f) No initials
1859
Small date
1860
(a) Copper, Young Head portrait, 60 over 59 in date
(b) Bronze, Bun Head portrait, outer circle composed of rounded beads
(c) Outer circle composed of toothed or elongated beads
(d) Designer's initials, LCW (Leonard Charles Wyon), below foot on reverse
(e) LCW below shield on reverse
(f) No initials on reverse
(g) Designer's name LC WYON, omitted from truncation on obverse, LCW on reverse

1861
(a) LCW on rock
(b) LC WYON on obverse only
(c) LCW on reverse only
(d) No name or initials
1863
Die number below date
1864
(a) Plain 4 in date
(b) Crosslets on 4 in date
1865
5 over 3 in date
1874
(a) 1860 portrait
(b) More matronly portrait, thicker neck and heavier cheek
(c) 1860 portrait, Ralph Heaton & Sons mint-mark, H, below date
(d) More matronly portrait, Heaton mint-mark below date
1875
Heaton mint-mark below date
1881
(a) 1874 matronly portrait
(b) More elderly portrait, thicker nose and heavy jowl
(c) Heaton mint-mark below date
1895
(a) Veiled Head portrait, trident 1mm from P of PENNY
(b) Trident 2mm from P of PENNY
(c) Sea omitted behind Britannia
(d) Sea delineated behind Britannia

Edward VII
1902
(a) High horizon on reverse (high tide)
(b) Low horizon on reverse (low tide)

George V
1912
Ralph Heaton & Sons mint-mark, H, to left of date
1918
(a) Heaton mint-mark to left of date
(b) Kings Norton Metal Company mint-mark, KN, to left of date, letters spaced

(c) Kings Norton mint-mark to left of date, letters close together
1919
(a) Heaton mint-mark to left of date
(b) Kings Norton mint-mark to left of date
1926
(a) 1911 portrait, designer's initials, BM (Bertram Mackennal), above M of IMP
(b) Modified head portrait, BM above I of IMP
1928
Smaller Head portrait introduced

George VI
1940
(a) Single exergual line
(b) Double exergual lines
1949
IND IMP omitted

Elizabeth II
1953
Outline of portrait in low relief
1954
Recut dies, outline of portrait sharper, BRITT OMN omitted (only one specimen recorded)

Three-halfpences

William IV
1835
5 over 4 in date

Victoria
1843
43 over 34 in date

Silver threepences

Victoria
1838
B for final R in BRITANNIAR
1868
R for initial B in BRITANNIAR
1887
(a) Young Head portrait
(b) Jubilee Head portrait
1893
(a) Jubilee Head portrait, open 3 in date
(b) Jubilee Head portrait, closed 3 in date
(c) Veiled Head portrait

Edward VII
1904
(a) Large ball at end of 3 on reverse
(b) Small ball at end of 3 on reverse

George V
1920
(a) .925 fine silver
(b) Debased to .500 fine silver
1926
(a) 1911 portrait
(b) Modified Head portrait
1927
New reverse, oakleaves and acorns (Proof only)

Nickel-brass threepences

Edward VIII
1937
Portrait of King Edward VIII

George VI
1937
Portrait of King George VI
1949
IND IMP omitted

Elizabeth II
1953
(a) Outline of portrait in low relief
(b) Recut dies, outline of portrait sharper
1954
BRITT OMN omitted

Groats

Victoria
1838
8 over horizontal 8 in date
1842
2 over 1 in date
1843
4 over 5 in date
1847
7 over 6 in date
1848
(a) 8 over 6 in date
(b) 8 over 7 in date
1849
9 over 8 in date

1888
Jubilee Head portrait

Sixpences

George III
1819
9 over 8 in date
1820
Inverted 1 in date

George IV
1821
B for first R in BRITANNIAR
1824
Shield in garter reverse
1826
(a) Laureate Head portrait by Benedetto Pistrucci
(b) Bare Head portrait by William Wyon

Victoria
1844
Large 44 in date
1848
(a) 8 over 6 in date
(b) 8 over 7 in date
1850
5 over 3 in date
1859
9 over 8 in date
1866
(a) Die number above date
(b) Die number omitted
1871
(a) Die number above date
(b) Die number omitted
1877
(a) Die number above date
(b) Die number omitted
1878
D for initial B in BRITANNIAR
1879
(a) Die number above date
(b) Die number omitted
1887
(a) Young Head portrait
(b) Jubilee Head portrait, shield in garter reverse
(c) Jubilee Head portrait, SIX PENCE in wreath reverse
1893
(a) Jubilee Head portrait

(b) Veiled Head portrait

George V
1920
(a) .925 fine silver
(b) Debased to .500 fine silver
1926
(a) 1911 portrait
(b) Modified Head portrait, designer's initials, BM (Bertram Mackennal), nearer to back of neck
1927
(a) 1911 reverse, lion in circle
(b) New reverse, oak-leaves and acorns (Proof only)

George VI
1947
Cupro-nickel
1949
IND IMP omitted, royal cypher changed to G R VI

Elizabeth II
1953
(a) Outline of portrait in low relief
(b) Recut dies, outline of portrait sharper
1954
BRITT OMN omitted

Shillings

George III
1817
E for R in GEOR
1819
9 over 8 in date

George IV
1823
Shield in garter reverse
1825
(a) Laureate Head portrait by Benedetto Pistrucci
(b) Bare Head portrait by William Wyon
1826
6 over 2 in date

Victoria
1839
(a) Designer's initials, WW (William Wyon), on truncation
(b) No initials

1848
8 over 6 in date
1850
50 over 46 in date
1866
B for first R in BRITANNIAR
1879
(a) Die number above date
(b) Die number omitted
1887
(a) Young Head portrait
(b) Small Jubilee Head portrait
1889
(a) Small Jubilee Head portrait
(b) Large Jubilee Head portrait

George V
1920
Debased to .500 fine silver
1926
(a) 1911 portrait
(b) Modified Head portrait, designer's initials, BM (Bertram Mackennal), nearer to back of neck
1927
(a) 1902 reverse, lion in circle
(b) New reverse, taller lion, circle omitted

George VI
1937-51
(a) English reverse, *lion statant guardant regally crowned*
(b) Scottish reverse, *lion sejant erect affronté regally crowned*
1947
Cupro-nickel
1949
IND IMP omitted

Elizabeth II
1953-66
(a) English reverse, *three leopards passant guardant*
(b) Scottish reverse, *lion rampant*
1953
(a) Outline of portrait in low relief
(b) Recut dies – outline of portrait sharper
1954
BRITT OMN omitted

Florins

Victoria

1848
Without DEI GRATIA
1851
Gothic type with D G
1867
BRITT instead of BRIT
1877
(a) Designer's initials, ww (William Wyon), below portrait
(b) No initials, 48 arcs in obverse ornamentation
(c) 42 arcs in obverse ornamentation
1879
(a) ww below portrait, 48 arcs in obverse ornamentation
(b) No initials, 38 arcs in obverse ornamentation
1887
(a) 33 arcs in obverse ornamentation
(b) 46 arcs in obverse ornamentation
(c) Jubilee Head portrait

George V
1920
Debased to .500 fine silver
1927
Modified Head portrait, new reverse design (Proof only)

George VI
1947
Cupro-nickel
1949
IND IMP omitted

Elizabeth II
1953
(a) Outline of portrait in low relief
(b) Recut dies, outline of portrait sharper
1954
BRITT OMN omitted

Halfcrowns

George III
1817
(a) Large or Bull Head portrait, thick neck
(b) Small Head portrait

George IV
1823
(a) Garnished shield reverse
(b) Shield in garter reverse

1824
(a) Laureate Head portrait by Benedetto Pistrucci
(b) Bare Head portrait by William Wyon, new reverse design

William IV
1834
(a) Designer's initials, ww (William Wyon), in upright capitals
(b) ww in script
1836
6 over 5 in date

Victoria
1848
8 over 6 in date
1849
(a) Large date
(b) Small date
1876
6 over 5 in date
1887
(a) Young Head portrait
(b) Jubilee Head portrait

George V
1920
(a) Debased to 50% silver, 40% copper, 10% nickel
(b) Change of alloy to 50% silver, 50% copper
1922
(a) Crown on reverse touches shield (1911 design)
(b) Groove between crown and shield
1926
(a) 1911 portrait
(b) Modified Head portrait, designer's initials, BM (Bertram Mackennal), nearer to back of neck
1927
(a) Modified Head portrait
(b) New portrait and new, thinner shield on reverse (Proof only)

George VI
1947
Cupro-nickel
1949
IND IMP omitted

Elizabeth II
1953
(a) Outline of portrait in low relief, 123 beads in rim decoration, I of DEI points to a space
(b) Recut dies, outline of portrait sharper, 127 beads in rim decoration, I of DEI points to a bead
1954
BRITT OMN omitted

Double-florins

Victoria
1887
(a) Roman I in date
(b) Arabic 1 in date
1888
(a) Second I in VICTORIA normal
(b) Second I in VICTORIA an inverted 1
1889
(a) Second I in VICTORIA normal
(b) Second I in VICTORIA an inverted 1

Crowns

George III
1818
(a) Regnal year LVIII on edge
(b) Regnal year LIX on edge
1819
(a) Regnal year LIX on edge
(b) 9 over 8 in date
(c) Regnal year LX on edge
1820
20 over 19 in date

George IV
1821
(a) SECUNDO on edge
(b) TERTIO on edge (error, Proof only)
1822
(a) SECUNDO on edge
(b) TERTIO on edge

Victoria
1847
(a) Young Head portrait
(b) Gothic Head portrait (Proof only)
1893-1900
Two regnal years in Roman numerals on edge for each date

Coin Grading

Although the value of a coin can be affected by a number of factors, the two main criteria upon which it depends are degrees of scarcity and condition. Of these, deciding what condition or 'grade' a coin is in is one of the most controversial and, for the newcomer to the hobby, difficult aspects of numismatics.

The ability to accurately grade a coin according to the amount of wear it has received only comes with experience, and even then opinions may sometimes be found to differ – grading is not an exact science. The fundamental principle to be followed is that the overall amount of wear sustained dictates the grade. Two coins of the same type and in the same grade will not necessarily look exactly alike – different wear patterns may be apparent. For example, if the obverses of two Victorian Old Head coins, both graded Fine, are inspected, one may show a well-defined crown but a rather weak necklace, while the other may have a weak crown but fairly well-defined drapery across the shoulder. In spite of these differences, both the coins will possess one common feature: the overall amount of wear on both will be about the same. Coins should be graded as a whole rather than by the appearance of individual features.

It should also be noted that each type of coin has its own grading characteristics and that while some coins will retain a lot of detail even when well worn, others will not. For example, the lines between Britannia's toes on a penny dated 1927 may still be visible whereas on one dated 1940 they may not, even though the later coin may have had less circulation. The reason for this is that the two Britannias are different types with the incuse lines on the earlier coin cut deeper.

Main grades

There are five main grades of condition, Very Good, Fine, Very Fine, Extremely Fine and Uncirculated. The degree of wear that each of these grades indicates is as follows:

VERY GOOD (VG)

A worn coin on which the main features of the design are still distinguishable with the date and legend readable. This grade is also sometimes termed 'Fair'.

FINE (F)

A coin showing signs of considerable wear on the highest points, but all other details, including the lettering, should still show clearly.

VERY FINE (VF)

A coin that has been in circulation very little, with only slight traces of wear on the highest points.

EXTREMELY FINE (EF)

A coin that has had only minimal circulation. Although it may appear Uncirculated, slight scuffing or other marks on the surface only just visible to the naked eye may be apparent and prevent it from being classified as such.

UNCIRCULATED (Unc and BU)

A mint-state coin that has never been in circulation but which is not necessarily perfect. It might show slight abrasion marks from being in contact with other coins in the mint bag, and other imperfections caused by its manufacture.

Uncirculated coins often still possess their original mint lustre on the surface in which case they may be termed 'Brilliant Uncirculated' (BU). Unless such coins are treated with special care, after a period of time exposed to the atmosphere, the lustre will gradually disappear. Uncirculated coins are sometimes advertised with a qualification to indicate how much of the original mint lustre they still retain, eg 'full mint lustre' or '50% lustre'. The amount of lustre retained, however, has no bearing on the classification of mint-state coins as Uncirculated and some numismatists describe all mint-state coins simply as Uncirculated whether or not they still possess their original lustre.

Prefixes, bi-grades and faults

The condition of a coin may not, however, fall exactly within one of the above grades in which case the relevant grade to which it most nearly conforms is given a prefix qualifying it. For example, a coin that is better than Very Fine but not quite Extremely Fine may be referred to as 'Good Very Fine' (GVF) or 'Nearly Extremely Fine' (NEF). It is also possible for the condition of a coin to be better on one side than on the other, both the grades concerned being quoted, that of the obverse usually first, eg NEF/EF. The reverse of these 'bi-grades' is most often the better side.

A coin in a certain grade may be described as being holed or scratched or as having an edge knock or other fault which, although not actually lowering its grade, will nevertheless detract from its desirability and therefore its value. Conversely, over the years an attractive 'toning' or 'patina' may develop on a coin making it more desirable. This will be referred to when describing the coin's condition, but again its actual grade will not be affected.

FDC and Proof

In addition to the five main grades, there is also the term FDC or 'Fleur-de-Coin' which is applied to a coin in absolutely perfect condition with no flaws or wear at all. Coins struck for general circulation, even in Uncirculated condition, rarely come into this category and the term is generally applied to Proof coins although even these, given the modern methods of mass production, may not be perfect.

The term 'Proof' describes a particular type of coin, *not* a condition. Such coins are specially struck collectors' pieces not intended for circulation. Highly polished dies and blanks are used in their manufacture so that they have a mirror-like finish when struck, and they are individually handled during production. Many Proof coins have a frosted relief, the design having been treated with acid or sandblasted so that it has a matt finish to make it stand out against the highly polished field surrounding it. Some Proof coins have an all-over matt finish.

Visual guide

Illustrated on the following six pages are the obverses of coins from Victoria to Elizabeth II in the various grades of condition and the main points of wear on each. Uncirculated coins are not remarked on except for one of Elizabeth II, as little can be said about them other than to emphasise that a coin is either Uncirculated or it is not.

VICTORIA YH

EF Minute wear in the following places: eyebrow, edge of hair near eyebrow, on hair above ear, highest parts of bun.

VF Coarse hairlines almost complete, edge of hair above eye indistinct. Headbands well defined, slight wear on nose, eyebrow, lips and truncation.

F Headbands only partly visible, some hairlines still visible behind ear and on bun, edge of ear no longer sharp, eyebrow well worn.

VG Very few hairlines visible, headbands virtually indistinct, ear poorly defined.

VICTORIA OH

EF Minute wear in the following places: hairlines, cheekbone, necklace, eyebrow, ear and highest parts of drapery.

VF Hairlines flattening slightly, highest parts of robe show slight but obvious wear, jewellery no longer sharp, slight wear on eyebrow and cheekbone.

F Edge of hair not well defined, folds of robe across head nearly smooth, side of face flattened but ear well defined.

VG Large area of face worn smooth, some wear on crown, jewellery well worn.

EDWARD VII

EF Minute wear on the following places: side of jaw, hair above ear, eyebrow, nose, edge of ear and moustache.

VF Edge of bald patch still distinct, distinct signs of flattening of hair above ear, side of jaw and moustache. Obvious but slight wear on eyebrow.

F Ear quite well defined, moustache nearly whole, a few hairlines still visible under chin but few elsewhere.

VG Ear beginning to wear smooth, virtually no hairlines visible, eye quite well defined.

GEORGE V

EF Minute wear in the following places: eyebrow, cheekbone, highest parts of hair in centre of head and above forehead, truncation and nose.

VF Top of ear beginning to flatten, edge of beard across cheek barely visible, hair above forehead and in centre of head slightly flattened, slight but obvious wear on eyebrow and cheekbone.

F Edge of hair above forehead still distinct, few hairlines still visible, wear on eyebrow and cheekbone very obvious.

VG Ear poorly defined, few, if any, hairlines visible, edge of hair above forehead indistinct.

GEORGE VI

EF Minute wear in the following places: highest parts of hairlines between ear and parting, eyebrow, end of nose, jawbone and truncation.

VF Slight flattening of hairlines just above ear, between ear and parting, above forehead. Slight but obvious wear on cheekbone, eyebrow, jawbone, chin and nose.

F Hairlines worn smooth except in the following places: on temple, behind ear and above parting. Hollow in hair above ear still visible.

VG Parting still visible, edge of ear poorly defined, virtually no hairlines.

ELIZABETH II

Unc No evidence of wear at all, a few very minor bag abrasions.

EF Minute wear in the following places: folds of ribbons behind head, outer edges of those leaves in the centre of head, highest part of shoulder, jawbone and on the hair above the forehead.

VF Slight but obvious wear on the outer edges of the leaves in the centre of head, eyebrow, folds of ribbons. Hairlines between edge of hair and leaves are beginning to flatten but outlines of all the leaves are still distinct. Top edge of dress only just visible.

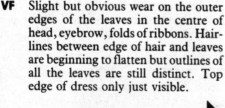

F Leaves and hairlines on both sides of wreath beginning to wear smooth. Top edge of dress indistinct.

Banknote Grading

The following system of banknote grading by numbers rather than by the conventional system of Fine, Very Fine, etc has been developed by Douglas Bramwell of Bramwell and Bramwell, a firm of London banknote dealers. It will be seen that this system gives a much more accurate and reliable indication of the condition of a banknote than does the conventional method of grading, each note being given a grade of 100 if in perfect condition from which so much is deducted for pin holes, soiling, etc to give the final grade. For example, a slightly soiled note with several folds, no damage to the surface or edges, and several pin holes would have a grade of 75. This figure is arrived at as follows:

Cleanliness	5
Folding	10
Surface	0
Edges	0
Body	$\frac{10}{25}$

100-25=75

Using the numerical system of grading the following would be the approximate equivalents of the grades used in the conventional system:

100	Uncirculated
90	Extremely Fine
75	Very Fine
55	Fine
30	Very Good

The prices in the list of British banknotes on page 248 are listed under the grades used in both systems. To use the numerical system, the table below gives the amounts to be deducted from 100 for a note according to the number of folds or pin holes it may have, amount of soiling, and folding or damaged edges.

Cleanliness:
- Slight soiling only just detectable ... 5
- Note considerably soiled and/or banker's marks ... 10
- Note very dirty, considerably reducing legibility ... 20

Folding:
- One or two folds leaving a slight crease ... 5
- Several more prominent folds ... 10
- Many folds ... 20

Surface:
- Slight and only just detectable damage ... 5
- Note damaged in several places or over considerable area ... 10
- Note extensively damaged over wide areas ... 20

Edges:
- Slight roughness or indentation ... 5
- Edges considerably damaged and/or tears not extending beyond margin ... 10
- Edges badly damaged or tears extending into design ... 20

Body:
- One or two pin holes ... 5
- Several pin holes or one or two larger holes ... 10
- Several larger holes ... 20

THE BLUE PAGES

The values listed in the following pages are, at the time of going to press, an analysis of dealers' and auctioneers' selling prices throughout the world. They have been processed — after considerable research — by computer, thus increasing their world-wide reputation for accuracy. It should be noted that they are not fixed standard prices or an indication of dealers' buying prices, nor are they offers to buy and sell on behalf of the publishers. They are a reliable guide to the current *selling prices* of the coins listed.

Asterisks (*) denote that coins are not generally offered for sale in the conditions specified and crosses (+) that no sales of the coins have been recorded from which a price could be calculated. Dashes (—) indicate that prices are not applicable. Unique coins and those of exceptional rarity, such as the 1933 and 1954 pennies, have not been listed, nor has any attempt been made to include every variety or Proof coin issued. Proof prices where listed are in FDC only.

Gold prices computed at a rate of £195.40 per oz, excluding VAT.

contents

grading

Grading is a method by which the numismatist describes the condition of a coin. Briefly, the degree of wear indicated by the grading terms used in the Blue Pages is as follows:

VERY GOOD (VG)

A worn coin on which the main features of the design are still distinguishable with the date and legend readable.

FINE (F)

A coin showing signs of considerable wear on the highest points, but all other details, including the lettering, should still show clearly.

VERY FINE (VF)

A coin that has been in circulation very little, with only slight traces of wear on the highest points.

EXTREMELY FINE (EF)

A coin that has had only minimal circulation. Although it may appear Uncirculated, slight scuffing or other surface marks will prevent it from being classified as such.

UNCIRCULATED (Unc)

A mint-state coin that has never been in circulation but which is not necessarily perfect and may show manufacturing imperfections.

FLEUR-DE-COIN (FDC)

A coin in absolutely perfect condition with no flaws or wear at all. Generally applied to Proof coins which have been specially struck in highly polished dies and blanks.

ILLUSTRATIONS

For more comprehensive advice, see our illustrated article Coin Grading (Page 94).

QUARTER-FARTHINGS

Victoria 1838-1901

	MINTAGE	F	VF	EF	UNC	PROOF
1839	3,840,000	£3.50	£17.00	£25.00	£40.00	—
1851		£4.75	£14.00	£30.00	£60.00	—
1852	2,215,680	£3.75	£15.00	£24.00	£42.00	—
1853		£5.25	£16.00	£30.00	£45.00	£250.00

THIRD-FARTHINGS

George IV 1821-1830

	MINTAGE	F	VF	EF	UNC	PROOF
1827	unrecorded	£3.50	£5.00	£15.00	£27.00	—

William IV 1831-1837

	MINTAGE	F	VF	EF	UNC	PROOF
1835	unrecorded	£1.00	£3.75	£15.00	£35.00	—

Victoria 1838-1901

Young Head

	MINTAGE	F	VF	EF	UNC	PROOF
1844	1,301,040	£5.50	£18.00	£55.00	£65.00	—
1844 RE for REG		+	+	+	+	—

Bun Head

	MINTAGE	F	VF	EF	UNC	PROOF
1866	576,000	£1.25	£4.00	£8.25	£16.00	—
1868	144,000	£0.75	£3.00	£9.00	£18.00	—
1876	162,000	£0.75	£3.75	£9.00	£20.00	—
1878	288,000	£1.50	£4.50	£8.00	£18.00	—
1881	144,000	£1.25	£3.50	£11.00	£17.00	—
1884	144,000	£1.00	£4.00	£8.25	£10.00	—
1885	288,000	£1.00	£4.50	£8.50	£12.00	—

Edward VII 1902-1910

	MINTAGE	F	VF	EF	UNC	PROOF
1902	288,000	£0.75	£2.50	£4.50	£6.25	—

George V 1911-1936

	MINTAGE	F	EF	VF	UNC	PROOF
1913	288,000	£1.00	£2.75	£3.50	£6.50	—

HALF-FARTHINGS

George IV 1821-1830

	MINTAGE	F	VF	EF	UNC	PROOF
1828	7,680,000	£3.75	£13.00	£40.00	£65.00	—
1830 large date	8,766,320	£6.00	£15.00	£40.00	£60.00	—
1830 small date		£3.50	£11.00	£40.00	£75.00	—

William IV 1831-1837

	MINTAGE	F	VF	EF	UNC	PROOF
1837	1,935,360	£15.00	£35.00	£165.00	£180.00	-

Victoria 1838-1901

1839   **1842-1856**

	MINTAGE	F	VF	EF	UNC	PROOF
1839	2,042,880	£1.00	£3.00	£16.00	£30.00	—
1842	unrecorded	£1.00	£3.75	£15.00	£22.00	—
1843	3,440,640	£1.00	£3.00	£4.50	£12.00	—
1844	6,451,200	£1.25	£2.50	£3.50	£9.00	—
1844 E of REGINA over N		£4.50	£10.00	£30.00	£50.00	—
1847	3,010,560	£1.00	£5.25	£12.00	£22.00	—
1851	unrecorded	£1.00	£4.50	£17.00	£35.00	—
1852	989,184	£1.00	£4.00	£18.00	£35.00	—
1853	955,224	£2.00	£7.00	£32.00	£50.00	£200.00
1854	677,376	£3.00	£13.00	£40.00	£70.00	—
1856	913,920	£3.00	£12.00	£40.00	£60.00	—

FARTHINGS

Charles II 1660-1685

Copper   **Tin**

	VG	F	VF	EF	PROOF
1672	£6.00	£15.00	£28.00	£175.00	—
1673	£4.50	£10.00	£30.00	£175.00	—
1674	£3.50	£13.00	£45.00	£175.00	—
1675	£3.25	£12.00	£60.00	£175.00	—
1679	£2.00	£20.00	£50.00	£220.00	—
1684 tin	£16.00	£40.00	£140.00	£480.00	—
1685 —					extremely rare

James II 1685-1688

Cuirassed   **Draped**

	VG	F	VF	EF	PROOF
1684 tin, cuirassed bust				extremely rare	
1685 — —	£20.00	£40.00	£135.00	£430.00	—
1686 — —	£22.00	£45.00	£160.00	£475.00	—
1687 — draped bust	£30.00	£55.00	£185.00	£525.00	—

William and Mary 1688-1694

Tin   **Copper**

	VG	F	VF	EF	PROOF
1689 tin, small busts				extremely rare	
1690 — large busts	£20.00	£47.00	£120.00	£450.00	—
1691 — —	£20.00	£45.00	£120.00	£475.00	—
1692 — —	£22.00	£50.00	£125.00	£500.00	—
1694 copper	£6.25	£12.00	£32.00	£380.00	—

William III 1694-1702

Date in exergue

	VG	F	VF	EF	PROOF
1695 date in exergue	£2.50	£9.50	£35.00	£220.00	—
1696 —	£2.00	£8.75	£30.00	£200.00	—
1697 —	£3.50	£8.50	£30.00	£200.00	—
1698 —	£10.00	£55.00	£175.00	£400.00	—
1698 date in legend	£4.00	£25.00	£75.00	£385.00	—
1699 —	£2.25	£9.50	£30.00	£200.00	—
1699 date in exergue	£2.00	£13.00	£45.00	£260.00	—
1700 —	£4.00	£12.00	£30.00	£200.00	—

Anne 1702-1714

	VG	F	VF	EF	PROOF
1714 not officially circulated	£20.00	£70.00	£150.00	£310.00	—

George I 1714-1727

'Dump'

Large flan

	VG	F	VF	EF	PROOF
1717 'dump'	£12.00	£55.00	£125.00	£345.00	—
1719 large flan	£5.50	£7.00	£28.00	£225.00	—
1720 —	£4.25	£7.25	£20.00	£160.00	—
1721 —	£2.25	£5.00	£30.00	£165.00	—
1722 —	£2.00	£10.00	£35.00	£175.00	—
1723 —	£2.00	£15.00	£30.00	£175.00	—
1724 —	£2.00	£7.00	£35.00	£175.00	—

George II 1727-1760

Young Head   **Old Head**

	VG	F	VF	EF	PROOF
1730 young head	£1.50	£5.50	£25.00	£85.00	—
1731 —	£1.75	£5.50	£25.00	£90.00	—
1732 —	£2.50	£6.00	£30.00	£90.00	—
1733 —	£2.00	£5.75	£25.00	£85.00	—
1734 —	£2.00	£6.00	£30.00	£90.00	—
1735 —	£1.75	£6.50	£20.00	£75.00	—
1736 —	£2.50	£6.00	£20.00	£85.00	—
1737 —	£1.25	£5.25	£15.00	£75.00	—
1739 —	£2.00	£7.00	£20.00	£75.00	—

	VG	F	VF	EF	PROOF
1741 old head, GEORGIVS	£1.50	£5.00	£28.00	£95.00	—
1744 — —	£1.75	£5.50	£28.00	£95.00	—
1746 — GEORGIVS	£2.75	£6.50	£18.00	£65.00	—
1749 — —	£1.00	£10.00	£20.00	£70.00	—
1750 — —	£3.00	£5.50	£25.00	£85.00	—
1754 — —	£2.00	£6.00	£13.00	£40.00	—

George III 1760-1820

1771-1775

	VG	F	VF	EF	PROOF
1771	£4.00	£15.00	£35.00	£100.00	—
1773	£1.50	£4.50	£10.00	£55.00	—
1774	£1.50	£4.50	£16.00	£75.00	—
1775	£2.25	£7.25	£15.00	£70.00	—

1799 **1806-1807**

	MINTAGE	F	VF	EF	UNC	PROOF
1799	unrecorded	£1.25	£11.00	£22.00	£30.00	—
1806	unrecorded	£2.00	£4.00	£15.00	£30.00	—
1807	unrecorded	£2.00	£3.50	£40.00	£55.00	—

George IV 1821-1830

First issue (1821-1826) **Second issue (1826-1830)**

	MINTAGE	F	VF	EF	UNC	PROOF
1821	2,688,000	£2.00	£3.25	£15.00	£30.00	—
1822	5,924,352	£1.50	£3.50	£9.50	£16.00	—
1823	2,365,440	£1.50	£3.75	£20.00	£25.00	—
1823 Roman I for 1		+	+	+	+	—

	MINTAGE	F	VF	EF	UNC	PROOF
1825	4,300,800	£1.50	£4.25	£15.00	£28.00	—
1826	6,666,240	£2.00	£4.75	£22.00	£100.00	—
1826 second issue		£1.50	£5.50	£21.00	£45.00	£110.00
1827	2,365,440	£2.00	£4.50	£20.00	£30.00	—
1828	2,365,440	£1.50	£4.50	£20.00	£50.00	—
1829	1,505,280	£3.00	£6.00	£30.00	£60.00	—
1830	2,365,440	£2.00	£4.00	£18.00	£32.00	—

William IV 1831-1837

	MINTAGE	F	VF	EF	UNC	PROOF
1831	2,688,000	£1.50	£5.00	£26.00	£40.00	£125.00
1834	1,935,360	£2.00	£3.50	£11.00	£50.00	—
1835	1,720,320	£1.50	£7.00	£18.00	£45.00	—
1836	1,290,240	£1.75	£6.50	£18.00	£60.00	—
1837	3,010,560	£1.25	£4.25	£16.00	£42.00	—

Victoria 1838-1901

Young Head

	MINTAGE	F	VF	EF	UNC	PROOF
1838	591,360	£2.50	£4.25	£17.00	£25.00	—
1839	4,300,800	£1.50	£5.00	£15.00	£24.00	£110.00
1840	3,010,560	£1.75	£5.25	£14.00	£25.00	—
1841	1,720,320	£2.00	£5.75	£14.00	£30.00	—
1842	1,290,240	£3.50	£6.25	£38.00	£45.00	—
1843	4,085,760	£2.00	£6.00	£15.00	£25.00	—
1843 Roman I for 1		+	+	+	+	—
1844	430,080	£16.00	£40.00	£150.00	£300.00	—
1845	3,225,600	£1.50	£5.50	£11.00	£26.00	—
1846	2,580,480	£2.25	£6.50	£35.00	£50.00	—
1847	3,879,720	£1.50	£4.75	£20.00	£25.00	—
1848	1,290,240	£1.25	£4.75	£16.00	£30.00	—
1849	645,120	£8.00	£25.00	£95.00	£115.00	—
1850	430,080	£3.50	£6.25	£23.00	£30.00	—
1851	1,935,360	£3.00	£11.00	£40.00	£60.00	—
1851 D of DEI over		£40.00	£120.00	£300.00	£500.00	—
1852	822,528	£3.00	£10.00	£40.00	£60.00	—
1853 WW raised	1,028,628	£2.00	£3.75	£18.00	£23.00	£250.00
1853 WW incuse		£1.75	£3.50	£12.00	£30.00	—
1854	6,504,960	£1.50	£5.75	£20.00	£25.00	—

FARTHINGS

	MINTAGE	F	VF	EF	UNC	PROOF
1855 WW raised	3,440,640	£4.00	£9.50	£24.00	£50.00	—
1855 WW incuse		£3.50	£7.50	£20.00	£50.00	—
1856	1,771,392	£3.00	£6.50	£30.00	£47.00	—
1856 R of VICT over E		£12.00	£45.00	£90.00	£200.00	—
1857	1,075,200	£1.75	£8.00	£14.00	£32.00	—
1858	1,720,320	£1.50	£3.50	£16.00	£25.00	—
1859	1,290,240	£5.25	£20.00	£45.00	£75.00	—
1860	unrecorded	+	+	+	+	—

Bun Head

	MINTAGE	F	VF	EF	UNC	PROOF
1860 beaded	2,867,200	£1.50	£2.25	£8.75	£12.00	—
1860 toothed		£0.75	£1.75	£9.00	£12.00	—
1861	8,601,600	£0.50	£4.25	£8.00	£12.00	—
1862	14,336,000	£1.50	£3.50	£10.00	£14.00	—
1863	1,433,600	£10.00	£22.00	£47.00	£140.00	—
1864	2,508,800	£1.25	£2.25	£9.25	£25.00	—
1865 5 over 2		£1.50	£2.50	£10.00	£25.00	—
1865 large 8	4,659,200	£2.00	£4.50	£10.00	£16.00	—
1865 small 8		£1.75	£4.50	£7.00	£15.00	—
1866	3,584,000	£0.75	£1.50	£7.75	£13.00	—
1867	5,017,600	£1.75	£3.50	£14.00	£20.00	—
1868	4,851,208	£1.75	£4.25	£13.00	£20.00	—
1869	3,225,600	£2.50	£7.25	£16.00	£30.00	—
1872	2,150,400	£1.75	£2.75	£11.00	£18.00	—
1873	3,225,620	£1.25	£3.00	£6.50	£15.00	—
1874 H	3,584,000	£1.25	£6.00	£11.00	£18.00	—
1874 H both Gs over		£27.00	£120.00	£200.00	£450.00	—
1875 large date	712,760	£7.00	£11.00	£19.00	£70.00	—
1875 small date		£12.00	£20.00	£50.00	£120.00	—
1875 H	6,092,800	£0.75	£1.50	£6.75	£10.00	—
1876 H	1,175,200	£4.00	£8.00	£22.00	£55.00	—
1878	4,008,540	£1.25	£3.50	£7.00	£10.00	—
1879	3,977,180	£1.00	£3.00	£6.25	£12.00	—
1880 4 berries	1,842,710	£2.00	£6.00	£12.00	£20.00	—
1880 3 berries		£1.50	£13.00	£30.00	£60.00	—
1881	3,494,670	£1.25	£2.25	£13.00	£17.00	—
1881 H	1,792,000	£2.00	£3.50	£6.75	£16.00	—
1882 H	1,792,000	£1.50	£3.50	£11.00	£15.00	—
1883	1,128,680	£4.00	£6.00	£16.00	£30.00	—
1884	5,782,000	£0.50	£1.50	£4.25	£7.50	—
1885	5,442,308	£0.60	£2.50	£4.50	£7.00	—
1886	7,707,790	£1.00	£2.00	£4.25	£9.25	—
1887	1,340,800	£1.75	£2.75	£6.75	£19.00	—
1888	1,887,250	£1.25	£2.25	£5.50	£10.00	—
1890	2,133,070	£1.50	£3.00	£7.50	£14.00	—
1891	4,959,690	£1.00	£3.25	£5.00	£6.50	—
1892	887,240	£3.00	£7.00	£15.00	£32.00	—
1893	3,904,320	£1.00	£2.00	£3.50	£9.00	—
1894	2,396,770	£1.00	£1.25	£6.50	£11.00	—
1895 young head	2,852,852	£3.75	£6.75	£30.00	£55.00	—
1895 veiled head		£1.00	£3.00	£5.75	£8.50	—
1896	3,668,610	£1.00	£2.75	£5.25	£7.50	—.
1897 brilliant finish	4,579,800	£1.00	£2.00	£5.00	£15.00	—
1897 black finish		£0.50	£1.00	£4.00	£5.50	—

Veiled Head

	MINTAGE	F	VF	EF	UNC	PROOF
1898	4,010,080	£0.75	£1.25	£4.00	£13.00	—
1899	3,864,616	£1.00	£1.75	£4.50	£8.50	—
1900	5,969,317	£1.00	£1.50	£3.25	£5.50	—
1901	8,016,459	£1.00	£1.50	£2.50	£4.75	—

Edward VII 1902-1910

	MINTAGE	F	VF	EF	UNC	PROOF
1902	5,125,120	£1.00	£1.50	£4.00	£6.50	—
1903	5,331,200	£1.00	£2.25	£4.00	£9.25	—
1904	3,628,800	£1.50	£2.50	£5.00	£12.00	—
1905	4,076,800	£1.50	£3.25	£5.25	£10.00	—
1906	5,340,160	£0.75	£1.25	£4.50	£9.25	—
1907	4,399,360	£1.00	£2.00	£5.00	£10.00	—
1908	4,264,960	£1.00	£2.25	£5.00	£9.50	—
1909	8,852,480	£1.00	£1.50	£3.50	£7.50	—
1910	2,298,400	£1.75	£3.25	£5.75	£12.00	—

George V 1911-1936

	MINTAGE	F	VF	EF	UNC	PROOF
1911	5,196,800	£1.25	£1.75	£3.00	£5.25	—
1912	7,669,760	£0.50	£1.00	£2.00	£5.50	—
1913	4,184,320	£0.65	£1.25	£2.00	£4.25	—
1914	6,126,988	£0.80	£1.25	£2.00	£4.50	—
1915	7,129,254	£0.75	£1.75	£3.75	£10.00	—
1916	10,993,325	£0.40	£1.00	£2.50	£4.00	—
1917	21,434,844	£0.30	£0.60	£1.50	£3.25	—
1918	19,362,818	£0.35	£0.50	£1.25	£3.25	—
1919	15,089,425	£0.25	£0.50	£1.25	£3.50	—
1920	11,480,536	£0.30	£0.55	£1.25	£3.00	—
1921	9,469,097	£0.30	£0.55	£1.00	£3.00	—
1922	9,956,983	£0.25	£0.60	£1.00	£3.00	—
1923	8,034,457	*	£0.35	£1.00	£3.00	—

FARTHINGS

	MINTAGE	F	VF	EF	UNC	PROOF
1924	8,733,414	*	£0.30	£1.00	£3.25	—
1925	12,634,697	*	£0.35	£1.00	£3.25	—
1926	9,792,397	£0.35	£0.60	£1.00	£3.25	—
1927	7,868,355	*	£0.35	£0.80	£2.25	—
1928	11,625,600	*	£0.30	£1.25	£3.00	—
1929	8,419,200	£0.30	£0.50	£1.00	£2.25	—
1930	4,195,200	*	£0.55	£1.75	£2.25	—
1931	6,595,200	*	£0.60	£0.80	£2.25	—
1932	9,292,800	*	£0.30	£0.60	£2.25	—
1933	4,560,000	*	£0.60	£1.00	£1.75	—
1934	3,052,800	£0.40	£0.75	£1.25	£3.50	—
1935	2,227,200	*	£1.25	£2.00	£3.75	—
1936	9,734,400	*	£0.30	£0.60	£3.00	—

George VI 1937-1952

	MINTAGE	F	VF	EF	UNC	PROOF
1937	8,131,200	*	£0.40	£0.75	£1.00	—
1937	26,402	—	—	—	—	£4.25
1938	7,449,600	*	£0.30	£1.50	£2.50	—
1939	31,440,000	*	£0.15	£0.40	£0.75	—
1940	18,360,000	*	£0.20	£0.40	£1.25	—
1941	27,312,000	*	£0.20	£0.45	£1.00	—
1942	28,857,600	*	£0.25	£0.45	£1.00	—
1943	33,345,600	*	£0.15	£0.40	£0.75	—
1944	25,137,600	*	£0.20	£0.40	£0.65	—
1945	23,736,000	*	£0.15	£0.40	£1.00	—
1946	24,364,800	*	£0.10	£0.35	£1.00	—
1947	14,745,600	*	£0.20	£0.40	£0.60	—
1948	16,622,400	*	£0.25	£0.50	£0.75	—
1949	8,424,000	*	£0.25	£0.40	£0.60	—
1950	10,324,800	*	£0.25	£0.35	£0.80	—
1950	17,513	—	—	—	—	£4.00
1951	14,016,000	*	£0.15	£0.35	£1.00	—
1951	20,000	—	—	—	—	£3.25
1952	5,251,200	*	*	£0.45	£0.80	—

Elizabeth II 1953-

	MINTAGE	F	VF	EF	UNC	PROOF
1953	6,131,037	*	*	£0.65	£1.25	—
1953	40,000	—	—	—	—	£3.25
1954	6,566,400	*	£0.25	£0.50	£0.75	—
1955	5,779,200	*	*	£0.40	£0.65	—
1956	1,996,800	*	*	£1.00	£1.25	—

HALFPENCE

Charles II 1660-1685

	VG	F	VF	EF	PROOF
1672	£4.00	£20.00	£55.00	£215.00	—
1673	£6.75	£32.00	£55.00	£215.00	—
1675	£6.50	£17.00	£50.00	£215.00	—

James II 1685-1688

	VG	F	VF	EF	PROOF
1685 tin	£20.00	£40.00	£135.00	£450.00	—
1686 —	£22.00	£45.00	£160.00	£500.00	—
1687 —	£20.00	£40.00	£135.00	£450.00	—

William and Mary 1688-1694

Tin   Copper

	VG	F	VF	EF	PROOF
1689 tin, small busts	£175.00	£350.00	£900.00	—	—
1690 — large busts, date on edge only	£20.00	£40.00	£115.00	£425.00	—
1691 — — date in ex and on edge	£20.00	£40.00	£115.00	£425.00	—
1692 — — —	£20.00	£50.00	£115.00	£425.00	—
1694 copper	£4.75	£15.00	£65.00	£275.00	—

William III 1694-1702

Right hand up   **Date after legend**   **Hand on knee**

	VG	F	VF	EF	PROOF
1695 date in exergue, right hand up	£3.50	£8.00	£30.00	£180.00	—
1696 — —	£2.50	£9.00	£25.00	£170.00	—
1697 — —	£4.00	£7.00	£25.00	£170.00	—
1698 —	£5.75	£11.00	£38.00	£185.00	—
1698 date after legend	£4.50	£9.00	£35.00	£175.00	—
1699 —	£3.50	£10.00	£34.00	£170.00	—
1699 date in exergue, hand on knee	£3.00	£7.00	£25.00	£165.00	—
1700 — —	£4.00	£8.25	£25.00	£165.00	—
1701 — —	£4.00	£8.00	£30.00	£170.00	—

George I 1714-1727

'Dump'   **Large flan**

	VG	F	VF	EF	PROOF
1717 'dump'	£4.50	£8.00	£35.00	£150.00	—
1718 —	£3.75	£8.00	£30.00	£135.00	—
1719 large flan	£4.00	£8.75	£35.00	£170.00	—
1720 —	£2.75	£8.25	£35.00	£170.00	—
1721 —	£2.00	£6.25	£35.00	£170.00	—
1722 —	£2.00	£5.25	£35.00	£170.00	—
1723 —	£2.25	£7.25	£35.00	£170.00	—
1724 —	£2.75	£8.50	£35.00	£170.00	—

George II 1727-1760

	VG	F	VF	EF	PROOF
1729 young head	£2.25	£5.00	£22.00	£90.00	—
1730 —	£2.00	£6.50	£20.00	£90.00	—
1731 —	£3.75	£6.50	£22.00	£90.00	—
1732 —	£1.00	£6.50	£22.00	£90.00	—
1733 —	£1.00	£5.25	£22.00	£90.00	—
1734 —	£1.50	£5.75	£20.00	£95.00	—

Young Head   **Old Head**

	VG	F	VF	EF	PROOF
1735 —	£0.75	£5.25	£20.00	£90.00	—
1736 —	£0.75	£8.50	£22.00	£90.00	—
1737 —	£0.75	£4.25	£30.00	£90.00	—
1738 —	£1.50	£6.25	£20.00	£80.00	—
1739 —	£1.75	£7.00	£22.00	£90.00	—
1740 old head, GEORGIUS	£0.50	£4.00	£20.00	£75.00	—
1742 — —	£0.50	£6.50	£20.00	£90.00	—
1743 — —	£2.00	£4.50	£26.00	£65.00	—
1744 — —	£0.50	£6.00	£20.00	£65.00	—
1745 — —	£0.75	£6.00	£18.00	£65.00	—
1746 — GEORGIVS	£1.75	£4.00	£23.00	£75.00	—
1747 — —	£1.50	£4.00	£20.00	£75.00	—
1748 — —	£0.50	£5.00	£18.00	£60.00	—
1749 — —	£0.50	£6.00	£18.00	£100.00	—
1750 — —	£1.25	£3.50	£18.00	£65.00	—
1751 — —	£1.25	£4.00	£16.00	£65.00	—
1752 — —	£2.25	£5.50	£23.00	£65.00	—
1753 — —	£1.25	£6.25	£18.00	£75.00	—
1754 — —	£0.55	£4.00	£18.00	£65.00	—

George III 1760-1820

	VG	F	VF	EF	PROOF
1770	£1.00	£4.00	£16.00	£65.00	—
1771	£1.25	£4.00	£11.00	£50.00	—
1772	£1.50	£3.00	£17.00	£50.00	—
1773	£1.75	£3.00	£10.00	£50.00	—
1774	£1.00	£7.50	£17.00	£55.00	—
1775	£1.25	£4.50	£15.00	£60.00	—

1770-1775   **1799**

	MINTAGE	F	VF	EF	UNC	PROOF
1799 5 guns	unrecorded	£1.75	£4.50	£20.00	£30.00	—
1799 6 guns	unrecorded	£1.50	£3.25	£13.00	£35.00	—
1799 9 guns	unrecorded	£1.75	£4.75	£16.00	£48.00	—
1806	unrecorded	£1.50	£3.50	£22.00	£45.00	—
1807	unrecorded	£1.50	£10.00	£27.00	£55.00	—

George IV 1821-1830

	MINTAGE	F	VF	EF	UNC	PROOF
1825	215,040	£9.00	£27.00	£70.00	£90.00	—
1826	9,031,630	£1.50	£7.50	£23.00	£45.00	£95.00
1827	5,376,000	£2.25	£18.00	£38.00	£70.00	—

William IV 1831-1837

	MINTAGE	F	VF	EF	UNC	PROOF
1831	806,400	£2.50	£5.50	£33.00	£60.00	£115.00
1834	537,600	£3.75	£8.00	£32.00	£70.00	—
1837	349,440	£2.50	£5.75	£23.00	£50.00	—

Victoria 1838-1901

Young Head

	MINTAGE	F	VF	EF	UNC	PROOF
1838	456,960	£0.75	£2.00	£15.00	£28.00	—
1839	268,800	—	—	—	—	£90.00
1841	1,075,200	£2.50	£7.00	£15.00	£23.00	—
1843	967,680	£1.25	£7.50	£40.00	£50.00	—
1844	1,075,200	£1.75	£3.00	£18.00	£40.00	—
1845	1,075,200	£15.00	£45.00	£150.00	£300.00	—
1846	860,160	£1.75	£5.25	£25.00	£40.00	—
1847	725,640	£1.75	£4.00	£21.00	£40.00	—
1848	} 322,560	£1.75	£6.00	£30.00	£40.00	—
1848 8 over 7		£1.75	£4.00	£14.00	£35.00	—

	MINTAGE	F	VF	EF	UNC	PROOF
1851	215,040	£1.00	£5.75	£20.00	£35.00	—
1851 dots above shield		£0.75	£2.00	£7.00	£20.00	—
1852	637,056	£1.25	£3.00	£23.00	£32.00	—
1852 dots above shield		£0.75	£2.75	£9.00	£25.00	—
1853	1,559,040	£2.00	£3.25	£8.00	£15.00	£125.00
1853 3 over 2		£3.75	£9.00	£21.00	£45.00	—
1854	12,354,048	£1.50	£2.25	£7.00	£20.00	—
1855	1,455,837	£1.50	£3.00	£8.50	£25.00	—
1856	1,942,080	£2.75	£4.25	£18.00	£35.00	—
1857	1,182,720	£2.00	£4.25	£10.00	£28.00	—
1857 dots above shield		£0.75	£4.00	£14.00	£27.00	—
1858	2,472,960	£2.25	£4.75	£8.75	£20.00	—
1858 small date		£0.75	£2.50	£14.00	£25.00	—
1858 8 over 6		£1.25	£4.75	£17.00	£40.00	—
1858 8 over 7		£1.50	£4.00	£11.00	£22.00	—
1859	1,290,240	£1.00	£5.25	£20.00	£27.00	—
1859 9 over 8		£4.00	£10.00	£20.00	£40.00	—
1860	unrecorded	+	+	+	+	—

Bun Head

	MINTAGE	F	VF	EF	UNC	PROOF
1860 beaded	6,630,400	£0.75	£3.75	£11.00	£26.00	—
1860 toothed		£4.50	£10.00	£22.00	£50.00	—
1861 no signature	54,118,400	£1.00	£3.25	£14.00	£20.00	—
1861 signature		£2.00	£3.75	£9.50	£30.00	—
1862	61,107,200	£1.00	£4.50	£13.00	£25.00	—
1863	15,948,800	£1.50	£4.00	£22.00	£45.00	—
1864	537,600	£1.75	£4.50	£27.00	£45.00	—
1865	8,064,000	£2.00	£6.00	£38.00	£50.00	—
1865 5 over 3		£12.00	£38.00	£120.00	£250.00	—
1866	2,508,800	£1.25	£5.00	£30.00	£37.00	—
1867	2,508,800	£2.25	£6.25	£40.00	£50.00	—
1868	3,046,400	£0.75	£5.75	£27.00	£50.00	—
1869	3,225,600	£3.25	£24.00	£85.00	£100.00	—
1870	4,350,739	£1.25	£4.50	£22.00	£45.00	—
1871	1,075,280	£7.00	£30.00	£85.00	£130.00	—
1872	4,659,410	£1.75	£4.00	£25.00	£35.00	—
1873	3,404,880	£1.00	£5.50	£25.00	£50.00	—
1874	1,347,655	£2.00	£8.50	£60.00	£70.00	—
1874 new portrait		£2.00	£8.00	£24.00	£45.00	—

Heaton Mint Mark

	MINTAGE	F	VF	EF	UNC	PROOF
1874 H	5,017,600	£3.00	£6.00	£21.00	£40.00	—
1875	5,430,815	£1.00	£2.50	£20.00	£37.00	—
1875 H	1,254,400	£2.50	£5.25	£27.00	£37.00	—

HALFPENCE

	MINTAGE	F	VF	EF	UNC	PROOF
1876 H	5,809,600	£1.25	£3.00	£20.00	£30.00	—
1877	5,209,505	£1.00	£4.75	£16.00	£21.00	—
1878	1,425,535	£2.00	£6.25	£40.00	£70.00	—
1879	3,582,545	£0.75	£3.50	£15.00	£20.00	—
1880	2,423,465	£1.25	£5.25	£25.00	£30.00	—
1881	2,007,515	£1.25	£11.00	£25.00	£35.00	—
1881 H	1,792,000	£0.75	£2.25	£20.00	£25.00	—
1882 H	4,480,000	£1.50	£2.25	£20.00	£28.00	—
1883	3,000,725	£1.25	£4.75	£22.00	£30.00	—
1884	6,989,580	£1.75	£4.50	£10.00	£25.00	—
1885	8,600,574	£1.25	£3.50	£12.00	£21.00	—
1886	8,586,155	£1.00	£5.00	£10.00	£22.00	—
1887	10,701,305	£1.25	£2.25	£10.00	£20.00	—
1888	6,814,670	£1.00	£5.00	£14.00	£18.00	—
1889	7,748,234	£1.00	£3.00	£11.00	£24.00	—
1889 9 over 8		£4.50	£25.00	£35.00	£80.00	—
1890	11,254,235	£0.75	£1.50	£11.00	£22.00	—
1891	13,192,260	£1.25	£5.00	£10.00	£20.00	—
1892	2,478,335	£0.75	£2.00	£18.00	£25.00	—
1893	7,229,344	£1.25	£4.75	£11.00	£21.00	—
1894	1,767,635	£1.00	£3.50	£22.00	£32.00	—

Veiled Head

	MINTAGE	F	VF	EF	UNC	PROOF
1895	3,032,154	£1.75	£2.75	£5.50	£10.00	—
1896	9,142,500	£0.75	£2.25	£4.75	£11.00	—
1897	8,690,315	£0.50	£1.50	£5.00	£7.75	—
1898	8,595,180	£0.50	£2.00	£4.50	£12.00	—
1899	12,108,001	£0.75	£1.00	£4.00	£10.00	—
1900	13,805,190	£0.50	£1.00	£3.00	£6.50	—
1901	11,127,360	£0.75	£1.50	£2.75	£4.50	—

Edward VII 1902-1910

	MINTAGE	F	VF	EF	UNC	PROOF
1902	13,672,960	£1.00	£1.50	£4.50	£7.50	—
1902 low horizon		£4.00	£11.00	£30.00	£45.00	—
1903	11,450,880	£1.25	£2.50	£7.25	£13.00	—
1904	8,131,200	£1.00	£2.50	£8.50	£22.00	—

	MINTAGE	F	VF	EF	UNC	PROOF
1905	10,124,800	£0.60	£3.50	£9.50	£20.00	—
1906	11,101,440	£0.45	£3.50	£7.00	£13.00	—
1907	16,849,280	£0.35	£1.50	£6.00	£11.00	—
1908	16,620,800	£0.30	£1.75	£8.00	£12.00	—
1909	8,279,040	£0.55	£1.25	£10.00	£18.00	—
1910	10,769,920	£0.40	£1.75	£6.75	£12.00	—

George V 1911-1936

	MINTAGE	F	VF	EF	UNC	PROOF
1911	12,570,880	£0.55	£2.75	£3.50	£9.00	—
1912	21,185,920	£0.35	£2.25	£5.75	£12.00	—
1913	17,476,480	£0.60	£1.00	£6.00	£15.00	—
1914	20,289,111	£0.50	£1.00	£4.00	£8.50	—
1915	21,563,040	£0.50	£2.00	£4.00	£14.00	—
1916	39,386,143	£0.25	£1.00	£5.25	£8.75	—
1917	38,245,436	£0.30	£0.75	£6.00	£13.00	—
1918	22,321,072	£0.30	£0.75	£4.00	£9.00	—
1919	28,104,001	£0.30	£0.75	£4.25	£13.00	—
1920	35,146,793	£0.30	£1.00	£4.25	£13.00	—
1921	28,027,293	£0.30	£1.50	£4.25	£9.50	—
1922	10,734,964	£0.30	£1.50	£6.75	£16.00	—
1923	12,266,282	£0.30	£1.25	£5.25	£12.00	—
1924	13,971,038	£0.30	£1.00	£5.50	£11.00	—
1925	12,216,123	£0.35	£1.00	£6.50	£13.00	—
1925 modified head		£0.65	£3.50	£10.00	£20.00	—
1926	6,172,306	£0.45	£2.50	£6.50	£10.00	—
1927	15,589,622	£0.50	£2.00	£5.00	£9.25	—

Smaller Head

	MINTAGE	F	VF	EF	UNC	PROOF
1928 smaller head	20,935,200	£0.20	£0.40	£2.25	£4.50	—
1929	25,680,000	£0.20	£1.50	£3.00	£5.75	—
1930	12,532,800	£0.20	£0.35	£2.50	£5.25	—
1931	16,137,600	£0.20	£0.75	£2.75	£5.00	—
1932	14,448,000	£0.50	£1.25	£3.00	£5.25	—
1933	10,560,000	£0.40	£0.60	£2.00	£5.50	—
1934	7,704,000	£0.40	£0.55	£3.50	£8.00	—
1935	12,180,000	£0.30	£0.75	£2.50	£4.50	—
1936	23,008,800	£0.55	£1.00	£1.75	£3.25	—

George VI 1937-1952

	MINTAGE	F	VF	EF	UNC	PROOF
1937	24,504,000	£0.20	£0.55	£1.00	£2.00	—
1937	26,402	—	—	—	—	£3.50
1938	40,320,000	£0.25	£0.45	£1.25	£3.00	—
1939	28,924,800	£0.25	£1.00	£2.50	£5.50	—
1940	32,162,400	£0.35	£0.75	£1.75	£5.00	—
1941	45,120,000	£0.20	£0.50	£2.00	£3.50	—
1942	71,908,800	£0.15	£0.55	£1.00	£2.00	—
1943	76,200,000	£0.25	£0.50	£1.00	£2.50	—
1944	81,840,000	£0.20	£0.50	£1.00	£2.00	—
1945	57,000,000	£0.25	£0.50	£1.00	£2.50	—
1946	22,725,600	£0.30	£0.50	£2.50	£4.00	—
1947	21,266,400	£0.25	£0.40	£0.75	£2.25	—
1948	26,947,200	£0.30	£0.45	£1.00	£2.00	—
1949	24,744,000	£0.20	£0.75	£1.25	£3.75	—
1950	24,153,600	£0.25	£0.35	£1.00	£3.50	—
1950	17,513	—	—	—	—	£4.00
1951	14,868,000	£0.25	£0.45	£1.25	£4.00	—
1951	20,000	—	—	—	—	£4.50
1952	33,278,400	£0.25	£0.60	£1.00	£2.00	—

Elizabeth II 1953-

	MINTAGE	F	VF	EF	UNC	PROOF
1953	8,926,366	*	£0.50	£1.00	£1.25	—
1953	40,000	—	—	—	—	£2.75
1954	19,375,000	*	£0.40	£1.25	£2.50	—
1955	18,799,200	*	£0.30	£1.50	£3.00	—
1956	21,799,200	*	£0.45	£1.50	£3.25	—
1957	43,684,800	*	£0.20	£0.50	£1.00	—
1957 calm sea		*	£0.50	£1.25	£7.25	—
1958	62,318,400	*	£0.10	£0.40	£0.60	—
1959	79,176,000	*	£0.10	£0.25	£0.40	—
1960	41,340,000	*	£0.10	£0.25	£0.40	—
1962	41,779,200	*	*	£0.05	£0.20	—
1963	45,036,000	*	*	£0.05	£0.25	—
1964	78,583,200	*	*	£0.15	£0.25	—
1965	98,083,200	*	*	£0.15	£0.25	—
1966	95,289,600	*	£0.05	£0.15	£0.25	—
1967 wide rim	146,491,200	*	*	*	£0.10	—
1967		*	£0.05	£0.10	£0.25	—
1970		—	—	—	—	£1.50

PENCE

George III 1760-1820

	MINTAGE	F	VF	EF	UNC	PROOF
1797	8,601,600	£5.50	£16.00	£60.00	£130.00	—

	MINTAGE	F	VF	EF	UNC	PROOF
1806	unrecorded	£2.25	£4.75	£24.00	£85.00	—
1807	unrecorded	£4.00	£8.75	£45.00	£95.00	—

George IV 1821-1830

	MINTAGE	F	VF	EF	UNC	PROOF
1825	1,075,200	£3.00	£12.00	£50.00	£110.00	—
1826	5,913,600	£4.00	£14.00	£40.00	£120.00	£195.00
1827	1,451,520	£32.00	£165.00	£900.00	+	—

William IV 1831-1837

	MINTAGE	F	VF	EF	UNC	PROOF
1831	806,400	£6.25	£28.00	£80.00	£140.00	£225.00
1834	322,560	£6.25	£37.00	£100.00	£165.00	—
1837	174,720	£8.25	£40.00	£150.00	£235.00	—

Victoria 1838-1901

Young Head

	MINTAGE	F	VF	EF	UNC	PROOF
1839	unrecorded	—	—	—	—	£210.00
1841 REG:	913,920	£5.50	£12.00	£23.00	£100.00	—
1841 REG no colon		£1.00	£10.00	£17.00	£42.00	—
1843 REG:	483,840	£20.00	£75.00	£285.00	£335.00	—
1843 REG no colon		£20.00	£70.00	£275.00	£450.00	—
1844	215,040	£3.50	£10.00	£30.00	£45.00	—
1845	322,560	£3.00	£16.00	£50.00	£65.00	—
1846 DEF :	483,840	£2.00	£7.75	£42.00	£60.00	—
1846 DEF:		£3.00	£9.00	£45.00	£70.00	—
1847 DEF :	430,080	£2.50	£6.00	£25.00	£55.00	—
1847 DEF:		£1.75	£5.50	£30.00	£50.00	—
1848		£1.75	£6.50	£27.00	£50.00	—
1848 8 over 6	161,280	£5.00	£17.00	£50.00	£140.00	—
1848 8 over 7		£4.75	£13.00	£28.00	£45.00	—
1849	268,800	£20.00	£75.00	£300.00	£500.00	—
1851 DEF :	268,800	£2.00	£8.00	£48.00	£60.00	—
1851 DEF:		£2.75	£6.25	£37.00	£80.00	—
1853 ornamental trident	1,021,440	£2.75	£8.25	£18.00	£33.00	£200.00
1853 — colon nearer DEF		£1.00	£5.50	£17.00	£34.00	—
1853 plain trident		£3.00	£5.00	£27.00	£40.00	—

	MINTAGE	F	VF	EF	UNC	PROOF
1854 ornamental trident .... }		£2.00	£7.00	£12.00	£30.00	—
1854 plain trident .... }	6,720,000	£1.25	£6.50	£18.00	£30.00	—
1854 — 4 over 3 .... }		£12.00	£30.00	£60.00	£95.00	—
1855 ornamental trident .... }		£1.00	£7.25	£16.00	£35.00	—
1855 plain trident .... }	5,273,856	£2.50	£5.00	£16.00	£30.00	—
1856 ornamental trident .... }		£5.25	£20.00	£75.00	£195.00	—
1856 plain trident .... }	1,212,288	£12.00	£28.00	£100.00	£300.00	—
1857 ornamental trident .... }		£2.00	£7.50	£20.00	£45.00	—
1857 plain trident .... }	752,640	£1.00	£3.25	£22.00	£40.00	—
1857 small date .... }		£1.00	£5.25	£15.00	£45.00	—
1858		£2.50	£8.75	£16.00	£27.00	—
1858 8 over 3 .... }		£5.75	£10.00	£35.00	£75.00	—
1858 8 over 6 .... }		£8.00	£25.00	£55.00	£100.00	—
1858 8 over 7 .... }	1,599,040	£1.25	£4.50	£8.50	£30.00	—
1858 small date .... }		£2.00	£7.25	£13.00	£45.00	—
1858 without WW .... }		£1.25	£6.25	£12.00	£35.00	—
1859 .... }		£1.50	£6.25	£20.00	£55.00	—
1859 small date .... }	1,075,200	£2.00	£8.50	£20.00	£60.00	—
1860 60 over 59	32,256	£60.00	£220.00	£425.00	+	—

Bun Head, beaded border

Bun Head, toothed border

	MINTAGE	F	VF	EF	UNC	PROOF
1860 beaded .... }		£1.25	£6.00	£20.00	£55.00	—
1860 LCW below foot .... }	5,053,440	£5.00	£26.00	£60.00	£120.00	—
1860 sig on obv & rev .... }		£1.25	£3.50	£10.00	£33.00	—
1860 sig on rev only .... }		£2.00	£4.00	£22.00	£45.00	—
1861 sig on obv & rev .... }		£1.50	£3.75	£20.00	£30.00	—
1861 no signature .... }		£2.00	£8.00	£12.00	£30.00	—
1861 sig on obv only .... }	36,449,280	£1.50	£6.00	£20.00	£45.00	—
1861 sig on rev only .... }		£1.50	£4.00	£14.00	£40.00	—
1862	50,534,400	£1.75	£5.75	£18.00	£30.00	—
1863	28,062,720	£1.75	£4.75	£18.00	£38.00	—

	MINTAGE	F	VF	EF	UNC	PROOF
1864 plain 4	3,440,640	£4.75	£22.00	£150.00	£250.00	—
1864 crosslet 4		£9.50	£40.00	£140.00	£300.00	—
1865	8,601,600	£3.50	£6.25	£35.00	£50.00	—
1865 5 over 3		£12.00	£48.00	£125.00	£350.00	—
1866	9,999,360	£1.50	£9.25	£27.00	£60.00	—
1867	5,483,520	£1.75	£6.25	£43.00	£75.00	—
1868	1,182,720	£2.00	£12.00	£80.00	£130.00	—
1869	2,580,480	£16.00	£80.00	£280.00	£440.00	—
1870	5,695,022	£2.00	£16.00	£47.00	£135.00	—
1871	1,290,318	£6.00	£25.00	£170.00	£275.00	—
1872	8,494,572	£1.25	£6.25	£25.00	£47.00	—
1873	8,494,200	£2.50	£7.75	£24.00	£47.00	—
1874	5,621,865	£2.25	£5.75	£40.00	£50.00	—
1874 new portrait		£2.50	£8.00	£30.00	£50.00	—
1874 H	6,666,240	£1.00	£6.50	£32.00	£55.00	—
1874 H new portrait		£1.50	£5.75	£25.00	£40.00	—
1875	10,691,040	£2.00	£9.00	£20.00	£45.00	—
1875 H	752,640	£8.00	£55.00	£175.00	£330.00	—
1876 H	11,074,560	£1.50	£8.75	£20.00	£50.00	—
1877	9,624,747	£2.50	£10.00	£16.00	£47.00	—
1878	2,764,470	£2.25	£6.50	£30.00	£55.00	—
1879	7,666,476	£1.25	£8.50	£22.00	£35.00	—
1880	3,000,831	£2.00	£7.50	£37.00	£60.00	—
1881	2,302,362	£1.25	£6.50	£33.00	£50.00	—
1881 new portrait		£4.00	£12.00	£40.00	£60.00	—
1881 H	3,763,200	£1.50	£4.25	£18.00	£35.00	—
1882 H	7,526,400	£1.25	£6.50	£19.00	£50.00	—
1883	6,237,438	£2.50	£6.25	£27.00	£50.00	—
1884	11,702,802	£1.75	£5.00	£14.00	£35.00	—
1885	7,145,862	£1.00	£2.75	£13.00	£23.00	—
1886	6,087,759	£1.25	£4.25	£17.00	£35.00	—
1887	5,315,085	£2.25	£6.25	£15.00	£35.00	—
1888	5,125,020	£1.50	£3.25	£15.00	£37.00	—
1889	12,559,737	£1.00	£3.50	£14.00	£30.00	—
1890	15,330,840	£1.00	£6.25	£13.00	£24.00	—
1891	17,885,961	£0.75	£4.00	£15.00	£26.00	—
1892	10,501,671	£1.00	£2.00	£12.00	£30.00	—
1893	8,161,737	£1.25	£4.50	£14.00	£32.00	—
1894	3,883,452	£2.00	£4.00	£21.00	£33.00	—

Veiled Head

	MINTAGE	F	VF	EF	UNC	PROOF
1895	5,395,830	£0.50	£3.25	£6.75	£11.00	—
1895 2 mm		£3.50	£16.00	£70.00	£140.00	—

	MINTAGE	F	VF	EF	UNC	PROOF
1896	24,147,156	£0.45	£3.75	£6.50	£11.00	—
1897	20,756,620	£0.30	£3.00	£5.00	£23.00	—
1898	14,296,836	£0.30	£4.50	£9.50	£18.00	—
1899	26,441,069	£0.30	£2.50	£5.50	£13.00	—
1900	31,778,109	£0.20	£2.00	£3.75	£7.50	—
1901	22,205,568	£0.55	£1.50	£3.50	£6.50	—

Edward VII 1902-1910

	MINTAGE	F	VF	EF	UNC	PROOF
1902	26,976,768	£1.25	£2.00	£3.50	£6.50	—
1902 low horizon		£1.00	£7.00	£20.00	£35.00	—
1903	21,415,296	£0.30	£3.25	£8.00	£17.00	—
1904	12,913,152	£0.35	£3.00	£12.00	£27.00	—
1905	17,783,808	£0.35	£2.00	£9.50	£25.00	—
1906	37,989,504	£0.35	£3.75	£8.25	£16.00	—
1907	47,322,240	£0.35	£2.25	£8.75	£16.00	—
1908	31,506,048	£0.55	£2.50	£12.00	£21.00	—
1909	19,617,024	£1.25	£3.25	£9.25	£20.00	—
1910	29,549,184	£0.30	£3.00	£7.00	£15.00	—

George V 1911-1936

	MINTAGE	F	VF	EF	UNC	PROOF
1911	23,079,168	£0.30	£2.00	£5.75	£9.25	—
1912	48,306,048	£0.25	£0.75	£4.00	£11.00	—

	MINTAGE	F	VF	EF	UNC	PROOF
1912 H	16,800,000	£1.75	£6.00	£15.00	£40.00	—
1913	65,497,812	£0.40	£3.50	£7.25	£15.00	—
1914	50,820,997	£0.50	£2.00	£5.50	£12.00	—
1915	47,310,807	£0.50	£1.25	£4.50	£17.00	—
1916	86,411,165	£0.40	£1.50	£4.25	£12.00	—
1917	107,905,436	£0.30	£1.75	£4.00	£9.50	—
1918	84,227,372	£0.20	£1.75	£4.25	£9.00	—

Heaton Mint Mark **Kings Norton Mint Mark**

	MINTAGE	F	VF	EF	UNC	PROOF
1918 H	3,660,800	£0.55	£9.00	£75.00	£160.00	—
1918 KN		£1.00	£12.00	£100.00	£200.00	—
1919	113,761,090	£0.20	£3.00	£4.50	£8.25	—
1919 H	5,209,600	£0.50	£7.00	£50.00	£125.00	—
1919 KN		£2.00	£24.00	£110.00	£215.00	—
1920	124,693,485	£0.50	£2.25	£4.00	£9.00	—
1921	129,717,693	£0.25	£2.50	£4.00	£8.00	—
1922	16,346,711	£0.65	£4.50	£10.00	£18.00	—

Modified Head

	MINTAGE	F	VF	EF	UNC	PROOF
1926	4,498,519	£1.00	£3.25	£15.00	£30.00	—
1926 modified head		£3.75	£65.00	£250.00	£450.00	—
1927	60,989,561	£0.45	£2.00	£3.50	£6.25	—

Smaller Head

	MINTAGE	F	VF	EF	UNC	PROOF
1928 smaller head	50,178,000	£0.40	£2.00	£3.00	£6.00	—
1929	49,132,800	£0.25	£1.00	£3.00	£6.25	—
1930	29,097,600	£0.30	£1.00	£3.75	£6.00	—
1931	19,843,200	£0.50	£1.50	£4.25	£7.50	—
1932	8,277,600	£1.00	£2.00	£12.00	£21.00	—
1934	13,965,600	£0.55	£2.00	£8.00	£15.00	—
1935	56,070,000	£0.35	£1.00	£2.50	£4.00	—
1936	154,296,000	£0.30	£0.55	£1.25	£3.25	—

George VI 1937-1952

	MINTAGE	F	VF	EF	UNC	PROOF
1937	88,896,000	£0.30	£0.55	£1.00	£2.25	—
1937	26,402	—	—	—	—	£4.00
1938	121,560,000	*	£0.40	£1.00	£2.25	—
1939	55,560,000	*	£0.35	£1.25	£4.25	—
1940	42,284,400	*	£0.30	£2.75	£6.50	—
1944	42,600,000	*	£0.30	£1.50	£8.25	—
1945	79,531,200	£0.25	£0.60	£2.25	£6.00	—
1946	66,855,600	*	£0.35	£1.00	£2.25	—
1947	52,220,400	*	£0.30	£0.75	£2.50	—

THREE-HALFPENCE

	MINTAGE	F	VF	EF	UNC	PROOF
1948	63,961,200	*	£0.30	£1.00	£2.00	—
1949	14,324,400	*	£0.45	£1.00	£2.50	—
1950	240,000	£2.75	£4.00	£9.00	£18.00	—
1950	17,513	—	—	—	—	£20.00
1951	120,000	£4.00	£7.00	£11.00	£15.00	—
1951	20,000	—	—	—	—	£17.00

Elizabeth II 1953-

	MINTAGE	F	VF	EF	UNC	PROOF
1953	1,308,400	*	£1.00	£2.00	£3.25	—
1953	40,000	—	—	—	—	£5.00
1961	48,313,400	*	£0.10	£0.25	£0.50	—
1962	143,308,600	*	*	£0.15	£0.25	—
1963	125,235,600	*	*	£0.05	£0.25	—
1964	153,294,000	*	*	£0.15	£0.25	—
1965	121,310,400	*	*	£0.10	£0.25	—
1966	165,739,200	*	*	£0.10	£0.20	—
1967	654,564,000	*	*	£0.10	£0.20	—
1970	unavailable	—	—	—	—	£2.50

THREE-HALFPENCE

William IV 1831-1837

	MINTAGE	F	VF	EF	UNC	PROOF
1834	800,448	£1.25	£4.25	£13.00	£30.00	—
1835	633,600	£1.00	£5.00	£16.00	£35.00	—
1835 5 over 4		£1.75	£10.00	£16.00	£40.00	—
1836	158,400	£0.75	£4.25	£18.00	£35.00	—
1837	30,624	£4.50	£20.00	£75.00	£100.00	—

Victoria 1838-1901

	MINTAGE	F	VF	EF	UNC	PROOF
1838	538,560	£1.00	£6.50	£18.00	£35.00	—
1839	760,320	£1.00	£5.50	£17.00	£30.00	—
1840	95,040	£1.00	£3.75	£35.00	£50.00	—
1841	158,400	£0.50	£2.75	£16.00	£35.00	—
1842	1,869,120	£0.75	£5.00	£23.00	£35.00	—
1843	475,200	£0.75	£4.25	£11.00	£13.00	—
1843 43 over 34		£2.00	£3.50	£16.00	£30.00	—
1860	160,000	£1.50	£5.75	£38.00	£45.00	—
1862	256,000	£3.25	£7.50	£34.00	£45.00	—

TWOPENCE

George III 1760-1820

	MINTAGE	F	VF	EF	UNC	PROOF
1797	722,160	£8.50	£24.00	£60.00	£270.00	—

THREEPENCE

William IV 1831-1837

	MINTAGE	F	VF	EF	UNC	PROOF
1834	unrecorded	£3.00	£7.50	£25.00	£45.00	—

	MINTAGE	F	VF	EF	UNC	PROOF
1835	unrecorded	£3.75	£9.00	£25.00	£40.00	—
1836	unrecorded	£2.50	£5.50	£23.00	£40.00	—
1837	unrecorded	£2.50	£8.50	£35.00	£45.00	—

Victoria 1838-1901

Young Head

	MINTAGE	F	VF	EF	UNC	PROOF
1838	unrecorded	£0.75	£5.25	£30.00	£50.00	—
1839	unrecorded	£1.00	£5.50	£40.00	£60.00	—
1840	unrecorded	£1.00	£5.50	£40.00	£55.00	—
1841	unrecorded	£1.00	£5.50	£50.00	£60.00	—
1842	unrecorded	£1.50	£6.00	£50.00	£70.00	—
1843	unrecorded	£1.50	£7.00	£30.00	£45.00	—
1844	unrecorded	£1.00	£6.00	£45.00	£55.00	—
1845	1,314,720	£2.25	£7.50	£18.00	£32.00	—
1846	47,520	£1.50	£6.50	£58.00	£65.00	—
1849	126,720	£1.25	£5.50	£45.00	£60.00	—
1850	950,400	£1.00	£3.75	£18.00	£35.00	—
1851	479,065	£1.00	£3.50	£35.00	£45.00	—
1853	31,680	£1.25	£5.50	£55.00	£65.00	—
1854	1,467,246	£1.25	£6.00	£35.00	£50.00	—
1855	383,350	£1.25	£8.25	£50.00	£60.00	—
1856	1,013,760	£1.25	£6.00	£35.00	£50.00	—
1857	1,758,240	£1.00	£5.50	£45.00	£60.00	—
1858	1,441,440	£1.75	£3.50	£35.00	£45.00	—
1859	3,579,840	£2.25	£6.25	£18.00	£32.00	—
1860	3,405,600	£1.25	£3.75	£28.00	£35.00	—
1861	3,294,720	£1.50	£9.00	£25.00	£35.00	—
1862	1,156,320	£1.00	£3.75	£35.00	£45.00	—
1863	950,400	£1.25	£6.00	£45.00	£55.00	—
1864	1,330,560	£1.00	£3.50	£30.00	£40.00	—
1865	1,742,400	£1.25	£7.75	£45.00	£50.00	—
1866	1,900,800	£1.50	£3.50	£30.00	£40.00	—
1867	712,800	£1.25	£3.50	£35.00	£40.00	—
1868		£2.75	£6.00	£25.00	£30.00	—
1868 BRITANNIAR	} 1,457,280	£14.00	£40.00	£120.00	+	
1869	unrecorded	£1.25	£13.00	£50.00	£60.00	—
1870	1,283,218	£0.75	£3.50	£20.00	£25.00	—
1871	999,633	£0.75	£3.50	£30.00	£35.00	—
1872	1,293,271	£0.50	£4.00	£20.00	£30.00	—
1873	4,055,550	£1.50	£2.75	£13.00	£25.00	—
1874	4,427,031	£1.25	£4.00	£18.00	£23.00	—
1875	3,306,500	£0.75	£2.50	£17.00	£25.00	—
1876	1,834,389	£1.00	£5.00	£16.00	£25.00	—
1877	2,622,393	£1.25	£2.00	£18.00	£25.00	—
1878	2,419,975	£1.00	£2.75	£16.00	£22.00	—
1879	3,140,265	£1.00	£3.25	£18.00	£21.00	—
1880	1,610,069	£1.00	£3.50	£18.00	£30.00	—
1881	3,248,265	£1.00	£4.50	£18.00	£30.00	—
1882	472,965	£1.00	£8.00	£35.00	£40.00	—
1883	4,369,971	£1.00	£5.00	£15.00	£20.00	—
1884	3,322,424	£1.25	£3.50	£13.00	£20.00	—

	MINTAGE	F	VF	EF	UNC	PROOF
1885	5,183,653	£1.25	£5.25	£10.00	£18.00	—
1886	6,152,669	£1.00	£5.00	£9.00	£17.00	—

Jubilee Head

	MINTAGE	F	VF	EF	UNC	PROOF
1887	2,780,761	£1.50	£5.50	£10.00	£18.00	—
1887 jubilee head		£1.00	£2.00	£5.00	£6.50	£33.00
1888	518,199	£1.25	£2.50	£10.00	£18.00	—
1889	4,587,010	£0.80	£1.50	£7.50	£11.00	—
1890	4,465,834	£0.80	£4.00	£8.75	£12.00	—
1891	6,323,027	£0.85	£4.00	£8.25	£14.00	—
1892	2,578,226	£1.00	£2.75	£9.00	£13.00	—
1893	3,067,243	£7.00	£28.00	£85.00	£120.00	—
1893 veiled head		£1.00	£2.75	£6.75	£9.50	£30.00

Veiled Head

	MINTAGE	F	VF	EF	UNC	PROOF
1894	1,608,603	£0.75	£1.50	£5.50	£18.00	—
1895	4,788,609	£0.65	£1.25	£6.25	£14.00	—
1896	4,598,442	£0.75	£1.00	£4.00	£10.00	—
1897	4,541,294	£1.00	£4.00	£7.25	£10.00	—
1898	4,567,177	£0.75	£1.75	£5.50	£11.00	—
1899	6,246,281	£1.00	£3.25	£6.25	£11.00	—
1900	10,644,480	£0.75	£1.25	£5.25	£9.50	—
1901	6,098,400	£0.75	£2.50	£5.25	£8.50	—

Edward VII 1902-1910

	MINTAGE	F	VF	EF	UNC	PROOF
1902	8,268,480	£0.75	£2.25	£4.00	£6.25	—
1903	5,227,200	£0.75	£1.75	£9.25	£14.00	—
1904	3,627,360	£2.00	£4.25	£28.00	£45.00	—
1905	3,548,160	£1.75	£6.25	£22.00	£35.00	—

THREEPENCE

	MINTAGE	F	VF	EF	UNC	PROO
1906	3,152,160	£2.00	£4.00	£20.00	£35.00	-
1907	4,831,200	£1.00	£3.75	£8.75	£14.00	-
1908	8,157,600	£1.00	£2.50	£7.00	£17.00	-
1909	4,055,040	£1.00	£4.25	£9.25	£14.00	-
1910	4,563,380	£0.75	£2.75	£7.25	£12.00	-

George V 1911-1936

	MINTAGE	F	VF	EF	UNC	PROO
1911	5,841,084	£0.80	£1.25	£4.00	£4.75	—
1912	8,932,825	£0.65	£1.50	£2.75	£5.50	—
1913	7,143,242	£0.60	£1.50	£3.25	£5.25	—
1914	6,733,584	£0.45	£1.25	£3.00	£6.50	—
1915	5,450,617	£0.60	£1.00	£3.25	£5.00	—
1916	18,555,201	£0.40	£1.50	£3.00	£4.25	—
1917	21,662,490	£0.55	£1.25	£2.50	£5.00	—
1918	20,630,909	£0.55	£1.25	£2.25	£4.25	—
1919	16,845,687	£0.40	£1.25	£3.00	£4.50	—
1920	16,703,597	£0.50	£1.50	£3.00	£5.50	—
1921	8,749,301	£0.50	£1.00	£3.00	£5.25	—
1922	7,979,998	£0.50	£1.00	£3.25	£6.00	—
1925	3,731,859	£1.00	£2.25	£11.00	£18.00	—
1926	4,107,910	£1.50	£3.00	£10.00	£25.00	—
1926 modified head		£1.00	£1.50	£4.75	£14.00	—

	MINTAGE	F	VF	EF	UNC	PROO
1927 new reverse	15,022	—	—	—	—	£30.0
1928	1,302,106	£1.25	£2.50	£7.75	£17.00	-
1930	1,319,412	£1.00	£2.00	£8.00	£14.00	-
1931	6,251,936	£0.35	£0.60	£1.00	£2.25	-
1932	5,887,325	£0.40	£0.75	£1.50	£3.00	-
1933	5,578,541	£0.35	£0.55	£1.25	£2.50	-
1934	7,405,954	£0.25	£0.55	£1.25	£2.50	-
1935	7,027,654	£0.30	£0.75	£1.25	£2.25	-
1936	3,328,670	£0.35	£0.60	£1.25	£2.25	-

George VI 1937-1952

	MINTAGE	F	VF	EF	UNC	PROO
1937	8,148,156	*	£0.60	£1.25	£1.75	—

134

	MINTAGE	F	VF	EF	UNC	PROOF
1937	26,402	—	—	—	—	£3.50
1938	6,402,473	*	£0.30	£1.25	£2.00	—
1939	1,355,860	*	£0.55	£2.50	£5.00	—
1940	7,914,401	*	£0.30	£1.25	£2.25	—
1941	7,979,411	*	£0.40	£1.25	£2.00	—
1942	4,144,051	£1.25	£2.50	£5.25	£9.25	—
1943	1,397,220	£1.50	£3.25	£6.50	£11.00	—
1944	2,005,553	£1.50	£5.00	£11.00	£21.00	—

Brass

	MINTAGE	F	VF	EF	UNC	PROOF
1937	45,707,957	*	£0.30	£0.75	£1.50	—
1937	26,402	—	—	—	—	£3.00
1938	14,532,332	*	£0.40	£3.00	£6.25	—
1939	5,603,021	£0.45	£1.00	£4.25	£20.00	—
1940	12,636,018	£0.30	£1.00	£2.50	£5.25	—
1941	60,239,489	£0.25	£0.50	£1.00	£3.00	—
1942	103,214,400	£0.20	£0.35	£1.00	£2.25	—
1943	101,702,400	£0.25	£0.45	£1.00	£2.00	—
1944	69,760,000	£0.25	£0.55	£1.25	£2.50	—
1945	33,942,466	*	£0.25	£2.00	£5.00	—
1946	620,734	£1.50	£4.50	£35.00	£130.00	—
1948	4,230,400	£0.40	£0.75	£6.50	£17.00	—
1949	464,000	£2.75	£16.00	£65.00	£135.00	—
1950	1,600,000	£0.70	£2.00	£12.00	£25.00	—
1950	17,513	—	—	—	—	£27.00
1951	1,184,000	£1.00	£3.00	£8.00	£25.00	—
1951	20,000	—	—	—	—	£30.00
1952	25,494,400	£0.30	£0.55	£1.25	£2.50	—

Elizabeth II 1953-

	MINTAGE	F	VF	EF	UNC	PROOF
1953	30,618,000	*	£0.20	£0.80	£1.25	—
1953	40,000	—	—	—	—	£4.00
1954	41,720,000	*	£0.30	£1.50	£3.25	—
1955	41,075,200	*	£0.25	£2.00	£4.00	—

	MINTAGE	F	VF	EF	UNC	PROO
1956	36,801,600	*	£0.20	£2.00	£4.25	-
1957	24,294,500	*	£0.25	£1.75	£3.00	-
1958	20,504,000	*	£0.25	£3.00	£6.50	-
1959	28,499,200	*	£0.20	£1.25	£3.00	-
1960	83,078,400	*	£0.15	£1.00	£1.25	-
1961	41,102,400	*	*	£0.20	£0.40	-
1962	51,545,600	*	*	£0.10	£0.30	-
1963	39,482,866	*	£0.05	£0.10	£0.25	-
1964	44,867,200	*	£0.05	£0.10	£0.25	-
1965	27,160,000	*	*	£0.10	£0.25	-
1966	53,160,000	*	*	£0.15	£0.20	-
1967	151,780,800	*	*	£0.10	£0.20	-
1970	unavailable	—	—	—	—	£2.0

GROATS

William IV 1831-1837

	MINTAGE	F	VF	EF	UNC	PROO
1836	unrecorded	£2.25	£7.00	£16.00	£19.00	-
1837	962,280	£2.00	£5.50	£16.00	£30.00	-

Victoria 1838-1901

	MINTAGE	F	VF	EF	UNC	PROOF
1838	2,150,280	£2.25	£5.00	£17.00	£23.00	—
1838 8 over horizontal 8		£1.25	£6.50	£20.00	£35.00	—
1839	1,461,240	£1.50	£3.50	£18.00	£34.00	£115.0
1840	1,496,880	£1.75	£6.00	£20.00	£30.00	—
1841	344,520	£1.00	£5.00	£32.00	£45.00	—
1842	724,680	£2.00	£4.00	£23.00	£30.00	—
1842 2 over 1		£4.00	£5.00	£25.00	£50.00	—
1843	1,817,640	£2.00	£9.00	£20.00	£40.00	—
1844	855,360	£1.50	£5.75	£24.00	£40.00	—
1845	914,760	£1.25	£4.00	£28.00	£35.00	—
1846	1,366,200	£1.25	£4.00	£27.00	£35.00	—
1847 7 over 6	225,720	£12.00	£40.00	£135.00	£160.00	—
1848	712,800	£0.80	£2.75	£22.00	£30.00	—
1848 8 over 6 or 7		£2.25	£9.00	£25.00	£45.00	—
1849	380,160	£1.50	£5.00	£22.00	£35.00	—
1849 9 over 8		£2.00	£7.00	£30.00	£50.00	—
1851	594,000	£13.00	£45.00	£150.00	£200.00	—
1852	31.300	£20.00	£75.00	£225.00	£350.00	—
1853	11,880	£32.00	£90.00	£265.00	£280.00	£300.0
1854	1,096,613	£2.00	£4.75	£20.00	£25.00	—
1855	646,041	£1.75	£4.00	£18.00	£25.00	—
1888 jubilee head	unrecorded	£6.25	£9.25	£21.00	£27.00	—

SIXPENCE

SIXPENCE

Charles II 1660-1685

	VG	F	VF	EF	PROOF
1674	£9.00	£16.00	£45.00	£150.00	—
1675	£6.50	£15.00	£45.00	£200.00	—
1676	£10.00	£20.00	£100.00	£300.00	—
1677	£6.00	£15.00	£45.00	£145.00	—
1678 8 over 7	£10.00	£17.00	£55.00	£200.00	—
1679	£12.00	£18.00	£65.00	£200.00	—
1680	£18.00	£25.00	£90.00	£300.00	—
1681	£9.00	£20.00	£45.00	£150.00	—
1682 2 over 1	£14.00	£18.00	£65.00	£190.00	—
1683	£6.00	£28.00	£55.00	£165.00	—
1684	£10.00	£18.00	£55.00	£180.00	—

James II 1685-1688

	VG	F	VF	EF	PROOF
1686 early shields	£10.00	£23.00	£100.00	£280.00	—
1687 —	£11.00	£28.00	£90.00	£280.00	—
1687 later shields	£10.00	£23.00	£80.00	£255.00	—
1688 —	£12.00	£28.00	£90.00	£285.00	—

William and Mary 1688-1694

	VG	F	VF	EF	PROOF
1693	£9.00	£20.00	£70.00	£220.00	—
1694	£14.00	£40.00	£140.00	£400.00	—

William III 1694-1702

	VG	F	VF	EF	PROOF
1695 first bust, early harp, large crowns	£4.00	£20.00	£55.00	£115.00	—
1696 — — —	£4.00	£7.25	£20.00	£50.00	—
1696 — — — B(Bristol)	£3.00	£13.00	£40.00	£70.00	—
1696 — — — C(Chester)	£3.50	£20.00	£45.00	£135.00	—
1696 — — — E(Exeter)	£4.00	£20.00	£60.00	£175.00	—
1696 — — — N(Norwich)	£3.50	£12.00	£40.00	£120.00	—
1696 — — — y(York)	£3.50	£12.00	£30.00	£90.00	—
1696 — — — Y(York)	£5.00	£20.00	£65.00	£175.00	—
1696 — later harp, large crowns	£6.00	£24.00	£75.00	£230.00	—
1696 — — — B(Bristol)	£10.00	£25.00	£75.00	£225.00	—
1696 — — small crowns	£12.00	£20.00	£65.00	£195.00	—
1696 — — — B(Bristol)	£10.00	£18.00	£55.00	£165.00	—
1696 — — — C(Chester)	£10.00	£35.00	£100.00	£300.00	—
1696 — — — N(Norwich)	£10.00	£30.00	£90.00	£275.00	—
1697 — — ..	£3.00	£8.50	£22.00	£70.00	—
1697 — — large crowns, B(Bristol)	£8.00	£20.00	£50.00	£125.00	—
1697 — — — C(Chester)	£8.00	£23.00	£60.00	£220.00	—
1697 — — — E(Exeter)	£6.00	£25.00	£70.00	£220.00	—
1697 — — small crowns, B(Bristol)	£3.00	£11.00	£45.00	£115.00	—
1697 — — — C(Chester)	£2.50	£12.00	£33.00	£115.00	—
1697 — — — E(Exeter)	£3.00	£15.00	£40.00	£130.00	—
1697 — — — N(Norwich)	£3.00	£11.00	£30.00	£90.00	—
1697 — — — y(York)	£4.00	£23.00	£75.00	£220.00	—
1697 second bust, later harp, small crowns	£12.00	£35.00	£120.00	£350.00	—
1697 third bust, later harp, large crowns	£2.50	£6.75	£20.00	£50.00	—
1697 — — — B(Bristol)	£5.00	£15.00	£45.00	£140.00	—
1697 — — — C(Chester)	£10.00	£25.00	£70.00	£200.00	—
1697 — — — E(Exeter)	£10.00	£30.00	£90.00	£270.00	—
1697 — — small crowns	£4.00	£10.00	£32.00	£90.00	—
1697 — — — C(Chester)	£14.00	£25.00	£65.00	£185.00	—
1697 — — — E(Exeter)	£6.00	£16.00	£50.00	£150.00	—
1697 — — — Y(York)	£7.00	£25.00	£80.00	£230.00	—
1698 — — large crowns	£3.25	£8.00	£30.00	£75.00	—
1698 — — — plumes in angles	£7.50	£12.00	£35.00	£105.00	—
1699 — — —	£12.00	£28.00	£80.00	£255.00	—
1699 — — — plumes in angles	£6.00	£14.00	£35.00	£130.00	—
1699 — — — roses in angles	£12.00	£25.00	£75.00	£230.00	—
1700 — —	£2.00	£9.00	£35.00	£75.00	—
1701 — — —	£5.00	£11.00	£35.00	£110.00	—

Anne 1702-1714

	VG	F	VF	EF	PROOF
Before Union reverse					
1703 VIGO	£4.00	£15.00	£40.00	£100.00	—
1705	£9.00	£20.00	£60.00	£200.00	—
1705 plumes in angles, shields point down	£6.00	£15.00	£35.00	£150.00	—
1705 — shields point up	£9.00	£20.00	£60.00	£175.00	—
1705 roses and plumes in angles	£5.00	£18.00	£60.00	£200.00	—
1707 —	£6.50	£16.00	£45.00	£125.00	—

Before Union reverse, plumes in angles

After Union reverse: English and Scottish shields impaled

	VG	F	VF	EF	PROOF
1707	£3.00	£9.00	£22.00	£55.00	—
1707 E(Edinburgh)	£6.00	£10.00	£30.00	£90.00	—
1707 plumes in angles	£5.00	£17.00	£35.00	£95.00	—
1708	£4.50	£18.00	£25.00	£95.00	—
1708 E(Edinburgh)	£7.75	£12.00	£40.00	£125.00	—
1708 E*(Edinburgh)	£8.00	£13.00	£35.00	£155.00	—
1708 — 'Edinburgh' bust	£8.00	£15.00	£55.00	£175.00	—
1708 plumes in angles	£5.00	£17.00	£40.00	£120.00	—
1710 roses and plumes in angles	£5.00	£15.00	£40.00	£150.00	—
1711	£6.75	£11.00	£30.00	£120.00	—

George I 1714-1727

Roses and plumes in angles

	VG	F	VF	EF	PROOF
1717 roses and plumes in angles	£6.00	£25.00	£80.00	£210.00	—
1720 — 20 over 17	£6.00	£20.00	£60.00	£210.00	—
1723 SS C in angles	£4.75	£14.00	£30.00	£65.00	—
1726 small roses and plumes in angles	£7.50	£20.00	£45.00	£135.00	—

George II 1727-1760

Young Head   **Old Head**

	VG	F	VF	EF	PROOF
1728 young head	£7.00	£35.00	£80.00	£240.00	—
1728 — plumes in angles	£5.00	£25.00	£70.00	£175.00	—
1728 — roses and plumes in angles	£4.00	£18.00	£25.00	£95.00	—
1731 — —	£6.00	£12.00	£30.00	£95.00	—
1732 — —	£3.75	£10.00	£35.00	£145.00	—

SIXPENCE

	VG	F	VF	EF	PROOF
1734——	£6.75	£25.00	£50.00	£140.00	—
1735——	£7.00	£25.00	£50.00	£140.00	—
1736——	£5.00	£20.00	£45.00	£130.00	—
1739—roses in angles	£4.25	£13.00	£30.00	£120.00	—
1741——	£5.50	£17.00	£30.00	£120.00	—
1743 old head, roses in angles	£7.00	£12.00	£40.00	£90.00	—
1745——	£8.75	£17.00	£45.00	£100.00	—
1745—LIMA	£4.25	£10.00	£30.00	£75.00	—
1746——	£5.00	£9.00	£25.00	£60.00	—
1750——	£8.25	£20.00	£45.00	£125.00	—
1751—	£5.75	£23.00	£65.00	£185.00	—
1757—	£2.75	£4.50	£11.00	£21.00	—
1758—	£4.25	£6.50	£11.00	£27.00	—

George III 1760-1820

	VG	F	VF	EF	PROOF
1787 hearts in shield	£1.50	£3.75	£7.50	£18.00	—
1787 no hearts in shield	£1.00	£3.50	£7.75	£14.00	—

	MINTAGE	F	VF	EF	UNC	PROOF
1816	unrecorded	£2.25	£9.00	£20.00	£30.00	—
1817	10,921,680	£2.25	£6.50	£18.00	£38.00	—
1818	4,284,720	£4.50	£7.25	£37.00	£55.00	—
1819	4,712,400	£1.50	£5.75	£22.00	£40.00	—
1820	1,488,960	£1.75	£5.75	£28.00	£40.00	—

George IV 1821-1830

Laureate Head, shield in garter

	MINTAGE	F	VF	EF	UNC	PROOF
1821 garnished shield	863,280	£5.00	£12.00	£48.00	£70.00	—
1821 BBITANNIAR		£25.00	£60.00	£180.00	£250.00	—

	MINTAGE	F	VF	EF	UNC	PROOF
1824 shield in garter	633,600	£4.25	£11.00	£45.00	£80.00	—
1825	483,120	£5.50	£15.00	£45.00	£70.00	—
1826	689,040	£10.00	£45.00	£140.00	£215.00	—
1826 bare head		£4.00	£7.00	£32.00	£55.00	£110.00

Bare Head

	MINTAGE	F	VF	EF	UNC	PROOF
1827	166,320	£8.50	£27.00	£95.00	£160.00	—
1828	15,840	£6.75	£20.00	£60.00	£120.00	—
1829	403,290	£5.50	£15.00	£40.00	£110.00	—

William IV 1831-1837

	MINTAGE	F	VF	EF	UNC	PROOF
1831	1,340,195	£5.50	£16.00	£38.00	£60.00	£100.00
1834	5,892,480	£3.00	£10.00	£33.00	£60.00	—
1835	1,552,320	£3.75	£10.00	£45.00	£65.00	—
1836	1,987,920	£5.25	£20.00	£90.00	£140.00	—
1837	506,880	£3.50	£15.00	£75.00	£100.00	—

Victoria 1838-1901

Young Head

	MINTAGE	F	VF	EF	UNC	PROOF
1838	1,607,760	£3.00	£9.00	£33.00	£50.00	—
1839	3,310,560	£2.50	£10.00	£35.00	£45.00	£130.00
1840	2,098,800	£2.50	£9.25	£40.00	£60.00	—
1841	1,386,000	£3.00	£15.00	£50.00	£70.00	—
1842	601,920	£2.50	£10.00	£35.00	£90.00	—
1843	3,160,080	£2.25	£11.00	£40.00	£65.00	—

SIXPENCE

	MINTAGE	F	VF	EF	UNC	PROOF
1844	3,975,840	£4.00	£7.50	£30.00	£50.00	—
1844 large 44		£4.75	£12.00	£45.00	£100.00	—
1845	3,714,480	£2.50	£9.00	£35.00	£45.00	—
1846	4,226,880	£3.50	£11.00	£37.00	£50.00	—
1848		£20.00	£65.00	£250.00	£300.00	—
1848 8 over 6	586,080	£10.00	£50.00	£200.00	£300.00	—
1848 8 over 7		£15.00	£60.00	£225.00	£300.00	—
1850	498,960	£2.50	£10.00	£50.00	£85.00	—
1851	2,288,107	£2.50	£10.00	£35.00	£50.00	—
1852	904,586	£2.25	£10.00	£40.00	£65.00	—
1853	3,837,930	£1.50	£8.75	£25.00	£50.00	£260.00
1854	840,116	£30.00	£100.00	£350.00	£400.00	—
1855	1,129,684	£1.75	£9.00	£35.00	£70.00	—
1856	2,779,920	£2.50	£7.75	£35.00	£60.00	—
1857	2,233,440	£3.25	£9.50	£35.00	£60.00	—
1858	1,932,480	£2.50	£10.00	£33.00	£65.00	—
1859	4,688,640	£1.50	£9.25	£35.00	£70.00	—
1859 9 over 8		£2.00	£9.50	£37.00	£70.00	—
1860	1,100,880	£2.50	£10.00	£35.00	£60.00	—
1862	990,000	£14.00	£55.00	£225.00	£275.00	—
1863	491,040	£8.00	£35.00	£115.00	£140.00	—
1864	4,253,040	£2.50	£8.75	£28.00	£60.00	—
1865	1,631,520	£3.50	£12.00	£50.00	£70.00	—
1866	4,140,080	£3.00	£8.50	£40.00	£55.00	—
1867	1,362,240	£3.25	£14.00	£40.00	£75.00	—
1868	1,069,200	£3.50	£14.00	£55.00	£80.00	—
1869	388,080	£3.50	£20.00	£75.00	£95.00	—
1870	479,613	£3.50	£22.00	£75.00	£85.00	—
1871	3,662,684	£4.25	£7.50	£35.00	£60.00	—
1872	3,382,048	£3.00	£8.00	£30.00	£60.00	—
1873	4,594,733	£1.50	£7.00	£35.00	£50.00	—
1874	4,225,726	£2.00	£8.50	£32.00	£45.00	—
1875	3,256,545	£1.50	£7.00	£35.00	£60.00	—
1876	841,435	£4.25	£14.00	£60.00	£80.00	—
1877	4,066,486	£1.50	£9.25	£30.00	£50.00	—
1878	2,624,525	£1.50	£7.25	£30.00	£50.00	—
1878 DRITANNIAR		£15.00	£50.00	£160.00	£400.00	—
1879	3,326,313	£4.25	£16.00	£55.00	£100.00	—
1879 without die no		£2.25	£10.00	£37.00	£60.00	—
1880	3,892,501	£1.25	£6.25	£16.00	£45.00	—
1881	6,239,447	£1.50	£7.50	£18.00	£28.00	—
1882	759,809	£3.50	£18.00	£60.00	£85.00	—
1883	4,986,558	£2.75	£5.00	£14.00	£30.00	—
1884	3,422,565	£2.75	£7.00	£13.00	£30.00	—
1885	4,652,771	£1.00	£9.00	£12.00	£35.00	—
1886	2,728,249	£1.00	£7.50	£12.00	£30.00	—
1887	3,675,607	£2.50	£9.25	£20.00	£25.00	—
1887 jubilee head withdrawn		£1.75	£2.50	£5.25	£7.00	£35.00
1887 jubilee head revised		£1.25	£2.25	£5.50	£6.50	

Jubilee Head (Withdrawn) 1887

Jubilee Head (Revised) 1887-1893

	MINTAGE	F	VF	EF	UNC	PROOF
1888	4,197,698	£2.50	£6.50	£13.00	£20.00	—
1889	8,738,928	£1.25	£4.50	£13.00	£22.00	—
1890	9,386,955	£2.00	£5.75	£12.00	£20.00	—

	MINTAGE	F	VF	EF	UNC	PROOF
1891	7,022,734	£2.50	£7.00	£19.00	£23.00	—
1892	6,245,746	£1.25	£3.75	£16.00	£22.00	—
1893	7,350,619	£65.00	£290.00	£835.00	£1,200	—
1893 veiled head	}	£1.75	£4.00	£9.25	£17.00	—
1893	1,312	—	—	—	—	£50.00
1894	3,467,704	£1.25	£3.25	£14.00	£25.00	—
1895	7,024,631	£1.25	£3.50	£15.00	£23.00	—
1896	6,651,699	£2.00	£3.00	£13.00	£20.00	—
1897	5,031,498	£1.00	£4.75	£11.00	£20.00	—
1898	5,914,100	£1.00	£2.50	£9.50	£22.00	—
1899	7,996,804	£1.25	£3.25	£12.00	£18.00	—
1900	8,984,354	£1.50	£4.75	£11.00	£18.00	—
1901	5,108,757	£1.00	£5.00	£8.50	£16.00	—

Edward VII 1902-1910

	MINTAGE	F	VF	EF	UNC	PROOF
1902	6,367,378	£2.00	£4.50	£11.00	£17.00	—
1902	15,123	—	—	—	—	£20.00
1903	5,410,096	£2.50	£3.00	£16.00	£32.00	—
1904	4,487,098	£2.00	£4.25	£30.00	£65.00	—
1905	4,235,556	£3.00	£6.50	£26.00	£55.00	—
1906	7,641,146	£2.00	£6.50	£17.00	£32.00	—
1907	8,733,673	£2.00	£4.25	£17.00	£28.00	—
1908	6,739,491	£2.00	£4.75	£32.00	£45.00	—
1909	6,584,017	£2.25	£6.00	£22.00	£35.00	—
1910	12,490,724	£1.75	£4.50	£13.00	£19.00	—

George V 1911-1936

	MINTAGE	F	VF	EF	UNC	PROOF
1911	9,155,310	£2.00	£5.00	£7.25	£14.00	—
1911	6,007	—	—	—	—	£28.00
1912	10,984,129	£1.75	£5.00	£15.00	£23.00	—
1913	7,499,833	£3.00	£8.25	£15.00	£27.00	—
1914	22,714,602	£1.25	£3.50	£7.50	£13.00	—
1915	15,694,597	£1.50	£3.75	£8.00	£16.00	—
1916	22,207,178	£1.25	£3.00	£7.75	£13.00	—

SIXPENCE

	MINTAGE	F	VF	EF	UNC	PROOF
1917	7,725,475	£2.00	£3.50	£13.00	£30.00	—
1918	27,553,743	£1.50	£2.75	£7.00	£12.00	—
1919	13,375,447	£2.00	£2.50	£7.50	£18.00	—
1920	14,136,287	£1.25	£6.50	£12.00	£22.00	—
1921	30,339,741	£1.50	£5.75	£8.75	£15.00	—
1922	16,878,890	£1.50	£4.25	£11.00	£19.00	—
1923	6,382,793	£1.75	£8.50	£18.00	£28.00	—
1924	17,444,218	£1.75	£4.75	£10.00	£13.00	—
1925	12,720,558	£1.25	£3.00	£12.00	£18.00	—
1926	21,809,621	£1.25	£4.00	£9.50	£17.00	—
1926 modified head	21,809,621	£0.75	£1.25	£6.50	£11.00	—
1927	8,924,873	£1.00	£3.25	£10.00	£13.00	—

	MINTAGE	F	VF	EF	UNC	PROOF
1927 new reverse	15,000	—	—	—	—	£15.00
1928	23,123,384	£0.40	£3.00	£5.25	£7.50	—
1929	28,319,326	£0.40	£1.50	£3.50	£8.00	—
1930	16,990,289	£0.60	£2.00	£4.00	£8.50	—
1931	16,873,268	£0.60	£4.50	£8.00	£10.00	—
1932	9,406,117	£0.75	£3.00	£12.00	£20.00	—
1933	22,185,083	£1.00	£3.00	£6.00	£9.00	—
1934	9,304,009	£1.00	£1.50	£6.50	£10.00	—
1935	13,995,621	£0.50	£0.75	£6.00	£8.00	—
1936	24,380,171	£0.55	£1.75	£2.75	£5.00	—

George VI 1937-1952

	MINTAGE	F	VF	EF	UNC	PROOF
1937	22,302,524	£0.55	£1.25	£2.00	£3.25	—
1937	26,402	—	—	—	—	£4.00
1938	13,402,701	£0.60	£1.25	£3.75	£6.00	—
1939	28,670,304	£0.60	£1.25	£2.00	£3.00	—
1940	20,875,196	£0.45	£1.00	£1.50	£3.75	—
1941	23,086,616	£0.60	£1.00	£2.00	£4.75	—
1942	44,942,785	£0.40	£1.25	£1.50	£2.00	—
1943	46,927,111	£0.35	£1.25	£1.50	£2.25	—
1944	36,952,600	£0.45	£1.00	£1.25	£2.00	—
1945	39,939,259	*	£0.55	£1.00	£2.00	—
1946	43,466,407	*	£0.55	£1.00	£2.00	—
1947	29,993,263	*	£0.25	£0.75	£2.25	—
1948	88,323,540	*	£0.25	£0.75	£2.50	—

IND: IMP: omitted 1949

	MINTAGE	F	VF	EF	UNC	PROOF
1949 new reverse	41,335,515	*	£0.30	£1.50	£3.50	—
1950	32,741,955	*	£0.30	£1.00	£3.00	—
1950	17,513	—	—	—	—	£3.50
1951	40,399,491	*	£0.45	£1.50	£3.50	—
1951	20,000	—	—	—	—	£4.00
1952	1,013,477	£1.50	£2.75	£8.00	£24.00	—

Elizabeth II 1953-

	MINTAGE	F	VF	EF	UNC	PROOF
1953	70,323,876	*	£0.30	£1.00	£1.25	—
1953	40,000	—	—	—	—	£2.50
1954	105,241,150	*	£0.20	£1.00	£2.00	—
1955	109,929,554	*	£0.20	£0.40	£1.00	—
1956	109,841,555	*	£0.20	£0.40	£1.50	—
1957	105,654,290	*	£0.20	£0.65	£1.50	—
1958	123,518,527	*	£0.20	£1.25	£2.50	—
1959	93,089,441	*	£0.20	£0.30	£0.65	—
1960	103,283,346	*	£0.20	£2.00	£2.75	—
1961	115,052,017	*	£0.20	£0.60	£2.50	—
1962	166,483,637	*	£0.15	£0.25	£0.45	—
1963	120,056,000	*	£0.15	£0.20	£0.40	—
1964	152,336,000	*	£0.10	£0.15	£0.40	—
1965	129,644,000	*	*	£0.10	£0.25	—
1966	175,676,000	*	*	£0.10	£0.30	—
1967	240,788,000	*	*	£0.10	£0.25	—
1970	unavailable	—	—	—	—	£1.75

SHILLINGS

Charles II 1660-1685

	VG	F	VF	EF	PROOF
1663 first bust	£15.00	£37.00	£65.00	£235.00	—
1663 variety of first bust	£9.00	£22.00	£60.00	£235.00	—
1666 — elephant below	£65.00	£140.00	£500.00	+	—
1666 guinea head, elephant below	£100.00	£350.00	£975.00	+	—
1668 variety of first bust	£30.00	£160.00	£400.00	£800.00	—
1668 second bust	£13.00	£33.00	£65.00	£235.00	—

Plume on obverse and reverse

	VG	F	VF	EF	PROOF
1670—	£20.00	£45.00	£175.00	£600.00	—
1671—	£23.00	£50.00	£220.00	£680.00	—
1671—plume on obv and rev	£35.00	£80.00	£340.00	£750.00	—
1672—	£12.00	£26.00	£120.00	£440.00	—
1673—	£20.00	£45.00	£175.00	£675.00	—
1673—plume on obv and rev	£35.00	£80.00	£400.00	£800.00	—
1674—	£20.00	£45.00	£175.00	£675.00	—
1674—plume on obv and rev	£35.00	£80.00	£350.00	£800.00	—
1674—plume on rev only	£50.00	£125.00	£450.00	£900.00	—
1674 third bust	£50.00	£125.00	£465.00	£900.00	—
1675—	£25.00	£75.00	£275.00	£885.00	—
1675 second bust	£35.00	£90.00	£300.00	£750.00	—
1675—plume on obv and rev	£35.00	£80.00	£400.00	£800.00	—
1676—	£14.00	£37.00	£90.00	£385.00	—
1676—plume on obv and rev	£35.00	£80.00	£340.00	£750.00	—
1677—	£15.00	£30.00	£90.00	£385.00	—
1677—plume on obv only	£50.00	£125.00	£500.00	£1,000	—
1678—	£20.00	£45.00	£175.00	£575.00	—
1679—	£15.00	£35.00	£100.00	£385.00	—
1679—plume on obv and rev	£35.00	£95.00	£430.00	£800.00	—
1679—plume on obv only	£35.00	£90.00	£385.00	£800.00	—
1680—plume on obv and rev	£60.00	£150.00	£550.00	+	—
1681—	£30.00	£50.00	£215.00	£660.00	—
1683 fourth bust	£30.00	£70.00	£200.00	£775.00	—
1684—	£15.00	£40.00	£175.00	£675.00	—

James II 1685-1688

	VG	F	VF	EF	PROOF
1685	£18.00	£28.00	£125.00	£350.00	—
1686	£12.00	£35.00	£125.00	£350.00	—
1687	£15.00	£35.00	£160.00	£400.00	—
1687 7 over 6	£15.00	£40.00	£160.00	£440.00	—
1688	£15:00	£40.00	£160.00	£440.00	—

William and Mary 1688-1694

	VG	F	VF	EF	PROOF
1692	£15.00	£30.00	£90.00	£425.00	—
1693	£11.00	£30.00	£85.00	£375.00	—

William III 1694-1702

Plumes in angles

	VG	F	VF	EF	PROOF
1695 first bust	£7.50	£18.00	£50.00	£150.00	—
1696 —	£4.50	£12.00	£25.00	£80.00	—
1696 — B(Bristol)	£5.00	£18.00	£45.00	£135.00	—
1696 — C(Chester)	£6.00	£17.00	£70.00	£150.00	—
1696 — E(Exeter)	£6.00	£23.00	£50.00	£150.00	—
1696 — N(Norwich)	£6.00	£20.00	£45.00	£150.00	—
1696 — y(York)	£6.00	£20.00	£50.00	£150.00	—
1696 — Y(York)	£7.00	£22.00	£60.00	£175.00	—
1696 third bust, C(Chester)	£23.00	£45.00	£140.00	£475.00	—
1697 first bust	£3.75	£9.00	£25.00	£80.00	—
1697 — B(Bristol)	£6.00	£20.00	£50.00	£150.00	—
1697 — C(Chester)	£6.00	£26.00	£50.00	£150.00	—
1697 — E(Exeter)	£7.50	£20.00	£50.00	£150.00	—
1697 — N(Norwich)	£5.00	£16.00	£45.00	£150.00	—
1697 — y(York)	£6.00	£20.00	£50.00	£150.00	—
1697 — Y(York)	£7.00	£22.00	£60.00	£175.00	—
1697 third bust	£4.00	£10.00	£23.00	£80.00	—
1697 — B(Bristol)	£7.00	£22.00	£60.00	£175.00	—
1697 — C(Chester)	£6.00	£20.00	£50.00	£150.00	—
1097 — E(Exeter)	£7.00	£22.00	£60.00	£175.00	—
1697 — N(Norwich)	£7.00	£25.00	£60.00	£175.00	—
1697 — y(York)	£7.00	£20.00	£60.00	£175.00	—
1697 variety of third bust	£5.50	£10.00	£25.00	£85.00	—
1697 — B(Bristol)	£7.00	£22.00	£60.00	£175.00	—
1697 — C(Chester)	£20.00	£50.00	£150.00	£450.00	—
1698 —	£7.00	£18.00	£50.00	£155.00	—
1698 — plumes in angles	£25.00	£55.00	£170.00	£525.00	—
1698 fourth bust	£12.00	£30.00	£100.00	£275.00	—
1699 —	£12.00	£25.00	£70.00	£275.00	—
1699 fifth bust	£12.00	£22.00	£60.00	£235.00	—
1699 — plumes in angles	£18.00	£40.00	£115.00	£355.00	—

SHILLINGS

	VG	F	VF	EF	PROOF
1699 — roses in angles	£25.00	£55.00	£165.00	£455.00	—
1700 —	£6.50	£15.00	£40.00	£135.00	—
1701 —	£7.00	£20.00	£60.00	£200.00	—
1701 — plumes in angles	£17.00	£40.00	£115.00	£360.00	—

Anne 1702-1714

After Union reverse

	VG	F	VF	EF	PROOF
Before Union reverse					
1702 first bust	£11.00	£32.00	£60.00	£225.00	—
1702 — plumes in angles	£10.00	£27.00	£100.00	£275.00	—
1702 — VIGO	£15.00	£25.00	£85.00	£240.00	—
1703 second bust, VIGO	£12.00	£23.00	£60.00	£140.00	—
1704 — plumes in angles	£12.00	£40.00	£125.00	£335.00	—
1705 —	£10.00	£27.00	£90.00	£275.00	—
1705 — plumes in angles	£8.00	£25.00	£60.00	£245.00	—
1705 — roses and plumes in angles	£13.00	£23.00	£75.00	£205.00	—
1707 — —	£14.00	£30.00	£100.00	£230.00	—
After Union reverse: English and Scottish arms impaled					
1707 second bust, E (Edinburgh)	£6.75	£15.00	£50.00	£155.00	—
1707 — E*(Edinburgh)	£16.00	£32.00	£110.00	£340.00	—
1707 third bust	£3.50	£12.00	£35.00	£95.00	—
1707 — plumes in angles	£6.00	£20.00	£60.00	£175.00	—
1707 — E(Edinburgh)	£6.25	£12.00	£40.00	£130.00	—
1708 second bust, E(Edinburgh)	£14.00	£33.00	£100.00	£290.00	—
1708 — E*(Edinburgh)	£6.00	£22.00	£60.00	£175.00	—
1708 — roses and plumes in angles	£20.00	£50.00	£150.00	£455.00	—
1708 third bust	£2.75	£12.00	£22.00	£80.00	—
1708 — plumes in angles	£6.00	£16.00	£30.00	£140.00	—
1708 — roses and plumes in angles	£8.00	£25.00	£70.00	£200.00	—
1708 — E(Edinburgh)	£10.00	£22.00	£80.00	£250.00	—
1708 'Edinburgh' bust, E*(Edinburgh)	£8.50	£25.00	£80.00	£250.00	—
1709 — —	£10.00	£25.00	£100.00	£275.00	—
1709 third bust	£4.00	£14.00	£50.00	£95.00	—
1710 — roses and plumes in angles	£7.50	£20.00	£50.00	£115.00	—
1710 fourth bust, roses and plumes in angles	£8.00	£25.00	£80.00	£250.00	—
1711 third bust	£11.00	£30.00	£150.00	£450.00	—
1711 fourth bust	£5.25	£14.00	£32.00	£85.00	—
1712 — roses and plumes in angles	£7.00	£15.00	£22.00	£95.00	—
1713 — — 3 over 2	£4.50	£25.00	£50.00	£150.00	—
1714 — —	£6.50	£12.00	£40.00	£95.00	—

George I 1714-1727

	VG	F	VF	EF	PROOF
1715 first bust, roses and plumes in angles	£4.50	£15.00	£45.00	£160.00	—
1716 — —	£12.00	£40.00	£120.00	£325.00	—
1717 — —	£4.50	£15.00	£45.00	£140.00	—
1718 — —	£4.00	£15.00	£40.00	£155.00	—
1719 — —	£12.00	£33.00	£120.00	£350.00	—

W.C.C. below bust

	VG	F	VF	EF	PROOF
1720——	£5.75	£15.00	£40.00	£175.00	—
1720—plain reverse	£4.00	£17.00	£45.00	£140.00	—
1721——	£30.00	£55.00	£200.00	£500.00	—
1721—roses and plumes in angles	£5.00	£18.00	£50.00	£180.00	—
1721——1 over 0	£5.00	£18.00	£60.00	£175.00	—
1722——	£6.00	£15.00	£50.00	£140.00	—
1723——	£5.25	£16.00	£50.00	£145.00	—
1723—SS C in angles	£6.50	£15.00	£24.00	£80.00	—
1723 second bust, SS C in angles	£3.50	£13.00	£40.00	£120.00	—
1723—roses and plumes in angles	£5.00	£16.00	£45.00	£155.00	—
1723—W.C.C. below	£45.00	£90.00	£300.00	£840.00	—
1724—roses and plumes in angles	£5.00	£18.00	£55.00	£155.00	—
1724—W.C.C. below	£60.00	£90.00	£330.00	£885.00	—
1725—roses and plumes in angles	£5.00	£18.00	£50.00	£155.00	—
1725—W.C.C. below	£50.00	£90.00	£325.00	£885.00	—
1726—roses and plumes in angles	£35.00	£100.00	£330.00	£1,000	—
1726—W.C.C. below	£40.00	£90.00	£325.00	£885.00	—
1727—roses and plumes in angles	£25.00	£90.00	£290.00	£830.00	—

George II 1727-1760

Young Head **Roses in angles** **Old Head**

	VG	F	VF	EF	PROOF
1727 young head, plumes in angles	£14.00	£32.00	£100.00	£300.00	—
1727—roses and plumes in angles	£6.75	£22.00	£50.00	£155.00	—
1728—	£23.00	£40.00	£140.00	£360.00	—
1728—roses and plumes in angles	£8.00	£30.00	£75.00	£190.00	—
1729——	£10.00	£30.00	£75.00	£190.00	—
1731——	£7.00	£27.00	£45.00	£150.00	—
1731—plumes in angles	£16.00	£40.00	£175.00	£440.00	—
1732—roses and plumes in angles	£15.00	£25.00	£75.00	£185.00	—
1734——	£6.75	£14.00	£32.00	£110.00	—
1735——	£4.00	£12.00	£45.00	£115.00	—
1736——	£7.50	£14.00	£28.00	£110.00	—
1737——	£4.00	£12.00	£40.00	£110.00	—
1739—roses in angles	£9.00	£12.00	£35.00	£125.00	—
1741——	£8.50	£14.00	£35.00	£150.00	—
1743 old head, roses in angles	£8.25	£16.00	£32.00	£80.00	—

	VG	F	VF	EF	PROOF
1745——.........................	£8.00	£18.00	£45.00	£150.00	—
1745—LIMA	£6.00	£16.00	£40.00	£80.00	—
1746——6 over 5	£10.00	£30.00	£85.00	£315.00	—
1747—roses in angles	£8.00	£11.00	£40.00	£90.00	—
1750——.........................	£5.00	£20.00	£40.00	£105.00	—
1751——.........................	£10.00	£30.00	£75.00	£205.00	—
1758——.........................	£5.75	£8.00	£15.00	£33.00	—

George III 1760-1820

'Northumberland'

	VG	F	VF	EF	PROOF
1763 'Northumberland'	£40.00	£95.00	£180.00	£400.00	—

	VG	F	VF	EF	PROOF
1787 no hearts in shield	£1.75	£5.25	£11.00	£23.00	—
1787—no stop over head	£1.50	£4.75	£12.00	£34.00	—
1787—no stops at date	£1.75	£4.25	£13.00	£38.00	—
1787 hearts in shield	£2.00	£4.00	£8.50	£22.00	—
1798 'Dorrien and Magens'	—	—	—	—	£3,000

	MINTAGE	F	VF	EF	UNC	PROOF
1816.........................	unrecorded	£5.00	£8.00	£27.00	£40.00	● —
1817.........................	23,031,360	£4.75	£13.00	£28.00	£40.00	—

	MINTAGE	F	VF	EF	UNC	PROOF
1818	1,342,440	£10.00	£20.00	£80.00	£140.00	—
1819	7,595,280	£4.25	£7.00	£35.00	£50.00	—
1820	7,975,440	£5.00	£11.00	£25.00	£45.00	—

George IV 1821-1830

Laureate Head, shield in garter

	MINTAGE	F	VF	EF	UNC	PROOF
1821 garnished shield	2,463,120	£6.50	£17.00	£47.00	£100.00	—
1823 shield in garter	693,000	£8.50	£47.00	£150.00	£200.00	—
1824	4,158,000	£5.75	£20.00	£60.00	£105.00	—
1825	2,459,160	£5.25	£13.00	£55.00	£85.00	—
1825 bare head		£4.50	£15.00	£30.00	£65.00	—

Bare Head

	MINTAGE	F	VF	EF	UNC	PROOF
1826	6,351,840	£4.00	£9.25	£32.00	£70.00	£200.00
1827	574,200	£9.00	£24.00	£110.00	£160.00	—
1829	879,120	£8.00	£13.00	£80.00	£140.00	—

William IV 1831-1837

	MINTAGE	F	VF	EF	UNC	PROOF
1831	unrecorded	—	—	—	—	£235.00
1834	3,223,440	£5.00	£17.00	£60.00	£120.00	—

SHILLINGS

	MINTAGE	F	VF	EF	UNC	PROOF
1835	1,449,360	£5.25	£33.00	£80.00	£150.00	—
1836	3,567,960	£4.00	£20.00	£70.00	£90.00	—
1837	478,160	£5.50	£30.00	£125.00	£160.00	—

Victoria 1838-1901

Young Head

	MINTAGE	F	VF	EF	UNC	PROOF
1838	1,956,240	£8.25	£20.00	£45.00	£80.00	—
1839	5,666,760	£7.00	£15.00	£60.00	£125.00	£235.00
1840	1,639,440	£9.00	£30.00	£130.00	£200.00	—
1841	875,160	£6.75	£28.00	£115.00	£135.00	—
1842	2,094,840	£6.75	£15.00	£45.00	£80.00	—
1843	1,465,200	£3.75	£20.00	£80.00	£135.00	—
1844	4,466,880	£7.00	£20.00	£50.00	£85.00	—
1845	4,082,760	£4.25	£15.00	£65.00	£80.00	—
1846	4,031,280	£4.50	£15.00	£50.00	£100.00	—
1848 8 over 6	1,041,480	£16.00	£50.00	£340.00	£400.00	—
1849	845,480	£3.50	£20.00	£55.00	£140.00	—
1850	685,080	£90.00	£300.00	£800.00	£1,400	—
1851	470,071	£18.00	£50.00	£220.00	£330.00	—
1852	1,306,574	£3.50	£13.00	£35.00	£70.00	—
1853	4,256,188	£6.00	£12.00	£40.00	£85.00	£400.00
1854	552,414	£35.00	£120.00	£365.00	£445.00	—
1855	1,368,499	£3.25	£15.00	£45.00	£85.00	—
1856	3,168,000	£7.50	£16.00	£40.00	£85.00	—
1857	2,562,120	£5.25	£15.00	£50.00	£75.00	—
1858	3,108,600	£6.00	£16.00	£45.00	£85.00	—
1859	4,561,920	£4.00	£23.00	£45.00	£85.00	—
1860	1,671,120	£9.00	£27.00	£80.00	£140.00	—
1861	1,382,040	£8.25	£20.00	£80.00	£140.00	—
1862	954,360	£12.00	£37.00	£90.00	£205.00	—
1863	859,320	£10.00	£55.00	£175.00	£250.00	—
1864	4,518,360	£3.00	£13.00	£43.00	£65.00	—
1865	5,619,240	£5.75	£17.00	£50.00	£75.00	—
1866	4,984,600	£3.25	£17.00	£47.00	£90.00	—
1867	2,166,120	£4.25	£22.00	£55.00	£90.00	—
1868	3,330,360	£4.00	£23.00	£55.00	£70.00	—
1869	736,560	£5.25	£16.00	£70.00	£110.00	—
1870	1,467,471	£3.50	£20.00	£65.00	£110.00	—
1871	4,910,010	£3.25	£11.00	£32.00	£60.00	—
1872	8,897,781	£3.00	£12.00	£25.00	£60.00	—
1873	6,489,598	£3.00	£15.00	£30.00	£65.00	—
1874	5,503,747	£3.00	£10.00	£30.00	£50.00	—
1875	4,353,983	£2.50	£13.00	£30.00	£55.00	—
1876	1,057,487	£2.50	£11.00	£40.00	£85.00	—
1877	2,980,703	£2.50	£8.75	£30.00	£50.00	—

	MINTAGE	F	VF	EF	UNC	PROOF
1878	3,127,131	£4.25	£13.00	£32.00	£45.00	—
1879	3,611,507	£3.75	£12.00	£38.00	£120.00	—
1880	4,842,786	£3.25	£9.50	£35.00	£45.00	—
1881	5,255,332	£4.50	£11.00	£32.00	£50.00	—
1882	1,611,786	£9.00	£22.00	£65.00	£140.00	—
1883	7,281,450	£3.00	£11.00	£27.00	£45.00	—
1884	3,923,993	£4.25	£12.00	£25.00	£50.00	—
1885	3,336,526	£2.75	£8.25	£27.00	£40.00	—
1886	2,086,819	£2.50	£11.00	£24.00	£40.00	—
1887	} 4,034,133	£6.25	£13.00	£50.00	£70.00	—
1887 jubilee head		£2.00	£4.00	£6.25	£8.50	—

Small Jubilee Head

	MINTAGE	F	VF	EF	UNC	PROOF
1887	1,084	—	—	—	—	£60.00
1888	4,526,856	£1.50	£7.25	£12.00	£27.00	—
1889 small head	} 7,039,628	£12.00	£60.00	£200.00	£300.00	—
1889 large head		£1.75	£8.50	£18.00	£32.00	—

Large Jubilee Head

	MINTAGE	F	VF	EF	UNC	PROOF
1890	8,794,042	£2.50	£9.00	£15.00	£32.00	—
1891	5,665,348	£4.50	£10.00	£20.00	£37.00	—
1892	4,591,622	£2.00	£6.50	£28.00	£50.00	—

Veiled Head

	MINTAGE	F	VF	EF	UNC	PROOF
1893 veiled head	7,039,074	£2.00	£5.50	£17.00	£23.00	—
1893	1,312	—	—	—	—	£65.00
1894	5,953,152	£2.00	£4.50	£18.00	£35.00	—

SHILLINGS

	MINTAGE	F	VF	EF	UNC	PROOF
1895	8,880,651	£1.75	£5.75	£20.00	£26.00	—
1896	9,264,551	£2.00	£7.75	£13.00	£25.00	—
1897	6,270,364	£3.25	£8.75	£17.00	£23.00	—
1898	9,768,703	£2.00	£3.75	£20.00	£38.00	—
1899	10,965,382	£2.00	£5.00	£16.00	£26.00	—
1900	10,937,590	£1.50	£4.50	£17.00	£23.00	—
1901	3,426,294	£1.75	£6.75	£13.00	£28.00	—

Edward VII 1902-1910

	MINTAGE	F	VF	EF	UNC	PROOF
1902	7,809,481	£2.50	£5.00	£15.00	£20.00	—
1902	13,123	—	—	—	—	£25.00
1903	2,061,823	£5.25	£25.00	£40.00	£95.00	—
1904	2,040,161	£3.00	£8.00	£37.00	£65.00	—
1905	488,390	£23.00	£60.00	£325.00	£600.00	—
1906	10,791,025	£2.00	£5.00	£22.00	£32.00	—
1907	14,083,418	£2.25	£3.75	£27.00	£38.00	—
1908	3,806,969	£1.50	£6.25	£55.00	£90.00	—
1909	5,664,982	£2.00	£5.25	£45.00	£90.00	—
1910	26,547,236	£1.50	£7.50	£15.00	£25.00	—

George V 1911-1936

	MINTAGE	F	VF	EF	UNC	PROOF
1911	20,065,901	£2.50	£5.50	£9.00	£16.00	—
1911	6,007	—	—	—	—	£37.00
1912	15,594,009	£2.25	£5.00	£16.00	£28.00	—
1913	9,011,509	£3.00	£5.00	£22.00	£50.00	—
1914	23,415,843	£2.25	£5.00	£8.00	£16.00	—
1915	39,279,024	£2.50	£3.50	£7.00	£13.00	—
1916	35,862,015	£2.50	£4.25	£8.00	£13.00	—
1917	22,202,608	£2.00	£6.25	£13.00	£18.00	—
1918	34,915,934	£2.00	£4.25	£7.50	£14.00	—
1919	10,823,824	£2.00	£5.75	£12.00	£18.00	—
1920	22,825,142	£1.75	£7.00	£15.00	£30.00	—
1921	22,648,763	£1.50	£5.00	£16.00	£50.00	—
1922	27,215,738	£1.25	£5.00	£16.00	£30.00	—
1923	14,575,243	£1.50	£4.00	£13.00	£20.00	—

COIN 1992 YEAR BOOK

	MINTAGE	F	VF	EF	UNC	PROOF
1924	9,250,095	£1.50	£6.75	£15.00	£33.00	—
1925	5,418,764	£3.25	£9.00	£35.00	£50.00	—
1926	22,516,453	£1.50	£3.75	£9.50	£24.00	—
1926 modified head		£1.75	£5.50	£12.00	£21.00	—
1927	9,247,344	£2.50	£8.00	£14.00	£26.00	—
1927 new reverse		£1.75	£7.50	£14.00	£18.00	—

	MINTAGE	F	VF	EF	UNC	PROOF
1927	15,000	—	—	—	—	£20.00
1928	18,136,778	£0.75	£3.25	£7.00	£11.00	—
1929	19,343,006	£2.00	£4.00	£7.50	£15.00	—
1930	3,172,092	£2.00	£7.25	£14.00	£27.00	—
1931	6,993,926	£1.50	£3.00	£8.00	£16.00	—
1932	12,168,101	£1.50	£3.00	£8.00	£11.00	—
1933	11,511,624	£1.00	£4.50	£6.00	£11.00	—
1934	6,138,463	£2.00	£7.00	£11.00	£22.00	—
1935	9,183,462	£1.00	£3.25	£6.00	£9.50	—
1936	11,910,613	£1.50	£2.25	£5.00	£8.00	—

George VI 1937-1952

English (Eng)　　　　　　　　　**Scottish (Scot)**

	MINTAGE	F	VF	EF	UNC	PROOF
1937 Eng	8,359,122	£1.00	£1.50	£4.00	£5.25	—
1937 Eng	26,402	—	—	—	—	£6.00
1937 Scot	6,748,875	*	£1.25	£3.25	£5.00	—
1937 Scot	26,402	—	—	—	—	£6.50
1938 Eng	4,833,436	*	£1.25	£7.00	£15.00	—
1938 Scot	4,797,852	*	£1.50	£5.50	£15.00	—
1939 Eng	11,052,677	*	£1.25	£2.00	£4.00	—
1939 Scot	10,263,892	*	£1.25	£2.00	£4.25	—
1940 Eng	11,099,126	*	£1.00	£2.00	£4.50	—
1940 Scot	9,913,089	*	£1.00	£2.50	£5.00	—
1941 Eng	11,391,883	*	£1.25	£2.00	£4.50	—
1941 Scot	8,086,030	*	£1.25	£2.50	£6.00	—
1942 Eng	17,453,643	*	£1.25	£2.00	£3.75	—
1942 Scot	13,676,759	*	£1.00	£1.50	£5.00	—
1943 Eng	11,404,213	*	£1.25	£2.25	£5.00	—
1943 Scot	9,824,214	*	£1.25	£2.50	£4.75	—
1944 Eng	11,586,751	*	£1.25	£1.75	£3.25	—
1944 Scot	10,990,167	*	£1.25	£2.00	£5.00	—
1945 Eng	15,143,404	*	£1.00	£2.00	£3.00	—
1945 Scot	15,106,270	*	£1.00	£2.00	£2.75	—
1946 Eng	18,663,797	*	£1.00	£1.50	£2.50	—
1946 Scot	16,381,501	*	£1.00	£1.50	£3.00	—

SHILLINGS

	MINTAGE	F	VF	EF	UNC	PROOF
1947 Eng	12,120,611	*	£0.30	£2.00	£6.50	—
1947 Scot	12,283,223	*	£0.30	£1.25	£4.00	—
1948 Eng	45,576,923	*	£0.30	£1.00	£4.00	—
1948 Scot	45,351,937	*	£0.30	£1.50	£3.75	—

IND: IMP omitted 1949

	MINTAGE	F	VF	EF	UNC	PROOF
1949 Eng	19,328,405	*	£0.30	£2.50	£8.25	—
1949 Scot	21,243,074	*	£0.50	£2.25	£9.00	—
1950 Eng	19,243,872	*	£0.30	£2.25	£4.50	—
1950 Eng	17,513	—	—	—	—	£5.00
1950 Scot	14,299,601	*	£0.30	£3.00	£6.25	—
1950 Scot	17,513	—	—	—	—	£7.00
1951 Eng	9,956,930	*	£0.30	£1.25	£5.00	—
1951 Eng	20,000	—	—	—	—	£5.50
1951 Scot	10,961,174	*	*	£1.50	£6.00	—
1951 Scot	20,000	—	—	—	—	£6.50

Elizabeth II 1953-

English (Eng)   **Scottish (Scot)**

	MINTAGE	F	VF	EF	UNC	PROOF
1953 Eng	41,942,894	*	*	£0.50	£1.00	—
1953 Eng	40,000	—	—	—	—	£3.50
1953 Scot	20,663,528	*	*	£0.75	£1.00	—
1953 Scot	40,000	—	—	—	—	£3.50
1954 Eng	30,262,032	*	*	£0.75	£2.00	—
1954 Scot	26,771,735	*	*	£0.75	£2.25	—
1955 Eng	45,259,908	*	*	£0.50	£1.50	—
1955 Scot	27,950,906	*	*	£1.00	£2.25	—
1956 Eng	44,907,008	*	*	£3.00	£5.50	—
1956 Scot	42,853,639	*	*	£3.00	£6.25	—
1957 Eng	42,774,217	*	*	£0.30	£1.50	—
1957 Scot	17,959,988	*	£1.00	£2.00	£17.00	—
1958 Eng	14,392,305	*	£1.00	£1.75	£16.00	—
1958 Scot	40,822,557	*	*	£0.50	£1.50	—
1959 Eng	19,442,778	*	*	£0.50	£1.00	—
1959 Scot	1,012,988	*	£0.75	£2.75	£15.00	—

	MINTAGE	F	VF	EF	UNC	PROOF
1960 Eng	27,027,914	*	*	£0.75	£1.00	—
1960 Scot	14,376,932	*	*	£1.00	£1.50	—
1961 Eng	39,816,907	*	*	£0.25	£1.00	—
1961 Scot	2,762,558	*	£0.50	£1.50	£5.25	—
1962 Eng	36,704,379	*	*	£0.10	£0.75	—
1962 Scot	17,475,310	*	*	£0.25	£1.00	—
1963 Eng	49,433,607	*	*	£0.25	£0.50	—
1963 Scot	32,300,000	*	*	£0.25	£0.50	—
1964 Eng	8,590,900	*	*	£0.15	£0.50	—
1964 Scot	5,239,100	*	*	£0.10	£0.75	—
1965 Eng	9,216,000	*	*	£0.15	£0.50	—
1965 Scot	2,774,000	*	*	£0.25	£0.75	—
1966 Eng	15,002,000	*	*	£0.15	£0.50	—
1966 Scot	15,604,000	*	*	£0.15	£0.50	—
1970 Eng Proof FDC	unavailable	—	—	—	—	£2.00
1970 Scot Proof FDC	unavailable	—	—	—	—	£2.75

FLORINS

Victoria 1838-1901

'Godless'—DEI: GRATIA omitted

	MINTAGE	F	VF	EF	UNC	PROOF
1848	unrecorded	—	—	—	—	+
1849	413,820	£6.25	£30.00	£57.00	£135.00	—

Gothic Script

	MINTAGE	F	VF	EF	UNC	PROOF
1851 mdcccli	1,540	+	+	+	+	—
1852 mdccclii	1,014,552	£4.25	£20.00	£80.00	£140.00	—
1853 mdcccliii	3,919,950	£3.50	£20.00	£80.00	£170.00	£1,100
1854 mdcccliv	550,413	£225.00	£500.00	£1,725	+	—
1855 mdccclv	831,017	£5.50	£40.00	£100.00	£180.00	—
1856 mdccclvi	2,201,760	£7.00	£20.00	£95.00	£225.00	—
1857 mdccclvii	1,671,120	£6.25	£25.00	£100.00	£180.00	—
1858 mdccclviii	2,239,380	£5.00	£23.00	£85.00	£165.00	—
1859 mdccclix	2,568,060	£8.50	£24.00	£100.00	£180.00	—
1860 mdccclx	1,475,100	£6.50	£40.00	£135.00	£225.00	—
1862 mdccclxii	594,000	£20.00	£100.00	£325.00	£450.00	—

FLORINS

	MINTAGE	F	VF	EF	UNC	PROOF
1863 mdccclxiii	938,520	£45.00	£160.00	£500.00	£600.00	—
1864 mdccclxiv	1,861,200	£5.50	£28.00	£95.00	£150.00	—
1865 mdccclxv	1,580,044	£5.75	£27.00	£110.00	£200.00	—
1866 mdccclxvi	914,760	£6.25	£30.00	£100.00	£225.00	—
1867 mdccclxvii	423,720	£15.00	£60.00	£160.00	£350.00	—
1868 mdccclxviii	896,940	£5.50	£27.00	£125.00	£225.00	—
1869 mdccclxix	297,000	£5.00	£25.00	£100.00	£165.00	—
1870 mdccclxx	1,080,648	£4.75	£25.00	£100.00	£180.00	—
1871 mdccclxxi	3,425,605	£4.25	£25.00	£100.00	£155.00	—
1872 mdccclxxii	7,199,690	£4.75	£20.00	£70.00	£135.00	—
1873 mdccclxxiii	5,921,839	£4.00	£30.00	£70.00	£140.00	—
1874 mdccclxxiv	1,642,630	£4.50	£20.00	£100.00	£180.00	—
1875 mdccclxxv	1,117,030	£5.75	£25.00	£100.00	£180.00	—
1876 mdccclxxvi	580,034	£5.25	£25.00	£110.00	£200.00	—
1877 mdccclxxvii	682,292	£8.75	£25.00	£110.00	£200.00	—
1877 no WW		£6.50	£30.00	£125.00	£250.00	—
1878 mdccclxxviii	1,786,680	£6.00	£20.00	£90.00	£180.00	—
1879 mdccclxxix	1,512,247	£7.00	£25.00	£110.00	£200.00	—
1879 no WW		£6.25	£25.00	£100.00	£185.00	—
1880 mdccclxxx	2,167,170	£5.25	£25.00	£100.00	£180.00	—
1881 mdccclxxxi	2,570,337	£7.25	£21.00	£65.00	£140.00	—
1883 mdccclxxxiii	3,555,667	£5.25	£18.00	£80.00	£125.00	—
1884 mdccclxxxiv	1,447,379	£4.75	£28.00	£85.00	£140.00	—
1885 mdccclxxxv	1,758,210	£4.00	£24.00	£85.00	£140.00	—
1886 mdccclxxxvi	591,773	£4.50	£20.00	£95.00	£140.00	—
1887 mdccclxxxvii	1,776,903	£13.00	£30.00	£165.00	£250.00	—
1887 jubilee head		£3.50	£6.75	£12.00	£25.00	—

Jubilee Head

	MINTAGE	F	VF	EF	UNC	PROOF
1887	1,084	—	—	—	—	£65.00
1888	1,547,540	£3.00	£6.75	£22.00	£40.00	—
1889	2,973,561	£2.75	£6.50	£24.00	£45.00	—
1890	1,684,737	£4.50	£26.00	£55.00	£100.00	—
1891	836,438	£6.50	£35.00	£120.00	£200.00	—
1892	283,401	£12.00	£25.00	£150.00	£265.00	—

Veiled Head

	MINTAGE	F	VF	EF	UNC	PROOF
1893	1,666,103	£2.25	£16.00	£26.00	£40.00	—
1893	1,312	—	—	—	—	£75.00

	MINTAGE	F	VF	EF	UNC	PROOF
1894	1,952,842	£4.00	£9.00	£45.00	£65.00	—
1895	2,182,968	£2.50	£8.25	£30.00	£60.00	—
1896	2,944,416	£4.25	£8.75	£24.00	£50.00	—
1897	1,699,921	£3.50	£13.00	£26.00	£45.00	—
1898	3,061,343	£2.50	£6.50	£30.00	£55.00	—
1899	3,966,953	£3.25	£9.50	£20.00	£50.00	—
1900	5,528,630	£3.50	£6.75	£30.00	£45.00	—
1901	2,648,870	£4.00	£14.00	£22.00	£46.00	—

Edward VII 1902-1910

	MINTAGE	F	VF	EF	UNC	PROOF
1902	2,189,575	£4.25	£11.00	£24.00	£42.00	—
1902	15,123	—	—	—	—	£45.00
1903	1,995,298	£3.25	£15.00	£33.00	£75.00	—
1904	2,769,932	£3.75	£15.00	£43.00	£105.00	—
1905	1,187,596	£12.00	£35.00	£115.00	£300.00	—
1906	6,910,128	£4.25	£11.00	£53.00	£100.00	—
1907	5,947,895	£4.00	£10.00	£55.00	£100.00	—
1908	3,280,010	£4.00	£25.00	£80.00	£120.00	—
1909	3,482,829	£7.00	£17.00	£75.00	£130.00	—
1910	5,650,713	£3.50	£7.75	£38.00	£70.00	—

George V 1911-1936

	MINTAGE	F	VF	EF	UNC	PROOF
1911	5,951,284	£2.50	£7.50	£16.00	£40.00	—
1911	6,007	—	—	—	—	£50.00
1912	8,571,731	£3.50	£5.00	£28.00	£60.00	—
1913	4,545,278	£3.00	£4.50	£35.00	£70.00	—
1914	21,252,701	£3.00	£6.00	£8.50	£23.00	—
1915	12,367,939	£3.00	£4.25	£12.00	£20.00	—
1916	21,064,337	£2.50	£6.00	£12.00	£20.00	—
1917	11,181,617	£2.25	£7.00	£14.00	£30.00	—
1918	29,211,792	£3.00	£5.00	£10.00	£20.00	—

	MINTAGE	F	VF	EF	UNC	PROOF
1919	9,469,292	£3.00	£7.00	£12.00	£27.00	—
1920	15,387,833	£1.50	£6.00	£21.00	£42.00	—
1921	34,863,895	£2.00	£9.00	£18.00	£32.00	—
1922	23,861,044	£3.00	£8.00	£17.00	£40.00	—
1923	21,546,533	£1.75	£4.50	£15.00	£23.00	—
1924	4,582,372	£3.00	£8.50	£23.00	£48.00	—
1925	1,404,136	£3.50	£12.00	£80.00	£140.00	—
1926	5,125,410	£3.50	£7.75	£27.00	£53.00	—

	MINTAGE	F	VF	EF	UNC	PROOF
1927 new reverse	101,497	—	—	—	—	£33.00
1928	11,087,186	£1.50	£3.50	£9.00	£15.00	—
1929	16,397,279	£1.50	£4.00	£8.00	£14.00	—
1930	5,753,568	£1.50	£4.00	£10.00	£22.00	—
1931	6,556,331	£1.50	£3.25	£10.00	£17.00	—
1932	717,041	£3.00	£12.00	£65.00	£130.00	—
1933	8,685,303	£2.25	£4.00	£6.50	£15.00	—
1935	7,540,546	£2.00	£4.50	£8.25	£11.00	—
1936	9,897,448	£2.00	£4.00	£6.25	£11.00	—

George VI 1937-1952

	MINTAGE	F	VF	EF	UNC	PROOF
1937	13,006,781	*	£1.50	£3.00	£4.75	—
1937	26,402	—	—	—	—	£7.75
1938	7,909,388	£1.50	£2.50	£5.00	£16.00	—
1939	20,850,607	*	£1.50	£2.50	£5.00	—
1940	18,700,338	*	£1.50	£2.50	£4.50	—
1941	24,451,079	*	£1.50	£2.25	£4.50	—
1942	39,895,243	*	£1.25	£2.00	£3.00	—
1943	26,711,987	*	£1.50	£2.75	£3.50	—
1944	27,560,005	*	£1.50	£2.00	£3.00	—
1945	25,858,049	*	£1.25	£2.50	£3.00	—
1946	22,300,254	*	£1.50	£2.00	£3.25	—
1947	22,910,085	*	£0.35	£1.50	£3.50	—
1948	67,553,636	*	£0.60	£1.00	£4.00	—

IND: IMP omitted 1949

	MINTAGE	F	VF	EF	UNC	PROOF
1949	28,614,939	*	£0.60	£1.75	£7.25	—
1950	24,357,490	*	£0.60	£1.75	£5.00	—
1950	17,513	—	—	—	—	£6.00
1951	27,411,747	*	£0.50	£2.50	£6.00	—
1951	20,000	—	—	—	—	£8.00

Elizabeth II 1953-

	MINTAGE	F	VF	EF	UNC	PROOF
1953	11,958,710	*	£0.50	£2.00	£2.75	—
1953	40,000	—	—	—	—	£4.50

BRITT: OMN: omitted 1954

	MINTAGE	F	VF	EF	UNC	PROOF
1954	13,085,422	*	£0.40	£5.00	£25.00	—
1955	25,887,253	*	£0.40	£1.50	£3.00	—
1956	47,824,500	*	£0.40	£1.50	£2.50	—
1957	33,071,282	*	£0.40	£4.00	£20.00	—
1958	9,564,580	*	£0.40	£2.75	£13.00	—
1959	14,080,319	*	£0.40	£4.00	£22.00	—
1960	13,831,782	*	£0.40	£1.00	£2.00	—

	MINTAGE	F	VF	EF	UNC	PROOF
1961	37,735,315	*	*	£0.75	£2.00	—
1962	35,147,903	*	*	£0.75	£1.25	—
1963	26,471,000	*	*	£0.75	£1.25	—
1964	16,539,000	*	*	£0.50	£0.75	—
1965	48,163,000	*	*	£0.50	£0.75	—
1966	83,999,000	*	*	£0.50	£0.75	—
1967	39,718,000	*	*	£0.40	£0.75	—
1970 Proof FDC	unavailable	—	—	—	—	£2.25

HALFCROWNS

Charles II 1660-1685

	VG	F	VF	EF	PROOF
1663 first bust	£24.00	£40.00	£175.00	£780.00	—
1664 second bust	£24.00	£80.00	£270.00	£975.00	—
1666 third bust, elephant below	£105.00	£430.00	£1,450	+	—
1668 — 8 over 4	£55.00	£90.00	£300.00	£900.00	—
1669 — 9 over 4	£40.00	£110.00	£300.00	£1,200	—
1670 —	£21.00	£27.00	£105.00	£680.00	—
1671 variety of third bust	£10.00	£28.00	£170.00	£465.00	—
1672 — V QVARTO	£22.00	£30.00	£130.00	£720.00	—
1672 fourth bust	£40.00	£50.00	£175.00	£700.00	—
1673 —	£10.00	£26.00	£90.00	£600.00	—
1674 —	£30.00	£80.00	£240.00	£940.00	—
1675 —	£16.00	£30.00	£165.00	£740.00	—
1676 —	£12.00	£25.00	£90.00	£500.00	—
1677 —	£11.00	£32.00	£95.00	£465.00	—
1678 —	£45.00	£105.00	£265.00	+	—
1679 —	£10.00	£28.00	£125.00	£455.00	—
1680 —	£50.00	£95.00	£300.00	+	—
1681 —	£20.00	£35.00	£175.00	£750.00	—
1682 —	£20.00	£50.00	£215.00	£780.00	—
1683 —	£12.00	£45.00	£120.00	£680.00	—
1684 — 4 over 3	£55.00	£90.00	£340.00	+	—

James II 1685-1688

	VG	F	VF	EF	PROOF
1685 first bust	£24.00	£45.00	£175.00	£380.00	—
1686 —	£30.00	£60.00	£185.00	£685.00	—

	VG	F	VF	EF	PROOF
1687 —	£21.00	£50.00	£150.00	£485.00	—
1687 second bust	£20.00	£45.00	£200.00	£600.00	—
1688 —	£22.00	£60.00	£160.00	£550.00	—

William and Mary 1688-1694

1st shield　　　　　　　　　　　　　　　**3rd shields**

	VG	F	VF	EF	PROOF
1689 first busts, first shield	£17.00	£40.00	£100.00	£335.00	—
1689 — second shield	£13.00	£28.00	£70.00	£300.00	—
1690 — —	£14.00	£35.00	£125.00	£450.00	—
1691 second busts, third shields	£10.00	£40.00	£150.00	£380.00	—
1692 — — QVARTO	£14.00	£35.00	£125.00	£450.00	—
1693 — —	£15.00	£30.00	£120.00	£600.00	—

William III 1694-1702

	VG	F	VF	EF	PROOF
1696 large shields, early harp	£10.00	£24.00	£55.00	£175.00	—
1696 — — B(Bristol)	£12.00	£23.00	£70.00	£210.00	—
1696 — — C(Chester)	£12.00	£26.00	£90.00	£275.00	—
1696 — — E(Exeter	£20.00	£30.00	£105.00	£375.00	—
1696 — — N(Norwich)	£27.00	£45.00	£175.00	£460.00	—
1696 — y(York)	£12.00	£25.00	£90.00	£275.00	—
1696 — ordinary harp	£25.00	£35.00	£140.00	£400.00	—
1696 — — C(Chester)	£30.00	£45.00	£155.00	£450.00	—
1696 — — E(Exeter)	£30.00	£40.00	£155.00	£500.00	—
1696 — — N(Norwich)	£35.00	£55.00	£210.00	£500.00	—
1696 small shields	£8.00	£15.00	£50.00	£175.00	—
1696 — B(Bristol)	£9.00	£20.00	£70.00	£235.00	—

B(Bristol)

	VG	F	VF	EF	PROOF
1696—C(Chester)	£20.00	£30.00	£120.00	£375.00	—
1696—E(Exeter)	£30.00	£45.00	£175.00	£500.00	—
1696—N(Norwich)	£14.00	£26.00	£95.00	£275.00	—
1696—y(York)	£14.00	£30.00	£125.00	£375.00	—
1697 large shields, ordinary harp	£13.00	£20.00	£55.00	£175.00	—
1697——B(Bristol)	£9.00	£35.00	£80.00	£225.00	—
1697——C(Chester)	£10.00	£22.00	£75.00	£255.00	—
1697——E(Exeter)	£12.00	£20.00	£70.00	£200.00	—
1697——N(Norwich)	£13.00	£23.00	£70.00	£255.00	—
1697——y(York)	£10.00	£20.00	£75.00	£230.00	—
1698 modified large shields, DECIMO	£11.00	£23.00	£45.00	£250.00	—
1699—	£9.00	£40.00	£120.00	£300.00	—
1700—	£7.00	£20.00	£60.00	£185.00	—
1701—	£10.00	£23.00	£70.00	£230.00	—
1701—plumes in angles	£14.00	£30.00	£100.00	£335.00	—

Anne 1702-1714

VIGO, before Union reverse

	VG	F	VF	EF	PROOF
Before Union reverse					
1703	£65.00	£265.00	£740.00	+	—
1703 VIGO	£23.00	£40.00	£70.00	£255.00	—
1704 plumes in angles	£25.00	£45.00	£150.00	£400.00	—
1705—	£18.00	£30.00	£135.00	£275.00	—
1706 roses and plumes in angles	£12.00	£33.00	£80.00	£250.00	—
1707—	£16.00	£35.00	£65.00	£265.00	—
After Union reverse: English and Scottish arms impaled					
1707	£14.00	£35.00	£55.00	£160.00	—
1707 E(Edinburgh)	£12.00	£23.00	£50.00	£175.00	—
1708	£9.00	£20.00	£55.00	£220.00	—
1708 E(Edinburgh)	£16.00	£28.00	£55.00	£175.00	—
1708 plumes in angles	£14.00	£35.00	£90.00	£255.00	—

	VG	F	VF	EF	PROOF
1709	£11.00	£22.00	£60.00	£170.00	—
1709 E(Edinburgh)	£35.00	£60.00	£215.00	£630.00	—
1710 roses and plumes in angles	£12.00	£27.00	£80.00	£240.00	—
1712—	£8.00	£30.00	£85.00	£225.00	—
1713	£12.00	£30.00	£70.00	£200.00	—
1713 roses and plumes in angles	£14.00	£25.00	£80.00	£225.00	—
1714—	£9.00	£22.00	£60.00	£200.00	—

George I 1714-1727

Small roses and plumes in angles

	VG	F	VF	EF	PROOF
1715 roses and plumes in angles	£20.00	£45.00	£140.00	£425.00	—
1717—	£20.00	£70.00	£185.00	£500.00	—
1720—20 over 17	£20.00	£55.00	£145.00	£500.00	—
1723 SS C in angles	£30.00	£65.00	£135.00	£485.00	—
1726 small roses and plumes in angles	£250.00	£575.00	£1,300	+	—

George II 1727-1760

Young Head   **Roses and plumes in angles**   **Old Head**

	VG	F	VF	EF	PROOF
1731 young head, roses and plumes in angles	£10.00	£30.00	£70.00	£285.00	—
1732——	£9.00	£30.00	£75.00	£300.00	—
1734——	£10.00	£30.00	£90.00	£330.00	—
1735——	£12.00	£30.00	£80.00	£330.00	—
1736——	£12.00	£35.00	£125.00	£425.00	—
1739—roses in angles	£12.00	£22.00	£90.00	£260.00	—
1741—	£12.00	£25.00	£75.00	£300.00	—
1743 old head, roses in angles	£12.00	£28.00	£65.00	£200.00	—
1745—	£10.00	£25.00	£55.00	£185.00	—
1745—LIMA	£13.00	£27.00	£50.00	£190.00	—
1746——	£12.00	£22.00	£33.00	£120.00	—

	VG	F	VF	EF	PROOF
1750—	£18.00	£40.00	£120.00	£400.00	—
1751—	£30.00	£50.00	£175.00	£475.00	—

George III 1760-1820

	F	VF	EF	UNC	PROOF
Half-dollar with oval counterstamp	£60.00	£135.00	£300.00	£450.00	—

Large Head

	MINTAGE	F	VF	EF	UNC	PROOF
1816 large head	unrecorded	£4.75	£18.00	£65.00	£160.00	—
1817	} 8,092,656	£10.00	£20.00	£50.00	£110.00	—
1817 small head		£7.25	£25.00	£65.00	£145.00	—

Small Head

	MINTAGE	F	VF	EF	UNC	PROOF
1818	2,905,056	£6.75	£30.00	£80.00	£140.00	—
1819	4,790,016	£8.25	£17.00	£60.00	£160.00	—
1820	2,396,592	£8.00	£35.00	£90.00	£200.00	—

George IV 1821-1830

Laureate Head, garnished shield

	MINTAGE	F	VF	EF	UNC	PROOF
1820 garnished shield	inc above	£7.50	£25.00	£85.00	£150.00	—
1821	1,435,104	£6.25	£20.00	£70.00	£170.00	—
1823	} 2,003,760	£215.00	£550.00	£1,800	£2,500	—
1823 shield in garter		£12.00	£35.00	£110.00	£160.00	—
1824	465,696	£9.00	£45.00	£160.00	£300.00	—

Bare Head

	MINTAGE	F	VF	EF	UNC	PROOF
1825	2,258,784	£9.00	£27.00	£70.00	£200.00	—
1826	2,189,088	£10.00	£18.00	£65.00	£175.00	£380.00
1828	49,890	£14.00	£35.00	£175.00	£275.00	—
1829	508,464	£12.00	£35.00	£150.00	£260.00	—

William IV 1831-1837

	MINTAGE	F	VF	EF	UNC	PROOF
1831	unrecorded	—	—	—	—	£455.00
1834	} 993,168	£8.00	£25.00	£95.00	£250.00	—
1834 WW in script		£6.00	£27.00	£80.00	£200.00	—

	MINTAGE	F	VF	EF	UNC	PROOF
1835	281,952	£11.00	£50.00	£175.00	£320.00	—
1836	1,588,752	£6.00	£20.00	£125.00	£200.00	—
1837	150,526	£20.00	£45.00	£200.00	£300.00	—

Victoria 1838-1901

Young Head

	MINTAGE	F	VF	EF	UNC	PROOF
1839	unrecorded	+	+	+	+	£535.00
1840	386,496	£12.00	£40.00	£165.00	£300.00	—
1841	42,768	£26.00	£95.00	£380.00	£600.00	—
1842	486,288	£10.00	£35.00	£135.00	£250.00	—
1843	454,608	£23.00	£60.00	£200.00	£300.00	—
1844	1,999,008	£6.75	£30.00	£135.00	£230.00	—
1845	2,231,856	£10.00	£26.00	£100.00	£220.00	—
1846	1,539,668	£11.00	£30.00	£140.00	£250.00	—
1848	367,488	£25.00	£80.00	£350.00	£500.00	—
1848 8 over 6		£30.00	£100.00	£400.00	£500.00	—
1849 large date	261,360	£7.00	£30.00	£175.00	£260.00	—
1849 small date		£16.00	£75.00	£200.00	£350.00	—
1850	484,613	£8.50	£50.00	£180.00	£400.00	—
1874	2,188,599	£5.50	£22.00	£60.00	£130.00	—
1875	1,113,483	£10.00	£27.00	£80.00	£140.00	—
1876	633,221	£7.50	£35.00	£85.00	£150.00	—
1877	447,059	£8.00	£18.00	£80.00	£145.00	—
1878	1,466,323	£5.50	£20.00	£75.00	£110.00	—
1879	901,356	£6.00	£23.00	£90.00	£160.00	—
1880	1,346,350	£7.00	£22.00	£80.00	£125.00	—
1881	2,301,495	£4.50	£18.00	£55.00	£110.00	—
1882	808,227	£5.00	£22.00	£80.00	£125.00	—
1883	2,982,779	£7.50	£26.00	£60.00	£95.00	—
1884	1,569,175	£5.75	£30.00	£70.00	£115.00	—
1885	1,628,438	£5.75	£17.00	£60.00	£130.00	—
1886	891,767	£9.00	£25.00	£60.00	£100.00	—
1887	1,438,046	£5.50	£20.00	£70.00	£100.00	—
1887 jubilee head		£4.00	£7.00	£11.00	£18.00	—

Jubilee Head

	MINTAGE	F	VF	EF	UNC	PROOF
1887	1,084	—	—	—	—	£115.00
1888	1,428,787	£2.75	£11.00	£27.00	£55.00	—
1889	4,811,954	£4.25	£14.00	£24.00	£45.00	—
1890	3,228,111	£3.25	£11.00	£38.00	£75.00	—
1891	2,284,632	£3.00	£13.00	£37.00	£60.00	—
1892	1,710,946	£2.75	£15.00	£42.00	£65.00	—

Veiled Head

	MINTAGE	F	VF	EF	UNC	PROOF
1893	1,792,600	£3.75	£15.00	£33.00	£50.00	—
1893	1,312	—	—	—	—	£125.00
1894	1,524,960	£4.25	£16.00	£40.00	£65.00	—
1895	1,772,662	£2.75	£8.50	£27.00	£55.00	—
1896	2,148,505	£4.00	£9.25	£23.00	£50.00	—
1897	1,678,643	£4.00	£8.50	£30.00	£42.00	—
1898	1,870,055	£4.50	£11.00	£27.00	£55.00	—
1899	2,865,872	£3.25	£8.00	£30.00	£47.00	—
1900	4,479,128	£3.25	£13.00	£25.00	£35.00	—
1901	1,516,570	£3.75	£9.00	£23.00	£50.00	—

Edward VII 1901-1910

	MINTAGE	F	VF	EF	UNC	PROOF
1902	1,316,008	£4.25	£12.00	£30.00	£55.00	—
1902	15,123	—	—	—	—	£60.00
1903	274,840	£20.00	£75.00	£300.00	£535.00	—
1904	709,652	£12.00	£50.00	£240.00	£400.00	—
1905	166,008	£45.00	£240.00	£730.00	£1,100	—
1906	2,886,206	£4.50	£16.00	£50.00	£150.00	—
1907	3,693,930	£5.25	£27.00	£70.00	£125.00	—
1908	1,758,889	£6.00	£17.00	£95.00	£150.00	—
1909	3,051,592	£5.00	£18.00	£70.00	£150.00	—
1910	2,557,685	£4.75	£13.00	£50.00	£75.00	—

George V 1911-1936

Crown Touches Shield, 1911-1922

	MINTAGE	F	VF	EF	UNC	PROOF
1911	2,914,573	£4.50	£7.00	£27.00	£65.00	—
1911	6,007	—	—	—	—	£75.00
1912	4,700,789	£4.00	£11.00	£27.00	£70.00	—
1913	4,090,169	£5.00	£10.00	£40.00	£90.00	—
1914	18,333,003	£3.50	£6.75	£12.00	£23.00	—
1915	32,433,066	£3.00	£4.50	£8.50	£20.00	—
1916	29,530,020	£3.00	£5.25	£11.00	£22.00	—
1917	11,172,052	£4.00	£7.50	£14.00	£30.00	—
1918	29,079,592	£3.00	£4.75	£8.00	£20.00	—
1919	10,266,737	£3.50	£7.00	£15.00	£35.00	—
1920	17,982,077	£1.75	£8.00	£17.00	£40.00	—
1921	23,677,889	£1.75	£7.75	£16.00	£50.00	—
1922	16,396,724	£2.50	£6.75	£18.00	£45.00	—
1923	26,308,526	£2.00	£6.50	£14.00	£23.00	—
1924	5,866,294	£2.25	£15.00	£30.00	£50.00	—
1925	1,413,461	£3.25	£25.00	£120.00	£200.00	—
1926	4,473,516	£3.50	£11.00	£30.00	£65.00	—
1926 modified head		£2.75	£6.00	£30.00	£60.00	—
1927	6,837,872	£3.00	£6.75	£17.00	£28.00	—

	MINTAGE	F	VF	EF	UNC	PROOF
1927 new reverse	15,000	—	—	—	—	£33.00
1928	18,762,727	£3.00	£6.00	£8.00	£13.00	—
1929	17,632,636	£3.00	£6.00	£8.00	£15.00	—
1930	809,051	£4.00	£8.50	£65.00	£180.00	—
1931	11,264,468	£2.75	£5.25	£9.50	£16.00	—
1932	4,793,643	£3.00	£10.00	£18.00	£25.00	—

	MINTAGE	F	VF	EF	UNC	PROOF
1933	10,311,494	£2.00	£6.25	£7.50	£15.00	—
1934	2,422,399	£3.00	£5.00	£22.00	£47.00	—
1935	7,022,216	£2.50	£5.25	£8.00	£12.00	—
1936	7,039,423	£2.50	£4.25	£7.25	£11.00	—

George VI 1937-1952

	MINTAGE	F	VF	EF	UNC	PROOF
1937	9,106,440	*	£2.00	£4.25	£6.00	—
1937	26,402	—	—	—	—	£9.00
1938	6,426,478	£1.50	£3.50	£6.00	£13.00	—
1939	15,478,635	£1.50	£2.00	£4.00	£7.00	—
1940	17,948,439	*	£2.00	£3.25	£6.00	—
1941	15,773,984	*	£2.00	£3.00	£6.00	—
1942	31,220,090	*	£2.00	£3.25	£4.00	—
1943	15,462,875	*	£2.00	£3.00	£6.75	—
1944	15,255,165	*	£2.00	£3.00	£4.00	—
1945	19,849,242	*	£2.00	£3.00	£4.00	—
1946	22,724,873	*	£2.00	£3.25	£4.00	—
1947	21,911,484	*	£0.75	£2.00	£3.50	—
1948	71,164,703	*	£0.30	£1.75	£3.00	—

IND: IMP omitted 1949

	MINTAGE	F	VF	EF	UNC	PROOF
1949	28,272,512	*	£0.60	£1.50	£6.50	—
1950	28,335,500	*	£0.50	£2.00	£5.50	—
1950	17,513	—	—	—	—	£7.00
1951	9,003,520	*	£0.60	£2.75	£6.75	—
1951	20,000	—	—	—	—	£8.00

Elizabeth II 1953-

	MINTAGE	F	VF	EF	UNC	PROOF
1953	4,333,214	*	£0.75	£1.25	£2.00	—
1953	40,000	—	—	—	—	£6.00

BRITT: OMN: omitted 1954

	MINTAGE	F	VF	EF	UNC	PROOF
1954	11,614,953	*	£0.75	£4.75	£14.00	—
1955	23,628,726	*	£0.50	£1.50	£3.25	—
1956	33,934,909	*	£0.50	£1.50	£3.25	—
1957	34,200,563	*	£0.50	£1.50	£2.75	—
1958	15,745,668	*	£0.60	£3.75	£12.00	—
1959	9,028,844	*	£0.75	£5.75	£13.00	—
1960	19,929,191	*	£0.40	£1.50	£3.25	—
1961	25,887,897	*	£0.40	£1.00	£1.50	—
1962	24,013,312	*	*	£0.60	£1.00	—
1963	17,625,200	*	*	£0.60	£1.00	—
1964	5,973,600	*	*	£0.80	£2.50	—
1965	9,778,440	*	*	£0.75	£1.25	—
1966	13,375,200	*	*	£0.50	£0.75	—
1967	33,058,400	*	*	£0.40	£0.60	—
1970		—	—	—	—	£3.00

DOUBLE FLORINS

Victoria 1838-1901

	MINTAGE	F	VF	EF	UNC	PROOF
1887 Roman I		£5.75	£10.00	£17.00	£28.00	—
1887 Roman I	483,347	—	—	—	—	£200.00
1887 Arabic 1		£8.50	£12.00	£18.00	£35.00	—
1887 Arabic 1		—	—	—	—	£200.00

	MINTAGE	F	VF	EF	UNC	PROOF
1888	} 243,340	£6.25	£20.00	£30.00	£50.00	—
1888 inverted 1 in VICT		£12.00	£20.00	£45.00	£140.00	—
1889	} 1,185,111	£6.00	£13.00	£37.00	£50.00	—
1889 inverted 1 in VICT		£10.00	£18.00	£50.00	£130.00	—
1890	782,146	£5.75	£10.00	£26.00	£60.00	—

CROWNS

Charles II 1660-1685

Elephant below bust

	VG	F	VF	EF	PROOF
1662 first bust, rose below	£20.00	£35.00	£190.00	£950.00	—
1662 —— 1662 on edge	£25.00	£45.00	£215.00	£1,100	—
1662 — no rose, 1662 on edge	£20.00	£50.00	£240.00	£1,250	—
1662 ——	£20.00	£45.00	£210.00	£1,000	—
1663 — new rev	£27.00	£50.00	£200.00	£1,000	—
1664 second bust	£28.00	£50.00	£280.00	£1,000	—
1665 — XVII	£75.00	£150.00	£650.00	+	—
1666 —	£25.00	£50.00	£225.00	£875.00	—
1666 — elephant below	£90.00	£125.00	£480.00	+	—
1667 —	£20.00	£35.00	£165.00	£1,000	—
1668 —	£15.00	£55.00	£135.00	£1,000	—
1669 —	£35.00	£90.00	£400.00	+	—
1670 —	£21.00	£45.00	£200.00	£1,100	—
1671 —	£25.00	£50.00	£160.00	£1,000	—
1671 third bust, V.TERTIO	£15.00	£35.00	£160.00	£950.00	—
1672 —	£13.00	£30.00	£110.00	£950.00	—
1673 — V.QUINTO	£10.00	£30.00	£150.00	£950.00	—
1675 — 5 over 3	£70.00	£200.00	£600.00	+	—

	VG	F	VF	EF	PROOF
1676—	£14.00	£35.00	£135.00	£950.00	—
1677—	£20.00	£40.00	£150.00	£950.00	—
1678—8 over 7	£40.00	£90.00	£400.00	—	
1679—	£28.00	£60.00	£160.00	£950.00	—
1679 fourth bust	£16.00	£35.00	£140.00	£950.00	—
1680 third bust	£30.00	£50.00	£180.00	£1,200	—
1680—80 over 79	£26.00	£50.00	£200.00	£1,000	—
1680 fourth bust	£20.00	£30.00	£160.00	£975.00	—
1681—	£20.00	£40.00	£200.00	£1,000	—
1682—2 over 1	£16.00	£40.00	£200.00	£1,000	—
1683—	£35.00	£110.00	£450.00	—	
1684—	£40.00	£85.00	£350.00	—	

James II 1685-1688

	VG	F	VF	EF	PROOF
1686 first bust	£35.00	£60.00	£240.00	£650.00	—
1687 second bust	£30.00	£45.00	£170.00	£450.00	—
1688—	£30.00	£45.00	£210.00	£400.00	—

William and Mary 1688-1694

	VG	F	VF	EF	PROOF
1691	£50.00	£125.00	£330.00	£1,000	—
1692	£65.00	£120.00	£280.00	£950.00	—

William III 1694-1702

	VG	F	VF	EF	PROOF
1695 first bust, first harp	£17.00	£32.00	£80.00	£300.00	—
1696 ——	£17.00	£40.00	£60.00	£230.00	—
1696 third bust, first harp	£14.00	£45.00	£100.00	£315.00	—
1697 — second harp	£115.00	£220.00	£800.00	+	—
1700 variety of third bust, third harp	£30.00	£40.00	£100.00	£430.00	—

Anne 1702-1714

After Union reverse, plumes in angles

	VG	F	VF	EF	PROOF
Before Union reverse					
1703 first bust, VIGO	£30.00	£100.00	£250.00	£775.00	—
1705 — plumes in angles	£50.00	£200.00	£450.00	£1,300	—
1706 — roses and plumes in angles	£30.00	£85.00	£180.00	£650.00	—
1707 ——	£23.00	£80.00	£245.00	£525.00	—
After Union reverse: English and Scottish arms impaled					
1707 second bust	£20.00	£45.00	£140.00	£450.00	—
1707 — E (Edinburgh)	£20.00	£45.00	£160.00	£465.00	—
1708 —	£16.00	£50.00	£170.00	£485.00	—
1708 — E (Edinburgh)	£26.00	£60.00	£150.00	£500.00	—
1708 — plumes in angles	£28.00	£60.00	£200.00	£700.00	—
1713 third bust, roses and plumes in angles	£25.00	£55.00	£200.00	£865.00	—

George I 1714-1727

SS C in angles

	VG	F	VF	EF	PROOF
1716 roses and plumes in angles	£50.00	£125.00	£265.00	£860.00	—
1718—8 over 6	£70.00	£175.00	£325.00	£1,000	—
1720—	£110.00	£200.00	£500.00	£1,200	—
1720—20 over 18	£70.00	£160.00	£335.00	£1,000	—
1723 SS C in angles	£60.00	£140.00	£275.00	£1,000	—
1726 roses and plumes in angles	£80.00	£160.00	£485.00	£1,000	—

George II 1727-1760

Young Head   **Roses in angles**   **Old Head, LIMA**

	VG	F	VF	EF	PROOF
1732 young head, roses and plumes in angles	£60.00	£80.00	£180.00	£600.00	—
1734——	£75.00	£115.00	£275.00	£630.00	—
1735——	£50.00	£80.00	£200.00	£535.00	—
1736——	£60.00	£80.00	£255.00	£700.00	—
1739—roses in angles	£45.00	£80.00	£270.00	£535.00	—
1741——	£45.00	£80.00	£245.00	£530.00	—

	VG	F	VF	EF	PROOF
1743 old head, roses in angles	£40.00	£80.00	£255.00	£800.00	—
1746 — LIMA	£40.00	£95.00	£200.00	£720.00	—
1750 —	£60.00	£150.00	£280.00	£865.00	—
1751 —	£60.00	£135.00	£330.00	£750.00	—

George III 1760-1820

	F	VF	EF	UNC	PROOF
Dollar with oval counterstamp	£50.00	£130.00	£230.00	£450.00	—
Dollar with octagonal counterstamp	£75.00	£150.00	£375.00	+	—

Bank of England Dollar

	MINTAGE	F	VF	EF	UNC	PROOF
1804 Britannia reverse	unrecorded	£40.00	£95.00	£165.00	£300.00	—

	MINTAGE	F	VF	EF	UNC	PROOF
1818 LVIII	} 155,232	£9.00	£25.00	£120.00	£245.00	—
1818 LIX		£13.00	£40.00	£135.00	£325.00	—
1819 LIX	} 683,496	£9.00	£40.00	£110.00	£200.00	—
1819 LIX 9 over 8		£9.00	£50.00	£180.00	£400.00	—
1819 LX		£8.00	£27.00	£120.00	£375.00	—
1820 LX	} 448,272	£11.00	£40.00	£110.00	£320.00	—
1820 LX 20 over 19		£20.00	£50.00	£200.00	£400.00	—

George IV 1821-1830

	MINTAGE	F	VF	EF	UNC	PROOF
1821 SECUNDO	} 437,976	£15.00	£45.00	£185.00	£475.00	—
1821 TERTIO		—	—	—	—	£2,000
1822 SECUNDO	} 124,929	£17.00	£85.00	£280.00	+	—
1822 TERTIO		£13.00	£50.00	£255.00	£1,000	—
1826 SEPTIMO	unrecorded	—	—	—	—	£2,300

William IV 1831-1837

	MINTAGE	F	VF	EF	UNC	PROOF
1831	unrecorded	—	—	—	—	£4,000
1834	unrecorded	—	—	—	—	+

Victoria 1838-1901

Young Head

	MINTAGE	F	VF	EF	UNC	PROOF
1839	unrecorded	—	—	—	—	£2,675
1844 VIII	94,248	£22.00	£110.00	£400.00	£1,000	—
1845 VIII	159,192	£17.00	£33.00	£290.00	£875.00	—
1847 XI	140,976	£17.00	£70.00	£430.00	£1,000	—

Gothic Script

	MINTAGE	F	VF	EF	UNC	PROOF
1847 UNDECIMO	8,000	—	—	—	—	£935.00
1847 plain edge	unrecorded	—	—	—	—	£1,525
1853 SEPTIMO	460	—	—	—	—	£3,500

Jubilee Head

	MINTAGE	F	VF	EF	UNC	PROOF
1887	173,581	£8.50	£20.00	£30.00	£50.00	—
1887	1,084	—	—	—	—	£370.00
1888	131,899	£10.00	£28.00	£60.00	£85.00	—
1889	1,807,224	£7.50	£16.00	£30.00	£70.00	—
1890	997,862	£7.50	£18.00	£42.00	£75.00	—
1891	556,394	£6.75	£18.00	£45.00	£90.00	—
1892	451,334	£8.00	£24.00	£80.00	£140.00	—

Veiled Head

	MINTAGE	F	VF	EF	UNC	PROOF
1893 LVI	497,845	£8.00	£28.00	£80.00	£120.00	—
1893 LVII		£10.00	£30.00	£175.00	—	—
1893 LVI	1,312	—	—	—	—	£345.00
1894 LVII	144,906	£6.00	£35.00	£120.00	£150.00	—
1894 LVIII		£5.75	£22.00	£105.00	£160.00	—
1895 LVIII	252,862	£7.00	£20.00	£95.00	£125.00	—
1895 LIX		£7.00	£27.00	£70.00	£125.00	—
1896 LIX	317,599	£12.00	£25.00	£125.00	£220.00	—
1896 LX		£7.00	£35.00	£95.00	£125.00	—
1897 LX	262,118	£8.75	£27.00	£75.00	£130.00	—
1897 LXI		£11.00	£30.00	£70.00	£135.00	—
1898 LXI	161,150	£13.00	£35.00	£170.00	£350.00	—
1898 LXII		£9.00	£40.00	£95.00	£160.00	—
1899 LXII	166,300	£8.25	£20.00	£100.00	£160.00	—
1899 LXIII		£7.50	£26.00	£80.00	£140.00	—
1900 LXIII	353,356	£9.25	£20.00	£90.00	£140.00	—
1900 LXIV		£9.25	£45.00	£75.00	£165.00	—

Edward VII 1902-1910

	MINTAGE	F	VF	EF	UNC	PROOF
1902	256,020	£24.00	£55.00	£80.00	£100.00	—
1902	15,123	—	—	—	—	£110.00

George V 1911-1936

	MINTAGE	F	VF	EF	UNC	PROOF
1927	15,030	—	—	—	—	£105.00
1928	9,034	£30.00	£55.00	£100.00	£140.00	—
1929	4,994	£40.00	£50.00	£85.00	£145.00	—
1930	4,847	£40.00	£70.00	£95.00	£160.00	—
1931	4,056	£50.00	£80.00	£115.00	£160.00	—
1932	2,395	£35.00	£70.00	£125.00	£235.00	—
1933	7,132	£33.00	£60.00	£90.00	£160.00	—
1934	932	£300.00	£400.00	£600.00	£925.00	—

	MINTAGE	F	VF	EF	UNC	PROOF
1935 incuse edge	714,769	£4.50	£6.50	£8.50	£15.00	—
1935 incuse edge, specimen	unrecorded	—	—	—	—	£20.00
1935 raised edge	2,500	—	—	—	—	£200.00

	MINTAGE	F	VF	EF	UNC	PROOF
1936	2,473	£40.00	£65.00	£165.00	£260.00	—

George VI 1937-1952

	MINTAGE	F	VF	EF	UNC	PROOF
1937	418,699	£6.00	£7.50	£10.00	£18.00	—
1937	26,402	—	—	—	—	£28.00

	MINTAGE	F	VF	EF	UNC	PROOF
1951	1,983,540	—	—	—	—	£4.25

Elizabeth II 1953-

	MINTAGE	F	VF	EF	UNC	PROOF
1953...	5,962,621	*	£1.00	£1.50	£2.50	—
1953...	40,000	—	—	—	—	£15.00

	MINTAGE	F	VF	EF	UNC	PROOF
1960...	1,024,038	*	£2.50	£3.25	£4.50	—
1960 polished dies.....................................	70,000	—	—	—	—	£9.00

	MINTAGE	F	VF	EF	UNC	PROOF
1965...	19,640,000	*	*	*	£0.60	—

HALF PENNY

Elizabeth II 1953-

1971-81   **1982-84**

	MINTAGE	F	VF	EF	UNC	PROOF
1971	1,394,188,250	*	*	*	£0.15	—
1973	365,680,000	*	*	*	£0.35	—
1974	365,448,000	*	*	*	£0.40	—
1975	197,600,000	*	*	*	£0.40	—
1976	412,172,000	*	*	*	£0.35	—
1977	unavailable	*	*	*	£0.15	—
1978	59,532,000	*	*	*	£0.20	—
1979	unavailable	*	*	*	£0.15	—
1980	unavailable	*	*	*	£0.20	—
1981	46,748,000	*	*	*	£0.40	—
1982 'new' omitted	unavailable	*	*	*	£0.15	—
1983	7,600,000	*	*	*	£0.30	—
1984	158,820	*	*	*	£1.00	—

ONE PENNY

Elizabeth II 1953-

	MINTAGE	F	VF	EF	UNC	PROOF
1971	1,521,666,250	*	*	*	£0.15	—
1973	280,196,000	*	*	*	£0.35	—
1974	330,892,000	*	*	*	£0.35	—
1975	221,604,000	*	*	*	£0.45	—
1976	241,800,000	*	*	*	£0.35	—
1977	285,430,000	*	*	*	£0.15	—
1978	292,770,000	*	*	*	£0.55	—
1979	459,000,000	*	*	*	£0.15	—
1980	416,304,000	*	*	*	£0.15	—
1981	301,800,000	*	*	*	£0.40	—
1982 'new' omitted	unavailable	*	*	*	£0.25	—
1983	243,002,000	*	*	*	£0.30	—
1984	154,759,625	*	*	*	£0.20	—

	MINTAGE	F	VF	EF	UNC	PROOF
1985	200,605,245	*	*	*	£0.10	—
1986	369,989,130	*	*	*	£0.10	—
1987	499,946,000	*	*	*	£0.10	—
1988	793,492,000	*	*	*	£0.10	—
1989	532,532,000	*	*	*	£0.10	—
1990	unavailable	*	*	*	£0.10	—

TWO PENCE

Elizabeth II 1953-

	MINTAGE	F	VF	EF	UNC	PROOF
1971	1,454,856,250	*	*	*	£0.15	—
1975	145,545,000	*	*	*	£0.35	—
1976	181,379,000	*	*	*	£0.35	—
1977	109,281,000	*	*	*	£0.20	—
1978	189,658,000	*	*	*	£0.70	—
1979	260,200,000	*	*	*	£0.20	—
1980	408,527,000	*	*	*	£0.20	—
1981	353,191,000	*	*	*	£0.15	—
1982 'new' omitted	205,000	*	*	*	£2.50	—
1983	637,100	*	*	*	£2.50	—
1984	158,820	*	*	*	£0.80	—

	MINTAGE	F	VF	EF	UNC	PROOF
1985	107,113,000	*	*	*	£0.15	—
1986	168,967,500	*	*	*	£0.15	—
1987	218,100,750	*	*	*	£0.15	—
1988	419,889,000	*	*	*	£0.15	—
1980	292,093,000	*	*	*	£0.15	—
1990	unavailable	*	*	*	£0.15	—

FIVE PENCE
Elizabeth II 1953-

	MINTAGE	F	VF	EF	UNC	PROOF
1968	98,868,250	•	•	•	£0.25	—
1969	120,270,000	•	•	•	£0.40	—
1970	225,948,525	•	•	•	£0.50	—
1971	81,783,475	•	•	•	£0.35	—
1975	141,539,000	•	•	•	£0.35	—
1977	24,308,000	•	•	•	£0.30	—
1978	61,094,000	•	•	•	£1.25	—
1979	155,456,000	•	•	•	£0.30	—
1980	220,566,000	•	•	•	£0.25	—
1982 'new' omitted	205,000	•	•	•	£3.50	—
1983	637,100	•	•	•	£3.00	—
1984	158,820	•	•	•	£1.20	—

	MINTAGE	F	VF	EF	UNC	PROOF
1985	178,375	•	•	•	£1.25	—
1986	unavailable	•	•	•	£1.15	—
1987	48,220,000	•	•	•	£0.40	—
1988	120,744,610	•	•	•	£0.40	—
1989	101,406,000	•	•	•	£0.40	—
1990	unavailable	•	•	•	£3.00	—
1990	unavailable	—	—	—	—	£18.00
1990 smaller size	unavailable	•	•	•	£0.35	—
1990 .925 silver, piedfort	unavailable	—	—	—	—	£25.00

TEN PENCE
Elizabeth II 1953-

	MINTAGE	F	VF	EF	UNC	PROOF
1968	336,143,250	•	•	•	£0.60	—
1969	314,008,000	•	•	•	£1.25	—

	MINTAGE	F	VF	EF	UNC	PROOF
1970	133,571,000	*	*	*	£1.40	—
1971	63,205,000	*	*	*	£1.60	—
1973	152,174,000	*	*	*	£1.40	—
1974	92,741,000	*	*	*	£1.50	—
1975	181,559,000	*	*	*	£2.25	—
1976	228,220,000	*	*	*	£1.25	—
1977	59,323,000	*	*	*	£0.85	—
1979	115,457,000	*	*	*	£0.85	—
1980	88,650,000	*	*	*	£0.85	—
1981	3,487,000	*	*	*	£0.55	—
1982 'new' omitted	205,000	*	*	*	£2.50	—
1983	637,100	*	*	*	£3.25	—
1984	158,820	*	*	*	£1.25	—

	MINTAGE	F	VF	EF	UNC	PROOF
1985	178,375	*	*	*	£1.25	—
1986	unavailable	*	*	*	£1.25	—
1987	172,425	*	*	*	£2.50	—
1988	unavailable	*	*	*	£1.50	—
1989	unavailable	*	*	*	£2.00	—
1990	unavailable	*	*	*	£0.75	—

TWENTY PENCE

Elizabeth II 1953-

	MINTAGE	F	VF	EF	UNC	PROOF
1982	740,815,000	*	*	*	£0.40	—
1982 .925 silver, piedfort	25,000	—	—	—	—	£55.00
1983	158,463,000	*	*	*	£0.60	—
1984	65,350,965	*	*	*	£0.65	—

	MINTAGE	F	VF	EF	UNC	PROOF
1985	74,273,699	*	*	*	£0.60	—
1986	unavailable	*	*	*	£1.00	—
1987	137,450,000	*	*	*	£0.50	—
1988	38,038,344	*	*	*	£0.60	—
1989	109,128,890	*	*	*	£0.65	—
1990	unavailable	*	*	*	£0.75	—

TWENTY-FIVE PENCE

Elizabeth II 1953-

	MINTAGE	F	VF	EF	UNC	PROOF
1972 Silver Wedding	7,452,100	•	•	•	£0.65	—
1972 Silver Wedding, .925 silver	100,000	—	—	—	—	£15.00

	MINTAGE	F	VF	EF	UNC	PROOF
1977 Silver Jubilee	} 36,989,000	•	•	•	£0.60	—
1977 Silver Jubilee, selected, in folder		•	•	•	£1.40	—
1977 Silver Jubilee, .925 silver	377,000	—	—	—	—	£11.00

	MINTAGE	F	VF	EF	UNC	PROOF
1980 Queen Mother	} 9,477,513	•	•	•	£0.50	—
1980 Queen Mother, selected, in folder .		•	•	•	£1.00	—
1980 Queen Mother, .925 silver	83,672	—	—	—	—	£28.00

	MINTAGE	F	VF	EF	UNC	PROOF
1981 Royal Wedding .... }		•	•	•	£0.50	—
1981 Royal Wedding, selected, in folder }	27,360,279				£1.00	—
1981 Royal Wedding, .925 silver	218,142	—	—	—	—	£26.00

FIFTY PENCE

Elizabeth II 1953-

Britannia reverse

1973 EEC reverse

	MINTAGE	F	VF	EF	UNC	PROOF
1969	188,400,000	•	•	•	£2.25	—
1970	19,461,500	•	•	•	£3.00	—
1973 EEC commemorative	89,775,000	•	•	•	£1.75	—
1973 EEC commemorative	356,616	—	—	—	—	£2.00
1976	43,746,500	•	•	•	£2.50	—
1977	49,536,000	•	•	•	£2.50	—
1978	72,005,500	•	•	•	£2.50	—
1979	58,680,000	•	•	•	£2.50	—
1980	89,086,000	•	•	•	£2.25	—
1981	74,002,000	•	•	•	£2.50	—
1982 'new' omitted	51,312,000	•	•	•	£1.75	—
1983	62,824,904	•	•	•	£2.25	—
1984	158,820	•	•	•	£4.00	—

	MINTAGE	F	VF	EF	UNC	PROOF
1985	679,603	•	•	•	£1.75	—
1986	unavailable	•	•	•	£2.00	—
1987	172,425	•	•	•	£2.75	—
1988	unavailable	•	•	•	£3.00	—
1989	unavailable	•	•	•	£3.00	—
1990	unavailable	•	•	•	£2.50	—

ONE POUND

Elizabeth II 1953-

1983 Royal Arms reverse

1984 Scottish reverse

	MINTAGE	F	VF	EF	UNC	PROOF
1983	443,053,510	•	•	•	£2.75	—
1983 selected, in folder	484,900	•	•	•	£2.75	—
1983 .925 silver	50,000	—	—	—	—	£30.00
1983 .925 silver, piedfort	10,000	—	—	—	—	£155.00
1984	146,256,501	•	•	•	£2.75	—
1984 selected, in folder	27,960	•	•	•	£3.75	—
1984 .925 silver	44,855	—	—	—	—	£22.00
1984 .925 silver, piedfort	15,000	—	—	—	—	£75.00

1985 Welsh reverse

1986 Northern Irish reverse

	MINTAGE	F	VF	EF	UNC	PROOF
1985	228,430,749	•	•	•	£2.25	—
1985 selected, in folder	24,850	•	•	•	£2.75	—
1985 .925 silver	50,000	—	—	—	—	£22.00
1985 .925 silver, piedfort	15,000	—	—	—	—	£70.00
1986	10,409,501	•	•	•	£2.25	—
1986 selected, in folder	19,908	•	•	•	£2.75	—
1986 .925 silver	50,000	—	—	—	—	£21.00
1986 .925 silver, piedfort	15,000	—	—	—	—	£60.00

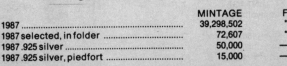

1987 English reverse

1988 Crowned Arms reverse

	MINTAGE	F	VF	EF	UNC	PROOF
1987	39,298,502	•	•	•	£2.25	—
1987 selected, in folder	72,607	•	•	•	£2.75	—
1987 .925 silver	50,000	—	—	—	—	£21.00
1987 .925 silver, piedfort	15,000	—	—	—	—	£55.00

	MINTAGE	F	VF	EF	UNC	PROOF
1988	7,118,825	•	•	•	£2.00	—
1988 selected, in folder	29,550	•	•	•	£2.75	—
1988 .925 silver	50,000	—	—	—	—	£21.00
1988 .925 silver, piedfort	15,000	—	—	—	—	£50.00
1989	70,290,550	•	•	•	£2.00	—
1989 .925 silver	22,275	—	—	—	—	£22.00
1989 .925 silver, piedfort	10,000	—	—	—	—	£60.00
1990	unavailable	•	•	•	£2.00	—
1990 .925 silver	unavailable	—	—	—	—	£21.00

TWO POUNDS

Elizabeth II 1953-

	MINTAGE	F	VF	EF	UNC	PROOF
1986	8,212,184	•	•	•	£4.25	—
1986 selected, in folder	520,191	•	•	•	£4.50	—
1986 .500 silver	125,000	•	•	•	£13.00	—
1986 .925 silver	75,000	—	—	—	—	£23.00
1986 .916 gold	17,500	—	—	—	—	£290.00

1989 Bill of Rights

1989 Claim of Right

	MINTAGE	F	VF	EF	UNC	PROOF
1989 Bill of Rights	4,397,074	•	•	•	£4.25	—
1989 Bill of Rights, selected, in folder	369,087	•	•	•	£4.50	—
1989 Bill of Rights .925 silver	25,000	—	—	—	—	£25.00
1989 Bill of Rights .925 silver, piedfort	unavailable	—	—	—	—	£40.00
1989 Claim of Right	345,828	•	•	•	£4.25	—
1989 Claim of Right, selected, in folder	74,682	•	•	•	£4.50	—
1989 Claim of Right .925 silver	24,852	—	—	—	—	£24.00
1989 Claim of Right .925 silver, piedfort	unavailable	—	—	—	—	£40.00

FIVE POUNDS

Elizabeth II 1953-

	MINTAGE	F	VF	EF	UNC	PROOF
1990 Queen Mother 90th birthday	unavailable	•	•	•	£7.00	—
1990 Queen Mother 90th birthday .925 silver	150,000	•	•	•	•	£28.75
1990 Queen Mother 90th birthday .916 gold	2,500	•	•	•	•	£750.00

HALF-SOVEREIGNS

George III 1760-1820

	MINTAGE	F	VF	EF	UNC	PROOF
1817	2,080,197	£52.00	£85.00	£200.00	£550.00	—
1818	1,030,286	£55.00	£95.00	£245.00	£600.00	—
1818 18 over 17		+	+	+	+	—
1820	35,043	£55.00	£90.00	£220.00	£650.00	—

George IV 1821-1830

	MINTAGE	F	VF	EF	UNC	PROOF
Laureate Head						
1821 ornate shield	231,288	£175.00	£420.00	£955.00	+	—
1823 plain shield	224,280	£65.00	£130.00	£385.00	£900.00	—
1824—	591,538	£58.00	£120.00	£325.00	£635.00	—
1825—	761,150	£60.00	£110.00	£335.00	£650.00	—
Bare Head						
1826	344,830	£60.00	£120.00	£300.00	£750.00	—
1826	unrecorded	—	—	—	—	£900.00
1827	492,014	£60.00	£150.00	£300.00	£750.00	—
1828	1,224,754	£55.00	£100.00	£270.00	£700.00	—

William IV 1831-1837

	MINTAGE	F	VF	EF	UNC	PROOF
1831 reduced diameter	unrecorded	—	—	—	—	£1,325
1834—	133,899	£90.00	£155.00	£425.00	£950.00	—
1835 normal diameter	772,554	£75.00	£150.00	£440.00	£900.00	—
1836—	146,865	£95.00	£225.00	£550.00	+	—
1836 6d die		£485.00	£935.00	£2,000	+	—
1837—	160,207	£90.00	£170.00	£465.00	£950.00	—

Victoria 1838-1901

	MINTAGE	F	VF	EF	UNC	PROOF
Young Head						
1838	273,341	£50.00	£75.00	£200.00	£425.00	—
1839	1,230	—	—	—	—	£1,000
1841	508,835	£65.00	£90.00	£255.00	£550.00	—
1842	2,223,352	£45.00	£60.00	£135.00	£275.00	—
1843	1,251,762	£55.00	£90.00	£250.00	£500.00	—
1844	1,127,007	£45.00	£70.00	£200.00	£325.00	—
1845	887,526	£85.00	£240.00	£785.00	£1,200	—
1846	1,063,928	£45.00	£80.00	£200.00	£350.00	—
1847	982,636	£45.00	£75.00	£200.00	£350.00	—
1848	410,595	£45.00	£75.00	£200.00	£375.00	—
1848 8 over 7		+	+	+	+	—
1849	845,112	£45.00	£65.00	£175.00	£350.00	—
1850	179,595	£75.00	£175.00	£475.00	£850.00	—
1851	773,573	£45.00	£65.00	£150.00	£300.00	—
1852	1,377,671	£45.00	£80.00	£175.00	£325.00	—
1853	2,708,796	£45.00	£60.00	£140.00	£275.00	—
1853	unrecorded	—	—	—	—	£2,450
1854	1,125,144	+	+	+	+	—

	MINTAGE	F	VF	EF	UNC	PROOF
1855	1,120,362	£45.00	£65.00	£140.00	£275.00	—
1856	2,391,909	£45.00	£65.00	£140.00	£275.00	—
1857	728,223	£45.00	£80.00	£175.00	£325.00	—
1858	855,578	£45.00	£60.00	£140.00	£300.00	—
1859	2,203,813	£45.00	£60.00	£140.00	£275.00	—
1860	1,131,500	£45.00	£60.00	£135.00	£275.00	—
1861	1,130,867	£45.00	£60.00	£150.00	£275.00	—
1862	unrecorded	+	£750.00	+	+	—
1863	1,571,574	£45.00	£65.00	£135.00	£275.00	—
1871	unrecorded	+	+	+	+	—
1880	1,009,049	£47.00	£60.00	£135.00	£250.00	—
1883	2,870,457	£45.00	£55.00	£115.00	£200.00	—
1884	1,113,756	£45.00	£55.00	£100.00	£225.00	—
1885	} 4,468,871	£45.00	£55.00	£100.00	£200.00	—
1885 5 over 3		+	+	+	+	—
1863 die no	inc above	£50.00	£80.00	£200.00	£425.00	—
1864—	1,758,490	£45.00	£60.00	£135.00	£275.00	—
1865—	1,834,750	£45.00	£60.00	£135.00	£275.00	—
1866—	2,058,776	£45.00	£60.00	£135.00	£275.00	—
1867—	992,795	£45.00	£60.00	£135.00	£275.00	—
1869—	1,861,764	£45.00	£60.00	£135.00	£275.00	—
1870—	1,159,544	£45.00	£68.00	£135.00	£275.00	—
1871—	2,062,970	£45.00	£60.00	£135.00	£250.00	—
1872—	3,248,627	£45.00	£60.00	£120.00	£250.00	—
1873—	1,927,050	£45.00	£55.00	£145.00	£275.00	—
1874—	1,884,432	£45.00	£68.00	£145.00	£275.00	—
1875—	516,240	£45.00	£55.00	£135.00	£275.00	—
1876—	2,785,187	£45.00	£60.00	£125.00	£225.00	—
1877—	2,197,482	£45.00	£55.00	£130.00	£225.00	—
1878—	2,081,941	£45.00	£62.00	£130.00	£225.00	—
1879—	35,201	£45.00	£75.00	£240.00	£375.00	—
1880—	inc above	£45.00	£55.00	£125.00	£225.00	—
1873 M(Melbourne)	165,034	£75.00	£115.00	£440.00	£650.00	—
1877—	80,016	£80.00	£135.00	£500.00	£850.00	—
1881—	42,009	£90.00	£200.00	£700.00	£1,200	—
1882—	107,522	£80.00	£135.00	£500.00	£850.00	—
1884—	48,009	£80.00	£185.00	£800.00	£1,000	—
1885—	11,003	£200.00	£300.00	£1,350	£2,250	—
1886—	38,008	£80.00	£135.00	£530.00	£950.00	—
1887—	64,013	£100.00	£235.00	£1,000	£1,250	—
1871 S(Sydney)	unrecorded	£65.00	£95.00	£400.00	£500.00	—
1872—	356,000	£65.00	£100.00	£400.00	£500.00	—
1875—	unrecorded	£65.00	£100.00	£375.00	£450.00	—
1879—	94,000	£70.00	£105.00	£425.00	£550.00	—
1880—	80,000	£70.00	£105.00	£440.00	£550.00	—
1881—	62,000	£85.00	£155.00	£600.00	£1,000	—
1882—	52,000	£180.00	£200.00	£1,000	£1,500	—
1883—	220,000	£65.00	£100.00	£345.00	£500.00	—
1886—	82,000	£70.00	£105.00	£430.00	£600.00	—
1887—	134,000	£65.00	£105.00	£420.00	£500.00	—
Jubilee Head						
1887	871,770	£40.00	£60.00	£70.00	£85.00	—
1887	797	—	—	—	—	£355.00
1890	2,266,023	£40.00	£50.00	£70.00	£80.00	—
1891	1,079,286	£40.00	£55.00	£80.00	£155.00	—
1892	13,680,486	£40.00	£50.00	£75.00	£85.00	—
1893	4,426,625	£40.00	£55.00	£80.00	£120.00	—
1887 M(Melbourne)	inc above	£45.00	£90.00	£260.00	£350.00	—
1893—	110,024	£45.00	£100.00	£300.00	£400.00	—

	MINTAGE	F	VF	EF	UNC	PROOF
1887 S (Sydney)	inc above	£45.00	£85.00	£230.00	£300.00	—
1889 —	64,000	£45.00	£100.00	£300.00	£400.00	—
1891 —	154,000	£45.00	£85.00	£230.00	£300.00	—

Veiled Head

	MINTAGE	F	VF	EF	UNC	PROOF
1893	inc above	£35.00	£45.00	£60.00	£75.00	—
1893	773	—	—	—	—	£400.00
1894	3,794,591	£35.00	£50.00	£60.00	£75.00	—
1895	2,869,183	£35.00	£50.00	£60.00	£70.00	—
1896	2,946,605	£35.00	£45.00	£60.00	£72.00	—
1897	3,568,156	£35.00	£45.00	£60.00	£75.00	—
1898	2,868,527	£35.00	£45.00	£60.00	£72.00	—
1899	3,361,881	£35.00	£45.00	£60.00	£75.00	—
1900	4,307,372	£35.00	£45.00	£60.00	£75.00	—
1901	2,037,664	£35.00	£45.00	£60.00	£75.00	—
1893 M (Melbourne)	unrecorded	+	+	+	+	—
1896 —	218,946	£40.00	£70.00	£185.00	£225.00	—
1899 —	97,221	£45.00	£75.00	£185.00	£300.00	—
1900 —	112,920	£45.00	£75.00	£200.00	£300.00	—
1900 P (Perth)	119,376	£45.00	£85.00	£275.00	£325.00	—
1893 S (Sydney)	250,000	£35.00	£65.00	£175.00	£200.00	—
1897 —	unrecorded	£35.00	£65.00	£175.00	£200.00	—
1900 —	260,000	£36.00	£60.00	£145.00	£180.00	—

Edward VII 1902-1910

	MINTAGE	F	VF	EF	UNC	PROOF
1902	4,244,457	*	£45.00	£50.00	£60.00	—
1902	15,123	—	—	—	—	£100.00
1903	2,522,057	*	£40.00	£46.00	£52.00	—
1904	1,717,440	*	£40.00	£46.00	£52.00	—
1905	3,023,993	*	£40.00	£46.00	£52.00	—
1906	4,245,437	*	£40.00	£46.00	£55.00	—
1907	4,233,421	*	£40.00	£46.00	£52.00	—
1908	3,996,992	*	£40.00	£46.00	£52.00	—
1909	4,010,715	*	£40.00	£46.00	£52.00	—
1910	5,023,881	*	£40.00	£46.00	£52.00	—
1906 M (Melbourne)	82,042	*	£55.00	£85.00	£175.00	—
1907 —	405,034	*	£55.00	£85.00	£175.00	—
1908 —		*	£55.00	£85.00	£200.00	—
1909 —	186,094	*	£55.00	£85.00	£175.00	—
1904 P (Perth)	60,030	£100.00	£175.00	£580.00	£1,000	—
1908 —	24,668	£90.00	£175.00	£600.00	£800.00	—
1909 —	44,022	£75.00	£140.00	£400.00	£500.00	—
1902 S (Sydney)	84,000	*	£60.00	£125.00	£250.00	—
1903 —	231,000	*	£55.00	£110.00	£175.00	—
1906 —	308,000	*	£55.00	£110.00	£175.00	—
1908 —	538,000	*	£55.00	£110.00	£155.00	—
1910 —	474,000	*	£55.00	£110.00	£170.00	—

George V 1911-1936

	MINTAGE	F	VF	EF	UNC	PROOF
1911	6,104,106	*	£40.00	£50.00	£55.00	—
1911	3,764	—	—	—	—	£200.00

	MINTAGE	F	VF	EF	UNC	PROOF
1912	6,224,316	*	£40.00	£50.00	£55.00	—
1913	6,094,290	*	£40.00	£50.00	£55.00	—
1914	7,251,124	*	£40.00	£45.00	£55.00	—
1915	2,042,747	*	£40.00	£45.00	£55.00	—
1915 M(Melbourne)	125,664	*	£55.00	£75.00	£125.00	—
1911 P(Perth)	130,373	*	£55.00	£75.00	£95.00	—
1915—	136,219	*	£55.00	£75.00	£95.00	—
1918—	unrecorded	£120.00	£200.00	£400.00	£560.00	—
1911 S(Sydney)	252,000	*	£50.00	£70.00	£90.00	—
1912—	278,000	*	£50.00	£65.00	£90.00	—
1914—	322,000	*	£50.00	£60.00	£70.00	—
1915—	892,000	*	£45.00	£55.00	£65.00	—
1916—	448,000	*	£45.00	£55.00	£65.00	—
1923 SA(Pretoria)	655	—	—	—	—	£475.00
1925—	946,615	*	£40.00	£45.00	£55.00	—
1926—	806,540	*	£40.00	£45.00	£55.00	—

George VI 1937-1952

	MINTAGE	F	VF	EF	UNC	PROOF
1937	5,501	—	—	—	—	£160.00

Elizabeth II 1953-

	MINTAGE	F	VF	EF	UNC	PROOF
1980	86,700	—	—	—	—	£52.00
1982	unavailable	*	*	*	£42.00	—
1982	21,590	—	—	—	—	£52.00
1983	19,710	—	—	—	—	£52.00
1984	19,505	—	—	—	—	£57.00
1985	15,800	—	—	—	—	£57.00
1986	25,000	—	—	—	—	£60.00
1987	20,687	—	—	—	—	£60.00
1988	22,500	—	—	—	—	£70.00
1989 Gold Sovereign Quincentenary	25,000	—	—	—	—	£100.00
1990	10,000	—	—	—	—	£80.00

SOVEREIGNS

George III 1760-1820

	MINTAGE	F	VF	EF	UNC	PROOF
1817	3,235,239	£85.00	£125.00	£370.00	£600.00	—
1818	2,347,230	£85.00	£150.00	£455.00	£900.00	—
1819	3,574	+	+	+	+	—
1820	931,994	£75.00	£125.00	£335.00	£580.00	—

George IV 1821-1830

	MINTAGE	F	VF	EF	UNC	PROOF
Laureate Head, St George						
1821	9,405,114	£75.00	£135.00	£340.00	£650.00	—
1822	5,356,787	£75.00	£135.00	£390.00	£750.00	—
1823	616,770	£110.00	£270.00	£1,100	+	—
1824	3,767,904	£75.00	£140.00	£400.00	£685.00	—
1825	4,200.343	£100.00	£300.00	£1.000	+	—

SOVEREIGNS

Bare Head, shield

	MINTAGE	F	VF	EF	UNC	PROOF
1825	inc above	£80.00	£135.00	£350.00	£750.00	—
1826	5,724,046	£75.00	£130.00	£300.00	£625.00	—
1826	unrecorded	—	—	—	—	£1,500
1827	2,266,629	£85.00	£140.00	£385.00	£800.00	—
1828	386,182	£500.00	£1,400	£2,900	+	—
1829	2,444,652	£85.00	£145.00	£385.00	£800.00	—
1830	2,387,881	£85.00	£135.00	£385.00	£725.00	—

William IV 1831-1837

	MINTAGE	F	VF	EF	UNC	PROOF
1831	598,547	£90.00	£165.00	£600.00	£1,000	—
1831	unrecorded	—	—	—	—	£2,000
1832	3,737,065	£100.00	£150.00	£375.00	£700.00	—
1833	1,225,269	£95.00	£150.00	£430.00	£850.00	—
1835	723,441	£85.00	£150.00	£450.00	£900.00	—
1836	1,714,349	£85.00	£150.00	£430.00	£850.00	—
1837	1,172,984	£85.00	£150.00	£465.00	£850.00	—

Victoria 1838-1901

Young Head, shield

	MINTAGE	F	VF	EF	UNC	PROOF
1838	2,718,694	£80.00	£95.00	£275.00	£600.00	—
1839	503,695	£105.00	£255.00	£820.00	+	—
1839	unrecorded	—	—	—	—	£2,47
1841	124,054	£420.00	£825.00	£2,535	+	—
1842	4,865,375	£60.00	£70.00	£140.00	£250.00	—
1843		£60.00	£70.00	£140.00	£275.00	—
1843 narrow shield	5,981,968	+	+	+	+	—
1843 3 over 2		+	+	+	+	—
1844	3,000,445	£65.00	£72.00	£145.00	£300.00	—
1845	3,800,845	£65.00	£72.00	£150.00	£300.00	—
1846	3,802,947	£65.00	£75.00	£140.00	£300.00	—
1847	4,667,126	£60.00	£70.00	£140.00	£250.00	—
1848	2,246,701	£65.00	£72.00	£140.00	£325.00	—
1849	1,755,399	£65.00	£70.00	£150.00	£325.00	—
1850	1,402,039	£65.00	£72.00	£170.00	£325.00	—
1851	4,013,624	£60.00	£72.00	£140.00	£250.00	—
1852	8,053,435	£60.00	£75.00	£125.00	£225.00	—
1853	10,597,993	£60.00	£75.00	£130.00	£225.00	—
1853	unrecorded	—	—	—	—	£4,25
1854	3,589,611	£60.00	£72.00	£130.00	£250.00	—
1855	8,448,482	£60.00	£75.00	£130.00	£200.00	—
1856	4,806,160	£60.00	£75.00	£130.00	£250.00	—
1857	4,495,748	£60.00	£75.00	£130.00	£235.00	—
1858	803,234	£70.00	£80.00	£180.00	£500.00	—
1859	1,547,603	£65.00	£70.00	£140.00	£300.00	—
1859 Ansell		£150.00	£350.00	£1,100	+	—
1860	2,555,958	£65.00	£70.00	£150.00	£325.00	—
1861	7,624,736	£62.00	£70.00	£130.00	£200.00	—
1862	7,836,413	£62.00	£72.00	£115.00	£225.00	—
1863	5,921,669	£62.00	£72.00	£115.00	£225.00	—
1863 '827'		+	+	+	+	—
1872	13,486,708	£60.00	£70.00	£125.00	£225.00	—
1863 die no	inc above	£60.00	£72.00	£130.00	£225.00	—
1863 — '827'	inc above	+	+	+	+	—
1864 —	8,656,352	£60.00	£70.00	£120.00	£175.00	—
1865 —	1,450,238	£60.00	£70.00	£135.00	£250.00	—

	MINTAGE	F	VF	EF	UNC	PROOF
1866—	4,047,288	£60.00	£70.00	£100.00	£200.00	—
1868—	1,653,384	£60.00	£70.00	£125.00	£200.00	—
1869—	6,441,322	£62.00	£72.00	£100.00	£200.00	—
1870—	2,189,960	£62.00	£70.00	£120.00	£180.00	—
1871—	8,767,250	£62.00	£75.00	£110.00	£175.00	—
1872—	inc above	£60.00	£72.00	£100.00	£175.00	—
1873—	2,368,215	£60.00	£72.00	£130.00	£225.00	—
1874—	520,713	£500.00	£1,100	+	+	—
1872 M(Melbourne)	} 748,180	£65.00	£75.00	£175.00	£325.00	—
1872—2 over 1		+	+	+	+	—
1874—	1,373,298	£65.00	£90.00	£170.00	£300.00	—
1880—	3,053,454	£140.00	£725.00	£1,725	£2,500	—
1881—	2,325,303	£70.00	£90.00	£285.00	£900.00	—
1882—	2,465,781	£65.00	£80.00	£150.00	£325.00	—
1883—	2,050,450	£80.00	£175.00	£525.00	£1,200	—
1884—	2,942,630	£66.00	£80.00	£150.00	£300.00	—
1885—	2,967,143	£66.00	£80.00	£170.00	£300.00	—
1886—	2,902,131	£400.00	£1,325	£2,750	£3,500	—
1887—	1,916,424	£300.00	£900.00	£2,250	£3,250	—
1871 S(Sydney)	2,814,000	£62.00	£82.00	£145.00	£250.00	—
1872—	1,815,000	£60.00	£80.00	£145.00	£275.00	—
1873—	1,478,000	£60.00	£72.00	£165.00	£250.00	—
1875—	2,122,000	£60.00	£85.00	£150.00	£250.00	—
1877—	1,590,000	£60.00	£75.00	£130.00	£250.00	—
1878—	1,259,000	£65.00	£72.00	£135.00	£300.00	—
1879—	1,366,000	£60.00	£72.00	£130.00	£250.00	—
1880—	1,459,000	£60.00	£75.00	£150.00	£275.00	—
1881—	1,360,000	£65.00	£75.00	£155.00	£355.00	—
1882—	1,298,000	£62.00	£68.00	£125.00	£250.00	—
1883—	1,108,000	£65.00	£75.00	£140.00	£300.00	—
1884—	1,595,000	£60.00	£70.00	£150.00	£250.00	—
1885—	1,486,000	£62.00	£75.00	£155.00	£250.00	—
1886—	1,667,000	£60.00	£75.00	£150.00	£250.00	—
1887—	1,000,000	£65.00	£80.00	£175.00	£325.00	—

Young Head, St George

	MINTAGE	F	VF	EF	UNC	PROOF
1871	inc above	*	£65.00	£90.00	£110.00	—
1872	inc above	*	£65.00	£90.00	£110.00	—
1873	inc above	*	£65.00	£95.00	£110.00	—
1874	inc above	*	£68.00	£105.00	£140.00	—
1876	3,318,866	*	£65.00	£90.00	£110.00	—
1878	1,091,275	*	£65.00	£100.00	£135.00	—
1879	20,013	£85.00	£155.00	£520.00	£1,400	—
1880	3,650,080	*	£65.00	£90.00	£110.00	—
1884	1,769,635	*	£65.00	£95.00	£110.00	—
1885	717,723	*	£65.00	£100.00	£140.00	—
1872 M(Melbourne)	inc above	*	£90.00	£175.00	£250.00	—
1873—	752,199	*	£70.00	£125.00	£150.00	—
1874—	inc above	*	£70.00	£125.00	£150.00	—
1875—	inc above	*	£65.00	£105.00	£130.00	—
1876—	2,124,445	*	£65.00	£110.00	£130.00	—
1877—	1,487,316	*	£70.00	£95.00	£130.00	—
1878—	2,171,457	*	£70.00	£90.00	£130.00	—
1879—	2,740,594	*	£70.00	£100.00	£130.00	—
1880—	inc above	*	£65.00	£90.00	£130.00	—
1881—	inc above	*	£70.00	£90.00	£130.00	—
1882—	inc above	*	£70.00	£90.00	£120.00	—
1883—	inc above	*	£70.00	£90.00	£135.00	—
1884—	inc above	*	£70.00	£90.00	£140.00	—
1885—	inc above	*	£70.00	£90.00	£130.00	—
1886—	inc above	*	£70.00	£90.00	£135.00	—
1887—	inc above	*	£70.00	£90.00	£130.00	—

SOVEREIGNS

	MINTAGE	F	VF	EF	UNC	PROO
1871 S(Sydney)	inc above	*	£75.00	£125.00	£145.00	-
1872—	inc above	*	£70.00	£125.00	£145.00	-
1873—	inc above	*	£70.00	£125.00	£145.00	-
1874—	1,899,000	*	£65.00	£100.00	£130.00	-
1875—	inc above	*	£65.00	£100.00	£130.00	-
1876—	1,613,000	*	£70.00	£100.00	£130.00	-
1879—	inc above	*	£70.00	£125.00	£145.00	-
1880—	inc above	*	£75.00	£95.00	£130.00	-
1881—	inc above	*	£65.00	£95.00	£130.00	-
1882—	inc above	*	£66.00	£95.00	£120.00	-
1883—	inc above	*	£66.00	£95.00	£130.00	-
1884—	inc above	*	£65.00	£95.00	£130.00	-
1885—	inc above	*	£70.00	£95.00	£135.00	-
1886—	inc above	*	£70.00	£90.00	£125.00	-
1887—	inc above	*	£64.00	£90.00	£130.00	-

Jubilee Head

	MINTAGE	F	VF	EF	UNC	PROO
1887..	1,111,280	*	£66.00	£85.00	£100.00	-
1887..	797	—	—	—	—	£520.0
1888..	2,777,424	*	£72.00	£85.00	£110.00	-
1889..	7,257,455	*	£66.00	£85.00	£100.00	-
1890..	6,529,887	*	£65.00	£85.00	£100.00	-
1891..	6,329,476	*	£65.00	£85.00	£100.00	-
1892..	7,104,720	*	£65.00	£85.00	£100.00	-
1887 M(Melbourne)	940,000	*	£65.00	£80.00	£130.00	-
1888—	2,830,612	*	£65.00	£85.00	£110.00	-
1889—	2,732,590	*	£65.00	£85.00	£110.00	-
1890—	2,473,537	*	£65.00	£85.00	£110.00	-
1891—	2,749,592	*	£65.00	£85.00	£110.00	-
1892—	3,488,750	*	£65.00	£85.00	£110.00	-
1893—	1,649,352	*	£65.00	£85.00	£130.00	-
1887 S(Sydney)	1,002,000	*	£75.00	£115.00	£135.00	-
1888—	2,187,000	*	£65.00	£105.00	£120.00	-
1889—	3,262,000	*	£65.00	£85.00	£110.00	-
1890—	2,808,000	*	£65.00	£80.00	£110.00	-
1891—	2,596,000	*	£65.00	£85.00	£110.00	-
1892—	2,837,000	*	£65.00	£90.00	£110.00	-
1893—	1,498,000	*	£65.00	£90.00	£110.00	-

Veiled Head

	MINTAGE	F	VF	EF	UNC	PROO
1893..	6,898,260	*	£65.00	£72.00	£100.00	-
1893..	773	—	—	—	—	£630.0
1894..	3,782,611	*	£65.00	£70.00	£100.00	-
1895..	2,285,317	*	£65.00	£70.00	£100.00	-
1896..	3,334,065	*	£65.00	£70.00	£100.00	-
1898..	4,361,347	*	£62.00	£70.00	£100.00	-
1899..	7,515,978	*	£65.00	£72.00	£95.00	-
1900..	10,846,741	*	£65.00	£72.00	£100.00	-
1901..	1,578,948	*	£65.00	£70.00	£100.00	-
1893 M(Melbourne)	1,914,000	*	£65.00	£70.00	£110.00	-
1894—	4,166,874	*	£62.00	£75.00	£100.00	-
1895—	4,165,869	*	£65.00	£70.00	£95.00	-
1896—	4,456,932	*	£65.00	£72.00	£100.00	-
1897—	5,130,565	*	£65.00	£75.00	£95.00	-
1898—	5,509,138	*	£65.00	£72.00	£95.00	-
1899—	5,579,157	*	£65.00	£72.00	£95.00	-
1900—	4,305,904	*	£65.00	£72.00	£100.00	-
1901—	3,987,701	*	£65.00	£75.00	£100.00	-
1899 P(Perth)	690,992	*	£65.00	£105.00	£140.00	-
1900—	1,886,089	*	£65.00	£75.00	£120.00	-
1901—	2,889,333	*	£65.00	£75.00	£120.00	-

	MINTAGE	F	VF	EF	UNC	PROOF
893 S(Sydney)	1,346,000	*	£65.00	£72.00	£100.00	—
894—	3,067,000	*	£65.00	£72.00	£100.00	—
895—	2,758,000	*	£65.00	£72.00	£100.00	—
896—	2,544,000	*	£65.00	£75.00	£110.00	—
897—	2,532,000	*	£65.00	£75.00	£100.00	—
898—	2,548,000	*	£65.00	£75.00	£100.00	—
899—	3,259,000	*	£65.00	£75.00	£100.00	—
900—	3,586,000	*	£66.00	£72.00	£100.00	—
901—	3,012,000	*	£65.00	£72.00	£100.00	—

Edward VII 1902-1910

	MINTAGE	F	VF	EF	UNC	PROOF
902	4,737,796	*	£62.00	£70.00	£95.00	—
902	15,123	—	—	—	—	£135.00
903	8,888,627	*	£62.00	£70.00	£80.00	—
904	10,041,369	*	£62.00	£70.00	£85.00	—
905	5,910,403	*	£62.00	£70.00	£80.00	—
906	10,466,981	*	£62.00	£70.00	£80.00	—
907	18,458,663	*	£62.00	£70.00	£80.00	—
908	11,729,006	*	£62.00	£70.00	£80.00	—
909	12,157,099	*	£62.00	£72.00	£80.00	—
910	22,379,624	*	£62.00	£70.00	£80.00	—
908 C(Ottawa)	636	+	+	+	+	—
909—	16,273	£70.00	£85.00	£205.00	£325.00	—
910—	28,012	£70.00	£85.00	£200.00	£320.00	—
902 M(Melbourne)	4,267,157	*	£60.00	£68.00	£75.00	—
903—	3,521,780	*	£60.00	£68.00	£72.00	—
904—	3,743,897	*	£60.00	£68.00	£75.00	—
905—	3,633,838	*	£60.00	£66.00	£75.00	—
906—	3,657,853	*	£60.00	£68.00	£75.00	—
907—	3,332,691	*	£60.00	£68.00	£80.00	—
908—	3,080,148	*	£60.00	£68.00	£75.00	—
909—	3,029,538	*	£60.00	£68.00	£75.00	—
910—	3,054,547	*	£60.00	£68.00	£80.00	—
902 P(Perth)	4,289,122	*	£60.00	£66.00	£75.00	—
903—	4,674,783	*	£60.00	£68.00	£75.00	—
904—	4,506,756	*	£60.00	£68.00	£75.00	—
905—	4,876,193	*	£60.00	£68.00	£75.00	—
906—	4,829,817	*	£60.00	£68.00	£75.00	—
907—	4,972,289	*	£60.00	£68.00	£75.00	—
908—	4,875,617	*	£60.00	£68.00	£75.00	—
909—	4,524,241	*	£60.00	£68.00	£75.00	—
910—	4,690,625	*	£60.00	£68.00	£75.00	—
902 S(Sydney)	2,813,000	*	£60.00	£68.00	£75.00	—
903—	2,806,000	*	£60.00	£68.00	£75.00	—
904—	2,986,000	*	£60.00	£68.00	£75.00	—
905—	2,778,000	*	£60.00	£68.00	£75.00	—
906—	2,792,000	*	£60.00	£68.00	£75.00	—
907—	2,539,000	*	£60.00	£68.00	£75.00	—
908—	2,017,000	*	£60.00	£68.00	£80.00	—
909—	2,057,000	*	£60.00	£68.00	£75.00	—
910—	2,135,000	*	£60.00	£68.00	£80.00	—

George V 1911-1936

	MINTAGE	F	VF	EF	UNC	PROO
Large Head						
1911	30,044,105	*	£62.00	£68.00	£75.00	–
1911	3,764	—	—	—	—	£280.0
1912	30,317,921	*	£60.00	£66.00	£80.00	–
1913	24,539,672	*	£60.00	£66.00	£75.00	–
1914	11,501,117	*	£60.00	£68.00	£80.00	–
1915	20,295,280	*	£60.00	£66.00	£80.00	–
1916	1,554,120	*	£65.00	£85.00	£115.00	–
1917	1,014,714	+	+	+	+	–
1925	4,406,431	*	£60.00	£68.00	£80.00	–
1911 C(Ottawa)	256,946	*	£65.00	£95.00	£110.00	–
1913—	3,715	£85.00	£230.00	£455.00	£900.00	–
1914—	14,891	£85.00	£225.00	£440.00	£600.00	–
1916—	6,111	+	+	£8,500	+	–
1917—	58,845	*	£70.00	£100.00	£125.00	–
1918—	106,516	*	£70.00	£100.00	£125.00	–
1919—	135,889	*	£70.00	£100.00	£125.00	–
1918 I(Bombay)	1,295,372	*	£65.00	£95.00	£115.00	–
1911 M(Melbourne)	2,851,451	*	£60.00	£68.00	£75.00	–
1912—	2,469,257	*	£60.00	£68.00	£75.00	–
1913—	2,323,180	*	£60.00	£68.00	£75.00	–
1914—	2,012,029	*	£60.00	£68.00	£75.00	–
1915—	1,637,839	*	£60.00	£68.00	£75.00	–
1916—	1,273,643	*	£60.00	£68.00	£75.00	–
1917—	934,469	*	£60.00	£68.00	£80.00	–
1918—	4,969,493	*	£60.00	£68.00	£75.00	–
1919—	514,257	*	£65.00	£90.00	£110.00	–
1920—	530,266	£200.00	£460.00	£975.00	£1,400	–
1921—	240,121	+	+	£4,000	£5,000	–
1922—	608,306	+	£1,200	£3,500	£4,750	–
1923—	510,870	*	£65.00	£75.00	£95.00	–
1924—	278,140	*	£65.00	£75.00	£95.00	–
1925—	3,311,662	*	£60.00	£68.00	£75.00	–
1926—	211,107	*	£65.00	£75.00	£95.00	–
1927—	310,156	+	+	+	+	–
1928—	413,208	£160.00	£300.00	£930.00	£1,400	–
1911 P(Perth)	4,373,165	*	£60.00	£68.00	£75.00	–
1912—	4,278,144	*	£60.00	£68.00	£75.00	–
1913—	4,635,287	*	£60.00	£68.00	£75.00	–
1914—	4,815,996	*	£60.00	£68.00	£75.00	–
1915—	4,373,596	*	£60.00	£68.00	£75.00	–
1916—	4,096,771	*	£60.00	£68.00	£75.00	–
1917—	4,110,286	*	£60.00	£68.00	£80.00	–
1918—	3,812,884	*	£60.00	£68.00	£75.00	–
1919—	2,995,216	*	£60.00	£70.00	£80.00	–
1920—	2,421,196	*	£60.00	£68.00	£75.00	–
1921—	2,134,360	*	£60.00	£68.00	£75.00	–
1922—	2,298,884	*	£60.00	£68.00	£80.00	–
1923—	2,124,154	*	£60.00	£68.00	£100.00	–
1924—	1,464,416	*	£60.00	£72.00	£80.00	–
1925—	1,837,901	*	£65.00	£75.00	£85.00	–
1926—	1,313,578	*	£65.00	£75.00	£85.00	–
1927—	1,383,544	*	£65.00	£75.00	£90.00	–
1928—	1,333,417	*	£65.00	£75.00	£85.00	–

	MINTAGE	F	VF	EF	UNC	PROOF
911 S(Sydney)	2,519,000	*	£60.00	£68.00	£75.00	—
912 —	2,227,000	*	£60.00	£68.00	£85.00	—
913 —	2,249,000	*	£60.00	£68.00	£75.00	—
914 —	1,774,000	*	£60.00	£68.00	£75.00	—
915 —	1,346,000	*	£60.00	£68.00	£75.00	—
916 —	1,242,000	*	£60.00	£68.00	£75.00	—
917 —	1,666,000	*	£60.00	£68.00	£75.00	—
918 —	3,716,000	*	£60.00	£68.00	£75.00	—
919 —	1,835,000		£60.00	£68.00	£75.00	—
920 —	360,000	+	+	+	+	—
921 —	839,000	£200.00	£380.00	£760.00	£1,200	—
922 —	578,000	£300.00	£750.00	£1,875	£4,750	—
923 —	416,000	£350.00	£765.00	£1,880	£4,750	—
924 —	394,000	£100.00	£285.00	£600.00	£1,000	—
925 —	5,632,000	*	£60.00	£72.00	£80.00	—
926 —	1,031,050	£500.00	£800.00	£2,300	£5,000	—
923 SA(Pretoria)	719	+	+	+	+	—
923 —	655	—	—	—	—	£755.00
924 —	3,184	+	+	£2,650	+	—
925 —	6,086,264	*	£60.00	£68.00	£72.00	—
926 —	11,107,611	*	£60.00	£68.00	£72.00	—
927 —	16,379,704	*	£60.00	£68.00	£75.00	—
928 —	18,235,057	*	£60.00	£68.00	£72.00	—

mall Head

	MINTAGE	F	VF	EF	UNC	PROOF
929 M(Melbourne)	436,719	£100.00	£260.00	£880.00	£1,000	—
930 —	77,547	£60.00	£70.00	£135.00	£200.00	—
931 —	57,779	£70.00	£90.00	£260.00	£500.00	—
929 P(Perth)	1,606,625	*	£65.00	£75.00	£85.00	—
930 —	1,915,352	*	£65.00	£75.00	£85.00	—
931 —	1,173,568	*	£65.00	£75.00	£85.00	—
929 SA(Pretoria)	12,024,107	*	£60.00	£75.00	£85.00	—
930 —	10,027,756	*	£60.00	£75.00	£85.00	—
931 —	8,511,792	*	£60.00	£75.00	£85.00	—
932 —	1,066,680	*	£66.00	£80.00	£110.00	—

George VI 1937-1952

	MINTAGE	F	VF	EF	UNC	PROOF
37	5,501	—	—	—	—	£365.00

Elizabeth II 1953-

	MINTAGE	F	VF	EF	UNC	PROOF
57	2,072,000	*	*	*	£70.00	—
58	8,700,140	*	*	*	£68.00	—
59	1,358,228	*	*	*	£70.00	—
62	3,000,000	*	*	*	£70.00	—
63	7,400,000	*	*	*	£68.00	—
64	3,000,000	*	*	*	£70.00	—
65	3,800,000	*	*	*	£68.00	—
66	7,050,000	*	*	*	£68.00	—
67	5,000,000	*	*	*	£70.00	—
68	4,203,000	*	*	*	£68.00	—
74	5,002,566	*	*	*	£70.00	—
76	4,150,000	*	*	*	£70.00	—
78	6,350,000	*	*	*	£70.00	—
79	9,100,000	*	*	*	£70.00	—
79	50,000	—	—	—	—	£80.00

	MINTAGE	F	VF	EF	UNC	PROO
1980	5,100,000	*	*	*	£68.00	—
1980	91,200	—	—	—	—	£80.0
1981	unavailable	*	*	*	£70.00	—
1981	32,960	—	—	—	—	£80.0
1982	unavailable	*	*	*	£70.00	—
1982	22,500	—	—	—	—	£80.0
1983	21,250	—	—	—	—	£95.0
1984	19,975	—	—	—	—	£105.0
1985	17,242	—	—	—	—	£100.0
1986	25,000	—	—	—	—	£105.0
1987	22,479	—	—	—	—	£100.0
1988	25,000	—	—	—	—	£120.0
1989 Gold Sovereign Quincentenary	27,500	—	—	—	—	£145.0
1990	10,000	—	—	—	—	£150.0

TWO POUNDS

George III 1760-1820

	MINTAGE	F	VF	EF	UNC	PROO
1820 pattern	unrecorded	—	—	—	—	£10,00

George IV 1821-1830

	MINTAGE	F	VF	EF	UNC	PROO
1823 St George rev	unrecorded	—	£280.00	£575.00	£900.00	-
1826 shield rev	unrecorded	—	—	—	—	£3,12

William IV 1831-1837

	MINTAGE	F	VF	EF	UNC	PROO
1831	225	—	—	—	—	£5,12

Victoria 1838-1901

	MINTAGE	F	VF	EF	UNC	PROO
1887 Jubilee head	91,345	£140.00	£160.00	£300.00	£375.00	
1887	797	—	—	—	—	£800.
1893 Veiled head	52,212	£180.00	£225.00	£455.00	£585.00	
1893	773	—	—	—	—	£1,0

Edward VII 1902-1910

	MINTAGE	F	VF	EF	UNC	PROC
1902	45,807	£160.00	£200.00	£345.00	£500.00	
1902	8,066	—	—	—	—	£550.

George V 1911-1936

	MINTAGE	F	VF	EF	UNC	PROC
1911	2,812	—	—	—	—	£620.

George VI 1937-1952

	MINTAGE	F	VF	EF	UNC	PROC
1937	5,501	—	—	—	—	£390.

Elizabeth II 1953-

	MINTAGE	F	VF	EF	UNC	PROOF
980	10,000	—	—	—	—	£230.00
982	2,500	—	—	—	—	£230.00
983	12,500	—	—	—	—	£220.00
985	5,849	—	—	—	—	£225.00
986 Commonwealth Games design	17,500	—	—	—	—	£290.00
987	14,301	—	—	—	—	£230.00
988	15,000	—	—	—	—	£290.00
989 Gold Sovereign Quincentenary	17,000	—	—	—	—	£290.00
990		—	—	—	—	£300.00

FIVE POUNDS

George III 1760-1820

	MINTAGE	F	VF	EF	UNC	PROOF
820 pattern	unrecorded	—	—	—	—	£20,500

George IV 1821-1830

	MINTAGE	F	VF	EF	UNC	PROOF
826	unrecorded	—	—	—	—	£7,750

Victoria 1838-1901

	MINTAGE	F	VF	EF	UNC	PROOF
839 'Una and the lion' rev, pattern	unrecorded	—	—	—	—	£17,250
887 jubilee head	53,844	£350.00	£440.00	£655.00	£850.00	—
887	797	—	—	—	—	£1,800
893 veiled head	20,405	£400.00	£500.00	£900.00	£1,500	—
893	773	—	—	—	—	£2,200

Edward VII 1902-1910

	MINTAGE	F	VF	EF	UNC	PROOF
902	34,911	£350.00	£450.00	£655.00	£760.00	—
902	8,066	—	—	—	—	£775.00

George V 1911-1936

	MINTAGE	F	VF	EF	UNC	PROOF
911	2,812	—	—	—	—	£1,275

George VI 1937-1952

	MINTAGE	F	VF	EF	UNC	PROOF
937	5,501	—	—	—	—	£675.00

Elizabeth II 1953-

	MINTAGE	F	VF	EF	UNC	PROOF
980	10,000	—	—	—	—	£440.00
981	5,400	—	—	—	—	£440.00
982	2,500	—	—	—	—	£440.00
984	15,104	•	•	•	£395.00	—
984	8,000	—	—	—	—	£435.00
985	13,626	•	•	•	£385.00	—
985	6,130	—	—	—	—	£460.00
986	17,500	•	•	•	£390.00	—
987	5,694	•	•	•	£440.00	—
988	unavailable	•	•	•	£440.00	—
989 Gold Sovereign Quincentenary	unavailable	•	•	•	£495.00	—
989—	5,000	—	—	—	—	£470.00
990	3,500	•	•	•	£450.00	—

QUARTER-GUINEAS

George I 1714-1727

	F	VF	EF	PROOF
1718	£35.00	£85.00	£165.00	—

George III 1760-1820

	F	VF	EF	PROOF
1762	£35.00	£75.00	£150.00	—

THIRD-GUINEAS

George III 1760-1820

	F	VF	EF	PROOF
1797 first head, date in legend	£30.00	£50.00	£115.00	—
1798 — —	£30.00	£50.00	£115.00	—
1799 — —	£35.00	£75.00	£185.00	—
1800 — —	£30.00	£50.00	£120.00	—
1801 — date below crown	£30.00	£50.00	£125.00	—
1802 — —	£30.00	£50.00	£125.00	—
1803 — —	£30.00	£50.00	£125.00	—
1804 second head, date below crown	£30.00	£50.00	£120.00	—
1806 — —	£30.00	£50.00	£120.00	—
1808 — —	£30.00	£50.00	£120.00	—
1809 — —	£30.00	£50.00	£125.00	—
1810 — —	£30.00	£50.00	£120.00	—
1811 — —	£125.00	£300.00	£655.00	—
1813 — —	£75.00	£150.00	£300.00	—

HALF-GUINEAS

Charles II 1660-1685

	F	VF	EF	PROOF
1669 first bust	£175.00	£500.00	£1,850	
1670 —	£150.00	£360.00	£1,525	
1671 —	£235.00	£670.00	£2,150	
1672 —	£220.00	£670.00	£2,150	
1672 second bust	£175.00	£400.00	£1,625	
1673 —	£300.00	£770.00	£2,250	
1674 —	£300.00	£770.00	£2,250	
1675 —	+	+	+	
1676 —	£175.00	£380.00	£1,525	
1676 — elephant and castle below	£350.00	£850.00	+	
1677 —	£175.00	£400.00	£1,625	
1677 — elephant and castle below	£300.00	£800.00	£2,400	
1678 —	£175.00	£400.00	£1,650	
1678 — elephant and castle below, 8 over 7	£230.00	£670.00	£2,150	
1679 —	£135.00	£350.00	£1,500	
1680 —	£300.00	£770.00	+	
1680 — elephant and castle below	+	+	+	
1681 —	£300.00	£770.00	£2,250	

	F	VF	EF	PROOF
682 —	£200.00	£600.00	£2,000	—
682 — elephant and castle below	£300.00	£825.00	£2,400	—
683 —	£175.00	£400.00	£1,625	—
683 — elephant and castle below	+	+	+	—
684 —	£135.00	£330.00	£1,500	—
684 — elephant and castle below	£175.00	£400.00	£1,650	—

James II 1685-1688

	F	VF	EF	PROOF
686	£175.00	£400.00	£1,425	—
686 elephant and castle below bust	£470.00	£1,500	+	—
687	£250.00	£575.00	£1,900	—
688	£200.00	£470.00	£1,600	—

William and Mary 1688-1694

	F	VF	EF	PROOF
689 first busts	£180.00	£465.00	£1,500	—
690 second busts	£200.00	£475.00	£1,600	—
691 —	£235.00	£575.00	£1,800	—
691 — elephant and castle below	£160.00	£460.00	£1,350	—
692 —	£200.00	£475.00	£1,600	—
692 — elephant below	+	+	+	—
692 — elephant and castle below	£135.00	£375.00	£1,230	—
693 —	+	+	+	—
694 —	£135.00	£375.00	£1,230	—

William III 1694-1702

	F	VF	EF	PROOF
695 early harp	£100.00	£280.00	£775.00	—
695 — elephant and castle below bust	£235.00	£575.00	£1,700	—
696 — —	£120.00	£325.00	£975.00	—
697 later harp	£165.00	£400.00	£1,250	—
698 —	£110.00	£260.00	£750.00	—
698 — elephant and castle below bust	£185.00	£475.00	£1,500	—
699 —	+	+	+	—
700 —	£110.00	£260.00	£750.00	—
701 —	£110.00	£260.00	£750.00	—

Anne 1702-1714

	F	VF	EF	PROOF
Before Union reverse				
702	£225.00	£550.00	£1,750	—
703 VIGO	£2,200	£5,000	+	—
705	£225.00	£550.00	£1,775	—
After Union reverse: English and Scottish arms impaled				
707	£160.00	£340.00	£960.00	—
708	£200.00	£460.00	£1,250	—
709	£135.00	£290.00	£825.00	—
710	£120.00	£270.00	£750.00	—
711	£135.00	£275.00	£760.00	—
712	£160.00	£340.00	£960.00	—
713	£135.00	£285.00	£800.00	—
714	£135.00	£285.00	£800.00	—

George I 1714-1727

	F	VF	EF	PROO
1715 first head	£150.00	£300.00	£760.00	—
1717 —	£125.00	£300.00	£735.00	—
1718 —	£100.00	£250.00	£680.00	—
1719 —	£100.00	£250.00	£680.00	—
1720 —	£175.00	£460.00	£975.00	—
1721 —	+	+	+	—
1721 — elephant and castle below	+	+	+	—
1722 —	£125.00	£300.00	£735.00	—
1723 —	+	+	+	—
1724 —	£175.00	£400.00	£875.00	—
1725 second head	£90.00	£230.00	£635.00	—
1726 —	£100.00	£300.00	£735.00	—
1727 —	£100.00	£300.00	£735.00	—

George II 1727-1760

	F	VF	EF	PROO
1728 young head	£150.00	£380.00	£950.00	—
1729 —	£125.00	£400.00	£1,000	—
1729 — E.I.C.	£250.00	£500.00	£1,550	—
1730 —	+	+	+	—
1730 — E.I.C.	£300.00	£1,000	+	—
1731 —	£200.00	£600.00	£1,525	—
1731 — E.I.C.	+	+	+	—
1732 —	£150.00	£425.00	£1,125	—
1732 — E.I.C.	+	+	+	—
1733 —	+	+	+	—
1734 —	£120.00	£350.00	£850.00	—
1735 —	+	+	+	—
1736 —	£125.00	£400.00	£1,000	—
1737 —	+	+	+	—
1738 —	£110.00	£325.00	£835.00	—
1739 —	£110.00	£325.00	£835.00	—
1739 — E.I.C.	+	+	+	—
1740 intermediate head	£200.00	£600.00	£1,500	—
1743 —	+	+	+	—
1745 —	£200.00	£600.00	£1,525	—
1745 — LIMA	£365.00	£960.00	£1,850	—
1746 —	£120.00	£350.00	£800.00	—
1747 old head	£160.00	£500.00	£1,125	—
1748 —	£130.00	£300.00	£675.00	—
1749 —	+	+	+	—
1750 —	£110.00	£280.00	£600.00	—
1751 —	£120.00	£335.00	£755.00	—
1752 —	£120.00	£335.00	£755.00	—
1753 —	£100.00	£250.00	£540.00	—
1755 —	£100.00	£250.00	£500.00	—
1756 —	£90.00	£225.00	£500.00	—
1758 —	£90.00	£230.00	£500.00	—
1759 —	£80.00	£180.00	£440.00	—
1760 —	£80.00	£180.00	£440.00	—

George III 1760-1820

	F	VF	EF	PROO
1762 first head	£150.00	£400.00	£1,200	—
1763 —	£200.00	£600.00	£1,380	—
1764 second head	£90.00	£230.00	£480.00	—
1765 — 5 over 4	£250.00	£600.00	£1,600	—

	F	VF	EF	PROOF
1766—	£100.00	£255.00	£500.00	—
1768—	£110.00	£280.00	£580.00	—
1769—	£100.00	£255.00	£500.00	—
1772—	+	+	+	—
1773—	£110.00	£280.00	£580.00	—
1774—	£175.00	£425.00	£1,250	—
1774 third head	+	+	+	—
1775—	£175.00	£440.00	£1,225	—
1775 fourth head	£70.00	£135.00	£275.00	—
1776—	£70.00	£135.00	£275.00	—
1777—	£65.00	£120.00	£250.00	—
1778—	£80.00	£140.00	£300.00	—
1779—	£95.00	£200.00	£500.00	—
1781—	£80.00	£140.00	£300.00	—
1783—	£300.00	£800.00	£2,250	—
1784—	£70.00	£135.00	£275.00	—
1785—	£65.00	£120.00	£250.00	—
1786—	£65.00	£120.00	£250.00	—
1787 fifth head, spade-shaped shield	£55.00	£115.00	£220.00	—
1788——	£55.00	£115.00	£220.00	—
1789——	£65.00	£125.00	£250.00	—
1790——	£55.00	£115.00	£220.00	—
1791——	£65.00	£125.00	£250.00	—
1792——	£350.00	£850.00	£2,500	—
1793——	£55.00	£115.00	£220.00	—
1794——	£60.00	£125.00	£250.00	—
1795——	£80.00	£170.00	£300.00	—
1796——	£65.00	£125.00	£250.00	—
1797——	£55.00	£115.00	£220.00	—
1798——	£55.00	£115.00	£220.00	—
1800——	£125.00	£350.00	£850.00	—
1801 sixth head, shield in garter	£45.00	£65.00	£125.00	—
1802——	£45.00	£70.00	£135.00	—
1803——	£45.00	£70.00	£135.00	—
1804 seventh head, shield in garter	£45.00	£65.00	£125.00	—
1805——	+	+	+	—
1806——	£45.00	£70.00	£135.00	—
1808——	£45.00	£70.00	£135.00	—
1809——	£45.00	£70.00	£135.00	—
1810——	£45.00	£70.00	£135.00	—
1811——	£75.00	£150.00	£340.00	—
1813——	£65.00	£135.00	£280.00	—

GUINEAS

Charles II 1660-1685

	F	VF	EF	PROOF
1663 first bust	£500.00	£1,475	£3,250	—
1663 — elephant below	£400.00	£1,155	£2,875	—
1664 second bust	£350.00	£950.00	£2,500	—
1664 — elephant below	+	+	+	—
1664 third bust	£200.00	£600.00	£2,000	—
1664 — elephant below	£250.00	£750.00	£2,200	—
1665 —	£200.00	£600.00	£2,000	—
1665 — elephant below	£250.00	£750.00	£2,200	—
1666 —	£200.00	£600.00	£2,000	—
1667 —	£200.00	£600.00	£2,000	—
1668 —	£200.00	£600.00	£2,000	—
1668 — elephant below	+	+	+	—
1669 —	£250.00	£750.00	£2,200	—
1670 —	£200.00	£600.00	£2,000	—

	F	VF	EF	PROOF
1671 —	£200.00	£600.00	£2,000	—
1672 —	£250.00	£750.00	£2,200	—
1672 fourth bust	£175.00	£500.00	£1,750	—
1673 third bust	£350.00	£975.00	£2,375	—
1673 fourth bust	£175.00	£500.00	£1,750	—
1674 —	£250.00	£750.00	£2,200	—
1674 — elephant and castle below	+	+	+	—
1675 —	£200.00	£600.00	£2,000	—
1675 — elephant and castle below	£250.00	£760.00	£2,250	—
1676 —	£150.00	£450.00	£1,625	—
1676 — elephant and castle below	£175.00	£500.00	£1,750	—
1677 —	£150.00	£450.00	£1,600	—
1677 — elephant below	+	+	+	—
1677 — elephant and castle below	£175.00	£500.00	£1,750	—
1678 —	£150.00	£450.00	£1,625	—
1678 — elephant below	+	+	+	—
1678 — elephant and castle below	£350.00	£950.00	£2,300	—
1679 —	£150.00	£450.00	£1,600	—
1679 — elephant and castle below	£255.00	£760.00	£2,250	—
1680 —	£150.00	£450.00	£1,600	—
1680 — elephant and castle below	£400.00	£1,200	£3,000	—
1681 —	£175.00	£500.00	£1,750	—
1681 — elephant and castle below	£250.00	£750.00	£2,200	—
1682 —	£175.00	£500.00	£1,750	—
1682 — elephant and castle below	£275.00	£800.00	£2,250	—
1683 —	£150.00	£450.00	£1,600	—
1683 — elephant and castle below	£400.00	£1,200	£3,000	—
1684 —	£175.00	£500.00	£1,750	—
1684 — elephant and castle below	£275.00	£800.00	£2,250	—

James II 1685-1688

	F	VF	EF	PROOF
1685 first bust	£185.00	£455.00	£1,500	—
1685 — elephant and castle below	£225.00	£655.00	£2,200	—
1686 —	£225.00	£600.00	£2,000	—
1686 — elephant and castle below	+	+	+	—
1686 second bust	£185.00	£455.00	£1,500	—
1686 — elephant and castle below	£300.00	£950.00	£3,500	—
1687 —	£185.00	£455.00	£1,500	—
1687 — elephant and castle below	£200.00	£500.00	£1,800	—
1688 —	£185.00	£455.00	£1,500	—
1688 — elephant and castle below	£200.00	£500.00	£1,800	—

William and Mary 1688-1694

	F	VF	EF	PROOF
1689	£200.00	£475.00	£1,425	—
1689 elephant and castle below busts	£200.00	£525.00	£1,500	—
1690	£200.00	£575.00	£1,675	—
1690 elephant and castle below busts	£280.00	£775.00	£2,000	—
1691	£230.00	£625.00	£1,700	—
1691 elephant and castle below busts	£230.00	£575.00	£1,700	—
1692	£230.00	£675.00	£2,000	—
1692 elephant below busts	£280.00	£775.00	£2,000	—
1692 elephant and castle below busts	£260.00	£625.00	£1,725	—
1693	£230.00	£625.00	£1,700	—
1693 elephant below busts	+	+	+	—
1693 elephant and castle below busts	+	+	+	—
1694	£200.00	£525.00	£1,500	—
1694 elephant and castle below busts	£260.00	£625.00	£1,800	—

William III 1694-1702

	F	VF	EF	PROOF
1695 first bust	£150.00	£380.00	£1,100	—
1695 — elephant and castle below	£200.00	£525.00	£1,500	—
1696 —	£185.00	£475.00	£1,350	—
1696 — elephant and castle below	+	+	+	—
1697 —	£185.00	£475.00	£1,350	—
1697 second bust	£185.00	£455.00	£1,250	—
1697 — elephant and castle below	£360.00	£1,000	+	—
1698 —	£150.00	£330.00	£950.00	—
1698 — elephant and castle below	£230.00	£600.00	£1,725	—
1698 — large date and rev lettering	£150.00	£380.00	£1,100	—
1699 —	£200.00	£525.00	£1,575	—
1699 — elephant and castle below	+	+	+	—
1700 —	£150.00	£330.00	£950.00	—
1700 — elephant and castle below	£400.00	£1,100	+	—
1701 —	£150.00	£330.00	£950.00	—
1701 — scrolled harp	£150.00	£380.00	£1,100	—
1701 — — elephant and castle below bust	+	+	+	—
1701 third bust	£325.00	£725.00	£2,625	—

Anne 1702-1714

Before Union reverse

	F	VF	EF	PROOF
1702	£175.00	£555.00	£1,850	—
1703 VIGO	£2,925	£7,375	+	—
1705	£280.00	£680.00	£2,250	—
1706	£275.00	£700.00	£2,350	—
1707	£325.00	£800.00	£2,600	—

After Union reverse: English and Scottish arms impaled

	F	VF	EF	PROOF
1707 first bust	£200.00	£425.00	£1,300	—
1707 — elephant and castle below	£400.00	£1,000	£2,625	—
1707 second bust	+	+	+	—
1708 first bust	+	+	+	—
1708 second bust	£180.00	£400.00	£1,200	—
1708 — elephant and castle below	£360.00	£925.00	£2,700	—
1709 —	£200.00	£450.00	£1,375	—
1709 — elephant and castle below	£330.00	£800.00	£2,450	—
1710 third bust	£150.00	£300.00	£850.00	—
1711 —	£150.00	£300.00	£850.00	—
1712 —	£200.00	£400.00	£1,200	—
1713 —	£150.00	£275.00	£800.00	—
1714 —	£150.00	£275.00	£800.00	—

George I 1714-1727

	F	VF	EF	PROOF
1714 first head	£300.00	£725.00	£2,125	—
1715 second head	£175.00	£375.00	£950.00	—
1715 third head	£150.00	£300.00	£900.00	—
1716 —	£200.00	£450.00	£1,000	—
1716 fourth head	£150.00	£300.00	£900.00	—
1717 —	£175.00	£360.00	£1,000	—
1718 —	+	+	+	—
1719 —	£150.00	£300.00	£900.00	—
1720 —	£150.00	£300.00	£900.00	—
1721 —	£175.00	£400.00	£1,100	—
1721 — elephant and castle below	+	+	+	—
1722 —	£150.00	£300.00	£900.00	—

	F	VF	EF	PROO
1722—elephant and castle below	+	+	+	–
1723—	£175.00	£400.00	£1,100	–
1723 fifth head	£200.00	£400.00	£1,100	–
1724—	£200.00	£400.00	£1,100	–
1725—	£200.00	£400.00	£1,100	–
1726—	£150.00	£360.00	£900.00	–
1726—elephant and castle below	£500.00	£1,200	+	–
1727—	£225.00	£525.00	£1,425	–

George II 1727-1760

	F	VF	EF	PROO
1727 first young head, small lettering	£360.00	£1,000	£2,300	–
1727—large lettering	£250.00	£650.00	£1,550	–
1728——	£300.00	£700.00	£1,725	–
1729 second young head	—	—	—	£3,60
1729—E.I.C.	£350.00	£900.00	£2,525	–
1730—	£200.00	£450.00	£1,550	–
1731—	£160.00	£400.00	£1,275	–
1731—E.I.C.	£250.00	£600.00	£1,700	–
1732—	£200.00	£500.00	£1,550	–
1732—E.I.C.	£250.00	£600.00	£1,700	–
1732—large obv lettering	£200.00	£500.00	£1,400	–
1732——E.I.C.	£300.00	£700.00	£1,800	–
1733——	£150.00	£375.00	£1,000	–
1734——	£150.00	£375.00	£1,000	–
1735——	£160.00	£360.00	£1,150	–
1736——	£180.00	£450.00	£1,300	–
1737——	£200.00	£500.00	£1,500	–
1738——	£180.00	£450.00	£1,300	–
1739 intermediate head	£150.00	£375.00	£950.00	–
1739—E.I.C.	£300.00	£700.00	£1,775	–
1740—	£160.00	£450.00	£1,300	–
1741—41 over 39	+	+	+	–
1743—	+	+	+	–
1745—	£225.00	£500.00	£1,500	–
1745—LIMA	£300.00	£600.00	£1,575	–
1746—	£200.00	£450.00	£1,100	–
1747 old head	£150.00	£360.00	£875.00	–
1748—	£125.00	£300.00	£875.00	–
1749—	£125.00	£300.00	£775.00	–
1750—	£150.00	£360.00	£780.00	–
1751—	£125.00	£300.00	£725.00	–
1752—	£125.00	£300.00	£725.00	–
1753—	£125.00	£300.00	£775.00	–
1755—	£175.00	£380.00	£925.00	–
1756—	£125.00	£280.00	£725.00	–
1758—	£115.00	£260.00	£675.00	–
1759—	£115.00	£260.00	£675.00	–
1760—	£120.00	£280.00	£700.00	–

George III 1760-1820

	F	VF	EF	PROO
1761 first head	£380.00	£860.00	£2,400	–
1763 second head	£250.00	£650.00	£1,300	–
1764—	£200.00	£550.00	£1,000	–
1765 third head	£100.00	£230.00	£500.00	–
1766—	£90.00	£180.00	£400.00	–
1767—	£110.00	£275.00	£580.00	–

	F	VF	EF	PROOF
1768—	£100.00	£200.00	£460.00	—
1769—	£100.00	£200.00	£460.00	—
1770—	£110.00	£255.00	£550.00	—
1771—	£100.00	£200.00	£475.00	—
1772—	£90.00	£175.00	£380.00	—
1773—	£90.00	£175.00	£380.00	—
1774 fourth head	£80.00	£150.00	£330.00	—
1775—	£80.00	£150.00	£330.00	—
1776—	£80.00	£150.00	£330.00	—
1777—	£80.00	£150.00	£330.00	—
1778—	£100.00	£190.00	£400.00	—
1779—	£90.00	£175.00	£375.00	—
1781—	£90.00	£175.00	£380.00	—
1782—	£90.00	£175.00	£375.00	—
1783—	£90.00	£175.00	£380.00	—
1784—	£90.00	£175.00	£375.00	—
1785—	£80.00	£150.00	£330.00	—
1786—	£80.00	£150.00	£330.00	—
1787 fifth head, spade-shaped shield	£80.00	£130.00	£250.00	—
1788—	£80.00	£130.00	£250.00	—
1789—	£80.00	£135.00	£275.00	—
1790—	£80.00	£130.00	£250.00	—
1791—	£80.00	£130.00	£250.00	—
1792—	£80.00	£135.00	£250.00	—
1793—	£80.00	£130.00	£250.00	—
1794—	£80.00	£130.00	£250.00	—
1795—	£100.00	£170.00	£400.00	—
1796—	£100.00	£175.00	£400.00	—
1797—	£90.00	£140.00	£275.00	—
1798—	£80.00	£130.00	£250.00	—
1799—	£100.00	£150.00	£350.00	—
1813 sixth head, shield in garter	£225.00	£340.00	£630.00	—

TWO GUINEAS

Charles II 1660-1685

	F	VF	EF	PROOF
1664 first bust	£360.00	£825.00	£3,250	—
1664—elephant below	£275.00	£650.00	£2,850	—
1665—	+	+	+	—
1669—	+	+	+	—
1671—	£400.00	£925.00	£3,500	—
1675 second bust	£380.00	£825.00	£3,250	—
1676—	£300.00	£675.00	£2,875	—
1676—elephant and castle below	£275.00	£650.00	£2,875	—
1677—	£255.00	£650.00	£2,850	—
1677—elephant and castle below	+	+	+	—
1678—	£250.00	£600.00	£2,600	—
1678—elephant below	+	+	+	—
1678—elephant and castle below	£300.00	£675.00	£2,750	—
1679—	£300.00	£675.00	£2,750	—
1680—	£400.00	£950.00	£3,500	—
1681—	£255.00	£650.00	£2,850	—
1682—	£255.00	£650.00	£2,850	—
1682—elephant and castle below	£250.00	£600.00	£2,025	—
1683—	£250.00	£600.00	£2,600	—
1683—elephant and castle below	£425.00	£950.00	£3,500	—
1684—	£375.00	£760.00	£3,000	—
1684—elephant and castle below	£400.00	£950.00	£3,500	—

James II 1685-1688

	F	VF	EF	PROOF
1687	£475.00	£1,360	£3,100	—
1688 8 over 7	£550.00	£1,475	£3,350	—

William and Mary 1688-1694

	F	VF	EF	PROOF
1691 elephant and castle below busts	+	+	+	—
1693	£400.00	£950.00	£3,000	—
1693 elephant and castle below busts	£655.00	£1,425	£4,000	—
1694	£400.00	£950.00	£3,000	—
1694 elephant and castle below busts	£655.00	£1,425	£4,000	—

William III 1694-1702

	F	VF	EF	PROOF
1701	£700.00	£1,725	£3,650	—

Anne 1702-1714

	F	VF	EF	PROOF
After Union reverse: English and Scottish arms impaled				
1709	£400.00	£975.00	£2,700	—
1711	£400.00	£975.00	£2,675	—
1713	£400.00	£975.00	£2,700	—
1714	£460.00	£1,000	£3,100	—

George I 1714-1727

	F	VF	EF	PROOF
1717	£560.00	£1,100	£3,125	—
1720	£560.00	£1,100	£3,125	—
1726	£475.00	£1,000	£3,000	—

George II 1727-1760

	F	VF	EF	PROOF
1734 young head, 4 over 3	£760.00	£2,000	+	—
1735 —	£300.00	£655.00	£1,450	—
1738 —	£200.00	£400.00	£950.00	—
1739 —	£200.00	£460.00	£1,000	—
1739 intermediate head	£200.00	£400.00	£950.00	—
1740 —	£200.00	£400.00	£950.00	—
1748 old head	£300.00	£700.00	£1,550	—
1753 —	£400.00	£950.00	£2,150	—

George III 1760-1820

	F	VF	EF	PROOF
1768 pattern	—	—	—	£22,000
1773 —	—	—	—	£22,000
1777 —	—	—	—	£22,000

FIVE GUINEAS

Charles II 1660-1685

	F	VF	EF	PROOF
1668 first bust	£700.00	£1,500	£3,850	—
1668 — elephant below	£700.00	£1,380	£3,650	—
1669 —	£750.00	£1,525	£3,875	—
1669 — elephant below	£960.00	£2,100	£4,625	—
1670 —	£700.00	£1,380	£3,650	—
1671 —	£800.00	£1,680	£3,875	—
1672 —	£700.00	£1,500	£3,850	—
1673 —	£700.00	£1,500	£3,850	—
1674 —	£800.00	£1,650	£4,000	—
1675 —	£750.00	£1,500	£3,800	—
1675 — elephant below	£960.00	£2,100	£4,625	—
1675 — elephant and castle below	+	+	+	—
1676 —	£800.00	£1,650	£3,850	—
1676 — elephant and castle below	£750.00	£1,550	£3,700	—
1677 —	£750.00	£1,550	£3,875	—
1677 — elephant below, 7 over 5	+	+	+	—
1677 — elephant and castle below	£800.00	£1,650	£3,875	—
1678 —	£700.00	£1,480	£3,850	—
1678 — elephant and castle below	£860.00	£1,775	£4,100	—
1678 second bust	£860.00	£1,775	£4,100	—
1679 —	£700.00	£1,400	£3,675	—
1680 —	£750.00	£1,550	£3,875	—
1680 — elephant and castle below	+	+	+	—
1681 —	£700.00	£1,400	£3,675	—
1681 — elephant and castle below	£860.00	£1,775	£4,100	—
1682 —	£700.00	£1,400	£3,675	—
1682 — elephant and castle below	£750.00	£1,550	£3,700	—
1683 —	£700.00	£1,500	£3,850	—
1683 — elephant and castle below	£860.00	£1,780	£4,125	—
1684 —	£700.00	£1,375	£3,600	—
1684 — elephant and castle below	£700.00	£1,380	£3,650	—

James II 1685-1688

	F	VF	EF	PROOF
1686	£960.00	£1,780	£4,000	—
1687	£900.00	£1,680	£3,850	—
1687 elephant and castle below bust	£1,000	£1,875	£4,300	—
1688	£860.00	£1,625	£3,800	—
1688 elephant and castle below bust	£1,000	£1,875	£4,300	—

William and Mary 1688-1694

	F	VF	EF	PROOF
1691	£760.00	£1,780	£4,000	—
1691 elephant and castle below busts	£860.00	£2,000	£4,650	—
1692	£760.00	£1,780	£4,000	—
1692 elephant and castle below busts	£900.00	£2,000	£4,650	—
1693	£760.00	£1,780	£4,000	—
1693 elephant and castle below busts	£1,100	£2,360	£5,200	—
1694	£825.00	£2,000	£4,280	—
1694 elephant and castle below busts	£1,000	£2,275	£5,000	—

FIVE GUINEAS

William III 1694-1702

	F	VF	EF	PROOF
1699 first bust	£860.00	£1,625	£3,200	—
1699 — elephant and castle below	£1,000	£1,900	£3,750	—
1700 —	£900.00	£1,650	£3,400	—
1701 second bust	£900.00	£1,650	£3,500	—

Anne 1702-1714

	F	VF	EF	PROOF
Before Union reverse				
1703 VIGO	£6,000	£15,000	£43,000	—
1705	£1,000	£2,280	£6,100	—
1706	£960.00	£2,000	£5,600	—
After Union reverse: English and Scottish arms impaled				
1706	£860.00	£1,900	£5,100	—
1709 broader shields	£950.00	£2,000	£5,600	—
1711 broader bust	£860.00	£1,900	£5,000	—
1713 —	£960.00	£2,000	£5,600	—
1714 —	£860.00	£1,900	£5,100	—

George I 1714-1727

	F	VF	EF	PROOF
1716	£1,000	£2,300	£5,000	—
1717	£1,260	£2,600	£5,200	—
1720	£1,250	£2,600	£5,200	—
1726	£1,000	£2,400	£5,000	—

George II 1727-1760

	F	VF	EF	PROOF
1729 young head	£750.00	£1,680	£3,550	—
1729 — E.I.C.	£800.00	£1,680	£3,550	—
1731 —	£900.00	£1,900	£3,840	—
1735 —	£860.00	£1,850	£3,800	—
1738 —	£820.00	£1,700	£3,600	—
1741 —	£700.00	£1,625	£3,300	—
1746 old head, LIMA	£520.00	£1,700	£3,850	—
1748 —	£700.00	£1,625	£3,300	—
1753 —	£700.00	£1,625	£3,300	—

George III 1760-1820

	F	VF	EF	PROOF
1770 pattern	—	—	—	£62,000
1773 —	—	—	—	£62,000
1777 —	—	—	—	£62,000

MAUNDY MONEY
Charles II 1660-1685

	F	VF	EF
Sets			
Undated milled	£45.00	£100.00	£155.00

Individual coins	F	VF	EF
Fourpence, undated milled	£8.00	£16.50	£31.50
Threepence, undated milled	£9.00	£18.50	£39.50
Twopence, undated milled	£7.00	£13.50	£26.50
Penny, undated milled	£9.50	£18.50	£41.50

Sets	F	VF	EF		F	VF	EF
1670	£32.00	£65.00	£190.00	1677	£30.00	£60.00	£180.00
1671	£30.00	£60.00	£180.00	1678	£35.00	£70.00	£215.00
1672	£32.00	£65.00	£190.00	1679	£32.00	£100.00	£190.00
1673	£30.00	£65.00	£180.00	1680	£30.00	£60.00	£180.00
1674	£30.00	£60.00	£180.00	1681	£35.00	£70.00	£205.00
1675	£30.00	£60.00	£180.00	1682	£32.00	£65.00	£190.00
1676	£30.00	£60.00	£155.00	1683	£30.00	£60.00	£180.00
				1684	£32.00	£65.00	£190.00

Individual coins	F	VF	EF
Fourpence, 1670-1684, from	£7.50	£13.50	£27.50
Threepence, 1670-1684, from	£5.25	£9.75	£30.50
Twopence, 1668-1684, from	£6.75	£12.00	£27.50
Penny, 1670-1684, from	£9.00	£19.50	£36.50

James II 1685-1688

Sets	F	VF	EF		F	VF	EF
1686	£35.00	£65.00	£155.00	1687	£35.00	£70.00	£150.00
				1688	£35.00	£70.00	£150.00

Individual coins	F	VF	EF
Fourpence, 1686-1688, from	£9.00	£14.75	£34.25
Threepence, 1685-1688, from	£7.00	£14.25	£32.75
Twopence, 1686-1688, from	£7.75	£14.25	£29.25
Penny, 1685-1688, from	£10.75	£20.75	£34.25

William and Mary 1688-1694

Sets	F	VF	EF		F	VF	EF
1689	£130.00	£280.00	£510.00	1692	£50.00	£105.00	£205.00
1691	£50.00	£105.00	£205.00	1693	£60.00	£115.00	£215.00
				1694	£50.00	£105.00	£205.00

Individual coins

	F	VF	EF
Fourpence, 1689-1694, from	£10.25	£21.75	£34.25
Threepence, 1689-1694, from	£9.00	£17.00	£30.75
Twopence, 1689-1694, from	£9.75	£17.75	£31.75
Penny, 1689-1694, from	£16.25	£26.75	£53.25

William III 1694-1702

Sets	F	VF	EF		F	VF	EF
1698	£50.00	£105.00	£180.00	1700	£60.00	£115.00	£195.00
1699	£60.00	£115.00	£195.00	1701	£50.00	£105.00	£180.00

Individual coins

	F	VF	EF
Fourpence, 1697-1702, from	£12.75	£21.75	£46.75
Threepence, 1698-1701, from	£12.25	£20.75	£44.25
Twopence, 1698-1701, from	£11.75	£18.00	£39.25
Penny, 1698-1701, from	£12.25	£19.75	£39.25

Anne 1702-1714

Sets	F	VF	EF		F	VF	EF
1703	£45.00	£75.00	£175.00	1708	£45.00	£75.00	£175.00
1705	£45.00	£75.00	£175.00	1709	£45.00	£75.00	£175.00
1706	£43.00	£70.00	£165.00	1710	£50.00	£80.00	£180.00
				1713	£45.00	£75.00	£140.00

Individual coins

	F	VF	EF
Fourpence, 1703-1713, from	£10.00	£16.50	£31.50
Threepence, 1703-1713, from	£9.25	£15.50	£30.50
Twopence, 1703-1713, from	£8.75	£15.50	£26.50
Penny, 1703-1713, from	£12.00	£22.50	£36.50

George I 1714-1727

Sets

	F	VF	EF		F	VF	EF
1723	£40.00	£95.00	£220.00	1727	£40.00	£95.00	£220.00

Individual coins

	F	VF	EF
Fourpence, 1717-1727, from	£11.50	£20.50	£39.50
Threepence, 1717-1727, from	£10.00	£21.00	£38.00
Twopence, 1717-1727, from	£6.50	£13.00	£23.00
Penny, 1716-1727, from	£6.50	£9.25	£16.50

George II 1727-1760

Sets

	F	VF	EF		F	VF	EF
1729	£30.00	£55.00	£125.00	1739	£27.00	£55.00	£105.00
1731	£30.00	£60.00	£125.00	1740	£27.00	£55.00	£110.00
1732	£27.00	£55.00	£110.00	1743	£27.00	£55.00	£110.00
1735	£27.00	£55.00	£110.00	1746	£27.00	£50.00	£115.00
1737	£27.00	£55.00	£110.00	1760	£30.00	£60.00	£125.00

Individual coins

	F	VF	EF
Fourpence, 1729-1760, from	£6.50	£13.25	£25.25
Threepence, 1729-1760, from	£7.25	£14.25	£24.75
Twopence, 1729-1760, from	£5.75	£9.25	£16.50
Penny, 1729-1760, from	£6.50	£9.50	£14.00

George III 1760-1820

Young Head

Sets

	F	VF	EF		F	VF	EF
1763	£26.00	£45.00	£105.00	1780	£26.00	£50.00	£105.00
1766	£26.00	£45.00	£115.00	1784	£26.00	£45.00	£115.00
1772	£26.00	£45.00	£115.00	1786	£26.00	£45.00	£100.00

MAUNDY MONEY

Individual coins

	F	VF	EF
Fourpence, 1763–1786, from	£4.75	£10.50	£19.00
Threepence, 1762–1786, from	£4.50	£7.00	£11.50
Twopence, 1763–1786, from	£5.00	£8.50	£12.50
Penny, 1763–1786, from	£3.50	£8.25	£11.75

Older Head, 'wire' numerals

Sets

	F	VF	EF
1792	£50.00	£80.00	£180.00

Individual coins

	F	VF	EF
Fourpence, 1792	£10.00	£17.50	£30.50
Threepence, 1792	£10.00	£17.50	£30.50
Twopence, 1792	£8.25	£14.00	£25.00
Penny, 1792	£5.25	£7.75	£11.50

Older Head, normal numerals

Sets

	F	VF	EF			F	VF	EF
1795	£20.00	£55.00	£80.00		1800	£20.00	£40.00	£75.00

Individual coins

	F	VF	EF
Fourpence, 1795 and 1800, from	£5.00	£9.00	£16.50
Threepence, 1795 and 1800, from	£4.25	£8.50	£19.50
Twopence, 1795 and 1800, from	£5.50	£6.75	£8.75
Penny, 1795 and 1800, from	£3.00	£6.00	£9.25

Laureate Head

Sets

	VF	EF	FDC			VF	EF	FDC
1817	£45.00	£80.00	£130.00		1818	£45.00	£80.00	£150.00
					1820	£45.00	£80.00	£140.00

George IV 1821-1830

Sets	VF	EF	FDC		VF	EF	FDC
1822	£30.00	£65.00	£130.00	1826	£30.00	£55.00	£105.00
1823	£30.00	£60.00	£105.00	1827	£30.00	£55.00	£105.00
1824	£30.00	£60.00	£115.00	1828	£30.00	£55.00	£105.00
1825	£30.00	£55.00	£100.00	1829	£30.00	£55.00	£105.00
				1830	£30.00	£55.00	£115.00

William IV 1831-1837

Sets	VF	EF	FDC		VF	EF	FDC
1831	£35.00	£80.00	£150.00	1834	£35.00	£75.00	£130.00
1831 proof	—	—	£245.00	1835	£35.00	£65.00	£125.00
1832	£35.00	£75.00	£140.00	1836	£35.00	£75.00	£140.00
1833	£35.00	£70.00	£135.00	1837	£35.00	£75.00	£140.00

Victoria 1838-1901

Young Head

Sets	MINTAGE	EF	FDC		MINTAGE	EF	FDC
1838	4,158	£35.00	£60.00	1852	4,158	£35.00	£60.00
1839	4,125	£35.00	£60.00	1853	4,158	£35.00	£60.00
1839 proof	unrecorded	—	£200.00	1853 proof	unrecorded	—	£300.00
1840	4,125	£35.00	£65.00	1854	4,158	£35.00	£60.00
1841	2,574	£40.00	£60.00	1855	4,158	£40.00	£70.00
1842	4,125	£35.00	£60.00	1856	4,158	£35.00	£60.00
1843	4,158	£35.00	£60.00	1857	4,158	£35.00	£60.00
1844	4,158	£35.00	£60.00	1858	4,158	£35.00	£60.00
1845	4,158	£35.00	£60.00	1859	4,158	£35.00	£60.00
1846	4,158	£35.00	£60.00	1860	4,158	£35.00	£60 00
1847	4,158	£40.00	£60.00	1861	4,158	£35.00	£60.00
1848	4,158	£35.00	£60.00	1862	4,158	£35.00	£55.00
1849	4,158	£40.00	£70.00	1863	4,158	£35.00	£55.00
1850	4,158	£35.00	£60.00	1864	4,158	£35.00	£55.00
1851	4,158	£35.00	£60.00	1865	4,158	£35.00	£55.00

MAUNDY MONEY

	MINTAGE	EF	FDC		MINTAGE	EF	FDC
1866	4,158	£35.00	£55.00	1877	4,488	£35.00	£50.00
1867	4,158	£35.00	£55.00	1878	4,488	£35.00	£55.00
1868	4,158	£35.00	£55.00	1879	4,488	£35.00	£55.00
1869	4,158	£35.00	£55.00	1880	4,488	£35.00	£55.00
1870	4,458	£35.00	£55.00	1881	4,488	£35.00	£55.00
1871	4,488	£35.00	£55.00	1882	4,146	£35.00	£50.00
1872	4,328	£35.00	£55.00	1883	4,488	£35.00	£55.00
1873	4,162	£35.00	£55.00	1884	4,488	£35.00	£50.00
1874	4,488	£35.00	£55.00	1885	4,488	£35.00	£55.00
1875	4,154	£35.00	£55.00	1886	4,488	£35.00	£55.00
1876	4,488	£35.00	£55.00	1887	4,488	£35.00	£55.00

Jubilee Head

Sets	MINTAGE	EF	FDC		MINTAGE	EF	FDC
				1890	4,488	£35.00	£55.00
1888	4,488	£40.00	£55.00	1891	4,488	£35.00	£50.00
1889	4,488	£35.00	£50.00	1892	4,488	£35.00	£55.00

Veiled Head

Sets	MINTAGE	EF	FDC		MINTAGE	EF	FDC
				1897	9,388	£30.00	£45.00
1893	8,976	£30.00	£45.00	1898	9,147	£30.00	£45.00
1894	8,976	£30.00	£40.00	1899	8,976	£35.00	£45.00
1895	8,877	£30.00	£45.00	1900	8,976	£30.00	£45.00
1896	8,476	£30.00	£40.00	1901	8,976	£30.00	£40.00

Edward VII 1902-1910

Sets	MINTAGE	EF	FDC		MINTAGE	EF	FDC
1902	8,976	£28.00	£38.00	1906	8,800	£30.00	£40.00
1902 proof	15,123	—	£42.00	1907	8,760	£30.00	£45.00
1903	8,976	£30.00	£45.00	1908	8,769	£30.00	£38.00
1904	8,976	£25.00	£45.00	1909	1,983	£35.00	£50.00
1905	8,976	£27.00	£38.00	1910	1,440	£35.00	£55.00

George V 1911-1936

Sets	MINTAGE	EF	FDC		MINTAGE	EF	FDC
1911	1,786	£25.00	£45.00	1923	1,430	£25.00	£42.00
1911 proof	6,007	—	£60.00	1924	1,515	£25.00	£45.00
1912	1,246	£25.00	£40.00	1925	1,438	£25.00	£42.00
1913	1,228	£25.00	£42.00	1926	1,504	£32.00	£45.00
1914	982	£25.00	£42.00	1927	1,647	£25.00	£40.00
1915	1,293	£25.00	£40.00	1928	1,642	£30.00	£45.00
1916	1,128	£25.00	£40.00	1929	1,761	£32.00	£45.00
1917	1,237	£25.00	£40.00	1930	1,724	£32.00	£45.00
1918	1,375	£25.00	£40.00	1931	1,759	£32.00	£45.00
1919	1,258	£25.00	£40.00	1932	1,835	£32.00	£45.00
1920	1,399	£25.00	£40.00	1933	1,872	£32.00	£45.00
1921	1,386	£25.00	£42.00	1934	1,887	£32.00	£45.00
1922	1,373	£25.00	£45.00	1935	1,928	£30.00	£45.00
				1936	1,323	£35.00	£50.00

George VI 1937-1952

Sets	MINTAGE	EF	FDC		MINTAGE	EF	FDC
1937	1,325	*	£45.00	1944	1,259	*	£45.00
1937 proof	20,901	—	£50.00	1945	1,355	*	£45.00
1938	1,275	*	£44.00	1946	1,365	*	£45.00
1939	1,234	*	£47.00	1947	1,375	*	£45.00
1940	1,277	*	£45.00	1948	1,385	*	£45.00
1941	1,253	*	£45.00	1949	1,395	*	£45.00
1942	1,231	*	£45.00	1950	1,405	*	£45.00
1943	1,239	*	£45.00	1951	1,468	*	£45.00
				1952	1,012	*	£45.00

Elizabeth II 1953-

Sets	MINTAGE	EF	FDC		MINTAGE	EF	FDC
1953	1,025	*	£225.00	1955	1,036	*	£51.00
1954	1,020	*	£50.00	1956	1,088	*	£49.00
				1957	1,094	*	£51.00

ENGLISH PROOF SETS

	MINTAGE	EF	FDC		MINTAGE	EF	FDC
1958	1,100	*	£50.00	1975	1,050	*	£55.00
1959	1,106	*	£45.00	1976	1,158	*	£55.00
1960	1,112	*	£45.00	1977	1,138	*	£65.00
1961	1,118	*	£45.00	1978	1,178	*	£55.00
1962	1,125	*	£50.00	1979	1,188	*	£55.00
1963	1,131	*	£45.00	1980	1,198	*	£55.00
1964	1,137	*	£50.00	1981	1,208	*	£55.00
1965	1,143	*	£50.00	1982	1,218	*	£55.00
1966	1,206	*	£50.00	1983	1,218	*	£60.00
1967	986	*	£45.00	1984	1,243	*	£55.00
1968	964	*	£45.00	1985	1,248	*	£55.00
1969	1,002	*	£50.00	1986	unavailable	*	£70.00
1970	980	*	£50.00	1987	unavailable	*	£75.00
1971	1,018	*	£55.00	1988	unavailable	*	£75.00
1972	1,026	*	£55.00	1989	unavailable	*	£75.00
1973	1,004	*	£50.00	1990	unavailable	*	£75.00
1974	1,042	*	£55.00				

ENGLISH PROOF SETS

George IV 1821-1830

	MINTAGE	PROOF
1826 ¼d to £5 (11 coins)	c400	£17,800

William IV 1831-1837

	MINTAGE	PROOF
1831 ¼d to £2 (14 coins)	c120	£16,250

Victoria 1838-1901

	MINTAGE	PROOF
1839 young head ¼d to £5 (15 coins)	300	£24,000
1853 — quarter-farthing to sovereign (16 coins)	unrecorded	£18,500
1887 jubilee head 3d to £5 (11 coins)	797	£4,300
1887 — 3d to crown (7 coins)	287	£860.00
1893 veiled head 3d to £5 (10 coins)	773	£5,000
1893 — 3d to crown (6 coins)	556	£900.00

Edward VII 1902-1910

	MINTAGE	PROOF
1902 maundy 1d to £5 (13 coins)	8,066	£1,475
1902 maundy 1d to sovereign (11 coins)	7,057	£385.00

George V 1911-1936

	MINTAGE	PROOF
1911 maundy 1d to £5 (12 coins)	2,812	£2,500
1911 maundy 1d to sovereign (10 coins)	952	£655.00
1911 maundy 1d to halfcrown (8 coins)	2,243	£300.00
1927 3d to crown (6 coins)	15,000	£200.00

George VI 1937-1952

	MINTAGE	PROOF
1937 half-sovereign to £5 (4 coins)	5,501	£1,500
1937 ¼d to crown inc maundy (15 coins)	20,901	£100.00
1950 ¼d to halfcrown (9 coins)	17,513	£35.00
1951 ¼d to crown (10 coins)	20,000	£50.00

Elizabeth II 1953-

	MINTAGE	PROOF
1953 ¼d to crown (10 coins)	40,000	£34.00
1970 ½d to halfcrown (8 coins)	750,000	£10.00
1971 ½p to 50p (6 coins)	350,000	£7.50
1972 ½p to 50p (7 coins)	150,000	£10.00
1973 ½p to 50p (6 coins)	100,000	£6.50
1974 ½p to 50p (6 coins)	100,000	£5.50
1975 ½p to 50p (6 coins)	100,000	£6.00
1976 ½p to 50p (6 coins)	100,000	£6.00
1977 ½p to 50p (7 coins)	193,800	£8.00
1978 ½p to 50p (6 coins)	88,100	£8.00
1979 ½p to 50p (6 coins)	81,000	£10.00
1980 half-sovereign to £5 (4 coins)	10,000	£775.00
1980 ½p to 50p (6 coins)	143,400	£7.00
1981 ½p to £5 (9 coins)	5,000	£520.00
1981 25p and sovereign (2 coins)	2,500	£130.00
1981 ½p to 50p (6 coins)	100,300	£7.50
1982 half-sovereign to £5 (4 coins)	2,500	£875.00
1982 ½p to 50p (7 coins)	106,800	£10.50
1983 half-sovereign to £2 (3 coins)	unavailable	£300.00
1983 ½p to £1 (8 coins)	107,800	£14.00
1984 half-sovereign to £5 (3 coins)	7,095	£600.00
1984 ½p to £1 (8 coins)	106,520	£12.00
1985 half-sovereign to £5 (4 coins)	5,849	£850.00
1985 1p to £1 in red case (7 coins)	102,015	£17.00
1985 1p to £1 in blue case (7 coins)		£12.00
1986 half-sovereign to gold £2 (3 coins)	12,500	£355.00
1986 1p to nickel-brass £2 in red case (8 coins)	125,000	£20.00
1986 1p to nickel-brass £2 in blue case (8 coins)		£16.00
1987 half-sovereign to £2 (3 coins)	12,500	£400.00
1987 1p to £1 in red case (7 coins)	88,659	£22.00
1987 1p to £1 blue case (7 coins)		£18.00
1987 Britannia Proofs, £100, £50, £25, £10 (4 coins)	£10,000	£900.00
1987 Britannia Proofs £25, £10, (2 coins)	11,100	£215.00
1988 half-sovereign to £2 (3 coins)	12,500	£500.00
1988 1p to £1 in red case (7 coins)	125,000	£24.00
1988 1p to £1 in blue case (7 coins)		£20.00
1988 Britannia Proofs (4 coins)	£3,505	£900.00
1988 Britannia Proofs (2 coins)	894	£215.00
1989 half-sovereign to £5 (4 coins)	5,000	£1,100
1989 half-sovereign to gold £2 (3 coins)	10,000	£500.00
1989 1p to nickel-brass £2 x 2 in red case (9 coins)	100,000	£28.00
1989 1p to nickel-brass £2 x 2 in blue case (9 coins)		£23.00
1989 Britannia Proofs (4 coins)	£2,268	£1,000
1989 Britannia Proofs (2 coins)	£451	£215.00
1990 half-sovereign to £5.00 (4 coins)	unavailable	£1,100
1990 half-sovereign to £2.00 (3 coins)	unavailable	£500.00
1990 2×2p Silver Proof (2 coins)	unavailable	£35.00
1990 1p to £1.00 in red case (8 coins)	unavailable	£29.00
1990 1 to £1.00 (8 coins)	unavailable	£22.00
1990 Britannia Proofs (4 coins)	unavailable	£1,000

ENGLISH SPECIMEN SETS

Elizabeth II 1953-

	MINTAGE	UNC
1953 ¼d to halfcrown (9 coins)	unavailable	£8.00
1968/71 ½p to 10p (5 coins)	unavailable	£1.00
1982 ½p to 50p (7 coins)	205,000	£5.00
1983 ½p to £1 (8 coins)	637,100	£7.25
1984 ½p to £1 (8 coins)	158,820	£5.00
1985 1p to £1 (7 coins)	178,375	£5.00
1986 1p to nickel-brass £2 (8 coins)	167,224	£8.00
1987 1p to £1 (7 coins)	172,425	£5.00
1988 1p to £1 (7 coins)	134,067	£5.75
1989 Bill of Rights and Claim of Right £2 (2 coins)	unavailable	£7.25
1989 1p to £1 (7 coins)	77,569	£6.00
1990 1p to £1 (8 coins)	unavailable	£6.25

island coinage prices

IRELAND

	MINTAGE	F	VF	EF	UNC	PROOF
Farthings						
1928	300,000	£1.50	£2.50	£3.50	£7.00	—
1928	6,001	—	—	—	—	£10.00
1930	288,000	£1.00	£2.00	£5.00	£8.00	—
1931	192,000	£3.00	£6.00	£8.00	£18.00	£250.00
1932	192,000	£5.00	£8.00	£12.00	£25.00	—
1933	480,000	£1.00	£1.75	£3.00	£6.00	—
1935	192,000	£5.00	£8.00	£16.00	£35.00	—
1936	192,000	£5.00	£8.00	£16.00	£45.00	—
1937	480,000	£0.80	£1.50	£2.50	£6.00	—
1939	768,000	£0.50	£1.00	£2.00	£4.50	£150.00
1940	192,000	£2.00	£4.00	£6.00	£9.00	—
1941	480,000	£0.50	£1.00	£1.60	£3.00	—
1943	480,000	£0.50	£0.80	£1.50	£2.50	—
1944	480,000	£0.75	£1.00	£2.00	£4.00	—
1946	480,000	*	£0.60	£1.00	£2.00	—
1949	192,000	*	£1.20	£3.00	£6.00	£160.00
1953	192,000	*	£0.30	£0.50	£1.50	£100.00
1959	192,000	*	*	£0.40	£1.00	£100.00
1966 from specimen set	96,000	*	*	£1.00	£2.50	
Halfpence						
1928	2,880,000	£1.00	£2.00	£4.00	£10.00	—
1928	6,001	—	—	—	—	£12.00
1933	720,000	£3.00	£10.00	£80.00	£360.00	—
1935	960,000	£1.50	£6.00	£35.00	£140.00	—
1937	960,000	£1.00	£2.00	£6.00	£18.00	—
1939	240,000	£6.00	£12.00	£25.00	£100.00	£250.00
1940	1,680,000	£0.40	£1.60	£25.00	£140.00	—
1941	2,400,000	£0.30	£0.80	£2.50	£14.00	—
1942	6,931,200	£0.20	£0.60	£2.00	£5.00	—
1943	2,668,800	£0.30	£1.00	£3.00	£12.00	—
1946	720,000	£0.75	£2.50	£12.00	£35.00	—
1949	1,344,000	£0.20	£0.80	£2.00	£8.00	—
1953	2,400,000	£0.10	£0.30	£0.50	£1.00	£100.00
1964	2,160,000	*	£0.10	£0.30	£0.80	—
1965	1,440,000	*	£0.10	£0.50	£1.60	—
1966	1,680,000	*	*	£0.20	£0.40	—
1967	1,200,000	*	*	£0.20	£0.60	—
Pence						
1928	9,000,000	£0.30	£1.00	£4.00	£10.00	—
1928	6,001	—	—	—	—	£16.00
1931	2,400,000	£0.50	£1.20	£10.00	£35.00	£300.00
1933	1,680,000	£1.00	£2.00	£16.00	£75.00	—
1935	5,472,000	£0.30	£1.00	£6.00	£16.00	—
1937	5,400,000	£0.30	£1.00	£10.00	£35.00	£300.00
1938	unique	—	—	—	—	£8,000
1940	312,000	£2.50	£7.50	£60.00	£900.00	—

IRELAND

	MINTAGE	F	VF	EF	UNC	PROOF
1941	4,680,000	£0.30	£0.50	£5.00	£20.00	—
1942	17,580,000	£0.20	£0.40	£2.00	£6.00	—
1943	3,360,000	£0.50	£1.50	£6.00	£16.00	—
1946	4,800,000	£0.20	£0.50	£3.00	£12.00	—
1948	4,800,000	£0.20	£0.40	£2.00	£6.00	—
1949	4,080,000	£0.20	£0.40	£2.00	£8.00	£180.00
1950	2,400,000	£0.20	£0.40	£2.50	£12.00	£180.00
1952	2,400,000	£0.20	£0.40	£1.00	£2.00	—
1962	1,200,000	£0.50	£1.00	£2.50	£5.00	£60.00
1963	9,600,000	*	£0.20	£0.40	£1.50	£120.00
1964	6,000,000	*	£0.20	£0.40	£1.00	£140.00
1965	11,160,000	*	*	£0.20	£0.50	—
1966	6,000,000	*	*	£0.20	£0.40	—
1967	2,400,000	*	*	£0.30	£0.50	—
1968	42,000,000	*	*	£0.20	£0.75	—

Threepence

	MINTAGE	F	VF	EF	UNC	PROOF
1928	1,500,000	£0.50	£1.00	£3.00	£10.00	—
1928	6,001	—	—	—	—	£12.00
1933	320,000	£1.50	£5.00	£30.00	£250.00	—
1934	800,000	£0.50	£1.50	£5.00	£25.00	—
1935	240,000	£1.50	£4.00	£25.00	£140.00	—
1939	64,000	£6.00	£15.00	£50.00	£160.00	£200.00
1940	720,000	£0.50	£1.00	£3.00	£24.00	—
1942	4,000,000	£0.30	£1.00	£5.00	£18.00	£180.00
1943	1,360,000	£0.50	£1.50	£10.00	£60.00	—
1946	800,000	£0.75	£2.00	£6.00	£20.00	—
1948	1,600,000	£0.40	£1.50	£15.00	£70.00	—
1949	1,200,000	£0.30	£0.80	£4.00	£14.00	£140.00
1950	1,600,000	£0.20	£0.50	£2.00	£12.00	£160.00
1953	1,600,000	£0.20	£0.50	£1.60	£6.00	—
1956	1,200,000	£0.20	£0.50	£1.60	£5.00	—
1961	2,400,000	*	£0.20	£1.00	£2.50	—
1962	3,200,000	*	£0.20	£1.00	£3.00	—
1963	4,000,000	*	£0.20	£0.60	£2.00	—
1964	4,000,000	*	*	£0.30	£1.00	—
1965	3,600,000	*	*	£0.20	£0.60	—
1966	4,000,000	*	*	*	£0.40	—
1967	2,400,000	*	*	*	£0.30	—
1968	12,000,000	*	*	*	£0.30	—

Sixpence

	MINTAGE	F	VF	EF	UNC	PROOF
1928	3,201,000	£0.40	£1.40	£4.00	£12.00	—
1928	6,001	—	—	—	—	£16.00
1934	600,000	£0.60	£2.00	£10.00	£60.00	—
1935	520,000	£0.75	£2.50	£12.00	£100.00	—
1939	876,000	£0.40	£1.50	£5.00	£35.00	—
1940	1,120,000	£0.40	£1.50	£5.00	£20.00	—
1942	1,320,000	£0.40	£1.50	£5.00	£25.00	—
1945	400,000	£1.00	£6.00	£30.00	£100.00	—
1946	720,000	£0.60	£5.00	£40.00	£250.00	—
1947	800,000	£0.50	£2.00	£12.00	£60.00	—
1948	800,000	£0.50	£1.50	£6.00	£25.00	£200.00
1949	600,000	£0.75	£2.00	£10.00	£24.00	—
1950	800,000	£0.50	£1.50	£10.00	£100.00	£200.00
1952	800,000	£0.50	£1.25	£3.00	£16.00	£100.00
1953	800,000	£0.50	£1.25	£3.00	£14.00	£90.00
1955	600,000	£0.75	£2.00	£6.00	£15.00	£90.00
1956	600,000	£0.50	£1.50	£3.00	£6.00	£100.00
1958	600,000	£0.50	£2.00	£6.00	£40.00	£200.00
1959	2,000,000	£0.20	£0.80	£2.00	£12.00	—
1960	2,020,000	£0.20	£0.60	£1.60	£8.00	—
1961	3,000,000	£0.20	£0.50	£1.50	£6.00	—
1962	4,000,000	£0.20	£0.75	£5.00	£30.00	—
1963	4,000,000	*	£0.20	£0.50	£2.00	—

	MINTAGE	F	VF	EF	UNC	PROOF
1964	6,000,000	*	£0.20	£0.50	£1.00	—
1966	2,000,000	*	*	£0.20	£0.60	—
1967	4,000,000	*	*	£0.20	£0.50	—
1968	8,000,000	*	*	*	£0.50	—
1969	2,000,000	*	*	*	£0.40	—

Shillings

	MINTAGE	F	VF	EF	UNC	PROOF
1928	2,700,000	£2.00	£4.00	£8.00	£18.00	—
1928	6,001	—	—	—	—	£24.00
1930	460,000	£2.50	£12.00	£100.00	£300.00	£400.00
1931	400,000	£2.50	£10.00	£60.00	£100.00	—
1933	300,000	£2.50	£12.00	£90.00	£275.00	—
1935	400,000	£2.00	£6.00	£16.00	£70.00	—
1937	100,000	£6.00	£20.00	£250.00	£750.00	—
1939	1,140,000	£1.60	£4.00	£8.00	£20.00	£250.00
1940	580,000	£1.60	£3.00	£8.00	£18.00	—
1941	300,000	£2.00	£4.00	£10.00	£25.00	—
1942	286,000	£2.00	£4.00	£8.00	£16.00	—
1951	2,000,000	£0.20	£1.00	£2.50	£7.00	£140.00
1954	3,000,000	£0.20	£0.60	£2.00	£5.00	£140.00
1955	1,000,000	£0.40	£1.40	£4.00	£10.00	—
1959	2,000,000	£0.20	£0.60	£4.00	£20.00	—
1962	4,000,000	£0.20	£0.50	£1.00	£4.00	—
1963	4,000,000	*	£0.20	£0.60	£3.00	—
1964	4,000,000	*	£0.20	£0.60	£2.00	—
1966	3,000,000	*	£0.20	£0.40	£1.00	—
1968	4,000,000	*	*	£0.40	£1.50	—

Florins

	MINTAGE	F	VF	EF	UNC	PROOF
1928	2,025,000	£3.50	£6.00	£14.00	£30.00	—
1928	6,001	—	—	—	—	£40.00
1930	330,000	£4.00	£15.00	£100.00	£350.00	£600.00
1931	200,000	£5.00	£18.00	£100.00	£300.00	—
1933	300,000	£4.50	£16.00	£100.00	£375.00	—
1934	150,000	£8.00	£30.00	£180.00	£500.00	£1,250
1935	390,000	£4.00	£12.00	£50.00	£160.00	—
1937	150,000	£6.00	£18.00	£120.00	£350.00	—
1939	1,080,000	£3.50	£5.00	£10.00	£20.00	£300.00
1940	670,000	£3.50	£5.00	£10.00	£25.00	—
1941	400,000	£4.00	£6.00	£12.00	£28.00	£300.00
1942	109,000	£5.00	£8.00	£14.00	£25.00	—
1943	unrecorded	£1,800	£2,500	£3,500	£6,000	—
1951	1,000,000	£0.30	£0.80	£4.00	£15.00	£160.00
1954	1,000,000	£0.30	£0.80	£4.00	£14.00	£180.00
1955	1,000,000	£0.30	£0.80	£4.00	£14.00	—
1959	2,000,000	£0.20	£0.60	£3.00	£10.00	—
1961	2,000,000	£0.20	£0.80	£4.00	£35.00	—
1962	2,400,000	£0.20	£0.50	£2.00	£8.00	—
1963	3,000,000	£0.20	£0.40	£1.00	£3.00	—
1964	4,000,000	£0.20	£0.40	£1.00	£2.50	—
1965	2,000,000	£0.20	£0.40	£0.80	£2.50	—
1966	3,625,000	*	*	£0.50	£1.50	—
1968	1,000,000	*	*	£1.00	£2.50	—

Halfcrowns

	MINTAGE	F	VF	EF	UNC	PROOF
1928	2,160,000	£5.00	£7.00	£14.00	£30.00	—
1928	6,001	—	—	—	—	£40.00
1930	352,000	£6.00	£14.00	£100.00	£300.00	—
1931	160,000	£8.00	£16.00	£100.00	£300.00	£400.00
1933	336,000	£6.00	£18.00	£120.00	£350.00	—
1934	480,000	£5.50	£10.00	£25.00	£90.00	—
1937	40,000	£30.00	£100.00	£500.00	£1,000	—
1939	888,000	£5.00	£7.00	£10.00	£25.00	£250.00
1940	752,000	£5.00	£7.00	£12.00	£28.00	—
1941	320,000	£5.50	£8.00	£16.00	£45.00	£300.00

IRELAND

	MINTAGE	F	VF	EF	UNC	PROOF
1942	285,600	£5.50	£8.00	£14.00	£24.00	—
1943	unrecorded	£60.00	£120.00	£250.00	£750.00	—
1951	800,000	£1.00	£2.00	£5.00	£20.00	£200.00
1954	400,000	£1.00	£2.50	£6.00	£20.00	£250.00
1955	1,080,000	£0.80	£1.60	£4.00	£14.00	—
1959	1,600,000	£0.60	£1.40	£2.50	£8.00	—
1961	1,600,000	£0.60	£1.40	£2.50	£10.00	—
1961 mule	unrecorded	£5.00	£10.00	£200.00	+	—
1962	3,200,000	£0.50	£1.00	£2.00	£7.00	£250.00
1963	2,400,000	£0.50	£1.00	£1.80	£4.00	—
1964	3,200,000	*	£0.50	£1.00	£2.00	—
1966	700,000	*	£0.50	£1.00	£2.40	—
1967	2,000,000	*	£0.50	£0.80	£1.60	—

Ten Shillings

	MINTAGE	F	VF	EF	UNC	PROOF
1966	2,000,000*	*	*	£5.00	£8.00	
1966	20,000	—	—	—	—	£12.50

*1,270,000 melted

Half Penny

	MINTAGE	F	VF	EF	UNC	PROOF
1971	100,500,000	*	*	*	£0.20	—
1975	10,500,000	*	*	*	£0.20	—
1976	5,464,000	*	*	*	£0.20	—
1978	20,302,000	*	*	*	£0.15	—
1980	20,616,000	*	*	*	£0.15	—
1982	9,660,000	*	*	*	£0.15	—
1985	2,784,000	*	*	*	£0.15	—
1986	6,750,000	*	*	*	£0.15	—

One Penny

	MINTAGE	F	VF	EF	UNC	PROOF
1971	100,500,000	*	*	*	£0.10	—
1974	10,000,000	*	*	*	£0.20	—
1975	10,000,000	*	*	*	£0.20	—
1976	38,164,000	*	*	*	£0.10	—
1978	25,746,000	*	*	*	£0.10	—
1979	21,766,000	*	*	*	£0.10	—
1980	86,712,000	*	*	*	£0.10	—
1982	54,189,000	*	*	*	£0.10	—
1985	19,242,000	*	*	*	+	—
1986	36,591,000	*	*	*	+	—

Two Pence

	MINTAGE	F	VF	EF	UNC	PROOF
1971	75,500,000	*	*	*	£0.10	£0.50
1975	20,010,000	*	*	*	£0.10	—
1976	5,414,000	*	*	*	£0.20	—
1978	12,000,000	*	*	*	£0.10	—
1979	32,373,000	*	*	*	£0.10	—
1980	59,828,000	*	*	*	£0.10	—
1982	30,435,000	*	*	*	£0.10	—
1985	14,469,000	*	*	*	+	—
1986	23,871,469	*	*	*	+	—

Five Pence

	MINTAGE	F	VF	EF	UNC	PROOF
1969	5,000,000	*	*	£0.10	£0.60	—
1970	10,000,000	*	*	*	£0.30	—
1971	8,000,000	*	*	*	£0.30	—
1974	7,000,000	*	*	*	£0.30	—
1975	10,000,000	*	*	*	£0.30	—
1976	20,616,000	*	*	*	£0.20	—
1978	28,536,000	*	*	*	£0.20	—
1980	22,190,000	*	*	*	£0.10	—
1982	24,404,000	*	*	*	£0.10	—
1985	4,202,000	*	*	*	+	—
1986	6,750,000	*	*	*	+	—

Ten Pence	MINTAGE	F	VF	EF	UNC	PROOF
1969	27,000,000	*	*	£0.20	£0.50	—
1971	4,000,000	*	*	*	£0.30	—
1973	2,500,000	*	*	*	£0.50	—
1974	7,500,000	*	*	*	£0.30	—
1975	15,000,000	*	*	*	£0.20	—
1976	9,433,000	*	*	*	£0.20	—
1978	30,905,000	*	*	*	£0.20	—
1980	44,605,000	*	*	*	£0.20	—
1982	7,374,000	*	*	*	£0.20	—
1985	4,100,000	*	*	*	+	—
1986	6,750,000	*	.	*	+	—

Twenty Pence

	MINTAGE	F	VF	EF	UNC	PROOF
1986	50,436,645	*	*	*	+	—
1988	unavailable	*	*	*	+	—

Fifty Pence

	MINTAGE	F	VF	EF	UNC	PROOF
1970	9,000,000	*	*	*	£1.60	—
1971	600,000	*	*	*	£1.60	—
1974	1,000,000	*	*	*	£2.00	—
1975	2,000,000	*	*	*	£1.00	—
1976	3,000,000	*	*	*	£1.00	—
1977	4,800,000	*	*	*	£1.00	—
1978	4,500,000	*	*	*	£1.00	—
1979	4,000,000	*	*	*	£1.00	—
1981	6,000,000	*	*	*	£0.75	—
1982	2,000,000	*	*	*	£0.75	—
1983	7,000,000	*	*	*	£0.60	—
1986	6,750,000	*	*	*	£0.60	—
1988	unavailable	*	*	*	£1.80	—

One Pound

	MINTAGE	F	VF	EF	UNC	PROOF
1990	unavailable	*	*	*	£1.40	—
1990	50,000	—	—	—	—	£12.50

Proof Sets

	MINTAGE	F	VF	EF	UNC	PROOF
1928 cased set of 8 coins, ¼d to halfcrown	6,001*	—	—	—	—	£120.00
1971 cased set of 6 coins, ½p to 50p	50,000	—	—	—	—	£5.00
*Only 4,006 issued						

Uncirculated Sets

	MINTAGE	F	VF	EF	UNC	PROOF
1982 set of 6 coins in wallet, ½p to 50p	unavailable	*	*	*	£2.00	—

GUERNSEY

One Double	MINTAGE	F	VF	EF	UNC	PROOF
1830	1,648,640	£0.60	£1.80	£6.50	£17.00	£100.00
1868	64,368	£2.50	£7.00	£18.00	£38.00	—
1868 68 over 30		£1.80	£4.50	£14.00	£32.00	—
1885 H	76,800	£0.50	£0.80	£1.80	£4.50	£60.00
1889 H	112,016	£0.20	£0.50	£1.00	£2.50	£55.00
1893 H	56,016	£0.50	£0.80	£2.00	£5.00	£60.00
1899 H	56,000	£0.50	£0.80	£1.80	£4.50	—
1902 H	84,000	£0.20	£0.40	£0.80	£1.80	—
1903 H	112,000	£0.10	£0.30	£0.60	£1.30	—
1911 H	67,200	£0.50	£1.00	£3.00	£4.50	—
1911 H new obv	67,400	£0.30	£0.80	£1.80	£3.50	—
1914 H	44,800	£0.80	£1.60	£4.50	£8.00	—
1929 H	79,100	£0.30	£0.50	£0.80	£1.60	—
1933 H	96,000	£0.30	£0.40	£0.60	£1.30	—
1938 H	96,000	£0.20	£0.30	£0.50	£1.20	—

GUERNSEY

Two Doubles

	MINTAGE	F	VF	EF	UNC	PROOF
1858	51,128	£8.00	£17.00	£45.00	+	—
1868 1 stalk	} 35,136	£3.00	£8.00	£25.00	£65.00	—
1868 3 stalks		£3.50	£8.00	£25.00	£65.00	—
1874	45,126	£2.50	£5.00	£15.00	£45.00	—
1885 H	76,800	£1.00	£2.00	£4.50	£9.00	£65.00
1889 H	35,616	£1.50	£2.50	£5.50	£12.00	£70.00
1899 H	35,636	£1.80	£3.50	£7.00	£16.00	—
1902 H	17,818	£3.00	£4.50	£13.00	£25.00	—
1903 H	17,818	£3.50	£5.50	£13.00	£25.00	—
1906 H	17,820	£5.00	£8.00	£17.00	£35.00	—
1908 H	17,780	£6.00	£9.00	£20.00	£38.00	—
1911 H	28,509	£3.00	£5.00	£9.00	£20.00	—
1914 H	28,509	£3.00	£5.00	£9.00	£20.00	—
1917 H	14,524	£17.00	£38.00	£75.00	+	—
1918 H	57,018	£0.60	£1.00	£2.50	£4.50	—
1920 H	57,018	£0.60	£1.00	£2.50	£4.00	—
1929 H	79,100	£0.20	£0.50	£1.60	£3.00	—

Four Doubles

	MINTAGE	F	VF	EF	UNC	PROOF
1830	655,200	£1.50	£3.50	£12.00	£30.00	£150.00
1858 H	114,060	£4.50	£11.00	£30.00	£75.00	—
1864 1 stalk	212,976	£0.50	£1.00	£6.00	£18.00	—
1864 3 stalks		£0.60	£1.50	£6.00	£18.00	—
1868	57,696	£1.20	£3.50	£10.00	£21.00	—
1874	69,216	£1.00	£2.50	£8.00	£21.00	—
1885 H	69,696	£1.00	£1.80	£7.00	£18.00	£65.00
1889 H	103,744	£0.40	£0.70	£2.50	£5.50	£65.00
1893 H	52,224	£1.20	£3.00	£7.00	£16.00	—
1902 H	104,534	£0.30	£0.90	£2.50	£4.50	—
1903 H	52,267	£1.00	£2.50	£5.50	£12.00	—
1906 H	52,226	£1.00	£2.50	£5.50	£12.00	—
1908 H	25,760	£4.00	£7.00	£14.00	£28.00	—
1910 H	52,267	£1.40	£2.50	£7.00	£14.00	—
1911 H	52,267	£1.50	£3.50	£8.00	£14.00	—
1914 H	209,067	£0.30	£0.60	£1.80	£4.00	—
1918 H	156,800	£0.30	£0.80	£2.50	£4.00	—
1920 H	156,800	£0.30	£0.70	£2.00	£3.50	—
1945 H	96,000	£0.30	£0.50	£1.20	£3.50	—
1949 H	19,200	£1.00	£2.00	£4.50	£7.00	—
1956	240,000	£0.20	£0.40	£0.90	£4.00	—

Eight Doubles

	MINTAGE	F	VF	EF	UNC	PROOF
1834	221,760	£3.00	£7.00	£22.00	£58.00	£190.00
1858 5 berries	} 111,496	£4.50	£12.00	£32.00	£92.00	£190.00
1858 4 berries		£5.50	£14.00	£32.00	£92.00	—
1864 1 stalk	} 284,736	£0.60	£1.60	£6.00	£20.00	£90.00
1864 3 stalks		£0.60	£1.60	£6.00	£20.00	—
1868	54,720	£2.50	£4.50	£16.00	£38.00	—
1874	73,248	£1.60	£3.00	£11.00	£26.00	—
1885 H	69,696	£1.50	£3.00	£8.00	£17.00	£80.00
1889 H	215,620	£0.50	£1.00	£2.50	£5.50	£75.00
1893 H	117,600	£0.80	£1.30	£4.00	£9.00	—
1902 H	235,200	£0.50	£1.00	£3.00	£5.50	—
1903 H	117,600	£0.90	£1.80	£4.50	£7.50	—
1910 H	91,467	£2.50	£4.50	£9.00	£17.00	—
1911 H	78,400	£3.00	£5.50	£12.00	£22.00	—
1914 H	156,800	£0.50	£0.80	£2.50	£5.50	—
1918 H	156,800	£0.50	£0.80	£2.50	£5.50	—
1920 H	156,800	£0.30	£0.50	£1.80	£4.00	—
1934 H	123,600	£0.30	£0.60	£1.80	£4.50	—
1934 H burnished flan	500	—	—	—	—	£40.00
1938 H	120,000	£0.30	£0.80	£1.80	£4.00	—
1945 H	192,000	£0.20	£0.50	£1.20	£3.50	—

	MINTAGE	F	VF	EF	UNC	PROOF
1947 H	240,000	£0.20	£0.30	£0.90	£2.50	—
1949 H	230,400	£0.20	£0.30	£0.90	£2.00	—
1956	494,600	£0.10	£0.20	£0.30	£1.70	—
1959	480,000	*	£0.10	£0.20	£1.20	—

Threepence

1956	508,675	*	£0.10	£0.40	£2.50	—
1959	480,000	*	£0.10	£0.20	£1.20	—

Five Shillings Token

1809	unrecorded	£1,200	£1,800	£2,800	+	—

Ten Shillings

1966	300,000	*	£0.60	£0.70	£1.20	—

Half Penny

1971	2,066,000	*	*	*	£0.10	—

One Penny

1971	1,922,000	*	*	*	£0.10	—
1977 'new' omitted	640,000	*	*	*	£0.10	—
1979	2,400,000	*	*	*	£0.10	—
1985 new type	60,000	*	*	*	£0.30	—
1986	1,010,000	*	*	*	£0.10	—
1987	5,000	*	*	*	£0.50	—
1988	500,000	*	*	*	£0.10	—
1989	1,000,000	*	*	*	£0.10	—
1990	5,000	*	*	*	£0.50	—

Two Pence

1971	1,680,000	*	*	*	£0.10	—
1977 'new' omitted	700,000	*	*	*	£0.10	—
1979	2,400,000	*	*	*	£0.10	—
1985 new type	60,000	*	*	*	£0.20	—
1986	510,000	*	*	*	£0.10	—
1987	5,000	*	*	*	£0.30	—
1988	500,000	*	*	*	£0.10	—
1989	620,000	*	*	*	£0.10	—
1990	380,000	*	*	*	£0.10	—

Five Pence

1968	800,000	*	*	*	£0.20	—
1977 'new' omitted	250,000	*	*	*	£0.30	—
1979	600,000	*	*	*	£0.10	—
1982	200,000	*	*	*	£0.10	—
1985 new type	35,000	*	*	*	£0.20	—
1986	100,000	*	*	*	£0.10	—
1987	300,000	*	*	*	£0.10	—
1988	405,000	*	*	*	£0.10	—
1989	5,000	*	*	*	£0.30	—
1990	2,400,000	*	*	*	£0.10	—

Ten Pence

1968	600,000	*	*	*	£0.30	—
1970	300,000	*	*	*	£0.50	—
1977 'new' omitted	480,000	*	*	*	£0.30	—
1979	659,000	*	*	*	£0.20	—
1982	200,000	*	*	*	£0.20	—
1984	400,000	*	*	*	£0.20	—
1985 new type	110,000	*	*	*	£0.30	—
1986	300,000	*	*	*	£0.20	—
1987	250,000	*	*	*	£0.20	—
1988	300,000	*	*	*	£0.20	—
1989	200,000	*	*	*	£0.20	—
1900	3,500	*	*	*	£0.50	—

GUERNSEY

	MINTAGE	F	VF	EF	UNC	PROOF
Twenty Pence						
1982	500,000	*	*	*	£0.40	—
1983	500,000	*	*	*	£0.40	—
1985 new type	35,000	*	*	*	£0.50	—
1986	10,000	*	*	*	£0.40	—
1987	5,000	*	*	*	£0.50	—
1988	5,000	*	*	*	£0.50	—
1989	92,500	*	*	*	£0.40	—
1990	112,500	*	*	*	£0.40	—
Twenty-five Pence						
1972 Silver Wedding	56,250	*	*	*	£4.50	—
1972 Silver Wedding, .925 silver	15,000	—	—	—	—	£12.00
1977 Silver Jubilee	207,400	*	*	*	£0.70	—
1977 Silver Jubilee, .925 silver	25,000	—	—	—	—	£10.00
1978 Royal Visit	105,220	*	*	*	£0.70	—
1978 Royal Visit .925 silver	25,000	—	—	—	—	£10.00
1980 Queen Mother	150,000	*	*	*	£0.60	—
1980 Queen Mother, .925 silver	25,000	—	—	—	—	£18.00
1981 Royal Wedding	113,717	*	*	*	£1.20	—
1981 Royal Wedding, .925 silver	12,341	—	—	—	—	£20.00
Fifty Pence						
1969	200,000	*	*	*	£1.00	—
1970	200,000	*	*	*	£1.00	—
1981 'new' omitted	200,000	*	*	*	£0.80	—
1982	150,000	*	*	*	£0.80	—
1983	200,000	*	*	*	£0.80	—
1984	200,000	*	*	*	£0.80	—
1985 new type	35,000	*	*	*	£1.20	—
1986	10,000	*	*	*	£1.20	—
1987	5,000	*	*	*	£1.50	—
1988	6,000	*	*	*	£1.50	—
1989	55,000	*	*	*	£1.00	—
1990	80,000	*	*	*	£1.00	—
One Pound						
1981 Guernsey lily	200,000	*	*	*	£1.80	—
1981 Guernsey lily, .916 gold	4,500	—	—	—	—	£115.00
1981 Guernsey lily, .916 gold, piedfort	500	—	—	—	—	£220.00
1983 HMS Crescent	269,000	*	*	*	£1.50	—
1985 new type	35,000	*	*	*	£1.80	—
1986	10,000	*	*	*	£1.80	—
1987	5,000	*	*	*	£2.00	—
1988	5,000	*	*	*	£2.00	—
1989	5,000	*	*	*	£2.00	—
1990	3,500	*	*	*	£2.00	—
Two Pounds						
1985 Liberation	50,000	*	*	*	£3.50	—
1985 Liberation, in pack/cover	25,000	*	*	*	£4.00	—
1985 Liberation, .925 silver	2,500	—	—	—	—	£28.00
1986 Commonwealth Games	10,000	*	*	*	£3.50	—
1986 Commonwealth Games, in pack	7,500	*	*	*	£4.00	—
1986 Commonwealth Games, .500 silver	50,000	*	*	*	£14.00	—
1986 Commonwealth Games, .925 silver	20,000	—	—	—	—	£25.00
1987 William the Conqueror	10,000	*	*	*	£3.50	—
1987 William the Conqueror, in pack/cover	7,500	*	*	*	£4.00	—
1987 William the Conqueror, .925 silver	2,500	—	—	—	—	£25.00
1987 William the Conqueror, .916 gold	90	—	—	—	—	+
1988 William II	7,500	*	*	*	£3.50	—
1988 William II, in pack	5,000	*	*	*	£4.00	—
1988 William II, .925 silver	2,500	—	—	—	—	£25.00

	MINTAGE	F	VF	EF	UNC	PROOF
1989 Henry II	10,000	*	*	*	£3.50	—
1989 Henry II, in pack	5,000	*	*	*	£4.00	—
1989 Henry II, .925 silver	2,500	—	—	—	—	£25.00
1989 Royal Visit, in pack	5,000	*	*	*	£4.00	—
1989 Royal Visit, .925 silver	5,000	—	—	—	—	£25.00
1990 Queen Mother, in pack	9,000	*	*	*	£4.00	—
1990 Queen Mother .925 silver	1,302	—	—	—	—	£25.00

Proof Sets

	MINTAGE	F	VF	EF	UNC	PROOF
1956 double set of 6 coins, 4 doubles to 3d	1,050	—	—	—	—	£32.00
1966 cased set of 4 coins, 2 doubles to 10/-	10,000	—	—	—	—	£10.00
1971 cased set of 6 coins, ½p to 50p	10,000	—	—	—	—	£8.00
1979 cased set of 6 coins, ½p to 50p	4,963	—	—	—	—	£12.00
1981 cased set of 6 coins, 1p to £1	10,000	—	—	—	—	£15.00
1985 cased set of 8 coins, 1p to £2	2,500	—	—	—	—	£24.00
1986 cased set of 8 coins, 1p to £2	2,500	—	—	—	—	£24.00
1987 cased set of 8 coins, 1p to £2	2,500	—	—	—	—	£22.00
1988 cased set of 8 coins, 1p to £2	2,500	—	—	—	—	£22.00
1989 cased set of 8 coins, 1p to £2	2,500	—	—	—	—	£22.00
1990 cased set of 7 coins, 1p to £1	700	—	—	—	—	£25.00

Uncirculated Sets

	MINTAGE	F	VF	EF	UNC	PROOF
1985 set of 7 coins, 1p to £1	10,000	*	*	*	£5.50	—
1986 set of 7 coins, 1p to £1	5,000	*	*	*	£5.50	—
1987 set of 7 coins, 1p to £1	7,500	*	*	*	£6.00	—
1988 set of 7 coins, 1p to £1	5,000	*	*	*	£6.00	—
1989 set of 7 coins, 1p to £1	5,000	*	*	*	£6.00	—
1990 set of 7 cons, 1p to £1	2,520	*	*	*	£8.00	—

JERSEY

	MINTAGE	F	VF	EF	UNC	PROOF
1/52 Shilling						
1841	116,480	£20.00	£40.00	£65.00	£110.00	+
1861	unrecorded	—	—	—	—	+
1/48 Shilling						
1877 H	288,000*	£7.00	£16.00	£35.00	£55.00	£120.00
1877	unrecorded	—	—	—	—	£170.00
* All withdrawn except for 38,400						
1/26 Shilling						
1841	232,960	£3.50	£8.00	£25.00	£48.00	£130.00
1844	232,960	£3.50	£8.00	£25.00	£48.00	—
1851	160,000	£3.00	£6.50	£16.00	£30.00	—
1858	173,333	£2.50	£5.50	£15.00	£25.00	£130.00
1861	173,333	£1.50	£4.00	£13.00	£22.00	£115.00
1866	173,333	£0.90	£2.00	£7.00	£16.00	£95.00
1870	160,000	£0.80	£2.00	£7.00	£16.00	£95.00
1871	160,000	£0.80	£2.00	£7.00	£16.00	£95.00
1/24 Shilling						
1877 H	336,000	£0.50	£1.50	£3.50	£8.00	£85.00
1877	unrecorded	—	—	—	—	£150.00
1888	120,000	£0.80	£1.60	£4.00	£10.00	—
1894	120,000	£0.50	£1.00	£3.50	£8.00	£85.00
1909	120,000	£1.20	£3.00	£7.50	£14.00	—
1911	72,000	£0.90	£2.00	£5.00	£10.00	—
1913	72,000	£0.90	£2.00	£5.00	£10.00	—
1923	72,000	£1.20	£3.00	£8.00	£14.00	—
1923 new design	72,000	£1.00	£2.00	£5.00	£9.00	—

JERSEY

	MINTAGE	F	VF	EF	UNC	PROOF
1926	120,000	£0.50	£1.00	£3.00	£5.00	—
1931	72,000	£0.60	£1.00	£2.50	£5.50	£65.00
1933	72,000	£0.60	£1.00	£2.50	£5.50	£65.00
1935	72,000	£0.60	£1.00	£2.50	£5.50	£65.00
1937	72,000	£0.50	£1.00	£2.50	£5.00	£60.00
1946	72,000	£0.40	£0.90	£2.50	£4.00	£50.00
1947	72,000	£0.40	£0.90	£2.50	£4.00	£50.00
¹⁄₁₃ Shilling						
1841	116,480	£7.00	£15.00	£40.00	£70.00	£170.00
1844	27,040	£10.00	£19.00	£58.00	£125.00	£200.00
1851	160,000	£3.50	£9.00	£24.00	£52.00	£150.00
1858	173,333	£3.50	£9.00	£22.00	£52.00	£150.00
1861	173,333	£3.00	£7.00	£20.00	£45.00	£150.00
1865	unrecorded	—	—	—	—	£270.00
1866	173,333	£1.00	£2.50	£8.00	£18.00	£120.00
1866 no LCW	unrecorded	—	—	—	—	£200.00
1870	160,000	£1.50	£3.00	£9.00	£17.00	£90.00
1871	160,000	£1.50	£3.00	£9.00	£17.00	£90.00
¹⁄₁₂ Shilling						
1877 H bronze	240,000	£0.50	£1.20	£4.00	£11.00	£80.00
1877 bronze	unrecorded	—	—	—	—	£130.00
1877 H nickel	unrecorded	—	—	—	—	£220.00
1877 nickel	unrecorded	—	—	—	—	£220.00
1881	75,153	£1.40	£3.50	£9.00	£22.00	—
1888	180,000	£0.80	£1.20	£4.00	£9.00	—
1894	180,000	£0.50	£1.00	£3.00	£7.00	£85.00
1909	180,000	£0.90	£1.50	£5.00	£12.00	—
1911	204,000	£0.40	£1.00	£3.50	£7.00	—
1913	204,000	£0.40	£0.90	£3.00	£7.00	—
1923	204,000	£0.30	£0.80	£2.50	£7.00	—
1923 new design	301,200	£0.20	£0.60	£2.00	£5.00	—
1926	82,800	£0.90	£2.00	£4.50	£10.00	—
1931	204,000	£0.20	£0.50	£1.60	£4.50	—
1933	204,000	£0.20	£0.50	£1.60	£4.50	£70.00
1935	204,000	£0.20	£0.50	£1.60	£4.50	£70.00
1937	204,000	£0.20	£0.40	£1.50	£4.00	£60.00
1946	204,000	£0.10	£0.20	£1.00	£3.00	£60.00
1947	444,000	*	£0.20	£0.80	£2.50	£60.00
1945 George VI commemorative	1,000,000	*	£0.10	£0.30	£1.00	£55.00
1945 Elizabeth II commemorative	720,000	*	£0.10	£0.30	£1.00	£50.00
1957	720,000	*	£0.10	£0.20	£0.50	—
1960	1,200,000	*	*	£0.10	£0.30	—
1960 mule, 1945 obv	unrecorded	—	—	—	—	£80.00
1964	1,200,000	*	*	*	£0.20	—
1966	1,200,000	*	*	*	£0.10	—
¼ Shilling						
1957	2,000,000	*	*	£0.10	£0.50	—
1964	1,200,000	*	*	£0.10	£0.30	—
1966	1,200,000	*	*	*	£0.20	—
Eighteen Pence						
1813	71,110	£25.00	£50.00	£90.00	£160.00	£270.00
Three Shillings						
1813	38,740	£40.00	£70.00	£115.00	£200.00	£320.00
Crowns						
1966	300,000	*	£0.30	£0.50	£1.20	—
Half Penny						
1971	3,000,000	*	*	*	£0.10	—
1980	200,000	*	*	*	£0.10	—
1981 'new' omitted	50,000	*	*	*	£0.30	—

	MINTAGE	F	VF	EF	UNC	PROOF
One Penny						
1971	4,500,000	*	*	*	£0.10	—
1980	3,000,000	*	*	*	£0.10	—
1981 'new' omitted	50,000	*	*	*	£0.30	—
1983 new type	500,000	*	*	*	£0.10	—
1984	1,000,000	*	*	*	£0.10	—
1985	1,000,000	*	*	*	£0.10	—
1986	2,000,000	*	*	*	£0.10	—
1987	1,500,000	*	*	*	£0.10	—
1988	1,000,000	*	*	*	£0.10	—
1989	1,500,000	*	*	*	£0.10	—
1990	2,000,000	*	*	*	£0.10	—
Two Pence						
1971	2,225,000	*	*	*	£0.10	—
1975	750,000	*	*	*	£0.10	—
1980	2,000,000	*	*	*	£0.10	—
1981 'new' omitted	50,000	*	*	*	£0.20	—
1983 new type	800,000	*	*	*	£0.10	—
1984	750,000	*	*	*	£0.10	—
1985	250,000	*	*	*	£0.10	—
1986	1,000,000	*	*	*	£0.10	—
1987	2,000,000	*	*	*	£0.10	—
1988	750,000	*	*	*	£0.10	—
1989	1,000,000	*	*	*	£0.10	—
1990	2,600,000	*	*	*	£0.10	—
Five Pence						
1968	3,600,000	*	*	*	£0.10	—
1980	800,000	*	*	*	£0.10	—
1981 'new' omitted	50,000	*	*	*	£0.30	—
1983 new type	400,000	*	*	*	£0.10	—
1984	300,000	*	*	*	£0.10	—
1985	600,000	*	*	*	£0.10	—
1986	200,000	*	*	*	£0.10	—
1988	400,000	*	*	*	£0.10	—
1990 new type	4,000,000	*	*	*	£0.10	—
Ten Pence						
1968	1,500,000	*	*	*	£0.20	—
1975	1,022,000	*	*	*	£0.30	—
1980	1,000,000	*	*	*	£0.20	—
1981 'new' omitted	50,000	*	*	*	£0.40	—
1983 new type	30,000	*	*	*	£0.40	—
1984	100,000	*	*	*	£0.30	—
1985	100,000	*	*	*	£0.30	—
1986	400,000	*	*	*	£0.20	—
1987	800,000	*	*	*	£0.20	—
1988	650,000	*	*	*	£0.20	—
1989	700,000	*	*	*	£0.20	—
1990	850,000	*	*	*	£0.20	—
Twenty Pence						
1982	200,000	*	*	*	£0.40	—
1982 .925 silver, piedfort	1,500	—	—	—	—	£26.00
1983	400,000	*	*	*	£0.30	—
1984	250,000	*	*	*	£0.30	—
1986	100,000	*	*	*	£0.30	—
1987	100,000	*	*	*	£0.30	—
1989	100,000	*	*	*	£0.30	—
1990	150,000	*	*	*	£0.30	—
Twenty-five Pence						
1977 Silver Jubilee	255,510	*	*	*	£0.70	—
1977 Silver Jubilee, .925 silver	35,000	—	—	—	—	£10.00

JERSEY

	MINTAGE	F	VF	EF	UNC	PROOF
Fifty Pence						
1969	480,000	*	*	*	£0.90	—
1980	100,000	*	*	*	£1.00	—
1981 'new' omitted	50,000	*	*	*	£1.00	—
1983 new type	50,000	*	*	*	£1.00	—
1984	50,000	*	*	*	£0.90	—
1985 Liberation	65,000	*	*	*	£0.90	—
1986	30,000	*	*	*	£0.90	—
1987	150,000	*	*	*	£0.90	—
1988	130,000	*	*	*	£0.90	—
1989	180,000	*	*	*	£0.90	—
1990	370,000	*	*	*	£0.90	—
One Pound						
1981 Battle of Jersey	200,000	*	*	*	£2.00	—
1981 Battle of Jersey, .925 silver	10,000	—	—	—	—	£12.00
1981 Battle of Jersey, .916 gold	5,000	—	—	—	—	£220.00
1983 St Helier	100,000	*	*	*	£1.60	—
1983 St Helier, .925 silver	10,000	—	—	—	—	£16.00
1983 St Helier, .916 gold	1,500	—	—	—	—	£300.00
1984 St Saviour	20,000	*	*	*	£1.60	—
1984 St Saviour, .925 silver	2,500	—	—	—	—	£16.00
1984 St Saviour, .916 gold	250	—	—	—	—	£300.00
1984 St Brelade	20,000	*	*	*	£1.60	—
1984 St Brelade, .925 silver	2,500	—	—	—	—	£16.00
1984 St Brelade, .916 gold	250	—	—	—	—	£300.00
1985 St Clement	25,000	*	*	*	£1.60	—
1985 St Clement, .925 silver	2,500	—	—	—	—	£16.00
1985 St Clement, .916 gold	250	—	—	—	—	£300.00
1985 St Lawrence	10,000	*	*	*	£1.60	—
1985 St Lawrence, .925 silver	2,500	—	—	—	—	£16.00
1985 St Lawrence, .916 gold	250	—	—	—	—	£300.00
1986 St Peter	10,000	*	*	*	£1.60	—
1986 St Peter, .925 silver	2,500	—	—	—	—	£16.00
1986 St Peter, .916 gold	250	—	—	—	—	£300.00
1986 Grouville	10,000	*	*	*	£1.60	—
1986 Grouville, .925 silver	2,500	—	—	—	—	£16.00
1986 Grouville, .916 gold	250	—	—	—	—	£300.00
1987 St Martin	10,000	*	*	*	£1.60	—
1987 St Martin, .925 silver	2,500	—	—	—	—	£16.00
1987 St Martin, .916 gold	250	—	—	—	—	£300.00
1987 St Ouen	10,000	*	*	*	£1.60	—
1987 St Ouen, .925 silver	2,500	—	—	—	—	£16.00
1987 St Ouen, .916 gold	250	—	—	—	—	£300.00
1988 Trinity	10,000	*	*	*	£1.60	—
1988 Trinity, .925 silver	2,500	—	—	—	—	£16.00
1988 Trinity, .916 gold	250	—	—	—	—	£300.00
1988 St John	10,000	+	+	+	£1.60	—
1988 St John, .925 silver	2,500	—	—	—	—	£16.00
1988 St John, .916 gold	250	—	—	—	—	£300.00
1989 St Mary	25,000	+	+	+	£1.60	—
1989 St Mary, .925 silver	2,500	—	—	—	—	£16.00
1989 St Mary .916 gold.....................	250	—	—	—	—	£300.00
Two Pounds						
1981 Royal Wedding	150,000	*	*	*	£3.00	—
1981 Royal Wedding, .925 silver	35,000	—	—	—	—	£21.00
1981 Royal Wedding, .916 gold	1,500	—	—	—	—	£220.00
1985 Liberation	5,000	*	*	*	£3.50	—
1985 Liberation, burnished, in pack ...	15,000	*	*	*	£4.50	—
1985 Liberation, .925 silver	2,500	—	—	—	—	£28.00
1985 Liberation, .916 gold	40	—	—	—	—	£950.00
1986 Commonwealth Games	5,000	*	*	*	£3.00	—
1986 Commonwealth Games, .500 silver	20,000	*	*	*	£10.00	—
1986 Commonwealth Games, .925 silver	20,000	—	—	—	—	£25.00

	MINTAGE	F	VF	EF	UNC	PROOF
1987 WWF	22,500	*	*	*	£3.00	—
1987 WWF, in pack	unavailable	*	*	*	£4.00	—
1987 WWF, .925 silver	25,000	—	—	—	—	£25.00
1989 Royal Visit	10,000	+	+	+	£3.00	—
1989 Royal Visit, .925 silver	3,000	—	—	—	—	£25.00
1990 Queen Mother 90th Birthday	10,000	*	*	*	£3.50	—
1990 Queen Mother 90th Birthday .925 silver	3,000	—	—	—	—	£25.00
1990 Queen Mother 90th Birthday .916 gold	90	—	—	—	—	£350.00
1990 Battle of Britain 50th Anniversary .925 silver	10,000	—	—	—	—	£25.00

Five Pounds

	MINTAGE	F	VF	EF	UNC	PROOF
1990 Battle of Britain 50th Anniversary .999 silver	5,000	—	—	—	—	£70.00

Proof Sets

	MINTAGE	F	VF	EF	UNC	PROOF
1957 double set of 4 coins, 1/12 & 1/4 sh	1,050	—	—	—	—	£30.00
1960 double set of 4 coins, 1/12 & 1/4 sh	2,100	—	—	—	—	£20.00
1964 double set of 4 coins, 1/12 & 1/4 sh	10,000	—	—	—	—	£6.00
1966 double set of 4 coins, 1/12 & 1/4 sh	15,000	—	—	—	—	£4.00
1966 double set of 2 crowns	15,000	—	—	—	—	£6.00
1972 cased set of 9 coins, 50p to £50	1,500	—	—	—	—	£500.00
1980 cased set of 6 coins, 1/2p to 50p	10,000	—	—	—	—	£12.00
1981 cased set of 7 coins, 1/2p to £1	15,000	—	—	—	—	£14.00
1983 cased set of 7 coins, 1p to £1, silver	5,000	—	—	—	—	£80.00
1990 cased set of 4 coins, £10 to £100 .999 gold	500	—	—	—	—	£900.00

Uncirculated Sets

	MINTAGE	F	VF	EF	UNC	PROOF
1972 set of 4 coins, 50p to £2.50	15,000	*	*	*	£15.00	—
1972 set of 9 coins, 50p to £50	8,500	*	*	*	£400.00	—
1983 set of 7 coins, 1p to £1	c25,000	*	*	*	£4.50	—
1987 set of 7 burnished coins, 1p to St M £1	unavailable	*	*	*	£6.00	—

ISLE OF MAN

Farthings

	MINTAGE	F	VF	· EF	UNC	PROOF
1839 copper	213,120	£6.00	£9.00	£16.00	£30.00	+
1841 copper mule	unrecorded	—	—	—	—	+
1860 copper mule	unrecorded	—	—	—	—	+
1864 copper mule	unrecorded	—	—	—	—	+

Halfpence

	MINTAGE	F	VF	EF	UNC	PROOF
1709 copper	c90,000	£50.00	£90.00	£160.00	+	—
1733 copper	unrecorded	£16.00	+	+	+	+
1733 bronze	60,000	£16.00	£25.00	£80.00	£170.00	+
1733 silver	unrecorded	£50.00	£90.00	£150.00	£200.00	+
1758 copper	72,000	£15.00	£30.00	£70.00	£130.00	+
1786 engrailed edge, copper	unrecorded	£7.00	£15.00	£40.00	£95.00	£120.00
1786 plain edge, copper	unrecorded	—	—	—	—	£225.00
1798 copper and bronze	unrecorded	£7.00	£14.00	£45.00	£95.00	£120.00
1798 copper-gilt, same flan as copper	unrecorded	—	—	—	—	+
1813 copper and bronze	unrecorded	£7.00	£14.00	£40.00	£90.00	£125.00
1813 copper-gilt, same flan as copper	unrecorded	—	—	—	—	+
1839 copper	214,080	£7.00	£11.00	£18.00	£35.00	+
1841 copper mule	unrecorded	—	—	—	—	+
1860 copper mule	unrecorded	—	—	—	—	+

Pence

	MINTAGE	F	VF	EF	UNC	PROOF
1709 copper	c90,000	£36.00	£80.00	£115.00	+	—
1709 silver	unrecorded	—	—	—	—	+
1733 copper	unrecorded	£13.00	+	+	+	+
1733 bronze	60,000	£13.00	£24.00	£80.00	£160.00	+
1733 silver	unrecorded	£70.00	£130.00	£210.00	£270.00	+

	MINTAGE	F	VF	EF	UNC	PROOF
1758 copper	60,000	£13.00	£22.00	£75.00	£135.00	+
1758 silver	c50	*	£180.00	£280.00	£340.00	+
1786 engrailed edge, copper	unrecorded	£12.00	£20.00	£45.00	£100.00	£150.00
1786 plain edge, copper	unrecorded	—	—	—	—	£325.00
1798 copper and bronze	unrecorded	£17.00	£30.00	£75.00	£130.00	£160.00
1798 copper-gilt (thin flan)	unrecorded	—	—	—	—	£450.00
1798 silver	unrecorded	—	—	—	—	+
1813 copper and bronze	unrecorded	£12.00	£20.00	£45.00	£110.00	£125.00
1813 copper-gilt, same flan as copper	unrecorded	—	—	—	—	+
1839 copper	80,640	£11.00	£18.00	£30.00	£50.00	+
1841 copper mule	unrecorded	—	—	—	—	+
1859 copper mule	unrecorded	—	—	—	—	+

Crowns

	MINTAGE	F	VF	EF	UNC	PROOF
1970 Manx cat	150,000	*	*	*	£2.00	—
1970 Manx cat, .925 silver	15,000	—	—	—	—	£15.00

Half-Sovereigns

	MINTAGE	F	VF	EF	UNC	PROOF
1965 Revestment Act	1,500	*	*	*	£40.00	—
1973	13,539	*	*	*	£30.00	—
1974	6,566	*	*	*	£30.00	—
1975	1,956	*	*	*	£35.00	—
1976	2,558	*	*	*	£35.00	—
1977	unavailable	*	*	*	£30.00	—
1979	unavailable	*	*	*	£30.00	—
1979	unavailable	—	—	—	—	£35.00
1980 Queen Mother countermark	7,500	—	—	—	—	£35.00
1981 Royal Wedding	40,000	*	*	*	£30.00	—
1981 Royal Wedding	30,000	—	—	—	—	£35.00
1982 Royal Baby countermark	70,000	*	*	*	£30.00	—
1982 Royal Baby countermark	30.000	—	—	—	—	£35.00
1984 new type	40,000	*	*	*	£30.00	—
1984 new type	30,000	—	—	—	—	£35.00

Sovereigns

	MINTAGE	F	VF	EF	UNC	PROOF
1965 Revestment Act	2,000	*	*	*	£60.00	—
1973	40,095	*	*	*	£50.00	—
1974	8,604	*	*	*	£50.00	—
1975	956	*	*	*	£55.00	—
1976	1,238	*	*	*	£55.00	—
1977	unavailable	*	*	*	£50.00	—
1979	unavailable	*	*	*	£50.00	—
1979	unavailable	—	—	—	—	£55.00
1980 Queen Mother countermark	5,000	—	—	—	—	£55.00
1981 Royal Wedding	30,000	*	*	*	£50.00	—
1981 Royal Wedding	40,000	—	—	—	—	£55.00
1982 Royal Baby countermark	70,000	*	*	*	£50.00	—
1982 Royal Baby countermark	40,000	—	—	—	—	£55.00
1984 new type	30,000	*	*	*	£50.00	—
1984 new type	20,000	—	—	—	—	£55.00

Two Pounds

	MINTAGE	F	VF	EF	UNC	PROOF
1973	3,612	*	*	*	£105.00	—
1974	1,257	*	*	*	£105.00	—
1975	456	*	*	*	£120.00	—
1976	578	*	*	*	£120.00	—
1977	unavailable	*	*	*	£105.00	—
1979	unavailable	*	*	*	£105.00	—
1979	unavailable	—	—	—	—	£110.00
1980 Queen Mother countermark	2,000	—	—	—	—	£110.00
1981 Royal Wedding	15,000	*	*	*	£105.00	—
1981 Royal Wedding	5,000	—	—	—	—	£110.00
1982 Royal Baby countermark	25,000	*	*	*	£105.00	—
1982 Royal Baby countermark	5,000	—	—	—	—	£110.00
1984 new type	10,000	*	*	*	£105.00	—
1984 new type	5,000	—	—	—	—	£110.00

	MINTAGE	F	VF	EF	UNC	PROOF
Five Pounds						
1965 Revestment Act	500	*	*	*	£250.00	—
1973	3,035	*	*	*	£250.00	—
1974	481	*	*	*	£250.00	—
1975	306	*	*	*	£270.00	—
1976	370	*	*	*	£270.00	—
1977	unavailable	*	*	*	£250.00	—
1979	unavailable	*	*	*	£250.00	—
1981 Royal Wedding	10,000	*	*	*	£250.00	—
1982 Royal Baby countermark	15,000	*	*	*	£250.00	—
1984 new type	5,000	*	*	*	£250.00	—
Half Penny						
1971	495,000	*	*	*	£0.30	—
1972	1,000	*	*	£7.50	£15.00	—
1973	1,000	*	*	£7.50	£15.00	—
1974	1,000	*	*	£7.50	£15.00	—
1975	825,000	*	*	*	£0.30	—
1976 new type, 'new' omitted	600,000	*	*	*	£0.20	—
1977 FAO	1,000,000	*	*	*	£0.20	—
1978	25,000	*	*	*	£0.20	—
1979	30,000	*	*	*	£0.20	—
1980 new type	unavailable	*	*	*	£0.10	—
1981	unavailable	*	*	*	£0.10	—
1981 World Food Day	unavailable	*	*	*	£0.10	—
1982	unavailable	*	*	*	£0.05	—
1983	unavailable	*	*	*	£0.05	—
1984 new type	unavailable	*	*	*	£0.05	—
1985 Sport countermark	unavailable	*	*	*	£0.05	—
One Penny						
1971	100,000	*	*	*	£0.40	—
1972	1,000	*	*	£7.00	£15.00	—
1973	1,000	*	*	£7.00	£15.00	—
1974	1,000	*	*	£7.00	£15.00	—
1975	855,000	*	*	*	£0.30	—
1976 new type, 'new' omitted	900,000	*	*	*	£0.20	—
1977	1,000,000	*	*	*	£0.20	—
1978	150,000	*	*	*	£0.20	—
1979	750,000	*	*	*	£0.20	—
1980 new type	unavailable	*	*	*	£0.20	—
1981	unavailable	*	*	*	£0.10	—
1982	unavailable	*	*	*	£0.05	—
1983	unavailable	*	*	*	£0.05	—
1984 new type	unavailable	*	*	*	£0.05	—
1985 Sport countermark	unavailable	*	*	*	£0.05	—
1986	unavailable	*	*	*	£0.05	—
1987	unavailable	*	*	*	£0.05	—
1988 new type	unavailable	*	*	*	+	—
Two Pence						
1971	100,000	*	*	£0.30	£0.50	—
1972	1,000	*	*	£8.00	£20.00	—
1973	1,000	*	£10.00	£18.00	£35.00	—
1974	1,000	*	*	£8.00	£20.00	—
1975	725,000	*	*	*	£0.30	—
1976 new type, 'new' omitted	800,000	*	*	*	£0.20	—
1977	1,000,000	*	*	*	£0.20	—
1978	250,000	*	*	*	£0.20	—
1979	550,000	*	*	*	£0.20	—
1980 new type	unavailable	*	*	*	£0.20	—
1981	unavailable	*	*	*	£0.10	—
1982	unavailable	*	*	*	£0.05	—
1983	unavailable	*	*	*	£0.05	—
1984 new type	unavailable	*	*	*	£0.05	—

ISLE OF MAN

	MINTAGE	F	VF	EF	UNC	PROOF
1985 Sport countermark	unavailable	*	*	*	£0.05	—
1986	unavailable	*	*	*	£0.05	—
1987	unavailable	*	*	*	£0.05	—
1988 new type	unavailable	*	*	*	+	—

Five Pence
1971	100,000	*	*	*	£0.60	—
1972	1,000	*	*	£7.00	£12.00	—
1973	1,000	*	*	£7.00	£12.00	—
1974	1,000	*	*	£7.00	£12.00	—
1975	1,400,000	*	*	*	£0.50	—
1976 new type, 'new' omitted	1,574,000	*	*	*	£0.30	—
1977	150,000	*	*	*	£0.30	—
1978	300,000	*	*	*	£0.20	—
1979	220,000	*	*	*	£0.20	—
1980 new type	unavailable	*	*	*	£0.20	—
1981	unavailable	*	*	*	£0.20	—
1982	unavailable	*	*	*	£0.15	—
1983	unavailable	*	*	*	£0.15	—
1984 new type	unavailable	*	*	*	£0.15	—
1985 Sport countermark	unavailable	*	*	*	£0.15	—
1986	unavailable	*	*	*	£0.15	—
1987	unavailable	*	*	*	£0.15	—
1988 new type	unavailable	*	*	*	+	—

Ten Pence
1971	100,000	*	*	*	£0.60	—
1972	1,000	*	*	£6.00	£11.00	—
1973	1,000	*	*	£6.00	£11.00	—
1974	1,000	*	*	£6.00	£11.00	—
1975	1,500,000	*	*	*	£0.70	—
1976 new type, 'new' omitted	2,800,000	*	*	*	£0.60	—
1977	150,000	*	*	*	£0.40	—
1978	600,000	*	*	*	£0.30	—
1979	30,000	*	*	*	£0.30	—
1980 new type	unavailable	*	*	*	£0.30	—
1981	unavailable	*	*	*	£0.30	—
1982	unavailable	*	*	*	£0.25	—
1983	unavailable	*	*	*	£0.25	—
1984 new type	unavailable	*	*	*	£0.25	—
1985 Sport countermark	unavailable	*	*	*	£0.25	—
1986	unavailable	*	*	*	£0.25	—
1987	unavailable	*	*	*	£0.25	—
1988 new type	unavailable	*	*	*	+	—

Twenty Pence
1982	unavailable	*	*	*	£0.40	—
1982	30,000	—	—	—	—	£5.00
1982 .925 silver	15,000	—	—	—	—	£10.00
1982 .916 gold	1,500	—	—	—	—	+
1982 platinum	250	—	—	—	—	+
1983	unavailable	*	*	*	£0.35	—
1984 new type	unavailable	*	*	*	£0.35	—
1985 Sport countermark	unavailable	*	*	*	£0.35	—
1986	unavailable	*	*	*	£0.35	—
1987	unavailable	*	*	*	£0.35	—
1988 new type	unavailable	*	*	*	+	—

Twenty-five Pence
1972 Silver Wedding, copper-nickel	70,000	*	*	*	£2.00	—
1972 Silver Wedding, silver	15,000	—	—	—	—	£12.00
1974 Churchill, copper-nickel	45,000	*	*	*	£1.00	—
1974 Churchill, silver	45,000	*	*	*	£7.00	—
1974 Churchill, silver	30,000	—	—	—	—	£10.00

	MINTAGE	F	VF	EF	UNC	PROOF
1975 Manx cat, copper-nickel	35,000	•	•	•	£1.00	—
1975 Manx cat, silver	unavailable	•	•	•	£6.00	—
1975 Manx cat, silver	30,000	—	—	—	—	£12.00
1976 Washington, copper-nickel	50,000	•	•	•	£1.00	—
1976 Washington, silver	50,000	•	•	•	£6.00	—
1976 Washington, silver	30,000	—	—	—	—	£9.00
1976 Tram, copper-nickel	50,000	•	•	•	£1.00	—
1976 Tram, silver	50,000	•	•	•	£6.00	—
1976 Tram, silver	30,000	—	—	—	—	£9.00
1977 Silver Jubilee, copper-nickel	100,000	•	•	•	£0.75	—
1977 Silver Jubilee, silver	70,000	•	•	•	£6.00	—
1977 Silver Jubilee, silver	30,000	—	—	—	—	£9.00
1977 Jubilee Fund, copper-nickel	100,000	•	•	•	£0.75	—
1977 Jubilee Fund, silver	70,000	•	•	•	£5.00	—
1977 Jubilee Fund, silver	30,000	—	—	—	—	£9.00
1978 Coronation, copper-nickel	100,000	•	•	•	£1.00	—
1978 Coronation, silver	70,000	•	•	•	£5.00	—
1978 Coronation, silver	30,000	—	—	—	—	£9.00
1979 Tercentenary, copper-nickel	100,000	•	•	•	£1.00	—
1979 Tercentenary, silver	70,000	•	•	•	£5.00	—
1979 Tercentenary, silver	30,000	—	—	—	—	£9.00
1979 Millennium: 5 coins						
1980 Olympics: 4 coins	} see under Proof and Uncirculated Sets					
1980 Derby, copper-nickel	100,000	•	•	•	£1.00	—
1980 Derby, silver	30,000	•	•	•	£5.00	—
1980 Derby, silver	20,000	—	—	—	—	£9.00
1980 Derby, gold	300	—	—	—	—	+
1980 Derby, platinum	400	—	—	—	—	+
1980 Queen Mother, copper-nickel	unavailable	•	•	•	£1.00	—
1980 Queen Mother, copper-nickel	100,000	—	—	—	—	£1.50
1980 Queen Mother, .500 silver	50,000	•	•	•	£5.00	—
1980 Queen Mother, .925 silver	30,000	—	—	—	—	£11.00
1980 Queen Mother, .375 gold, 22mm	50,000	—	—	—	—	£12.00
1980 Queen Mother, .916 gold, 22mm	10,000	—	—	—	—	£55.00
1981 Year of the Disabled: 4 coins						
1981 Royal Wedding: 2 coins						
1981 Award Scheme: 4 coins	see under Proof and Uncirculated Sets					
1982 World Cup: 4 coins						
1982 Italy Victory, copper-nickel	unavailable	•	•	•	£2.00	—
1982 Italy Victory, copper-nickel	20,000	—	—	—	—	£2.50
1982 Italy Victory, .925 silver	5,000	—	—	—	—	£15.00
1982 Italy Victory, .375 gold, 22mm	3,000	—	—	—	—	£20.00
1982 Maritime Heritage: 4 coins						
1983 Manned Flight: 4 coins						
1984 Olympics: 4 coins						
1984 College of Arms: 4 coins						
1984 C'wealth Conference: 4 coins	see under Proof and Uncirculated Sets					
1985 Queen Mother: 6 coins						
1986 World Cup: 6 coins						
1986 Royal Wedding: 2 coins						
1987 America's Cup: 5 coins						
1987 US Presidency, copper-nickel	unavailable	•	•	•	£2.00	—
1988 Navigation: 6 coins						
1988 Australia Bicentenary: 6 coins						
1988 Manx Cat: 1 coin						
1989 Mutiny on the Bounty: 4 coins						
1989 Star of India, America's Cup: 1 coin						

Fifty Pence

	MINTAGE	F	VF	EF	UNC	PROOF
1971	110,000	•	•	•	£1.20	—
1972	1,000	•	•	•	£15.00	—
1973	1,000	•	•	£7.00	£15.00	—
1974	1,000	•	•	£7.00	£15.00	—
1975	227,000	•	•	•	£1.20	—

ISLE OF MAN

	MINTAGE	F	VF	EF	UNC	PROOF
1976 new type, 'new' omitted	250,000	*	*	*	£1.00	—
1977	50,000	*	*	*	£0.90	—
1978	25,000	*	*	*	£0.90	—
1979 Millennium, copper-nickel	100,000	*	*	*	£1.40	—
1979 Millennium, silver	70,000	*	*	*	£5.00	—
1979 Millennium, silver	30,000	—	—	—	—	£9.00
1979 Millennium, platinum	1,000	—	—	—	—	£280.00
1979 Royal Visit (edge ins), copper-nickel	50,000	*	*	*	£1.00	—
1979 Royal Visit (edge ins), silver	10,000	*	*	*	£5.00	—
1979 Royal Visit (edge ins), silver	5,000	—	—	—	—	£9.00
1979 Royal Visit (edge ins), platinum	500	—	—	—	—	£300.00
1980 new type	unavailable	*	*	*	£1.00	—
1980 New York Ex (edge ins), CuNi	20,000	*	*	*	£1.75	—
1980 New York Ex (edge ins), silver	5,000	—	—	—	—	£8.00
1980 New York Ex (edge ins), gold	250	—	—	—	—	£180.00
1980 New York Ex (edge ins), platinum	50	—	—	—	—	£300.00
1980 Christmas, copper-nickel	30,000	*	*	*	£1.50	—
1980 Christmas, silver	5,000	—	—	—	—	£9.00
1980 Christmas, gold	250	—	—	—	—	£180.00
1980 Christmas, platinum	50	—	—	—	—	£300.00
1981	unavailable	*	*	*	£1.50	—
1981 TT Races, copper-nickel	30,000	*	*	*	£2.75	—
1981 TT Races, silver	5,000	—	—	—	—	£10.00
1981 TT Races, gold	250	—	—	—	—	£180.00
1981 TT Races, platinum	50	—	—	—	—	£300.00
1981 Christmas, copper-nickel	30,000	*	*	*	£1.50	—
1981 Christmas, silver	5,000	—	—	—	—	£10.00
1981 Christmas, gold	250	—	—	—	—	£180.00
1981 Christmas, platinum	50	—	—	—	—	£300.00
1982	unavailable	*	*	*	£1.00	—
1982 TT Races, copper-nickel	unavailable	*	*	*	£2.25	—
1982 TT Races, copper-nickel	30,000	—	—	—	—	£2.50
1982 TT Races, silver	5,000	—	—	—	—	£10.00
1982 TT Races, gold	250	—	—	—	—	£180.00
1982 TT Races, platinum	50	—	—	—	—	£300.00
1982 Christmas, copper-nickel	unavailable	*	*	*	£1.50	—
1982 Christmas, copper-nickel	30,000	—	—	—	—	£2.50
1982 Christmas, silver	5,000	—	—	—	—	£9.00
1982 Christmas, gold	250	—	—	—	—	£180.00
1982 Christmas, platinum	50	—	—	—	—	£300.00
1983	unavailable	*	*	*	£1.00	—
1983 TT Races, copper-nickel	unavailable	*	*	*	£2.00	—
1983 TT Races, copper-nickel	30,000	—	—	—	—	£2.50
1983 TT Races, silver	5,000	—	—	—	—	£10.00
1983 TT Races, gold	250	—	—	—	—	£180.00
1983 TT Races, platinum	50	—	—	—	—	£300.00
1983 Christmas, copper-nickel	unavailable	*	*	*	£1.50	—
1983 Christmas, copper-nickel	30,000	—	—	—	—	£2.50
1983 Christmas, silver	5,000	—	—	—	—	£9.00
1983 Christmas, gold	250	—	—	—	—	£180.00
1983 Christmas, platinum	50	—	—	—	—	£300.00
1984 new type	unavailable	*	*	*	£0.90	—
1984 TT Races, copper-nickel	unavailable	*	*	*	£2.00	—
1984 TT Races, copper-nickel	30,000	—	—	—	—	£2.50
1984 TT Races, silver	5,000	—	—	—	—	£10.00
1984 TT Races, gold	250	—	—	—	—	£180.00
1984 TT Races, platinum	50	—	—	—	—	£300.00
1984 Christmas, copper-nickel	unavailable	*	*	*	£1.50	—
1984 Christmas, copper-nickel	30,000	—	—	—	—	£2.50
1984 Christmas, silver	5,000	—	—	—	—	£9.00
1984 Christmas, gold	250	—	—	—	—	£180.00
1984 Christmas, platinum	50	—	—	—	—	£300.00
1985 Sport countermark	unavailable	*	*	*	£0.90	—
1985 Christmas, copper-nickel	unavailable	*	*	*	£1.25	—
1985 Christmas, copper-nickel	30,000	—	—	—	—	£2.50

	MINTAGE	F	VF	EF	UNC	PROOF
1985 Christmas, silver	5,000	—	—	—	—	£10.00
1985 Christmas, gold	250	—	—	—	—	£180.00
1985 Christmas, platinum	50	—	—	—	—	£300.00
1986	unavailable	*	*	*	£0.90	—
1986 Christmas, copper-nickel	unavailable	*	*	*	£1.20	—
1986 Christmas, copper-nickel	30,000	—	—	—	—	£2.50
1986 Christmas, silver	5,000	—	—	—	—	£10.00
1986 Christmas, gold	250	—	—	—	—	£180.00
1986 Christmas, platinum	50	—	—	—	—	£300.00
1987	unavailable	*	*	*	£0.90	—
1987 Christmas, copper-nickel	unavailable	*	*	*	£0.90	—
1987 Christmas, copper-nickel	30,000	—	—	—	—	£3.50
1987 Christmas, silver	5,000	—	—	—	—	£10.00
1987 Christmas, gold	250	—	—	—	—	£180.00
1987 Christmas, platinum	50	—	—	—	—	£300.00
1988 new type	unavailable	*	*	*	+	—

One Pound

	MINTAGE	F	VF	EF	UNC	PROOF
1978 virenium	326,851	*	*	*	£1.80	—
1978 virenium	150,000	—	—	—	—	£2.00
1978 silver	100,000	—	—	—	—	£5.00
1978 platinum	1,000	—	—	—	—	£90.00
1979 virenium	70,000	*	*	*	£1.80	—
1979 Millennium, virenium	100,000	—	—	—	—	£2.00
1979 Millennium, silver	75,000	—	—	—	—	£5.00
1979 Millennium, platinum	1,000	—	—	—	—	£90.00
1980 inc TT and DMIHE(N) cmks, virenium.	unavailable	*	*	*	£1.80	—
1980 virenium	100,000	—	—	—	—	£2.00
1980 silver	75,000	—	—	—	—	£5.00
1980 gold	5,000	—	—	—	—	£60.00
1980 platinum	1,000	—	—	—	—	£90.00
1981 virenium	unavailable	*	*	*	£1.60	—
1981 virenium	100,000	—	—	—	—	£2.00
1981 silver	75,000	—	—	—	—	£5.00
1981 gold	5,000	—	—	—	—	£60.00
1981 platinum	1,000	—	—	—	—	£90.00
1982 virenium	unavailable	*	*	*	£11.00	—
1983 Peel, virenium	unavailable	*	*	*	£1.60	—
1983 Peel, virenium	unavailable	—	—	—	—	£3.50
1984 Castletown, virenium	unavailable	*	*	*	£1.60	—
1985 Ramsey, Sport cmk, virenium	unavailable	*	*	*	£1.60	—
1986 Douglas, virenium	unavailable	*	*	*	£1.60	—
1987 Viking warrior, virenium	unavailable	*	*	*	£1.60	—
1988 new type, virenium	unavailable	*	*	*	£1.60	—

Two Pounds

	MINTAGE	F	VF	EF	UNC	PROOF
1986 virenium	unavailable	*	*	*	£3.00	—
1987 virenium	unavailable	*	*	*	£3.00	—
1988 new type, virenium	unavailable	*	*	*	£3.00	—

Five Pounds

	MINTAGE	F	VF	EF	UNC	PROOF
1981 virenium	unavailable	*	*	*	£7.50	—
1981 virenium	30,000	—	—	—	—	£11.00
1981 silver	15,000	—	—	—	—	£12.00
1981 gold	1,000	—	—	—	—	£275.00
1981 platinum	500	—	—	—	—	£450.00
1982 virenium	unavailable	*	*	*	+	—
1983 virenium	unavailable	*	*	*	£7.00	—
1984 new type, virenium	unavailable	*	*	*	£7.00	—
1985 Sport countermark, virenium	unavailable	*	*	*	£7.00	—
1986 virenium	unavailable	*	*	*	£7.00	—
1987 virenium	unavailable	*	*	*	£7.00	—
1988 new type, virenium	unavailable	*	*	*	£7.00	—

ISLE OF MAN

	MINTAGE	F	VF	EF	UNC	PROOF

Proof Sets

	MINTAGE	F	VF	EF	UNC	PROOF
1965 Revestment Act, 3 coins, gold	1,000	—	—	—	—	£350.00
1971 6 coins, base	10,000	—	—	—	—	£6.00
1973 4 coins, gold	1,250	—	—	—	—	£450.00
1974 4 coins, gold	2,500	—	—	—	—	£450.00
1975 6 coins, platinum	600	—	—	—	—	£900.00
1975 4 coins, gold	200	—	—	—	—	£475.00
1976 new designs, 6 coins, platinum	600	—	—	—	—	£900.00
1977 Silver Jubilee, 6 coins, silver	10,000	—	—	—	—	£12.00
1977 4 coins, gold	1,250	—	—	—	—	£450.00
1978 7 coins, platinum	600	—	—	—	—	£1,000
1978 8 coins, base	50,000	—	—	—	—	£4.50
1979 4 coins, gold	1,000	—	—	—	—	£450.00
1979 Millennium, 7 coins, silver	10,000	—	—	—	—	£12.00
1979 Millennium, 7 coins, platinum	500	—	—	—	—	£1,000
1979 Millennium, 5 crowns:						
silver	10,000	—	—	—	—	£35.00
gold	300	—	—	—	—	*
platinum	100	—	—	—	—	*
1980 Olympics, 4 crowns:						
copper-nickel	30,000	—	—	—	—	£6.00
.925 silver	10,000	—	—	—	—	£30.00
gold	300	—	—	—	—	*
platinum	100	—	—	—	—	*
1980 new designs, 7 coins, base	25,000	—	—	—	—	£5.00
1980 new designs, 7 coins, silver	10,000	—	—	—	—	£15.00
1980 new designs, 7 coins, gold	300	—	—	—	—	*
1980 new designs, 7 coins, platinum	500	—	—	—	—	£1,000
1980 Queen Mother cmk, 4 coins, gold	250	—	—	—	—	£475.00
1981 Year of the Disabled, 4 crowns:						
copper-nickel	50,000	—	—	—	—	£6.00
.925 silver	15,000	—	—	—	—	£30.00
.375 gold, 22mm	10,000	—	—	—	—	£70.00
.916 gold, 22mm	1,000	—	—	—	—	£250.00
platinum	100	—	—	—	—	*
1981 Royal Wedding, 2 crowns:						
copper-nickel	50,000	—	—	—	—	£3.00
.925 silver	15,000	—	—	—	—	£20.00
.375 gold, 22mm	10,000	—	—	—	—	£35.00
.916 gold, 22mm	1,000	—	—	—	—	£120.00
platinum	100	—	—	—	—	*
1981 Royal Wedding, 4 coins, gold	1,000	—	—	—	—	£475.00
1981 Award Scheme, 4 crowns:						
copper-nickel	50,000	—	—	—	—	£6.00
.925 silver	15,000	±	—	—	—	£30.00
.375 gold, 22mm	10,000	—	—	—	—	£65.00
.916 gold, 22mm	1,000	—	—	—	—	£250.00
platinum	100	—	—	—	—	*
1982 World Cup, 4 crowns:						
copper-nickel	50,000	—	—	—	—	£6.00
.925 silver	15,000	—	—	—	—	£30.00
.375 gold, 22mm	10,000	—	—	—	—	£65.00
.916 gold, 22mm	1,000	—	—	—	—	£250.00
platinum	100	—	—	—	—	*
1982 Royal Baby cmk, 9 coins, base	25,000	—	—	—	—	£20.00
1982 Royal Baby cmk, 7 coins, silver	9,000	—	—	—	—	
1982 Royal Baby cmk, 9 coins, silver	1,000	—	—	—	—	
1982 Royal Baby cmk, 7 coins, gold	250	—	—	—	—	
1982 Royal Baby cmk, 9 coins, gold	250	—	—	—	—	
1982 Royal Baby cmk, 7 coins, platinum	400	—	—	—	—	
1982 Royal Baby cmk, 9 coins, platinum	100	—	—	—	—	
1982 Royal Baby cmk, 4 coins, gold	500	—	—	—	—	

	MINTAGE	F	VF	EF	UNC	PROOF
1982 Maritime Heritage, 4 crowns:						
copper-nickel	50,000	—	—	—	—	£6.00
.925 silver	10,500	—	—	—	—	£35.00
.375 gold, 22mm	5,500	—	—	—	—	£65.00
.916 gold, 22mm	500	—	—	—	—	£250.00
platinum	50	—	—	—	—	+
1983 Manned Flight, 4 crowns:						
copper-nickel	50,000	—	—	—	—	£6.00
.925 silver	10,500	—	—	—	—	£40.00
.375 gold, 22mm	5,500	—	—	—	—	£65.00
.916 gold, 22mm	500	—	—	—	—	£250.00
platinum	50	—	—	—	—	+
1983 9 coins, base	25,000	—	—	—	—	£10.00
1983 9 coins, silver	5,000	—	—	—	—	+
1983 9 coins, gold	150	—	—	—	—	+
1983 9 coins, platinum	100	—	—	—	—	+
1983-1986 Town Tribute, 4 £1 coins:						
.925 silver	29,050	—	—	—	—	£25.00
.925 silver, piedfort	4,950	—	—	—	—	+
.375 gold	4,950	—	—	—	—	+
.375 gold, piedfort	950	—	—	—	—	+
.916 gold	950	—	—	—	—	+
.916 gold, piedfort	250	—	—	—	—	+
platinum	450	—	—	—	—	+
platinum, piedfort	50	—	—	—	—	+
1984 Olympics, 4 crowns:						
copper-nickel	50,000	—	—	—	—	£6.00
silver-clad copper-nickel	20,000	—	—	—	—	£12.00
.925 silver	15,000	—	—	—	—	£30.00
.375 gold, 22mm	10,000	—	—	—	—	£65.00
.916 gold, 22mm	1,000	—	—	—	—	£250.00
platinum	100	—	—	—	—	+
1984 new designs, 7 coins, base	25,000	—	—	—	—	£9.00
1984 new designs, 9 coins, base	inc above	—	—	—	—	£14.00
1984 new designs, 7 coins, silver	5,000	—	—	—	—	£20.00
1984 new designs, 9 coins, silver	inc above	—	—	—	—	£25.00
1984 new designs, 7 coins, gold	150	—	—	—	—	+
1984 new designs, 9 coins, gold	inc above	—	—	—	—	+
1984 new designs, 7 coins, platinum	100	—	—	—	—	+
1984 new designs, 9 coins, platinum	inc above	—	—	—	—	+
1984 College of Arms, 4 crowns:						
copper-nickel	50,000	—	—	—	—	£6.00
silver-clad copper-nickel	20,000	—	—	—	—	£10.00
.925 silver	15,000	—	—	—	—	£30.00
.375 gold, 22mm	10,000	—	—	—	—	£65.00
.916 gold, 22mm	1,000	—	—	—	—	£250.00
platinum	100	—	—	—	—	+
1984 C'wealth Conference, 4 crowns:						
copper-nickel	50,000	—	—	—	—	£6.00
silver-clad copper-nickel	20,000	—	—	—	—	£10.00
.925 silver	15,000	—	—	—	—	£30.00
.375 gold, 22mm	10,000	—	—	—	—	£65.00
.916 gold, 22mm	1,000	—	—	—	—	£250.00
platinum	100	—	—	—	—	+
1984 new designs, 4 coins, gold	500	—	—	—	—	£475.00
1985 Sport cmk, 7 coins, base	25,000	—	—	—	—	£8.00
1985 Sport cmk, 9 coins, base	inc above	—	—	—	—	£14.00
1985 Sport cmk, 7 coins, silver	5,000	—	—	—	—	£20.00
1985 Sport cmk, 9 coins, silver	inc above	—	—	—	—	£30.00
1985 Sport cmk, 7 coins, gold	150	—	—	—	—	+
1985 Sport cmk, 9 coins, gold	inc above	—	—	—	—	+
1985 Sport cmk, 7 coins, platinum	100	—	—	—	—	+
1985 Sport cmk, 9 coins, platinum	inc above	—	—	—	—	+

	MINTAGE	F	VF	EF	UNC	PROOF
1985 Queen Mother, 6 crowns:						
copper-nickel	50,000	—	—	—	—	£7.00
silver-clad copper-nickel	20,000	—	—	—	—	£10.00
.925 silver	15,000	—	—	—	—	£40.00
.375 gold, 22mm	10,000	—	—	—	—	£95.00
.916 gold, 22mm	1,000	—	—	—	—	£325.00
platinum	100	—	—	—	—	+
1986 World Cup, 6 crowns:						
copper-nickel	50,000	—	—	—	—	£7.00
silver-clad copper-nickel	20,000	—	—	—	—	£12.00
.925 silver	15,000	—	—	—	—	£45.00
.375 gold, 22mm	10,000	—	—	—	—	£95.00
.916 gold, 22mm	1,000	—	—	—	—	£325.00
platinum	100	—	—	—	—	+
1986 Royal Wedding, 2 crowns:						
copper-nickel	50,000	—	—	—	—	£5.00
silver-clad copper-nickel	20,000	—	—	—	—	£8.50
.925 silver	15,000	—	—	—	—	£25.00
.375 gold, 22mm	10,000	—	—	—	—	£35.00
.916 gold, 22mm	1,000	—	—	—	—	£120.00
platinum	100	—	—	—	—	+
1987 America's Cup, 5 crowns:						
silver-clad copper-nickel	20,000	—	—	—	—	+
.925 silver	15,000	—	—	—	—	+
1988 Steam Navigation, 6 crowns						
1988 Australia Bicentenary, 6 crowns						
1988 Manx Cat, 1 crown						
1989 Mutiny on the Bounty, 4 crowns						
1989 Star of India, America's Cup, 1 crown						

Uncirculated Sets

	MINTAGE	F	VF	EF	UNC	PROOF
1965 Revestment Act, 3 coins, gold	1,500	•	•	•	£325.00	—
1971 6 coins in wallet, base	50,000	•	•	•	£2.50	—
1973 4 coins, gold	2,500	•	•	•	£425.00	—
1974 4 coins, gold	250	•	•	•	£425.00	—
1975 6 coins in wallet, base	20,000	•	•	•	£2.50	—
1975 6 coins, silver	20,000	•	•	•	£10.00	—
1975 4 coins, gold	200	•	•	•	£450.00	—
1976 new designs, 6 coins in wallet, base	20,000	•	•	•	£1.50	—
1976 new designs, 6 coins, base	unavailable	•	•	•	£2.50	—
1976 new designs, 6 coins, silver	20,000	•	•	•	£10.00	—
1976 4 coins, gold	unavailable	•	•	•	+	—
1977 6 coins in wallet, base	50,000	•	•	•	£1.50	—
1977 4 coins, gold	180	•	•	•	£425.00	—
1978 7 coins, silver	10,000	•	•	•	£10.00	—
1979 4 coins, gold	unavailable	•	•	•	£425.00	—
1979 Millennium, 5 crowns:						
copper-nickel	100,000	•	•	•	£6.00	—
silver	25,000	•	•	•	£25.00	—
1980 Olympics, 4 crowns:						
copper-nickel	70,000	•	•	•	£5.50	
gold	1,500	•	•	•	+	
1980 new designs, 7 coins, base	25,000	•	•	•	£3.00	
1981 Year of the Disabled, 4 crowns:						
copper-nickel	unavailable	•	•	•	£5.50	
.925 silver	20,000	•	•	•	£25.00	
1981 Royal Wedding, 2 crowns:						
copper-nickel	unavailable	•	•	•	£2.50	
.925 silver	20,000	•	•	•	£15.00	
1981 Award Scheme, 4 crowns:						
copper-nickel	unavailable	•	•	•	£5.50	
.925 silver	20,000	•	•	•	£25.00	

	MINTAGE	F	VF	EF	UNC	PROOF
1982 World Cup, 4 crowns:						
copper-nickel	unavailable	*	*	*	£5.50	—
.925 silver	20,000	*	*	*	£25.00	—
1982 Maritime Heritage, 4 crowns:						
copper-nickel	unavailable	*	*	*	£5.50	—
.925 silver	15,000	*	*	*	£25.00	—
1983 Manned Flight, 4 crowns:						
copper-nickel	unavailable	*	*	*	£5.50	—
.925 silver	15,000	*	*	*	£30.00	—
1984 Olympics, 4 crowns:						
copper-nickel	unavailable	*	*	*	£5.50	—
1984 College of Arms, 4 crowns:						
copper-nickel	unavailable	*	*	*	£5.50	—
1984 C'wealth Conference, 4 crowns:						
copper-nickel	unavailable	*	*	*	£5.50	—
1984 new designs, 4 coins, gold	unavailable	*	*	*	£425.00	—
1985 Queen Mother, 6 crowns:						
copper-nickel	unavailable	*	*	*	£7.50	—
1986 World Cup, 6 crowns:						
copper-nickel	unavailable	*	*	*	£7.50	—
1986 Royal Wedding 2 crowns:						
copper-nickel	unavailable	*	*	*	£3.50	—
1987 America's Cup, 5 crowns:						
copper-nickel	unavailable	*	*	*	£6.50	—
.925 silver	20,000	*	*	*	+	—
1988 new designs, 9 coins, base	unavailable	*	*	*	+	—
1988 Steam Navigation, 6 crowns						
1988 Australia Bicentenary, 6 crowns						
1988 Manx Cat, 1 crown						
1989 Mutiny on the Bounty, 4 crowns						
1989 Star of India, America's Cup, 1 crown						

LUNDY

	MINTAGE	F	VF	EF	UNC	PROOF
Half Puffin						
1929	50,000	£0.90	£1.75	£3.80	£6.50	—
Puffin						
1929	50,000	£1.20	£2.25	£4.35	£7.50	—
Proof Sets						
1965 double set of 4 coins, spurious issue	3,000	—	—	—	—	£14.00

british banknote prices

The following prices are based on an average of dealers' current selling prices and the latest auction realisations. In many cases more than one variety of a type is known and the first and last prefix serials will usually command a premium. The prices quoted are therefore those of the commonest type with a mid-series prefix.

KEY TO SYMBOLS

LNN = Prefix consisting of Letter, Number, Number, eg N28
NNM = Some letters, particularly M and A, are sometimes used exclusively to signify replacement notes. Where this is the case the particular letters are given and the fact noted
'G' = A small letter placed on the reverse of the note, usually to identify a particular type of printing or machine. Other such letters are 'R' and 'L'
*   = Face value – a common note in a low grade and therefore not usually collected in that condition
+   = Exceedingly rare and not recently seen on the market

	F 55	VF 75	EF 90	UNC 100
TREASURY 10 SHILLING NOTES				
Bradbury type 1 red 5in x 2½in	£130.00	£230.00	£300.00	£420.00
Bradbury type 2 5½in x 3in	£55.00	£90.00	£180.00	£250.00
Bradbury type 2 Arabic overprint	£165.00	£295.00	£450.00	+
Bradbury type 3 green/brown, black dot	£80.00	£140.00	£280.00	£400.00
Bradbury type 3 green/brown, black dash	£70.00	£120.00	£260.00	£350.00
Bradbury type 3 green/brown, red dot	£250.00	£400.00	£600.00	+
Bradbury type 3 green/brown, red dash	£75.00	£140.00	£185.00	£250.00
Warren Fisher type 1 red dash	£45.00	£85.00	£125.00	£160.00
Warren Fisher type 1 red dot	£65.00	£125.00	£155.00	£190.00
Warren Fisher type 2 'No' omitted	£20.00	£40.00	£55.00	£75.00
Warren Fisher type 3 Northern Ireland	£25.00	£55.00	£75.00	£125.00
TREASURY 1 POUND NOTES				
Bradbury type 1 black 5in x 2½in	£150.00	£285.00	£360.00	£525.00
Bradbury type 2 6in x 3¼in	£75.00	£125.00	£175.00	£250.00
Bradbury type 2 Arabic overprint	£1,000	£1,800	+	+
Bradbury type 3 green/brown	£20.00	£40.00	£60.00	£80.00
Warren Fisher type 1	£16.00	£33.00	£50.00	£65.00
Warren Fisher type 2 boxed watermark	£15.00	£30.00	£45.00	£55.00
Warren Fisher type 3 Northern Ireland	£20.00	£45.00	£65.00	£85.00
BANK OF ENGLAND 10 SHILLING NOTES				
Mahon Britannia type	£20.00	£40.00	£60.00	£90.00
Catterns	£12.00	£24.00	£40.00	£52.00
Peppiatt LNN	£12.00	£24.00	£40.00	£52.00
Peppiatt NNL	£12.00	£24.00	£40.00	£52.00
Peppiatt mauve war issue	£6.00	£12.00	£18.00	£24.00
Peppiatt NNL post-war issue	£15.00	£30.00	£60.00	£85.00
Peppiatt NNL threaded	£5.00	£10.00	£14.00	£18.00
Peppiatt NNA threaded (replacement)	£100.00	£200.00	£300.00	£400.00
Beale NNL	£5.00	£10.00	£13.00	£17.00
Beale NNA (replacement)	£25.00	£45.00	£60.00	£85.00
Beale LNNL	£4.00	£8.00	£11.00	£15.00
O'Brien LNNL	£3.00	£6.00	£9.00	£12.00
O'Brien NNA (replacement)	£20.00	£40.00	£55.00	£70.00
O'Brien portrait type LNN	*	£3.00	£5.00	£7.00
O'Brien portrait type MNN (replacement)	£7.00	£15.00	£28.00	£40.00

	F 55	VF 75	EF 90	UNC 100
Hollom LNN	*	£3.00	£5.00	£7.00
Hollom MNN (replacement)	£7.00	£14.00	£23.00	£30.00
Hollom NNL	*	£3.00	£5.00	£7.00
Fforde NNL	*	*	£3.00	£5.00
Fforde MNN (replacement)	*	£3.00	£7.00	£11.00
Fforde LNNL	*	*	£3.00	£5.00

BANK OF ENGLAND 1 POUND NOTES

	F 55	VF 75	EF 90	UNC 100
Mahon Britannia type	£16.00	£31.00	£47.00	£65.00
Catterns LNN	£8.00	£15.00	£25.00	£35.00
Catterns NNL	£16.00	£38.00	£75.00	£105.00
Peppiatt NNL	£6.00	£12.00	£25.00	£30.00
Peppiatt, pre-war issue, LNNL	£6.00	£11.00	£18.00	£25.00
Peppiatt pale blue war issue	£3.00	£7.00	£13.00	£22.00
Peppiatt blue war issue	*	£4.00	£7.00	£10.00
Peppiatt post-war issue, green LNNL	£7.00	£15.00	£22.00	£32.00
Peppiatt threaded LNNL	*	£8.00	£11.00	£14.00
Peppiatt SNNS (replacement)	£36.00	£95.00	£145.00	£185.00
Beale LNNL	*	*	£4.00	£7.00
Beale SNNS (replacement)	£5.00	£14.00	£24.00	£42.00
O'Brien LNNL	*	*	£4.00	£7.00
O'Brien SNNS + SNNT (replacement)	£4.00	£16.00	£35.00	£45.00
O'Brien portrait type LNN	*	*	£4.00	£6.00
O'Brien MNN (replacement)	*	£8.00	£14.00	£20.00
O'Brien NNL	*	*	£4.00	£6.00
O'Brien LNNL	*	£12.00	£18.00	£24.00
O'Brien 'R' reverse	£30.00	£70.00	£120.00	£175.00
Hollom LNNL	*	*	£4.00	£6.00
Hollom MNNR (replacement)	£6.00	£14.00	£25.00	£35.00
Hollom MNN (replacement)	£6.00	£15.00	£25.00	£35.00
Hollom NNM (replacement)	*	£10.00	£15.00	£22.00
Hollom 'G' reverse	*	£3.00	£6.00	£10.00
Hollom 'G' reverse MNNL (replacement)	*	£12.00	£18.00	£25.00
Fforde LNNL	*	*	£4.00	£7.00
Fforde MNNL (replacement)	*	£10.00	£18.00	£25.00
Fforde LNNM (replacement)	*	£5.00	£11.00	£14.00
Fforde 'G' reverse	*	*	£4.00	£8.00
Fforde 'G' reverse MNNL (replacement)	£5.00	£15.00	£28.00	£40.00
Fforde 'G' reverse LNNM (replacement)	*	£18.00	£27.00	£36.00
Page LNNL	*	*	£3.00	£6.00
Page LNNM (replacement)	*	£5.00	£11.00	£14.00
Page LLNN	*	*	£3.00	£6.00
Page MLNN (replacement)	*	*	£5.00	£8.00
Page, state robes type, LNN	*	*	£3.00	£5.00
Page MNN (replacement)	£20.00	£50.00	£75.00	£100.00
Page NNL	*	*	£3.00	£5.00
Page LNNL	*	*	£4.00	£7.00
Somerset LLNN	*	*	£3.00	£5.00

BANK OF ENGLAND 5 POUND NOTES

	F 55	VF 75	EF 90	UNC 100
Nairne black on white type	£87.00	£150.00	£230.00	£325.00
Harvey	£35.00	£65.00	£85.00	£110.00
Mahon	£45.00	£80.00	£145.00	£185.00
Catterns	£30.00	£65.00	£125.00	£165.00
Peppiatt	£25.00	£35.00	£60.00	£80.00
Peppiatt threaded thick paper	£25.00	£35.00	£55.00	£70.00
Peppiatt thin paper	£25.00	£35.00	£55.00	£75.00
Beale	£25.00	£35.00	£50.00	£70.00
O'Brien LNN	£25.00	£35.00	£55.00	£75.00
O'Brien LNNL	£25.00	£35.00	£50.00	£70.00
O'Brien, Britannia type, shaded symbols on reverse	*	£10.00	£14.00	£18.00
O'Brien outline symbols reverse	*	£10.00	£14.00	£18.00

BRITISH BANKNOTES

	F	VF	EF	UNC
Hollom portrait type, LNN	*	£9.00	£12.00	£17.00
Hollom MNN (replacement)	£20.00	£35.00	£55.00	£70.00
Fforde LNN	*	£7.00	£12.00	£17.00
Fforde MNN (replacement)	£20.00	£35.00	£50.00	£65.00
Fforde NNL	*	£7.00	£12.00	£17.00
Fforde NNM (replacement)	£20.00	£35.00	£50.00	£65.00
Page NNL	*	£9.00	£14.00	£20.00
Page NNM (replacement)	£20.00	£35.00	£65.00	£80.00
Page state robes, type LNN	*	*	£12.00	£17.00
Page MNN (replacement)	£18.00	£30.00	£55.00	£80.00
Page 'L' reverse NNL	*	*	£12.00	£17.00
Page 'L' reverse NNM (replacement)	£18.00	£30.00	£55.00	£80.00
Page 'L' reverse LLNN	*	*	£11.00	£16.00
Somerset LLNN	*	*	£12.00	£16.00
Somerset wide thread	*	*	£11.00	£15.00
Gill LLNN	*	*	*	£13.00
Gill, Stephenson reverse, LNN	*	*	*	£7.00

BANK OF ENGLAND 10 POUND NOTES

	F	VF	EF	UNC
Nairne black on white type	£170.00	£290.00	£390.00	£540.00
Harvey	£50.00	£130.00	£185.00	£240.00
Mahon	£65.00	£160.00	£210.00	£285.00
Catterns	£45.00	£125.00	£185.00	£240.00
Peppiatt	£40.00	£85.00	£135.00	£165.00
Hollom portrait type	*	*	£25.00	£34.00
Fforde	*	*	£22.00	£32.00
Page LNN	*	*	£21.00	£31.00
Page MNN (replacement)	*	£15.00	£25.00	£35.00
Page state robes type LNN	*	*	£20.00	£30.00
Page MNN (replacement)	£25.00	£35.00	£50.00	£65.00
Somerset LNN	*	*	£24.00	£32.00
Somerset NNL	*	*	£24.00	£32.00
Somerset LLNN	*	*	£18.00	£24.00
Somerset LLNN windowed thread	*	*	*	£22.00
Gill LLNN	*	*	*	£15.00

BANK OF ENGLAND 20 POUND NOTES

	F	VF	EF	UNC
Fforde	*	£38.00	£72.00	£100.00
Fforde MNN (replacement)	£70.00	£95.00	£155.00	£200.00
Page	*	£34.00	£45.00	£75.00
Page MNN (replacement)	*	£65.00	£95.00	£125.00
Somerset LNN	*	£30.00	£45.00	£60.00
Somerset windowed thread, NNL	*	*	£35.00	£45.00
Gill NNL	*	*	*	£32.00

BANK OF ENGLAND 50 POUND NOTES

	F	VF	EF	UNC
Somerset	*	*	£70.00	£95.00
Somerset windowed thread	*	*	*	£70.00
Gill, LNN	*	*	*	£60.00

british gallantry award medals

General comments

When putting a price on a gallantry award, it is essential to bear in mind the following:

1 Many awards are not named, therefore the badge, cross or medal by itself, without evidence supporting the award or details of the recipient, is worth a great deal less. The prices given are for verified awards.

2 The citation relating to the award affects its value. Those given for a specific act of gallantry are worth a great deal more than general citations. When a citation is not available, the circumstances of the award can usually be found in regimental histories.

3 In many cases gallantry awards are sold as part of a group which could include medals which are themselves valuable, thus giving an inflated idea of the value of the award on its own.

4 It is important to remember that the policy for gallantry awards was often more liberal in the past than in recent years, also that the DSC, MC, DFC, AFC, DSM, MM, DFM and AFM were created during WWI; previously there were only the DSO for junior officers and the DCM for ORs. Therefore these were awarded in cases where lesser awards would have been given in later years.

5 When the award is made to a service other than the one for which it was intended (ie the DFC to the RN or the Army), the value is greatly increased.

6 Most of the gallantry awards can be awarded bars to denote further acts of gallantry. The value of these has not been given because it varies so much according to the circumstances of each case.

7 The difference between 1st and 2nd type is as follows:

	1st type
George V	Bare head
George VI	
(crosses)	GRI
Medals	Including INDIAE IMP
Elizabeth II	Legend D G BR OMN REGINA F D

	2nd type
George V	Crowned head
George VI	
(crosses)	GVIR
Medals	No mention of India in the legend
Elizabeth II	Legend DEI REGINA F D

8 Finally the MSM has been included, although its main purpose was to reward long service of senior NCOs, during the period 1916-28, it was also awarded for services in the field which did not meet the requirements of the MM or DCM and even in a few cases for gallantry, not in the field. This is the most common type of this medal.

Victoria Cross (1856). Named

The rarest of all gallantry awards, its value varies so much in each case that it is not possible to put a value on it. To illustrate this a VC to a WWI air ace sold for £99,000 in November 1988 whilst one to a WWI Pte in the Lancashire Fusiliers sold for only £18,700 in September 1990.

George Cross (1940). Named

Holders of the Empire Gallantry Medal could exchange it for the GC. Few GCs have been awarded and the price varies a great deal in each case, similar to the VC. As a general rule Military awards post 1940 are the most valuable ones, especially those given for bomb disposal work, followed by exchange awards to the Military. Civilian awards are worth less.

The Most Excellent Order of the British Empire (Military Division) 1917. Unnamed

The OBE and the MBE have been awarded for gallantry, particularly in the case of escaped POWs, agents working behind the enemy lines, and foreign nationals helping in these activities. It is only since 1957 that there has been a visible indication of such awards on the ribbon in the form of an emblem with two silver oak leaves. Previously one had to rely on the citation, not always available, and often of a very general nature. The Military Division is indicated by a central vertical grey stripe on the ribbon.

With gallantry emblem

OBE	Rar
MBE	£1,000-£2,00

For gallantry without emblem

OBE	Rar
MBE	£1,000-£1,50

Medal of the Order of the British Empire. Military Division (1918-22). Unnamed

In this case only the Military Division i indicated by a red central stripe on th ribbon.

British Empire Medal (Military Division) (1922). Named

George V	£250.00-£350.
George VI 1st type	Ra
2nd type	Ra
Elizabeth II (since 1957 gallantry awards bear the silver emblem)	£1,000-£1,5

Medal of the Order of the British Empire for Gallantry (1922). Named

(This medal was replaced by the George Cross in 1940)

George V	Rare
George VI	Ra

Distinguished Service Order (1886). Unnamed

George V	£300.00-£400.00
George VI 1st type	£400.00-£600.00
George VI 2nd type	£1,000-£1,5
Elizabeth II	£1,500-£2,0

Distinguished Service Cross (1914). Unnamed

George V	£200.00-£300.00
George VI 1st type	£300.00-£400.00
George VI 2nd type	£1,000-£1,5
Elizabeth II	£1,500-£2,0

Military Cross (1914). Unnamed

George V	£150.00-£200.00
George VI 1st type	£200.00-£350.00
George VI 2nd type	£750.00-£1,0
Elizabeth II	£1,000-£1,5

Distinguished Flying Cross (1918). Unnamed

George V	£500.00-£750.00	George VI 2nd type £800.00-£1,000
George VI 1st type	£250.00-£350.00	Elizabeth II £1,000-£1,500

Air Force Cross (1918). Unnamed

George V	£600.00-£800.00	George VI 2nd type £600.00-£800.00
George VI 1st type	£350.00-£500.00	Elizabeth II £600.00-£800.00

Distinguished Conduct Medal (1854). Named

George V 1st type	£100.00-£200.00	George VI 2nd type £1,500-£2,000
George V 2nd type	£1,500-£1,800	Elizabeth II 1st type £1,500-£2,000
George VI 1st type	£400.00-£500.00	Elizabeth II 2nd type £1,200-£1,500

Distinguished Conduct Medal (Colonial & Dominions) (1894). Named

(This medal was awarded up to 1942 only)

George V awards to King's African Rifles	£400.00-£500.00
George V awards to West African Frontier Force	£450.00-£600.00
George VI (1st type only)	£450.00-£500.00
George VI awards to King's African Rifles	£400.00-£500.00
George VI awards to West African Frontier Force	£500.00-£600.00

Conspicuous Gallantry Medal (1855). Named

George V	Rare	George VI 2nd type (Flying est 1942) £2,000-£3,000
George VI 1st type	Rare	Elizabeth II (Flying) £2,500-£3,500

George Medal (1940). Named

George VI 1st type	£450.00-£600.00	Elizabeth II 1st type £1,000-£1,500
George 2nd type	£500.00-£650.00	Elizabeth 2nd type £1,000-£1,500

Distinguished Service Medal (1914). Named

George V	£150.00-£200.00	Elizabeth II 1st type £1,500-£2,000
George VI 1st type	£190.00-£275.00	Elizabeth II 2nd type £1,200-£1,500
George VI 2nd type	£1,000-£1,500	

Military Medal (1916). Named

George V 1st type	£40.00-£60.00	George VI 2nd type £750.00-£1,000
George V 2nd type	£1,000-£1,250	Elizabeth II 1st type £750.00-£1,000
George VI 1st type	£250.00-£350.00	Elizabeth II 2nd type £750.00-£1,000

Distinguished Flying Medal (1918). Named

George V 1st type	£900.00-£1,000	George VI 2nd type £1,000-£1,250
George V 2nd type	£1,500-£2,000	Elizabeth II £1,250-£1,500
George VI 1st type	£300.00-£400.00	

Air Force Medal (1918). Named

George V 1st type	£600.00-£800.00	George VI 1st type £600.00-£800.00
George V 2nd type	£750.00-£1,000	George VI 2nd type £500.00-£750.00
		Elizabeth II £750.00-£850.00

Queen's Gallantry Medal (1974). Named

Elizabeth II Military awards	£1,000-£1,500

Meritorious Service Medal (1845). Named

George V	£30.00-£50.00

british war medal prices

WORLD WAR I

1914 Star		
Bar 5th AUG-22nd NOV 1914	£10.00 –	£18.
Without bar	£8.00 –	£15.
1914-15 Star	£4.00 –	£8.
British War Medal 1914-20		
Silver	£5.00 –	£10.
Bronze	£20.00 –	£40.
Victory Medal	£2.00 –	£3.
South African issue	£10.00 –	£15.
Mercantile Marine War Medal 1914-1918	£8.00 –	£12.
Territorial War Medal 1914-1919	£25.00 –	£40

The above are for medals issued to the Army or the Navy (except, of course, the Mercantile Marine W
Medal). The 1914 and 1914-15 Stars, the British War Medal and the Victory Medal are worth about double whe
issued to the RFC or the RNAS.

Allied Subjects Medal 1914-18		
Silver	£500.00 –	£650
Bronze	£300.00 –	£400
British Red Cross Commemorative Medal of the 1914-1918 War	£4.00 –	£5.
Special Constabulary LS & GC Medal, George V		
clasp THE GREAT WAR 1914-18	£6.00 –	£8
Canadian Memorial Cross 1914-18	£15.00 –	£20

INDIA GENERAL SERVICE MEDAL 1936-1939

(Never issued without a bar)

Royal Mint issue		
Bar NORTH WEST FRONTIER 1936-37	£35.00 –	£60
Bar NORTH WEST FRONTIER 1937-39	£32.00 –	£60.
Both bars	£70.00 –	£90.
Calcutta issue		
Bar NORTH WEST FRONTIER 1936-37	£20.00 –	£30
Bar NORTH WEST FRONTIER 1937-39	£20.00 –	£30
Both bars	£30.00 –	£40

WORLD WAR II

1939-45 Star	£2.00 –	£3.
Bar BATTLE OF BRITAIN (if verified)	£300.00 –	£400
Atlantic Star	£8.00 –	£10.
Bar AIR CREW EUROPE (if verified)	£100.00 –	£150
Bar FRANCE & GERMANY (if verified)	£20.00 –	£25.

ir Crew Europe Star	£80.00 –	£100.00
Bar ATLANTIC or FRANCE & GERMANY (if verified)	£100.00 –	£150.00
frica Star	£6.00 –	£8.00
Bar NORTH AFRICA 1942-43, EIGHTH ARMY or FIRST ARMY	£8.00 –	£10.00
urma Star	£6.00 –	£8.00
Bar PACIFIC (if verified)	£15.00 –	£18.00
acific Star	£12.00 –	£15.00
Bar BURMA (if verified)	£18.00 –	£20.00
aly Star	£5.00 –	£6.00
rance & Germany Star	£7.00 –	£9.00
efence Medal	£2.50 –	£5.00
Canadian issue in silver	£10.00 –	£12.00
ar Medal	£2.50 –	£5.00
Canadian issue in silver	£10.00 –	£12.00
ustralian Service Medal	£12.00 –	£15.00
anadian Volunteer Service Medal	£12.00 –	£15.00
with clasp	£15.00 –	£20.00
dia Service Medal	£10.00 –	£15.00
ew Zealand War Service Medal	£12.00 –	£15.00
outh Africa War Service Medal	£32.00 –	£45.00
frica Service Medal	£10.00 –	£15.00
outhern Rhodesia Service Medal	£90.00 –	£140.00
ng's Medal for Courage in the Cause of Freedom 1939-45	£400.00 –	£600.00
ng's Medal for Service in the Cause of Freedom 1939-45	£300.00 –	£475.00

KOREA 1950-1953

orean War Medal	£40.00 –	£60.00
to the Gloucestershire Regiment	£150.00 –	£175.00
Canadian issue in silver	£60.00 –	£80.00
South African issue	£325.00 –	£375.00
Southern Rhodesian issue	Rare	
ited Nations Korean Medal	£12.00 –	£18.00

NAVAL GENERAL SERVICE MEDAL
1915-1964

(Never issued without a bar)

orge V 1911-1936		
Bar PERSIAN GULF 1909-14	£42.00 –	£65.00
Bar IRAQ 1919-20	£300.00 –	£400.00
Bar N W PERSIA 1919-20	£400.00 –	£500.00
Bar N W PERSIA 1920	£400.00 –	£500.00
orge VI 1937-1952		
Bar PALESTINE 1936-1939	£32.00 –	£55.00
Bar S E ASIA 1945-46	£40.00 –	£60.00
Bar PALESTINE 1945-48	£50.00 –	£75.00
Bar MALAYA	£35.00 –	£48.00
Bar YANGTZE 1949	£300.00 –	£400.00
to HMS Amethyst	£400.00 –	£550.00
Bar MINESWEEPING 1945-51	£65.00 –	£100.00
zabeth II 1953—		
Bar MALAYA	£35.00 –	£45.00
ar BOMB & MINE CLEARANCE 1945-53	£275.00 –	£300.00
ar BOMB & MINE CLEARANCE MEDITERRANEAN	£350.00 –	£400.00
ar CYPRUS	£30.00 –	£40.00
ar NEAR EAST	£50.00 –	£70.00
ar ARABIAN PENINSULA	£50.00 –	£60.00
ar BRUNEI	£100.00 –	£130.00

GENERAL SERVICE MEDAL
1918-1964

(Army and RAF — never issued without a bar)

George V 1911-1936

Bar SOUTH PERSIA	£40.00 –	£50.00
Bar KURDISTAN	£30.00 –	£60.00
Bar IRAQ	£25.00 –	£40.00
Bar N W PERSIA	£30.00 –	£55.0
Bar SOUTHERN DESERT — IRAQ	£150.00 –	£200.0
Bar NORTHERN KURDISTAN	£350.00 –	£400.0

George VI 1937-1952

Bar PALESTINE	£18.00 –	£35.00
Bar S E ASIA 1945-46 named	£45.00 –	£60.00
unnamed	£15.00 –	£18.00
Bar BOMB AND MINE CLEARANCE 1945-49	£150.00 –	£200.0
Bar PALESTINE 1945-48	£15.00 –	£35.00
Bar MALAYA	£16.00 –	£20.00

Elizabeth II 1953—

Bar BOMB AND MINE CLEARANCE 1949-56	£120.00 –	£130.0
Bar MALAYA	£15.00 –	£25.0
Bar CYPRUS	£12.00 –	£20.0
Bar NEAR EAST	£28.00 –	£45.0
Bar ARABIAN PENINSULA	£18.00 –	£35.0
Bar BRUNEI	£70.00 –	£80.

GENERAL SERVICE MEDAL
1962

(Issued to all three services)

Bar BORNEO	£20.00 –	£30.
Bar RADFAN	£40.00 –	£60.
Bar SOUTH ARABIA	£20.00 –	£30.
Bar SOUTH VIETNAM (Australian Forces only)	£200.00 –	£250.0
Bar NORTHERN IRELAND	£18.00 –	£25.
Bar DHOFAR	£120.00 –	£160.
Bar MALAY PENINSULA	£22.00 –	£30.
Bar LEBANON	£500.00 –	£600.
Bar GULF	Rare	

VIETNAM

Australian Service Medal for Vietnam (1964)	£80.00 –	£100.0
South Vietnam Service Medal	£8.00 –	£10.

RHODESIA 1979-1980

Rhodesia Medal	£250.00 –	£300.

SOUTH ATLANTIC 1982

South Atlantic Medal	£100.00 –	£150.
with rosette	£120.00 –	£175.

NUMISMATIC DICTIONARY

by C W HILL

Æ – Numismatic symbol for copper bronze, brass or coins of this colour.

AR – Numismatic symbol for silver coins.

AV – Numismatic symbol for gold coins.

Agonistic – Descriptive term for coins which commemorate a religious festival at which games were held.

Alliance – Term applied to some ancient Greek coins struck in common by two or more cities or states.

Androcephalous – Descriptive term for images, such as the Sphynx, which incorporate a man's head.

Angel (originally angel-nobel) – Gold coin equal to one-third of a pound, introduced by Edward IV in 1465. Its name was derived from the obverse design, showing St Michael slaying Satan in the form of a dragon on the obverse. The angel was minted regularly until the reign of Charles I.

Annulet – Ring. Often used as a symbol on coins with various significations.

Assay – Test to ascertain the weight and purity, etc, of precious metal.

B – Mint-mark of the Bristol Mint found on silver coins of William III.

B.M. – Initials of Sir Bertram Mackennal, designer.

B.P. – Initials of Benedetto Pistrucci, designer and engraver.

BU – Brilliant Uncirculated. Grade.

Base – Term applied to non-precious metals such as copper.

Bawbee – Scottish coin introduced by James V in 1538. Made of billon, it was equal to six Scottish pence or one English halfpenny. It was last minted as a copper coin for William III.

Becker, Karl – Notorious forger of ancient coins and medals who worked near Frankfurt between 1815 and 1825.

Billon – Alloy of copper and silver.

Blank – Coin-shaped piece of metal which has been prepared for minting but is as yet unstruck.

Bodle – Scottish copper coin worth one sixth of an English penny. Minted 1642-97, its name may have been derived from Bothwell, Master of the Mint.

Boehm, Sir Joseph – Sculptor and designer of many public monuments. Designed the Jubilee Head portrait on the coins of Queen Victoria, 1887-92. Born Vienna 1834, died 1890.

Bonnet – A variety of the Scottish gold ducat issued in 1539 and 1540. So-called because it depicts James V sporting a flat bonnet. First coin of the British Isles to show the date.

Boulton, Matthew – Founder of the Soho Mint in Birmingham (1762) and striker of the Cartwheel coinage.

Breeches Money – Nickname given to the gold and silver coins minted during the Commonwealth period, 1649-1660. Their reverse design showed the English cross of St George and the Irish harp on two shields joined at the top. The resultant shape was similar to men's baggy breeches, hence the name.

BRITT. and BRITT. OMN. – BRITT is the abbreviated plural form of Britanniarum ('of the Britains', ie Britain and its foreign possessions) and OMN is an appreciation of the service given by the colonies during the Boer War.

Broad – Term used for a hammered gold coin worth 20s 0d, originally called a unite. A reference to the size of the coins, which were large and thin, the word was used well into the reign of Charles II.

Brock, Sir Thomas – Sculptor and designer of many portrait busts, statues and public monuments. Designed the Veiled Head portrait on the coins of Queen Victoria, 1893-1901. Born Worcester 1847, died 1922.

Brockage – Mis-struck coin featuring the inverted impression, as well as the normal, of either the obverse or reverse design only. Caused by a previous coin lodging in the coinage press and acting as an inverted die when the piece in question is being struck.

Bull Head – Nickname given to the portrait of George III on the halfcrowns minted in 1816 and 1817. The portrait, by Benedetto Pistrucci, showed the King's head from behind his right shoulder, emphasising his heavy features and giving him a thick neck like a bull.

Bun Head – Nickname given to the portrait of Queen Victoria on the bronze coins issued between 1860 and 1894. These showed the Queen with her hair gathered in a 'bun'.

C – Mint-mark of the Chester Mint found on silver coins of William III.

C – Mint-mark of the Ottawa Mint found on gold sovereigns of Edward VII and George V.

C.T. – Initials of Cecil Thomas, designer.

Cache – Term loosely used for treasure trove or any hoard of coins.

Cartwheels – Nickname given to the large penny and twopenny coins minted by Matthew Boulton in 1797 at his 'manufactory' at Soho, near Birmingham. The pennies contained 1oz of copper and the twopences 2oz, so that their metal content was equivalent to their face value. The coins were never reissued, not only because they were so cumbersome but also because as the price of copper rose unscrupulous merchants could make a profit by melting the coins to obtain the metal.

Chisel Cut – Small nick often found on ancient coins, probably made by merchants testing the metal's purity.

Chop Mark – Private symbol made by a native merchant of Hong Kong guaranteeing the genuineness of a dollar passing through his hands.

Clipping – The illegal removal by unscrupulous persons of particles from the edge of a valuable coin for personal gain. Despite severe penalties, the practice was rife in the days of hammered coinage. In an endeavour to prevent it,

Henry III introduced the Long Cross Penny in 1247, but the practice was not finally eliminated until the introduction of grained edges on milled coins during the reign of Charles II.

Coinage Design – Term used when a piece incorporates an obverse and reverse that are upside-down in relation to one another.

Communion Token – A token, usually of lead, pewter or white metal, issued in Scotland and in some Scottish communities overseas to indicate that a Presbyterian churchgoer was to be admitted to the communion service. The tokens usually bore the name of the church by which they were issued, a Biblical text and sometimes the name of the minister. In recent years they have been replaced by printed cards.

Convention Money – Currency shared by two or more medieval European cities.

Copper Nose – Nickname given to the silver coins issued during the last years of Henry VIII's reign and for a few years after his death in 1547. The coins were so debased, containing about 75% copper to 25% silver, that when they became worn the coppery tinge was clearly visible. As the coins had a full-face or three-quarter face portrait of the King, the copper showed most plainly on the most prominent feature of the design, his nose.

Countermark – Number, letter or device stamped on a coin subsequent to its issue guaranteeing or changing its value, or rendering it current in a country other than that for which it was issued.

Cowry – Small sea-shell used in the East and on the African coast as currency.

Crown – The first English crown was a gold coin introduced in 1526 by Henry VIII and valued at 4s 6d. Gold crowns were last minted during the reign of Charles I but silver crowns were introduced in 1551, as part of a new coinage for Edward VI. Since the introduction of decimal currency in 1971 the 25 pence commemorative coins have replaced the crown and are still officially known by that name. Nowadays the term is also generally applied to any silver or cupronickel coin of large size.

Crown Gold – Gold used for English currency which has an alloy of two carats, ie 22 carats fine.

Cuirassed – Wearing body armour.

Cumberland Jack – When Princess Victoria succeeded to the British throne in 1837, she was not entitled to rule also in Hanover, which had belonged to the British Crown since the accession of George I in 1714, because the Salic Law, banning women from the succession, was in force there. Instead her nearest male relative, the Duke of Cumberland, went to become King of Hanover. He was widely unpopular for his illiberal political views and because he was believed to have murdered his valet. Small brass medalets showing him on horseback, sometimes with a monkey's face, and inscribed with the words TO HANOVER were issued by his political opponents. These are popularly known as Cumberland Jacks.

Cupro-nickel – Alloy consisting of 75% copper and 25% nickel.

Currency Bar – Sword-shaped block of iron used as money in ancient times.

De.S. – George William de Saulles, designer.

Dandiprat – Any very small coin.

Debase – To lower the intrinsic value of a coin by altering its purity.

Decimal – Currency using denominations in units of ten.

Decoration – Mostly awarded for gallantry (VC, GC, MC, etc), and in a few cases to long service officers (TD, VRD, etc).

Depreciation – The lowering in value of one currency in relation to another.

De Saulles, George William – (1862-1903) Engraver for John Pinches 1884, and at the Royal Mint 1892. Designed the portrait of Edward VII on British and colonial coins, 1902-10, and the standing Britannia reverse of the Edwardian florin. Medals include Edward VII Coronation, South Africa 1899-1902 and Ashanti 1900.

Device – Pattern or emblem used in an heraldic sense on coins.

Die – Metal stamp or punch engraved with the obverse or reverse design from which coins are struck.

Die-flaw – Raised mark on the surface of a coin unintentionally caused by a pit or crack in the die.

Die Number – Minute number on a coin from which the die can be traced.

Dioscuri – Castor and Pollux, the Heavenly Twins and sons of Zeus.

Dollar, counterstamped – To alleviate the chronic shortage of silver, Spanish-American 8 reales pieces were overstruck in 1797 with an oval countermark bearing the head of George III rendering them current for 4s 9d as British regal coinage. Spanish-American 4 reales pieces were also similarly counter stamped. In 1799 an octagonal countermark was used on the dollar to counteract forgery, and in 1804 Spanish dollars were entirely overstruck to create a token 5 shilling piece, inscribed FIVE SHILLING DOLLAR.

Double-Florin – A silver coin introduced in 1887 as a step towards the decimalisation of the currency. Equal to two florins or four shillings, the double-florins were unpopular because they were easily confused with the crowns, or 5 shilling pieces, which measured only 2¾mm more in diameter. The double-florin was discontinued in 1890.

Dump – Generally, any small, thick coin.

Duodecimal – Currency which uses denominations in units of twelve.

Dyce, William – Portrait painter. Designed the reverse of the 1847 and 1853 Gothic crowns and of the 1848 Godless florin. Born Aberdeen 1806, died 1864.

E – Mint-mark of the Exeter Mint found on silver coins of William III.

E and E*– Mint-marks of the Edinburgh Mint found on silver coins of Queen Anne dated 1707-1709.

EF – Extremely Fine. Grade.

E.F. – Initials of Edgar Fuller, designer.

E.I.C. – Provenance mark of the East India Company on George II gold coins denoting that the gold was supplied by the Company.

Elephant (& Castle) – Provenance mark of the African ('Guinea') Co found on gold and silver coins of Charles II to 1675 and, with a castle, on those of Charles II to George II.

Engrailing – The succession of dots or similar curved indentations on the edge of a coin.

Essay – Trial piece.

Exergue – Section below and apart from the main design of a coin in which the date, value, etc, may be inscribed.

F – Fine. Grade.

FDC – Fleur-de-Coin. Grade.

Farthing – It was common practice in Anglo-Saxon and Norman times to obtain small change by cutting silver pennies into halves or quarters. The latter were known as farthings, from the Anglo-Saxon word *feorthing*, meaning a fourth part. Round silver farthings were introduced in England by Edward I in 1279. By the 16th century the rise in the price of silver had made the minting of farthings uneconomic and they were discontinued during the reign of Edward VI. Farthings were re-introduced as copper coins, manufactured under licence for James I and as regal coins for Charles II in 1672. From 1860 they were made of bronze and the last were issued in 1956.

Field – All that part of a coin not occupied by the design or legend.

Filler – Coin of poor condition used to complete a collection temporarily until a better specimen is acquired.

Flan – Term used to refer to the piece of metal, or blank, after it has been struck.

Florin – First minted in Florence in 1252 as a gold coin, this derived its name, *fiorino* in Italian, from the flower, a lily, on its reverse. In 1344 it was introduced in England as a gold coin worth 6s 0d but was never reissued. The first English silver florins were issued in 1849, though Pattern coins dated 1848 are also known. The florins were intended to replace the halfcrowns as a step towards a decimal currency. They survive as the decimal 10 pence.

G.L. – Initials of Gilbert Ledward, designer.

Gardner, William – Specialist in heraldry and calligraphy. Designed the reverses of the English and Scottish shillings, 1953-66, of the brass threepence, 1953-67, and of the decimal 20 pence, also other Commonwealth coins. Medal designs include the George VI Medal for Courage in the Cause of Freedom. Born Northumberland 1914.

Geat or **Git** – Channel through which molten metal runs in moulding process.

Ghost – Image of the design on one side of a coin visible on the other.

Ghost Penny – Nickname given to the first pennies of George V, minted between 1911 and 1927. Because of the size of the portrait on the obverse a ghost of this could be seen on the reverse of the coins. This was eliminated by the introduction of a smaller portrait in 1928 on both the halfpenny and penny.

Gillick, Mary – Sculptress specialising in bronze relief memorials. Designed the portrait of Queen Elizabeth II on British coins, 1953-67, also used on other Commonwealth coins. Born Nottingham 1881, died 1965.

Godless Florin – The traditional inscription DEI GRATIA FID.DEF., meaning 'By the Grace of God, Defender of the Faith', was omitted from the design of the silver florins issued in 1849. Described by many of the clergy as 'Godless' or 'Graceless', the coins were replaced in 1851 by florins of a new design which included the inscription.

Gothic Crown – Name given to the crowns minted in 1847 and 1853. The portrait of Queen Victoria by William Wyon showing her in a crown and an elaborately embroidered dress, and the Early English style of lettering used for the inscriptions, reflected the Gothic revival in art and architecture.

Gothic Florin – Companion coin to the Gothic crown, the florin was minted between 1851 and 1887.

Graceless florin – Another name for the Godless florin.

Graining – The serrations around the edge of a coin.

Groat – A silver coin worth fourpence which was introduced in 1279 by Edward I. Its name was derived from its French counterpart, the *gros tournois*, which had been minted twenty years earlier at Tours. Although not popular at first because it represented too large a sum to be convenient for the poorer classes, the groat was reissued in 1351 by Edward III and was minted regularly until 1662. It then survived as one of the Maundy coins, some of which circulated. In 1836 the groat was revived as an ordinary coin but was discontinued as such after 1855, except for a small issue in 1888 for use in British Guiana and the West Indies.

Guinea – Gold coin introduced in 1663 as a 20 shilling piece and originally known as a Guinea pound because much of the gold for minting it was brought from the Guinea coast of West Africa. Its value fluctuated with the price of gold between 20s 0d and 30s 0d until it was finally fixed at 21s 0d in 1717. The guinea was last minted in 1813 and was replaced in 1817 by the sovereign.

Gun Money – Name given to coins minted in Ireland in 1689 and 1690 during the abortive attempt of James II to regain his throne from William III. Lacking gold and silver with which to pay his troops, James ordered coins to be minted of copper, brass and gun-metal in values of sixpence, shilling, halfcrown and crown. They were to be redeemed at face value for gold and silver coins after James had defeated the usurper. To ensure that the redemption should be organised equitably, the gun money coins were inscribed with the month as well as the year of their issue. After the defeat of James II in 1690, William III ordered the gun money to be accepted at the value of its metal content, so that the crown was valued at 1d, the halfcrown at ¾d, and the shillings and sixpences at a ¼d each.

H – Mint-mark of Ralph Heaton & Sons' Birmingham Mint found on British bronze and other colonial coins.

H.P. – Initials of Thomas Humphrey Paget, designer.

Halfcrown – Introduced as a gold coin by Henry VIII and minted regularly until the reign of James I. The halfcrown was also minted in silver by Edward VI and survived in this form until it was demonetised in 1970 preparatory to the introduction of decimal currency.

Half-farthing – A small copper coin intended for use in Ceylon but made legal

tender in Great Britain in 1842. It was first minted in 1828 but discontinued after 1856, although there was a small issue of Proof coins in 1868.

Halfpenny – Minted as a silver coin by a few of the Viking and Saxon kings but not a regular feature of the English coinage until the reign of Edward I. As the price of silver rose, the halfpennies became so small as to be a nuisance in circulation, those of Charles I measuring only 10mm in diameter. The first regal copper halfpennies were minted in 1672 and the coins have survived as the bronze decimal ½ pence.

Hammered – Term used to describe the age-old hand method by which coins were minted before the advent of machinery. The coins were struck by a heavy blow being delivered with a mallet to the blank, which was held between the obverse and reverse dies by tongs.

Hardhead – A billon coin first struck under Mary Queen of Scots. It served as small change, with a value of 1½d.

Hat Piece – A gold coin of James VI of Scotland worth 80s 0d which derived its name from the very tall hat worn by the King in the obverse portrait.

Helm – Edward III gold quarter-florin the obverse of which depicted a helmet surmounted by a lion.

I – Mint-mark of the Bombay Mint found on gold sovereigns of George V.

Incuse – Impressed, stamped in.

Intaglio – Hollowed out.

Ironside, Christopher – Designer and medallist. Designed the reverses of the British decimal coins. Born London 1913.

J.B.M. – Initials of Jean Baptiste Merlen, designer.

J.E.B. – Initials of Sir Joseph Boehm, designer.

Jack – Card counter made to resemble the sovereign.

Janiform – Two-faced head.

Jetton – A counter or token used in games or, during medieval times, as a means of calculating sums of money on chequered boards at the Exchequer.

Jubilee Head – The portrait of Queen Victoria designed by Sir Joseph Boehm for the gold and silver coins issued between 1887, the year of her Golden Jubilee, and 1892. Although dignified and life-like, the portrait was criticised because the Queen was wearing a disproportionately small crown.

Jugate – Having two or more heads joined or overlapping.

K. – Initial of Conrad Heinrich Kuchler, designer.

K.G. – Initials of Kruger Gray, designer.

K.N. – Mint-mark of the Kings Norton Metal Company's Birmingham Mint found on pennies of George V – 1918/19.

Key Date – Coin the date of which is more scarce and therefore of greater value than others in the same series.

Knife-Money – Chinese currency consisting of replicas, about 7in long, of a billhook representing the value of that tool.

L.C.W. – Initials of Leonard Charles Wyon, designer.

Laureate – Bearing a wreath of laurel leaves.

Laurel – Third coinage sovereign, or unite, of James I so called because the King is depicted wearing a laurel wreath crown.

Ledward, Gilbert – Sculptor and designer of several war memorials. Designed the reverse of the 1953 Coronation Crown. Born Chelsea 1888, died 1960.

Legend – Wording on the edge of a coin.

Leopard – Name given to the gold half-florin of Edward III, whose obverse shows a facing lion, known heraldically as a leopard.

Lima – Inscribed below the portrait of George II on gold and silver coins minted in 1745 and 1746 to indicate that the bullion used for these came from the capture of two French treasure ships, the Louis Erasme and the Marquis d'Antin, which had come from Peru. The ships were captured by two British privateers, the Prince Frederick and the Duke, which took the bullion to Bristol from whence it was transported to the Tower of London for use by the Royal Mint. As much of the bullion comprised pieces of eight bearing the Lima mint-mark, a request was made that the word 'Lima' be placed on the coins minted from them, to mark the event.

Lion – Silver denier of the Anglo-Gallic series which earned its name from the lion passant guardant present in the arms of Aquitaine. Demi-lions were also issued. A Scottish gold coin issued up to 1589 was known as a lion-noble. Half-lions were also struck.

Long Cross Penny – Replaced the Short Cross Penny. To deter unscrupulous people from clipping slivers of metal from the edges of silver pennies, Henry III in 1247 ordered the arms of the cross on the reverse of the coins to be extended to the edge of the design. If more than one end of the arms of the cross were missing, the coins ceased to be legal tender.

M – Mint-mark of the Melbourne Mint found on gold half-sovereigns and sovereigns of Victoria, Edward VII and George V.

M.G. – Initials of Mary Gillick, designer.

MM – Abbreviation for mint-mark.

Machin, Arnold – Sculptor and ceramic artist. Designed the portrait of Queen Elizabeth II on the British decimal and other Commonwealth coins. Born Stoke-on-Trent.

Mackennal, Sir Bertram – Sculptor of many public monuments and portrait busts. Designed the portrait of George V on British and colonial coins, 1911-36. Medal designs include the Coronation Medal of George V 1911, the portrait of George V on the second issue Polar Medal 1904, etc. Born Melbourne, Australia, 1863, died 1931.

Maklouf, Raphael – Israeli sculptor. Designed the two new portraits of Queen Elizabeth II for use on the coinage from 1985 onwards.

Mascle – Voided lozenge frequently used as a mint-mark, etc.

Matrix – Mould for making die punches.

Maundy Money – The small silver coins, 1, 2, 3 and 4 pence, which are specially minted for distribution to elderly men and women at a service on Maundy Thursday, the day before Good Friday. The number of coins distributed is dependent on the monarch's age.

Medal – Metal piece, not necessarily round in shape and usually attached to a ribbon awarded for military or other services or to commemorate a coronation, jubilee or other major event.

Medal Design – Term used when obverse and reverse are upright when placed on a horizontal plane.

Medallion – Metal coin-like piece struck commercially as a memento, but not as an award or reward.

Merk – A colloquial derivation of mark. The half-merk was a Scottish silver coin first issued by James VI in 1572 and valued at 6s 8d. Merks and double-merks were issued in 1578-80 and became known as thistle half-dollars and thistle dollars because of their reverse thistle design. Quarter-merks were also struck, and later 4 merks by Charles II.

Metcalfe, Percy – Sculptor and medallist. Designed the reverse of the 1935 George V Silver Jubilee crown and the Irish 1928, 1935 and decimal coinage series, also 1934 Australia florin. Born Wakefield 1895, died 1969.

Milled – Term used for machine-made coins produced in a coining press as opposed to by the hand-hammered method. No connection with milling.

Mint-mark – The initial, name or device included in the design of a coin to indicate when, where or by whom it has been minted.

Mis-strike – Coin on which the design has not been struck centrally on the flan.

Model – Imitation, usually brass, of Victorian coinage used in Christmas crackers or as a card counter but sometimes as a serious suggestion for an improved coinage.

Modified Effigy – Modified portrait of George V with sharper detail in the design first introduced on the halfpenny in 1925 and on the rest of the coinage from 1926. On the halfpenny and penny the Modified Effigy was replaced in 1928 by the Small Head to eliminate ghosting.

Mule – Hybrid coin. Piece featuring non-matching obverse and reverse.

N – Mint-mark of the Norwich Mint found on silver coins of William III.

Nemon, Oscar – Sculptor and medallist. Designed the reverse of the 1965 Churchill crown. Born Yugoslavia 1906.

Nike – Goddess of Victory. Frequent device on Greek and Roman coins.

Noble – Gold coin introduced in 1344 by Edward III, superseding the florin. It was valued at 6s 8d, one third of a pound, which for many years remained the standard fee for the professional services of a lawyer. The noble was replaced in 1465 by the angel.

Numismatics – Science and study of coins and medals.

Numismatist – Student of numismatics.

Obolus – Latin for halfpenny.

Obsidional Money – Coins minted for the garrison of a besieged town. Refers particularly to the siege pieces issued during the Civil War for the Royalist forces besieged in Carlisle, Colchester, Newark, Pontefract and Scarborough. Similar emergency coins were James II's Irish gun money.

Obverse – That side of a coin featuring the more important device or the bust of the reigning monarch or head of state.

Old Head – see Veiled Head.

Order – Originally a fraternity of knights headed by the sovereign, now the highest form of recognition (except for gallantry in the UK) given by a state to an individual, which in the UK grants a knighthood with the higher classes. Insignia, generally in the form of stars and sash, for the first three classes.

Overstrike – Piece whose design has been implanted on that of another coin instead of on a blank.

P – Mint-mark of the Perth Mint found on gold half-sovereigns and sovereigns of Victoria, Edward VII and George V.

PM – Mint-mark of the Pobjoy Mint. This is found on post-1973 Isle of Man coinage issues.

P.M. – Initials of Percy Metcalfe, designer.

Paget, Thomas Humphrey – Designed the unissued coinage of Edward VIII, 1936; the **Golden Hind** reverse of the halfpenny, 1937-67, and the portrait of George VI on many Commonwealth coins. Also the 1953 Rhodesia crown and 1966 Irish 10 shillings. Born Croxley Green 1893, died 1974.

Patina – The colouring – usually green – on a coin caused by oxidisation of the metal.

Pattern – Unofficial design struck as a suggested coin type.

Penny – Based on the Roman denarius, the English penny was a silver coin introduced during the 8th century by two little-known Anglo-Saxon kings of Kent and popularised by the powerful King Offa of Mercia. Because of the rising price of silver and the need for a greater number of coins as trade and commerce increased, the silver penny was steadily reduced in size. The pennies of Elizabeth I were only about one-third the weight of those of William the Conqueror, and the metal was much debased. The first regal copper pennies were not issued until 1797. The silver penny survives in the Maundy money.

Pheon – Heraldic term for a barbed arrowhead, directed downwards.

Piece de Plaisir – Fancy piece. Coin struck in limited quantity for a special purpose and usually in a noble metal.

Piedfort – Type of Pattern struck on a thick flan.

Pile – Lower die incorporating the obverse design used in the hammering process of coin production.

Pinchbeck – Cheap brass imitation of gold.

Pistole – Struck from African gold in the reign of William III, the pistole and half-pistole were Scottish coins worth £12 and £6 respectively. Charles I also issued a gold pistole in the Irish money of necessity series. The origin of the name is uncertain, but may have evolved from the Spanish *pistola*, a metal plate.

Pistrucci, Benedetto – Cameo-engraver and medallist, succeeded Thomas Wyon as engraver at the Royal Mint 1817. Designed the gold and silver coinage of George III, 1816-20, and of George IV, 1820-25, including the celebrated 'St George and Dragon' still used on the reverse of British gold coins. Medal designs include the Queen Victoria Coronation Medal 1838, and dies for the Waterloo Medallion 1849. Born Italy 1784, died 1855.

Plack – A Scottish billon coin debased drastically over the years and left virtually worthless, its name has found its way into a proverbial expression meaning

'to the last farthing'. The word takes its name from the French *plaque* meaning disk or plate.

Planchet – Metal disc.

Plugged Money – Tin farthings and halfpennies of Charles II and James II with a copper plug to prevent counterfeiting.

Plume – Provenance mark found on British coins denoting that the coinage metal came from Welsh mines.

Pollard – Counterfeit penny struck in base silver and imported from Europe during the reign of Edward I.

Potin – Base alloy not containing silver.

Pound – Originated as a weight, the amount of silver needed to mint 240 pennies. It was introduced as a coin, the gold pound sovereign, during the reign of King Henry VII. The present sovereign is the successor of this coin, although a large silver pound was minted as a temporary measure during the Civil War due to a shortage of gold.

Poynter, Sir Edward – Painter. Designed the reverse of the shilling and florin 1893-1901. Born Paris 1836, died 1919.

Privy – Secret mark on a coin used to indicate the moneyer of an issue.

Proof – A coin not intended for circulation, minted from specially polished dies and blanks which give it a mirror-like finish.

Provenance Mark – Symbol denoting the source of the metal used to make a coin.

Quarter-farthing – Minted between 1839 and 1853 for use in Ceylon, where it was the equivalent of half a Cingalese doit or half an Indian pie. Proof coins were also minted in 1868.

Rad – Abbreviation for radiate.

Rev – Abbreviation for reverse.

Radiate – Having rays or beams emanating from the head. Symbol of real or assumed divinity.

Ramatanka – Indian temple coin or medal depicting the religious epic, the Ramayana.

Relief – Raised design.

Re-strike – Coin struck from dies previously, although not normally current, temporarily, used.

Reverse – That side of a coin featuring the least important device.

Rider – A Scottish gold coin first issued under James III and taking its name from the obverse design of the King riding a charger apparently at some speed. James VI also issued riders but with a modified design, the horse having slowed down somewhat.

Rose – Provenance mark found on British coins denoting that the coinage metal came from English mines.

Roses and Plumes – Provenance mark found on British coins denoting that the coinage metal came from English and Welsh mines.

Ryal – Worth 30s 0d, the first ryals issued under Mary were withdrawn to facilitate the circulation of a more acceptable second issue showing the name of Mary Queen of Scots before that of her husband, Henry Darnley, the first juxtaposition of names having implied that he was joint ruler. Ryals were known in England as rose nobles.

– – Mint-mark of the Sydney Mint found on gold half-sovereigns and sovereigns of Victoria, Edward VII and George V.

.A. – Mint-mark of the Pretoria Mint found on gold half-sovereigns and sovereigns of George V.

S C – Provenance mark on silver coins of George I struck from metal obtained from Peru by the South Sea Company.

Saltire – Term for the cross of St Andrew.

Sceat – A small silver coin minted in the southern kingdoms of Anglo-Saxon England during the 7th and 8th centuries. In Northumbria the equivalent coin was the styca.

Scissel – The clippings of metal left after a blank has been cut.

Shilling – Introduced as a silver coin worth twelve pence during the reign of Henry VIII. At first known as a testoon, from the Italian *testa* and the Old French *teste*, meaning a head, because it had a portrait of the King on the obverse. It survives as the decimal 5 pence piece coin.

Short Cross Penny – Silver coin whose name was derived from the small cross within a beaded circle on the reverse. Introduced in 1180 by Henry II, the Short Cross Penny was replaced in 1247 by the Long Cross Penny.

Simon, Thomas – Medallist and engraver, Chief Engraver at the Royal Mint 1646. Designed the gold and silver coins of Oliver Cromwell, 1656-58, and the 'Petition Crown' of 1663 with the portrait of Charles II. Engraved the Great Seals for Cromwell and Charles II. Born Yorkshire 1623, died 1665.

Sixpence – One of the new silver coins introduced by Edward VI in 1551 as part of a scheme to improve the coinage after the debasement which had taken place during the reign of his predecessor, Henry VIII. The sixpence was minted regularly until 1967.

Soho – Mint-mark of Matthew Boulton's Soho, Birmingham, Mint found on the Cartwheel coinage of 1797 and the later copper coins of George III. The mint operated the new machinery installed by Boulton and James Watt, but it declined after Boulton's death in 1809, and was purchased by Heaton's in the 1850s.

Sovereign – A gold coin introduced by Henry VII and so called because its obverse had a portrait of the King seated on his throne. Although originally valued at 20s 0d, the sovereign later fluctuated in value, weight and fineness. It was superseded by the guinea in 1663 but was revived in 1817 during the extensive re-coinage of that year. The sovereign is still minted as a legal tender bullion coin.

Spade Guinea – Name given to the George III guineas minted between 1787 and 1799 because the shield on the reverse resembled a garden spade or the spades in a pack of cards. Many brass imitations of the spade guineas were made in Victorian times for use as counters in card games or as children's toy coins.

Specie – Metal as opposed to paper money.

Stater – Name given to the gold coins which circulated in southern England before the Roman occupation. The coins were crudely made copies of the gold and silver staters of ancient Greece, some featuring a portrait of Apollo or a chariot.

Styca – Contemporary with the silver sceat, the styca was a small coin of debased silver, later of copper, which circulated in Northumbria. Some were minted by the Archbishops of York.

T.B. – Initials of Sir Thomas Brock, designer.

Testoon – From the Italian *testa* and the Old French *teste*, meaning head, this term was applied to coins which gave great importance to the head of the monarch. Because of its resemblance to such foreign coins, the shilling of Henry VII became known as a testoon. A silver coin valued at 12 pence the Scottish testoon was the forerunner of the English shilling.

Third-farthing – A small copper coin minted for use in Malta to replace the grano, a local coin worth one-third of the British farthing. First issued in 1827, the third-farthing was minted at intervals until 1913, the issues after 1860 being made of bronze.

Third-guinea – Introduced as a 7 shilling coin in 1797 because a shortage of silver made the minting of crowns and halfcrowns uneconomic. The third-guinea was discontinued when the guinea series was replaced by the sovereign and half-sovereign.

Thomas, Cecil – Sculptor and medallist. Designed the crowned portrait of Queen Elizabeth II for overseas coinages, and the Elizabeth II Coronation Medal. Born London 1903.

Three-farthings – A small silver coin issued only during the reign of Elizabeth I.

Three-halfpence – A small silver coin issued during the reign of Elizabeth I. Revived in 1834, also as a silver coin, for use in Ceylon, British Guiana and the West Indies. Last minted in 1862, though a few Proofs dated 1870 are known.

Threepence – One of the new silver coins, introduced by Edward VI. The silver threepence survives as one of the Maundy coins but for general circulation it was superseded after 1944 by the twelve-sided nickel-brass threepence. This had been introduced in 1937 and both types of threepence circulated until the rising cost of silver led to the silver threepence being discontinued. The brass threepence was demonetised after the change to decimal currency in 1971.

Thrymsa – Meaning three, or one-third thrymsas were of Merovingian and Byzantine origin and these designs were copied on to gold coins by the Anglo-Saxons. The inscriptions finally became illegible and the Latin legend wa replaced by one in the Runic alphabet Because of the constant rising price o gold, the thrymsa was replaced by th silver sceat.

Token – An unofficial coin issued by private citizen or a company, usually at time when there is a shortage of lega tender coins.

Token Coinage – Coins which do no represent in intrinsic value th denomination upon them.

Touch Piece – Coin or medalet given b royalty to scrofula – the 'king's evil' sufferers.

Treasure Trove – Any hoard of gold o silver coins or articles which is deemed b a coroner and jury to have bee deliberately hidden and of which th owner cannot be traced. (See Collectin and the Law).

Trussel – Upper die which incorporates th reverse design used in the hammerin process.

Turner – A copper variety of the twopenn piece struck for use in Scotland, this is corruption of the French *gros tournoi* and was first issued by James I. Thes coins were later to become known a bodles.

Type – Coin of a particular main design

Unc – Uncirculated. Grade.

Unicorn – Scottish gold coin initiall struck in the reign of James III an deriving its name from the obverse figu of a unicorn. Originally valued at 18s 0 it rose to 22s 0d during the reign of Jam V.

Uniface – Coin having the design on on side only, the other side being blank.

Unite – Gold coin valued at 20s 0d fir struck by James I and so called because was inscribed with a Latin quotatic from the Book of Ezekiel, FACIAM E GENTEM VNAM ('I *will make them o nation*'), referring to the union of t English and Scottish crowns in 1603.

VF – Very Fine. Grade.

VG – Very Good. Grade.

VOC – Initials of the Vereenigde Oostindische Compagnie – United East India Company.

Variety – A coin having a variation in the design when compared with another of the same type.

Veiled Head – The portrait of Queen Victoria on the coins minted between 1893 and the end of her reign in 1901. Designed by Sir Thomas Brock, sculptor and designer, the portrait showed her wearing a coronet over which was draped a long veil.

Vigo – Inscribed below the portrait of Queen Anne on some of the gold and silver coins minted in 1702 and 1703 to indicate that the bullion used for these had been captured by Admiral Sir George Rooke in a raid on treasure ships in the Spanish port of Vigo.

Vis-a-Vis – Face to face.

W. – Initial of Thomas Wyon, designer and engraver.

W.C.C. – Provenance mark of the Welsh Copper Company found on coins of George I.

W.G. – Initials of William Gardner, designer.

W.P. – Initials of Wilson Parker, designer.

W.W. – Initials of William Wyon, designer.

Wampum – Beads or discs made from sea-shells and used as currency by the North American Indians and other primitive races. Wampum is still used in the South Sea Islands.

Wire Money – Name given to the Maundy coins issued for George III in 1792 because the figures of value on the reverse were unsually thin.

Wolsey's Groat – Name given to the silver groat or fourpence, minted by Cardinal Wolsey while he was Archbishop of York. The ecclesiastical mints at Canterbury, Durham and York were permitted to issue small silver coins in denominations of a half-groat, or twopence, a penny and a halfpenny. The ambitious Cardinal overreached himself by ordering groats to be minted. They were in the same design as the regal groats but with the addition of a cardinal's hat and the initials TW on the reverse. This infringement of the royal prerogative formed part of the case against Wolsey when he was charged with high treason.

Wynne, David – Sculptor and medallist. Designed the reverse of the 1973 EEC 50 pence. Born 1926.

Wyon, Allan-Gairdner – Sculptor and medallist, great-grandson of Thomas Wyon. Designed the King George V Coronation Medal 1911 and Lloyd's Medal for Bravery at Sea 1940. Born London 1882, died 1962.

Wyon, Leonard Charles – Eldest son of William Wyon whom he succeeded as Chief Engraver at the Royal Mint in 1851. Designed numerous coins and medals including Patterns for British decimal coinage, 1859; the bronze coinage Bun Head portrait of Queen Victoria, 1860-94; many colonial coinages; Arctic Medal 1857; Ashanti War Medal 1873-74; London Police Medals 1887, 1897. Born London 1826, died 1891.

Wyon, Thomas – Engraver and medallist, uncle of William Wyon. Designed the reverse of the George III Bull Head halfcrown of 1816 and numerous trade tokens, also Dr William Turton's medal for Nelson 1805 and several in honour of George III. Born Birmingham 1767, died 1830.

Wyon, William – Engraver and medallist, nephew of Thomas Wyon. Designed numerous British coins including the Bare Head of George IV, 1825-29, the Young Head portrait of Queen Victoria, 1838-87, and the obverses of the Godless florin, 1848-49, and Gothic florin and crown, 1847-87. Medals include the Punjab War Medal 1851. Born Birmingham 1795, died 1851.

Y and y – Mint-marks of the York Mint found on silver coins of William III.

Young Head – The portrait of Queen Victoria by William Wyon which was used on most of the coins minted for her between her accession in 1837 and the introduction of the Bun Head on the bronze coins in 1860 and of the Jubilee Head used on the gold and silver coins in 1887.

World Mint-Marks

ARGENTINA
M	–Mendoza
RA	–Rioja
SE	–Santiago del Estero
PTS	–Potosi, Bolivia (1813-1815)

AUSTRALIA
A	–Perth
D	–Denver, USA (1942-1943)
H	–Heaton
I	–Calcutta (1916-1918)
M	–Melbourne (1916-1921)
P	–Perth
PL	–Royal Mint, London (1951)
S	–Sydney
S	–San Francisco, USA (1942-1943)

Dot before and after PENNY and I on obverse
–Bombay (1942-1943)
Dot before and after HALFPENNY and I on obverse
–Bombay (1942-1943)
Dot before and after PENNY
–Bombay (1942-1943)
Dot after HALFPENNY
–Perth
Dot before SHILLING
–Perth (1946)
Dot above scroll on reverse
–Sydney (1920)
Dot below scroll on reverse
–Melbourne (1919-1920)
Dot between designer's initials KG
–Perth (1940-1941)
Dot after AUSTRALIA
–Perth (1952-1953)
I under bust
–Bombay (1942-1943)

Coins also struck without mint-marks at: London (1910-1915), Melbourne (1921-1956), Perth (1922 penny and 1955 halfpenny), and Sydney (1919-1926).

AUSTRIA
A	–Vienna (1765-1872)
AH-AG	–Carlsburg, Transylvania (1765-1776)
AH-GS	–Carlsburg (1776-1780)
A-S	–Hall, Tyrol (1765-1774)
AS-IE	–Vienna (1745)
AW	–Vienna (1764, 1768)
B	–Kremnitz, Hungary (1765-1857)
B-L	–Nagybanya, Hungary (1765-1771)
B-V	–Nagybanya (1772-1780)
C	–Carlsburg (1762-1764)
C	–Prague, Bohemia (1766-1855)
C-A	–Carlsburg (1746-1766)
C-A	–Vienna (1774-1780)
CG-AK	–Graz, Styria (1767-1772)
CG-AR	–Graz (1767)
C-K	–Vienna (1765-1773)
CM	–Kremnitz (1779)
CVG-AK	–Gratz (1767-1772)
CVG-AR	–Gratz (1767)
D	–Graz (1765-1772)
D	–Salzburg (1800-1809)
E	–Carlsburg (1765-1867)
EC-SK	–Vienna (1766)
EvM-D	-Kremnitz (1765-1774)
EvS-AS	–Prague (1765-1773)
EvS-IK	–Prague (1774-1780)
F	–Hall (1765-1807)
G	–Graz (1761-1763)
G	–Gunzburg, Burgau (1764-1779)
G	–Nagybanya (1766-1851, on coins of Joseph II only until 1780
G-K	–Graz (1767-1772)
G-R	–Graz (1746-1767)
GTK	–Vienna (1761)
H	–Hall (on coins of Maria Theresa and Franz I 1760-1780)
H	–Gunsburg (1765-1805, on coins of Joseph II only until 1780)

H-A	–Hall (1746-1765)
H-G	–Carlsburg (1765-1777)
H-S	–Carlsburg (1777-1780)
IB-FL	–Nagybanya (1765-1771)
IB-IV	–Nagybanya (1772-1780)
IC-FA	–Vienna (1774-1780)
IC-IA	–Vienna (1780)
IC-SK	–Vienna (1765-1773)
I-K	–Graz (1765-1767)
I-K	–Vienna (Franz I posthumous year B = 1767)
IZV	–Vienna (1763-1765)
K	–Kremnitz (1760-1763)
K-B	–Kremnitz (1619-1765)
K-D	–Kremnitz (1765)
K-M	–Kremnitz (1763-1765)
M	–Milan, Lombardy (1780-1859)
N	–Nagybanya (1780)
N-B	–Nagybanya (1630-1777, 1849)
O	–Oravicza, Hungary (1783-1816, copper only)
P	–Prague (1760-1763)
P-R	–Prague (1746-1767)
PS-IK	–Prague (1774-1780)
S	–Hall (1765-1780, no copper)
S	–Schmöllnitz, Hungary (1763-1816, copper only)
S-C	–Gunzburg (1765-1774)
SC-G	–Gunzburg (1765)
S-F	–Gunzburg (1775-1780)
S-G	–Gunzburg (1764-1765)
S-IE	–Vienna (1745)
SK-PD	–Kremnitz (1774-1780)
TS	–Gunzburg (1762-1788)
	–Venice, Venetia (1805-1866)
VC-S	–Hall (1774-1780)
VS-K	–Prague (1774-1780)
VS-S	–Prague (1765-1773)
V	–Vienna (1748-1763)
V-I	–Vienna (1746-1771)

OLIVIA
,PTS,or PTR	–Porosi

BRAZIL
B	–Bahia
C	–Cuiaba
G	–Goias
M	–Minas Geraes

P	–Pernambuco
R	–Rio de Janeiro
SP	–Sao Paulo

BRITISH HONDURAS
H	–Heaton

BRITISH NORTH BORNEO
H	–Heaton

BRITISH WEST AFRICA
H	–Heaton
KN	–King's Norton
S.A.	–South Africa
G	–J R Gaunt, Birmingham

CANADA
C	–Ottawa
H	–Heaton

Coins without a mint-mark and struck before 1908 were struck at the Royal Mint; those without a mint-mark struck after 1908 were struck at Ottawa

CEYLON
H	–Heaton
B	–Bombay

CHILE
S	–Santiago
VA	–Val distra

COLOMBIA
B.B	–Bogota
M	–Medellin
NR	–(neuvo Reino) Sante Fe de Bogota
P or PN	–Popayan
SM	–Santa Marta

COSTA RICA
CR	–San Jose
S or SD	–San Domingo

DENMARK
Crown or Heart
	–Copenhagen
●Orb	–Altona (1839-1848)

EAST AFRICA
H	–Heaton
KN	–King's Norton
I	–Bombay

K	–ICI (Knoch) Ltd
A	–Ackroyd & Best Ltd

FIJI
S	–San Francisco

FRANCE
A	–Paris
AA	–Metz
B	–Rouen
BB	–Strasburg
C	–Castelarrasin
C	–Caen
CC	–Genoa
CL	–Genoa
Cornucopia and torch	
	–Paris (1901-1930); Vincennes
Cornucopia and wing	
	–Paris (1931); Vincennes
Cow	–Pau
D	–Lyons
G	–Geneva
G	–Poitiers (pre-1789)
H	–La Rochelle
I	–Limoges
K	–Bordeaux
L	–Bayonne
M	–Toulouse
MA	–Marseilles
N	–Montellier
O	–Riom
P	–Dijon
Q	–Perpignan
R	–Orleans (pre 1789)
R cwnd	–Rome
T	–Nantes
TRA and/or fish	
	–Utrecht
U	–Turin
V	–Troyes
W	–Lille
X	–Amiens (1740)
Zigzag	–Poissy
9	–Rennes

GERMANY
Mints post 1871
A	–Berlin
B	–Hannover (1866-1878)
B	–Vienna (1938-1945)
C	–Frankfurt am Main
	(1866-1879)
D	–Munich (1872-)

E	–Dresden (1872-1887)
E	–Muldenhutte (1887-)
F	–Stuttgart (1872-)
G	–Karlsruhe (1872-)
H	–Darmstadt (1872-1882)
J	–Hamburg (1873-)

Dusseldorf mint-marks (Julich-Berg)
A.K.	–1749-1766
C.L.S.	–1767-1770
P.M.	–1771-1783
P.R.	–1783-1804

Prussian mint-marks
A	–Berlin, Brandenburg (1750-)
A.E.	–Breslau, Silesia (1743-1751)
A.G.P.	–Cleve, Rhineland (1742-1743)
A.H.E.	–See A.E.
A.L.S.	–Berlin (1749)
B	–Breslau (1750-1826)
B	–Bayreuth, Franconia
	(1796-1804)
B	–Hannover (1866-78)
C	–Cleve (1750-1806)
C	–Frankfurt am Main
	(1866-1879)
C.H.I.	–Berlin (1749-1763)
D	–Aurich, East-Friesland
	(1750-1806)
D	–Dusseldorf, Rhineland
	(1816-1848)
E	–Koenigsberg, East Prussia
	(1750-1798)
E.G.N.	–Berlin (1725-1749)
F	–Magdeburg, Lower Saxony
	(1750-1806)
G	–Stettin, Pomerania (1750-1806)
G	–Glatz, Silesia (1807-1809)
G.K.	–Cleve (1740-1755)
S	–Schwaback, Franconia
	(1792-1794)
W	–Breslau (1743)

Saxon mint-marks
B	–Dresden, Prussian Occupation
	(1756-1759)
B	–Dresden (1861-1872)
C	–Dresden (1779-1804)
E.C., E.D.C	
	–Leipzig (1753-1763)
F ·	–Dresden (1845-1858)
F.W.oF	–Dresden (1734-1763)
G	–Dresden (1833-1844)

H	–Dresden (1804-1812)
I.C.	–Dresden (1779-1804)
I.D.B	–Dresden, Prussian Occupation (1756-1759)
I.E.C.	–Dresden (1779-1804)
I.F.oF.	–Leipzig (1763-1765)
I.G.G.	–Leipzig (1752)
I.G.S.	–Dresden (1716-1734, 1813-32)
L	–Leipzig (1761-1762)
S	–Dresden (1813-1832)
S.G.H.	–Dresden (1804-1812)

GREAT BRITAIN
B	–Bristol (William III)
C	–Chester (William III)
E	–Exeter (William III)
E	–Edinburgh (Anne)
E*	–Edinburgh (Anne)
H	–Heaton, Birmingham
KN	–King's Norton, Birmingham
N	–Norwich (William III)
y	–York (William III)
Y	–York (William III)

GUATEMALA
C or G	–Guatemala (1733-1776)
NG	–Nuevo (1777-)

HONDURAS
I or TEG –Tegueigalpa

HONG KONG
H	–Heaton
KN	–King's Norton

ISLE OF MAN
PM –Pobjoy

JAMAICA
C	–Ottawa
H	–Heaton

MALAYA AND BRITISH BORNEO
H	–Heaton
KN	–King's Norton

MALAYA
I –Calcutta

MAURITIUS
H	–Heaton
S.A.	–Pretoria, South Africa

MEXICO
A or As	–Alamos
C or CN	–Culiacan
C^E	–Real del Catorce
CH or CA	–Chilhulhua
D or Do	–Durango
Eo or Mo	–Tlalpam
GA	–Guadalajara
GC	–Guadelupe y Calvo
Go	–Guanajuato
Ho	–Hermosillo
M,M or Mo	–Mexico City
MX	–Mexico City
O, OA or OKA	–Oaxaca
Pi	–San Luis Potosi
S:L.P.	–San Luis Potosi
TC	–Tierra Caliente
Z or Zs	–Zacatecas

MOMBASA
C.M.	–Heaton
H	–Heaton

NETHERLANDS
Austrian Netherlands 1700-1793
Hand	–Antwerp
Head	–Brussels
Lion	–Bruges
W	–Vienna

Kingdom of the Netherlands
B	–Brussels (1814-1830)
Caduceus	–Utrecht
D	–Denver, USA
Mercury staff	–Utrecht
P	–Philadelphia, USA
S	–San Francisco, USA

NICARAGUA
NR –Leon de Nicaragua

NORWAY
Hammers –Kongsberg

PERU
C, Co or CUZO	–Cuzco
L, LM, LR, or LIMAE	–Lima

ME	–Lima
P	–Lima (1568-1570)

RUSSIA

MM	–Moscow
CIIIS	–St Petersburg

Additional Copper Mints

A-M	–Annensk (1762-1796)
C-M	–Sestroretsk (1762-1796)
E-M	–Ekaterinburg (1762-1810)
K-M	–Kolyvan (1762-1810)
M-M	–Moscow (1762-1796)
TM	–Feodosia, Crimea (1762-1796)
NM	–Izhorsk (1811-1821)
CM	–Suzon (1825-1855)
BM or M.W.	
	–Warsaw (1825-1855)
C.JI.M	–St Petersburg (1825-1855)

SARAWAK

H	–Heaton

SOUTH AFRICA

S.A.	–Pretoria

SPAIN

Aqueduct	
	–Segovia
B	–Burgos (to 1700)
B	–Barcelona (1808-)
BA	–Barcelona
C cwnd	–Cadiz
C	–Cataluna
C	–Cuenca
C with a centre	
	–Cuenca
C	–Reus (1808-)
CA	–Zaragoza
G	–Granada
GNA	–Gerona
ILD	–Lerida
J	–Jubia
M cwnd	–Madrid
M	–Madrid
MD ligate	–Madrid
P	–Palma, Majorca (1812)
PPA	–Pamplona
Pomegranate	
	–Granada
S	–Seville
Scallop	–Corunna
Shield with vertical shading, crown above	
	–Tarragona

Shield quartered, with vertical shading
and star above M or star above castle
–Palma

Star, five pointed	
	–Madrid (1895-)
Star, six pointed	
	–Madrid
Star, seven pointed	
	–Seville (1833-)
Star, eight pointed	
	–Barcelona (1833-)
T	–Toledo
TOR:SA	–Tortosa
V	–Valencia
Wavy Lines	
	–Valladolid

STRAITS SETTLEMENTS

H	–Heaton

SWITZERLAND

Helvetian Republic 1793-1803

B	–Bern
S	–Solothurn

TONGA

PM	–Pobjoy

UNITED STATES OF AMERICA

C	–Charlotte, North Carolina
CC	–Carson City, Nevada
D	–Dahlonega, Georgia (1838-1861)
D	–Denver, Colorado (1906-)
O	–New Orleans
P	–Philadelphia
S	–San Francisco

Dealer Directory

Dealer Directory is divided into two sections. The first is an alphabetical list of dealers' names and addresses throughout the United Kingdom and the Republic of Ireland. The second, which begins on page 296, is a Dealers' Specialities section arranged geographically by country and county.

It should be noted that the counties used in the postal addresses in the first section are not necessarily those under which the dealers' names will appear in the specialities section. For example, Stockport has to have Cheshire included in the postal address in accordance with GPO regulations, yet it is in the metropolitan county of Greater Manchester, and is thus listed under that heading in the specialities section.

Dealers not included in the Directory but who wish to be in *Coin 1993 Year Book* should write to the Editor, Sovereign House, Brentwood, Essex CM14 4SE. There is no charge.

AGORA IN ASTARTE

	Britannia Hotel
	Grosvenor Square
	London
	W1A 3AN
Telephone	071-409 1875
Hours	10.30-17.00
Closed	Sat Sun
Member	ADA

AIREDALE COINS

	PO Box 7
	Bingley
	West Yorkshire
	BD16 4ST
Telephone	Bradford [0274] 563869
Hours	08.00-17.00
	Postal only
Regular ads	Coin Monthly
Member	ANA BNTA

ALFRED S ALLEN & CO

	PO Box 4
	South Ockendon
	Essex
	RM15 4JE
Telephone	South Ockendon [0708] 852943
Hours	Postal only

ALISTAIR GIBB

	5 West Albert Road
	Kirkcaldy
	Fife
	Scotland
	KY1 1DL
Telephone	Kirkcaldy [0592] 269045
Hours	Postal only
Member	IBNS

ANCIENT WORLD

	16 High Petergate
	York
	Yorkshire
	YO1 2EH
Telephone	York [0904] 624062
Hours	10.00-17.00
Regular ads	Coin Monthly
Member	BNTA

ANTIQUE BOUTIQUE

	54-59 Merrion Centre
	Leeds
	West Yorkshire
Telephone	Leeds [0532] 444174
Hours	09.30-17.30
Half-day	Wed 09.30-13.30
Closed	Sun

ARNOLDS ANTIQUES

	58 High Street
	Ventnor
	Isle of Wight
	PO38 1LT
Telephone	Ventnor [0983] 852514
Hours	24 hour answer phone

ART OF ARTS LTD (UK)

	Westhouse Chambers
	3 Sandpit Road
	Braintree
	Essex
	CM7 7LY
Telephone	Braintree [0376] 28000
Fax	[0376] 27502
Hours	09.00-17.00
Regular ads	Coin Monthly

ARTHUR COBWRIGHT
91 Derby Road
Bramcote
Nottinghamshire
NG9 3GW

Hours	Postal only
Regular ads	Coin Monthly

AURELIO TRIVELLA
11 Glebe Road
Handsacre
Staffordshire
WF15 4HD

Telephone	Lichfield [0543] 490439
Hours	Postal only
Regular ads	Coin Monthly

N J AVES
PO Box 811
Yeovil
Somerset
BA20 1FU

Telephone	Yeovil [0935] 72368
Fax	[0935] 78898
Hours	Postal only

BAIRD & CO
304 High Street
Stratford
London
E15 1AJ

Telephone	081-555 5217
Fax	081-534 3583
Telex	897170 Bairco
Hours	09.00-17.30
Closed	Sat Sun
Member	BNTA

A H BALDWIN & SONS LTD
11 Adelphi Terrace
London
WC2N 6BJ

Telephone	071-930 6879
Fax	071-930 9450
Hours	09.00-17.00
Closed	Sat Sun
Member	ANA BADA BNTA IAPN

BANKING MEMORABILIA
PO Box 14
Carlisle
Cumbria
CA3 8DZ

Telephone	Carlisle [069 96] 465
Hours	09.00-18.00
Closed	Sun
Regular ads	Coin Monthly
Member	IBNS

D G BARNEY
Greenfield
Colyton Hill
Colyton
Devon
EX13 6HY

Telephone	Colyton [0297] 52702
Hours	Postal only
Regular ads	Coin Monthly

G BARRINGTON SMITH
Cross Street
Oadby
Leicestershire
LE2 4DD

Telephone	Leicester [0533] 719181
Fax	[0533] 712114
Hours	08.30-17.15
Closed	Sat Sun

BARRY BOSWELL BRITISH BANKNOTES
24 Townsend Lane
Upper Boddington
Daventry
Northamptonshire
NN11 6DR

Telephone	Byfield [0327] 61877
Hours	Postal only
Regular ads	Coin Monthly

BATH STAMP & COIN SHOP
Pulteney Bridge
Bath
Avon
BA2 4AY

Telephone	Bath [0225] 463073
Hours	Mon-Sat 09.30-17.30
Closed	Sun
Member	BNTA

BAUDEY & BRICHER
Unit A28/29
Lower Ground Floor
Grays Mews Antique Market
1-7 Davies Mews
London
WIY 1AR

Telephone	071-629 2823
Hours	10.30-17.30
Closed	Sat Sun
Member	BNTA (J C Baudey)

BAXTERS COIN & STAMP EXCHANGE
20/22 Hepworths Arcade
Silver Street
Hull
North Humberside
HU1 1JU

Telephone	Hull [0482] 223875
Hours	10.00-17.00
Closed	Thu

R P & P J BECKETT
'Maes-y-Derw'
Capel Dewi
Llandyssul
Dyfed
Wales
SA44 4PJ

Hours	Postal only

BERKSHIRE COIN CENTRE

35 Castle Street
Reading
Berkshire
RG1 7SB

Telephone	Reading [0734] 575593
Hours	10.00-16.00
Half-day	Sat
Closed	Sun
Regular ads	Coin Monthly

BIRCHIN LANE GOLD COIN COMPANY

6 Castle Court
St Michael's Alley (off Cornhill)
City of London
EC3V 9DS

Telephone	071-621 0370 & 071-283 3981
Fax	071-621 0379
Hours	10.00-16.30
Closed	Sat Sun
Regular ads	Coin Monthly

BOOKMARK

1 Quay Street
Haverfordwest
Dyfed
Wales
SA61 1BG

Telephone	Haverfordwest [0437] 762633
Closed	Sun

J BRIDGEMAN COINS

129a Blackburn Road
Accrington
Lancashire

Telephone	Accrington [0254] 384757
Closed	Wed Sun

BRIGHTON COIN COMPANY

38 Ship Street
Brighton
Sussex
BN1 1AB

Telephone	Brighton [0273] 733365
Hours	Mon-Fri 09.45-17.30
	Sat 09.45-15.30
Closed	Sun
Member	ANA BNTA

BRITANNIA ENTERPRISES

28 Raglan Place
Burnopfield
Newcastle
Tyne & Wear
NE16 6NN

Telephone	Burnopfield [0207] 71869
Hours	Postal only

BRITANNIA JEWELLERY CO

234 Yorkshire Street
Rochdale
Lancashire
OL16 2DP

Telephone	Rochdale [0706] 341046/55507
Hours	10.00-17.00
Closed	Sun

BRITISH NUMISMATIC TRADE ASSOCIATION LTD

PO Box 82
Coventry
CV5 6SW

Telephone	Coventry [0203] 677976
Fax	[0203] 677985

A F BROCK & COMPANY

269 London Road
Hazel Grove
Stockport
Cheshire
SK7 4PL

Telephone	Manchester [061] 456 5050/5112
Hours	09.30-17.30
Closed	Sun
Regular ads	Coin Monthly

BROOKLANDS COLLECTIONS

10 Sea View Street
Cleethorpes
South Humberside
DN35 8QP

Telephone	Grimsby [0472] 692804
Hours	Mon Tue Wed Fri Sat 10.00-17.00
	Thu Sun (April to Dec) 14.00-17.00

E J & C A BROOKS

36 Kiln Road
South Benfleet
Essex
SS7 1TB

Telephone	South Benfleet [0268] 753835
Hours	Anytime
	Evenings up to 23.00
Member	BNTA IBNS

S BURROUGHS PRECIOUS METALS

1 Vallance Street
Mansfield Woodhouse
Nottinghamshire
NG19 8EQ

Telephone	Mansfield [0623] 657744
Hours	Postal only

BUTLER & CO

111 Promenade
Cheltenham
Gloucestershire
GL50 1NN

Telephone	Cheltenham [0242] 522272
Hours	Open Sat only

BYZANTIUM NUMISMATISTS

Fitling Grange
Fitling
North Humberside
HU12 9AJ

Telephone	Hornsea [0964] 527035
Hours	Postal only

THE CAMBRIDGE STAMP CENTRE LTD

9 Sussex Street
Cambridge
Cambridgeshire
CB4 4HU

Telephone	Cambridge [0223] 63980
Hours	09.00-17.30
Closed	Sun

CAPRICORN

PO Box 726
Easton
Portland
Dorset
DT5 2HU

Telephone	Portland [0305] 824237
Hours	18.00-22.00
	Postal only
Regular ads	Coin Monthly

CASTLE COINS

47a High Street South
Dunstable
Bedfordshire
LU6 3RZ

Telephone	Dunstable [0582] 602778
Hours	10.00-17.00

CASTLE CURIOS

165 Wellgate
Rotherham
South Yorkshire
S60 4DT

Hours	11.00-17.00
Closed	Mon Tue Sun

CASTLE GALLERIES (JOHN C LODGE)

81 Castle Street
Salisbury
Wiltshire
SP1 3SP

Telephone	Salisbury [0722] 333734
Hours	Tue Thu Fri 09.00-17.00
	Sat 09.30-16.00
Closed	Mon Wed

CATHEDRAL COINS

23 Kirkgate
Ripon
North Yorkshire
HG4 1PB

Telephone	Ripon [0765] 701400
Hours	10.00-17.00

CAVECELLAR LTD

5 Conifer Close
Silica Lodge
Scunthorpe
South Humberside
DN17 2AH

Telephone	Scunthorpe [0724] 857811
Hours	24 hour answer phone
	Postal only
Regular ads	Coin Monthly

CHELSEA COINS LTD

PO Box 2
Fulham Road
London
SW10 9PQ

CHRIS BELTON

PO Box 356
Christchurch
Dorset
BH23 2YD

Telephone	Christchurch [0202] 478592
Hours	09.00-21.00
	Postal only
Regular ads	Coin Monthly

CHRISTIE, MANSON & WOODS LTD

8 King Street
St James's
London
SW1Y 6QT

Telephone	071-839 9060
Telex	London 916429

CHRISTOPHER EIMER

PO Box 352
London
NW11 7SU

Telephone	081-458 9933
Hours	Postal only
Member	ANA BNTA

CLIVE DENNETT

66 St Benedicts Street
Norwich
Norfolk
NR2 4AR

Telephone	Norwich [0603] 624315
Hours	Mon-Fri 09.00-17.30
	Sat 09.00-16.00
Closed	Thu Sun
Member	BNTA

M COESHAW

PO Box 115
Leicester
Leicestershire
LE3 8JJ

Telephone	Leicester [0533] 873808
Member	ANA BNTA IBNS

COIN & COLLECTORS CENTRE

PO Box 22
Pontefract
West Yorkshire
WR8 1YT

Telephone	Pontefract [0977] 704112
Hours	Postal only
Regular ads	Coin Monthly

COIN INVESTMENTS

PO Box 20
Sevenoaks
Kent
TN14 7DZ

Telephone	Knockholt [0959] 34413
Hours	Postal only

THE COIN MART

	73 Ballabrooie Avenue
	Douglas
	Isle of Man
Telephone	Douglas [0624] 629089 evenings
Hours	19.00-23.00
Member	IBNS

COIN & STAMP CENTRE

	13 Centurion House
	St Johns Street
	Colchester
	Essex
	CO2 7AH
Telephone	Colchester [0206] 41232
Hours	09.00-17.00
Closed	Sun

COINS & MILITARIA

	The High Street
	Brasted
	Nr Westerham
	Kent
	TN16 1JA
Telephone	Westerham [0959] 62592
Hours	10.00-17.30
Closed	Wed Sun

COINCRAFT

	45 Great Russell Street
	London
	WC1B 3LU
Telephone	071-636 1188 & 071-637 8785
Fax	071-323 2860
Hours	09.30-17.00
Half-day	Sat 10.00-14.30
Closed	Sun
Member	ANA IBNS

B B M COINS

	8 & 9 Lion Street
	Kidderminster
	Hereford & Worcester
	DY10 1PT
Telephone	Kidderminster [0562] 744118
Hours	10.00-17.00
Closed	Tue Sun

B R M COINS

	3 Minshull Street
	Knutsford
	Cheshire
	WA16 6HG
Telephone	Knutsford [0565] 651480
	& Northwich [0606] 74522
Closed	Sun

K B COINS

	50 Lingfield Road
	Stevenage
	Hertfordshire
	SG1 5SL
Telephone	Stevenage [0438] 312661
Hours	09.00-18.00
	Callers by appointment
Regular ads	Coin Monthly
Member	BNTA

M T R COINS (M T RAY)

	22a Kingsnorth Close
	Newark
	Nottingham
	Nottinghamshire
	NG24 1PS
Telephone	Newark [0636] 703152
Hours	Postal only

R & J COINS

	21b Alexandra Street
	(Entrance in Market Place)
	Southend on Sea
	Essex
	SS1 1DA
Telephone	Southend on Sea [0702] 345995
Hours	10.00-16.00
Closed	Wed Sun

R & L COINS

	521 Lytham Road
	Blackpool
	Lancashire
	FY4 1RJ
Telephone	Blackpool [0253] 43081
Hours	09.00-17.00
	By appointment Sat
Closed	Sun
Regular ads	Coin Monthly
Member	BNTA

COINS OF BEESTON

	PO Box 19
	Beeston
	Nottinghamshire
	BG9 2NE
Hours	Postal only
Regular ads	Coin Monthly

COINS OF CANTERBURY

	PO Box 47
	Faversham
	Kent
	ME13 7HX
Telephone	Faversham [0795] 531980
Hours	Postal only

COINS INTERNATIONAL

	1 & 2 Melbourne Street
	Leeds
	West Yorkshire
	LS2 7PS
Telephone	Leeds [0532] 434230
Fax	[0532] 345544
Hours	09.30-17.00
Closed	Sat Sun
Regular ads	Coin Monthly
Member	BNTA

COINS & MEDALS (REGD)

	10 Cathedral Street
	Dublin 1
	Irish Republic
Telephone	Dublin [0001] 744033
Half-day	Mon
Closed	Sun
Member	ANA BNTA IAPN

COINTACT SERVICES
155 Parklands Drive
Loughborough
Leicestershire
LE11 2TA
Telephone	Loughborough [0509] 261352
Hours	Postal only

COLIN COOKE
257 Brooklands Road
Manchester
M23 9HF
Telephone	Manchester [061] 973 2395
Fax	[061] 962 2864
Hours	09.00-18.00
	Postal only
Half-day	Sat
Closed	Sun
Regular ads	Coin Monthly

COLIN JAMES O'KEEFE
15 Pettits Place
Dagenham
Essex
RM10 8NL
Hours	Postal only

COLIN NARBETH & SON LTD
20 Cecil Court
Leicester Square
London
WC2N 4HE
Telephone	071-379 6975
Hours	10.30-17.00
Closed	Sun
Regular ads	Coin Monthly
Member	ANA IBNS

COLISEUM COINS
30 Staunton Avenue
Hayling Island
Hampshire
PO11 0EN
Telephone	Hayling Island [0705] 464332
Hours	Postal only
	Callers by appointment
Regular ads	Coin Monthly

COLLECTA COINS LIMITED
PO Box 101
Northampton
Northamptonshire
NN1 3LT
Telephone	Northampton [0604] 766607/27076
Hours	09.00-21.00
Regular ads	Coin Monthly

COLLECTORS' CORNER
East Street
Crescent Road
Faversham
Kent
ME13 8AD
Telephone	Faversham [0795] 539721
Hours	10.00-15.00
Half-day	Mon Thu
Closed	Sat Sun
Regular ads	Coin Monthly

COLLECTORS' CORNER
13 Market Avenue
Huddersfield
West Yorkshire
HD1 2BB
Telephone	Huddersfield [0484] 428359
Hours	09.30-16.30
Closed	Wed Sun

COLLECTORS' CORNER
Watford Market
(off Watford High Street)
Watford
Hertfordshire
Telephone	081-904 0552
Hours	09.00-17.00
Closed	Mon Wed Thu Sun

COLLECTORS' FORUM
237 South Street
Romford
Essex
RM1 2BE
Telephone	Romford [0708] 723357
Hours	09.30-18.00
Half day	Thu 09.30-14.00
Closed	Sun
Member	BNTA

CONSTANTIA CB
15 Church Road
Northwood
Middlesex
HA6 1AR
Hours	Postal only

A J CONSULTANTS
PO Box 19
Beeston
Nottingham
Nottinghamshire
NG9 2NE
Hours	Postal only

COSMO COINS (INC COSMOPOLITAN COLLECTORS GROUP)
PO Box 3
Lutterworth
Leicestershire
LE17 4FU
Telephone	Lutterworth [0455] 554387
Hours	Postal only

COTREL MEDALS
7 Stanton Road
Bournemouth
Dorset
BH10 5DS
Telephone	Bournemouth [0202] 516801
Hours	09.00-21.00
	Postal only

K A CUDWORTH

8 Park Avenue
Clayton West
Huddersfield
West Yorkshire
HD8 9PT

Telephone	Huddersfield [0484] 862679
Hours	Mon-Fri 09.00-21.00
	Postal only

DAVID ALLEN MCIM
COINS AND COLLECTABLES

PO Box 125
Pinner
Middlesex
HA5 2TX

Telephone	081-866 6796
Hours	Postal only

DAVID L CAVANAGH

49 Cockburn Street
Edinburgh
EH1 1PB

Telephone	Edinburgh [031] 226 3391
Hours	10.30-17.00
Closed	Sun

DAVID FLETCHER LTD

PO Box 64
Coventry
CV5 6SN

Telephone	Coventry [0203] 715425
Fax	[0203] 677985
Hours	09.00-13.00
	14.00-18.00
	Postal only
Closed	Sat Sun
Regular ads	Coin Monthly
Member	ANA BNTA

DAVID KEABLE & CO

5 The Crescens
Sanderstead Road
Croydon
Surrey
CR2 OPB

Telephone	081-657 5399
Hours	Postal only
Regular ads	Coin Monthly
Member	ANA BNTA IBNS

DAVID MILLER (COINS & ANTIQUITIES)

51 Carlisle Avenue
St Albans
Hertfordshire
AL3 5LX

Telephone	St Albans [0727] 52412
Fax	[0727] 52412
Hours	09.00-17.30 by appointment
Regular ads	Coin Monthly
Member	ANA BNTA

DAVID C PINDER

20 Princess Road West
Leicester
LE1 6TP

Telephone	Leicester [0533] 702439
Hours	Postal only

DAVID R RUDLING

112 Hollingdean Terrace
Brighton
East Sussex
BN1 7HE

Telephone	Brighton [0273] 506877
Hours	Postal only

DAVIDSON MONK FAIRS

PO Box 201
Croydon
Surrey
CR9 7AQ

Telephone	081-656 4583
Regular ads	Coin Monthly

B J DAWSON (COINS) REGD

52 St Helens Road
Bolton
Lancashire
BL3 3NH

Telephone	Bolton [0204] 63732
Hours	Mon Tue Sat 09.30-16.00
	Thu Fri 09.30-17.30
Half-day	Wed
Closed	Sun
Member	BNTA

DECUS COINS

The Haven
Brockweir
Chepstow
Gwent
Wales
NP6 7NN

Telephone	Tintern [0291] 689216
Hours	09.00-20.00
	Postal only
Regular ads	Coin Monthly

C J DENTON

PO Box 25
Orpington
Kent
BR6 8PU

Telephone	Orpington [0689] 873690
Hours	Postal only
Regular ads	Coin Monthly
Member	ANA BNTA FRNS

C J & A J DIXON LTD

1st Floor
23 Prospect Street
Bridlington
East Yorkshire
YO15 2AE

Telephone	Bridlington [0262] 676877
Fax	[0262] 606600
Hours	09.00-17.00
Closed	Sun
Member	BNTA

DOLPHIN COINS
	2c Englands Lane
	Hampstead
	London
	NW3 4TG
Telephone	071-722 4116
Fax	071-483 2000
Telex	267033 D COINS
Hours	09.30-17.00
	Sat by appointment only
Closed	Sun
Regular ads	Coin Monthly
Member	ANA BNTA

DON MAC RAE COINS
	PO Box 233
	Uxbridge
	Middlesex
	UB9 4HY
Telephone	Uxbridge [0895] 832625
Hours	Postal only
Regular ads	Coin Monthly

DON OLIVER GOLD COINS
	The Coin Gallery
	Stanford House
	23 Market Street
	Stourbridge
	West Midlands
	DY8 1AB
Telephone	Stourbridge [0384] 373899
Hours	10.00-17.00
Half-day	Sat
Closed	Thu Sun
Regular ads	Coin Monthly

DORSET COIN CO LTD
	PO Box 7
	West Moors
	Wimborne
	Dorset
	BH22 0NE
Telephone	Ferndown [0202] 871753
Hours	Postal only
Regular ads	Coin Monthly
Member	BNTA

DRIZEN COINS
	1 Hawthorns
	Leigh-on-Sea
	Essex
	SS9 4JT
Telephone	Southend [0702] 521094
Hours	09.00-21.00
	Postal only
Regular ads	Coin Monthly

DUNELME COINS & MEDALS
	(County Collectors' Centre)
	7 Durham Road
	Esh Winning
	Durham
	Co Durham
	DH7 9NW
Telephone	Durham [091] 373 4446
	Telephone for appointments

Half-day	Wed
Closed	Sun
Member	BNTA

DYAS COINS & MEDALS
	30 Shaftmoor Lane
	Acocks Green
	Birmingham
	B27 7RS
Telephone	Birmingham [021] 707 2808
Fax	[021] 707 8312
Hours	Fri 10.30-18.30
	Sun 10.30-13.00
Closed	Mon Tue Wed Thu Sat

EAGLE COINS
	Winterhaven
	Mourneabbey
	Mallow
	Cork
	Eire
Telephone	Mallow [010 353 22] 29385
Hours	Postal only

EDDIE BAXTER BOOKS
	10 The Close
	Glastonbury
	Somerset
	BA6 9HZ
Telephone	Glastonbury [0458] 31662
Hours	Postal only

EDEN COINS
	PO Box 73
	Oldbury
	Warley
	Birmingham
	West Midlands
	B68 0BT
Telephone	Birmingham [021] 422 5357
Hours	Postal only

EDINBURGH COIN SHOP
	2 Polwarth Crescent
	Edinburgh
Telephone	Edinburgh [031] 229 2915/229 3007
Hours	10.00-17.30
Closed	Sun
Regular ads	Coin Monthly
Member	ANA LM

ELM HILL STAMPS & COINS
	27 Elm Hill
	Norwich
	Norfolk
	NR3 1HN
Telephone	Norwich [0603] 627413
Hours	09.00-16.45
Half-day	Sat
Closed	Sun

ELVIDGE TEAL
	8 Brora Close
	Bletchley
	Milton Keynes
	Buckinghamshire
	MK2 3HD

Telephone	Milton Keynes [0908] 373905
Fax	[0908] 584419
Hours	24 hour answer phone
Regular ads	Coin Monthly

ELY STAMP & COIN SHOP

	27 Fore Hill
	Ely
	Cambridgeshire
	CB7 1AA
Telephone	Ely [0353] 663919
Hours	09.30-17.30
Closed	Tue Sun

EUROPA NUMISMATICS

	PO Box 119
	High Wycombe
	Buckinghamshire
	HP11 1QL
Telephone	High Wycombe [0494] 437307
Hours	09.00-17.00
Closed	Sun
Member	ANA BNTA

EVESHAM STAMP & COIN CENTRE

	(Inside Magpie Antiques)
	Paris House
	61 High Street
	Evesham
	Worcestershire
	WR11 4DA
Telephone	Evesham [0386] 41631
Hours	09.00-17.30
Closed	Sun

FAR EAST COINS LTD

	8 Farleycroft
	55 Ashburton Road
	Croydon
	Surrey
	CR0 6AQ
Telephone	081-656 9559
Hours	Postal only

FARTHING SPECIALIST (REGD)

	Parr Lane
	Unsworth
	Bury
	Lancashire
	BL9 8PJ
Telephone	Manchester [061] 766 4347
Hours	Postal only
Regular ads	Coin Monthly
Member	BNTA

H FINE & SON LTD

	Victoria House
	93 Manor Farm Road
	Wembley
	Middlesex
	HA0 1XB
Telephone	081-997 5055
Fax	081-997 8410
Hours	09.00-17.00
	Postal only
Closed	Sat Sun

FORMAT OF BIRMINGHAM LTD

	18/19 Bennetts Hill
	Birmingham
	West Midlands
	B2 5QJ
Telephone	Birmingham [021] 643 2058
Fax	[021] 643 2210
Hours	09.30-17.00
Closed	Sat
Member	ANA BNTA IAPN IBNS

FOX & CO

	30 Princes Street
	Yeovil
	Somerset
	BA20 1EQ
Telephone	Yeovil [0935] 72323
Hours	09.00-17.30
Closed	Sun
Member	BNTA

FRANK MILWARD

	2 Ravensworth Road
	Mortimer
	Berkshire
	RG7 3UU
Telephone	Mortimer [0734] 322843
Hours	09.00-19.00
	Postal only
Half-day	Sat
Closed	Sun
Member	ANA BNTA

B FRANK & SON

	3 South Avenue
	Ryton
	Tyne & Wear
	NE40 3LD
Telephone	Tyneside [091] 413 8749
Hours	Postal only
Member	ANA IBNS

FYODOR

	67 Caledonian Road
	London
	N1 9BT
Hours	Postal only
Regular ads	Coin Monthly

GALATA COINS LTD

	The Old White Lion
	Market Street
	Llanfyllin
	Powys
	Wales
	SY22 5BX
Telephone	Llanfyllin [0691 84] 765
Hours	09.00-18.00
	Postal only
Closed	Sat Sun
Member	ANA BNTA

GANCE

24 Hatton Garden
London
EC1N 8BQ

Telephone	071-242 3151
Hours	10.00-16.00
Half-day	Fri
Closed	Sat Sun

GEMINI JEWELLERY, STAMPS & COINS

3 Golden Parade
Wood Street
Walthamstow
London
E17

Telephone	081-520 2968
Hours	10.00-18.00
Closed	Thu Sun
Member	ARICS

GEOFFREY WEDGWOOD LTD

35 Westfield Street
St Helens
Merseyside
WA10 1QA

Telephone	St Helens [0744] 55900
Hours	09.30-17.00
Closed	Thu Sun
Regular ads	Coin Monthly

GEORGE RANKIN COIN CO LTD

325 Bethnal Green Road
London
E2 6AH

Telephone	071-729 1280
Fax	071-729 5023
Hours	10.00-18.00
Half-day	Thu
Closed	Sun
Regular ads	Coin Monthly
Member	ANA BNTA

GEORGE SOWDEN

Coins Galore
The Lizard
Nr Helston
Cornwall
TR12 7NU

Telephone	The Lizard [0326] 290300
Hours	Postal only

GEORGE & JANE WHITE

29 Shortacre
Basildon
Essex
SS14 2LR

Telephone	Basildon [0268] 522923
Hours	Postal only
Member	IBNS

GIUSEPPE MICELI COIN & MEDAL CENTRE

173 Wellingborough Road
Northampton
Northamptonshire
NN1 4DX

Telephone	Northampton [0604] 39776
Hours	09.00-18.00
Closed	Sun
Regular ads	Coin Monthly
Member	OMRS

GLADSTONE

69 Castle Street
Cranborne
Dorset
BH21 5QA

Telephone	Cranborne [07254] 441
Hours	Postal only
Closed	Sun

GLASGOW STAMP SHOP

7 Scott Street
Glasgow
Lanarkshire
Scotland
G3 6NU

Telephone	Glasgow [041] 332 5100
Hours	10.30-14.30
Closed	Mon Sun

GLAZENWOOD

37 Augustus Way
Witham
Essex
CM8 1HH

GLENDINING'S

101 New Bond Street
London
W1Y 9LG

Telephone	071-493 2445
Fax	071-491 9181
Hours	08.30-17.00
Half-day	Sat
Closed	Sun
Regular ads	Coin Monthly
Member	ANA BNTA

GOLD INVESTMENTS LTD

Baltic Exchange
24/28 St Mary Axe
London
EC3A 8DE

Telephone	071-283 7752
Hours	09.30-17.00
Closed	Sat Sun

GOLD SILVER SHOP

1 Cross Street
Gorseinon
Nr Swansea
Glamorgan
Wales

Telephone	Gorseinon [0792] 891874
Mobile	[0806] 504558
Hours	10.00-12.00
	14.00-16.00
Closed	Sun

GOULBORN COLLECTION
44 Highfield Park
Rhyl
Clwyd
Wales
LL18 3NH
Telephone   Rhyl [0745] 344856
Hours   Postal only

GRAEME & LINDA MONK
PO Box 201
Croydon
Surrey
CR9 7AQ
Telephone   081-656 4583
Fax   081-656 4583
Hours   Postal only
Members   ANA BNTA

GRANTA STAMP & COIN SHOP
28 Magdalene Street
Cambridge
Cambridgeshire
CB3 0AF
Telephone   Cambridge [0223] 315044
Hours   10.30-18.30
Half-day   Sun

GRANTHAM COINS
PO Box 60
Grantham
Lincolnshire
Telephone   Grantham [0476] 870565
Hours   Postal only
Regular ads   Coin Monthly
Member   BNTA

GROVE PHILATELICS, COINS & ANTIQUITIES
Suite 4
Grove House
Blackheath Grove
London
SE3 0DG
Telephone   081-463 0063
Hours   Postal only

R I GROVES
82 Burntscarth Green
Locharbriggs
Dumfries
Dumfriesshire
Scotland
DG1 1UL
Telephone   Amisfield [0387] 710636
Hours   Postal only

A HALSE
The Headlands
Chepstow Road
Lanestone
Newport
Gwent
Wales
NP6 2JN

Telephone   Llanwern [0633] 413238
Fax   [0222] 521650
Hours   Postal only

A D HAMILTON & CO
7 St Vincent Place
Glasgow
Scotland
G77 5JA
Telephone   Glasgow [041] 221 5423
Fax   [041] 248 6019
Hours   09.00-17.30
Closed   Sun
Member   ANA BNTA

P HANSON
160 Princess Road
Buckhurst Hill
Essex
IG9 5DJ

J HARDIMAN & SON
6 Warwick Road
Anerley
London
SE20 7YL
Telephone   081-778 2678/4159
Hours   Postal only
Member   BNTA

HARRY WALKER
74 Ferry Road
Barrow-in-Furness
Cumbria
LA14 2QE
Telephone   Barrow-in-Furness [0229] 825048
Hours   Postal only

R G HOLMES
11 Cross Park
Ilfracombe
Devon
EX34 8BJ
Telephone   Ilfracombe [0271] 864474
Hours   Postal only

HOMELAND HOLDING LTD
Homeland
St John
Jersey
Channel Islands
JE3 4AB
Fax   [0534] 65339
Hours   09.00-12.00
Half-day   Mon Tue Wed Thu Fri
Regular ads   Coin Monthly
Member   IBNS

HUDSON
28 Howard Close
Braintree
Essex
CM7 6DS
Hours   Postal only

HUMBER COINS REGD

	PO Box 16
	Scunthorpe
	South Humberside
	DN15 7AA
Telephone	Scunthorpe [0724] 763990
Hours	Postal only
Member	BNTA

D D & A INGLE

	380 Carlton Hill
	Nottingham
	Nottinghamshire
Telephone	Nottingham [0602] 873325
Hours	09.30-17.00
Half-day	Sun

INTERCOL LONDON

	43 Templars Crescent
	London
	N3 3QR
Telephone	081-349 2207
Fax	081-346 9539
Hours	Postal only
Member	ANA BNTA IBNS

JAK

	31 Vapron Road
	Mannamead
	Plymouth
	Devon
	PL3 5NJ
Telephone	Plymouth [0752] 665405
Hours	Postal only
Regular ads	Coin Monthly
Member	IBNS

JAMES & C BRETT

	17 Dale Road
	Lewes
	East Sussex
	BN7 1LH
Hours	Postal only
Regular ads	Coin Monthly

JAMES GARRIOCK

	38 Hazel Close
	Bemerton Heath
	Salisbury
	Wiltshire
	SP2 9JJ
Telephone	Salisbury [0722] 325935
Hours	Postal only
Regular ads	Coin Monthly

JAMES IN IPSWICH LTD

	47 St Nicholas Street
	Ipswich
	Suffolk
	IP1 1TW
Telephone	Ipswich [0473] 231095
Hours	09.00-17.00
Closed	Wed Sat

JAMES OF NORWICH

	33 Timberhill
	Norwich
	Norfolk
	NR1 3LA
Telephone	Norwich [0603] 624817
Fax	[0603] 663750
Hours	09.00-17.00
Closed	Sun
Regular ads	Coin Monthly
Member	IBNS

JAN LIS

	Beaver Coin Room
	57 Philbeach Gardens
	London
	SW5 9ED
Telephone	071-373 4553
Fax	071-373 4555
Hours	By appointment
Member	BNTA

F J JEFFERY & SON LTD

	61 Locking Close
	Melksham
	Wiltshire
	SN12 6XS
Telephone	Melksham [0225] 703143
Hours	Postal only
Regular ads	Coin Monthly

JEREMY TENNISWOOD

	28 Gordon Road
	Aldershot
	Hampshire
	GU11 1ND
Telephone	Aldershot [0252] 319791
Hours	10.00-17.00
	Sat 09.00-17.00
Closed	Wed Sun

JERSEY COIN CO LTD

	26 Halkett Street
	St Helier
	Jersey
	Channel Islands
Telephone	Jersey [0534] 25743
Hours	09.00-17.00
Half-day	Thu

S P M JEWELLERS

	9 Bedford Place
	Southampton
	Hampshire
	SO1 2DB
Telephone	Southampton [0703] 223255/227923
Hours	09.15-17.00
Sat	09.15-16.00
Closed	Mon Sun
Member	BNTA

D J JEWELLERY
166-168 Ashley Road
Parkstone
Poole
Dorset
BH14 9BY

Telephone	Poole [0202] 745148
Regular ads	Coin Monthly
Member	NAG

JOAN ALLEN ELECTRONICS LTD
190 Main Road
Biggin Hill
Kent
TN16 3BB

Telephone	Biggin Hill [0959] 71255
Closed	Sun

JOHN GAUNT
21 Harvey Road
Bedford
Bedfordshire
MK41 9LF

Telephone	Bedford [0234] 217686
Hours	By appointment

JOHN L HOMAN
Oxford Grange
Marsh Lane
Barrow Haven
Barrow-on-Humber
South Humberside
DN19 7ER

Telephone	Barrow-on-Humber [0469] 32109
Hours	09.00-20.00
	Postal only
Closed	Sun
Regular ads	Coin Monthly

JOHN OF SATIN
27 Osborne Road
Cale Green
Stockport
Cheshire
SK2 6RQ

Telephone	Manchester [061] 477 1064
Hours	Postal only
Regular ads	Coin Monthly

JOHN WELSH
PO Box 1
Uttoxeter
Staffordshire

Telephone	Uttoxeter [0889] 563554
Hours	13.00-20.00
	Postal only
Half-day	Mon Tue Wed Thu Fri Sat
Closed	Sun
Regular ads	Coin Monthly

JUMBO COINS
22 Woodend Lane
Stalybridge
Cheshire
SK15 2SR

Telephone	Manchester [061] 338 5741
Hours	14.00-19.00
Closed	Mon Tue Wed Thu

J R KADOW
Liverton House
Liverton
Nr Newton Abbot
Devon
TQ12 6HR

Telephone	Bickington [062682] 1756
Hours	Postal only

KENDONS
10 London Road
Grays
Essex
RM17 5XY

Telephone	Grays Thurrock [0375] 371200
Hours	09.30-17.30
Closed	Mon Tue Wed

KNIGHTSBRIDGE COINS
43 Duke Street
St James's
London
SW1Y 6DD

Telephone	071-930 8215/7597
Fax	071-930 8214
Hours	10.00-17.30
Regular ads	Coin Monthly
Member	ANA BNTA IAPN

LANCASHIRE COIN & MEDAL CO
31 Adelaide Street
Fleetwood
Lancashire
FY7 6AD

Telephone	Fleetwood [0253] 779308
Hours	Postal only
Regular ads	Coin Monthly

LANCE CHAPLIN
17 Wanstead Lane
Ilford
Essex
IG1 3SB

Telephone	081-554 7154
Hours	Postal only
Regular ads	Coin Monthly

LAURIE BAMFORD
272 Melfort Road
Thornton Heath
Surrey
CR7 7RR

Telephone	081-684 6515
Hours	Callers by appointment
	Postal only

LES HUGHES

	17 Carfield
	Clay Brow
	Skelmersdale
	Lancashire
	WN8 9DR
Telephone	Skelmersdale [0695] 33089
	Evenings only
Hours	Postal only
	08.00-16.00 Preston Market
Half-day	Tue
Closed	Thu

LIBRITZ STAMPS

	70 London Road
	Apsley
	Hemel Hempstead
	Hertfordshire
	HP3 9SD
Telephone	Hemel Hempstead [0442] 242691
Hours	10.00-18.00
Closed	Sun

LIGHTHOUSE PUBLICATIONS (UK)

	4 Beaufort Road
	Reigate
	Surrey
	RH2 9DJ
Telephone	Reigate [0737] 244222
Fax	[0737] 24743

LINDNER PUBLICATIONS LTD

	26 Queen Street
	Cubbington
	Leamington Spa
	Warwickshire
	CV32 7NA
Telephone	Leamington Spa [0926] 425026
Fax	[0926] 422706
Hours	09.00-13.00
Closed	Sat Sun
Regular ads	Coin Monthly

LIVERPOOL COIN & MEDAL CO

	68 Lime Street
	Liverpool
	Merseyside
	L1
Telephone	Liverpool [051] 708 8441
Hours	10.00-17.00
Closed	Sun

LLOYD BENNETT

	PO Box 2
	Monmouth
	Gwent
	Wales
	NP5 3YE
Telephone	Monmouth [0600] 890634
Hours	09.00-16.00
	Tue Abergavenny Market
	Fri Sat Monmouth Market
Closed	Sun
Member	BNTA

LUBBOCKS

	315 Regent Street
	London
	W1R 7YB
Telephone	071-580 9922 & 071-637 7922
Fax	071-637 7602
Hours	By appointment
Closed	Sat Sun
Member	ANA BNTA IAPN IBNS INTO

MALCOLM BORD

	16 Charing Cross Road
	London
	WC2H 0HR
Telephone	071-836 0631 & 071-240 0479
Hours	09.00-17.30
Closed	Sun
Member	ANA BNTA

MALCOLM ELLIS

	Petworth Road
	Witley
	Nr Godalming
	Surrey
	GU8 5LK
Telephone	Wormley [0428] 682896
Hours	Postal only

MALCOLM R GORDON MEDALS & MILITARIA

	33 Victoria Road
	South Woodford
	London
	E18 1LJ
Telephone	081-530 6229
Fax	081-989 1114
Hours	10.00-18.00
Closed	Sun
Member	OMRS

MALTHOUSE COINS & ANTIQUITIES

	3 Malthouse Row
	Church Road
	Wereham
	Downham Market
	Nr King's Lynn
	Norfolk
	PE33 9AP
Telephone	Downham Market [0366] 501057
Hours	08.00-23.00
	Postal only
Regular ads	Coin Monthly

MANCHESTER COIN & MEDAL CENTRE

	Antique Gallery
	Royal Exchange Building
	Cross Street
	Manchester
Telephone	Manchester [061] 832 9535
Hours	10.15-16.45

MANNIN COLLECTIONS LTD
5 Castle Street
Peel
Isle of Man
Telephone   Douglas [0624] 843 897
Hours   10.00-17.00
Half-day   Thu
Closed   Sun

MARK CARTER
PO Box 470
Slough
Berkshire
SL3 6RR
Telephone   Slough [0753] 34777
Hours   09.00-21.00
Postal only

I MARKOVITS – ENAMELLED COINS
1-3 Cobbold Mews
London
W12 9LB
Telephone   081-749 3000
Member   BJA

MARRON COINS
7 Beacon Close
Sheffield
South Yorkshire
S9 1AA
Telephone   Sheffield [0742] 433500
Hours   Postal only
Regular ads   Coin monthly

MARSH COINS
3 Fitzroy Place
Glasgow
Strathclyde
Scotland
G3 7RH
Hours   Postal only
Regular ads   Coin Monthly

M MARSTON & CO (GOLDCOINS)
M Chaplin Ltd
Suite 202
100 Hatton Garden
London
EC1N 8NX
Telephone   071-242 7357
24 hour answer phone
Closed   Sat Sun

C J MARTIN (COINS) LTD
85 The Vale
Southgate
London
N14 6AT
Telephone   081-882 1509
Hours   Postal only
Regular ads   Coin Monthly
Member   BNTA

McKNIGHT & CO
3 Rugby Place
Kemptown
Brighton
East Sussex
BN2 5JB
Telephone   Brighton [0273] 685824
Hours   Postal only
Regular ads   Coin Monthly

MICHAEL BEAUMONT
PO Box 8
Carlton
Nottinghamshire
NG4 4QZ
Telephone   Nottingham [0602] 878361
Hours   Postal only
Member   BNTA

MICHAEL COINS
6 Hillgate Street
London
W8 7SR
Telephone   071-727 1518
Hours   10.00-17.00
Closed   Sat Sun

MICHAEL DICKINSON
Richard House
30-32 Mortimer Street
London
WIN 7RA
Telephone   081-441 7175
Hours   09.00-19.00
Postal only
Member   ANA BNTA

MICHAEL E EWINS
Meyrick Heights
20 Meyrick Park Crescent
Bournemouth
Dorset
BH3 7AQ
Telephone   Bournemouth [0202] 290674
Hours   Postal only
Regular ads   Coin Monthly

MICHAEL O'GRADY
9-11 Kensington High Street
London
W8 5NP
Telephone   081-969 8842
Hours   Postal only
Regular ads   Coin Monthly
Member   IBNS

MICHAEL TRENERRY LTD
Newhaven House
1 Northfield Drive
Truro
Cornwall
TR1 2BS
Telephone   Truro [0872] 77977
Hours   Callers by appointment only
Regular ads   Coin Monthly
Member   BNTA

MIDLAND MEDALS

	12 Commerce House
	Vicarage Lane
	Water Orton
	Birmingham
	B46 1RR
Telephone	Birmingham [021] 7475983
Fax	[0564] 784245
Hours	10.00-17.00
	Postal only

MINIATURE MEDALS

	30 Coventry Road
	Burbage
	Leicestershire
	LE10 2HP
Telephone	Hinckley [0455] 239262
Hours	09.00-18.00
	Postal only

MODERN COINS & STAMPS

	24 Market Hall
	Arndale Centre
	Luton
	Bedfordshire
	LU1 2TA
Telephone	Luton [0582] 412839
Hours	09.00-17.00
Half-day	Wed

C MOORE LTD

	The Broadway
	St Ives
	Cambridgeshire
	PE17 4BX
Telephone	St Ives [0480] 63753
Closed	Thu

D H MORLEY

	PO Box 276
	Luton
	Bedfordshire
	LU3 4EL
Telephone	Luton [0582] 490697
Hours	Postal only
	Callers by appointment

CAPT L E MULCROW

	138 St Williams Way
	Rochester
	Kent
	ME1 2PE
Telephone	Medway [0634] 407076
Hours	Postal only
Regular ads	Coin Monthly

MULLHULLAND IGNATIOUS

	PO Box 19
	Beeston
	Nottinghamshire
	NG9 2NE
Hours	Postal only

NATHAN HARRIS COINS & MEDALS

	PO Box 58
	West PDO
	Nottingham
	Nottinghamshire
	NG7 1AJ
Telephone	Nottingham [0602] 473099
Hours	Postal only

NEW FOREST LEAVES

	Bisterne Close
	Burley
	Ringwood
	Hampshire
	BH24 4BA
Telephone	Burley [04253] 3315

NIGEL A CLARK

	Hedgecourt House
	Felbridge
	East Grinstead
	West Sussex
	RH19 2QQ
Telephone	East Grinstead [0342] 315483
Hours	Postal only

NORTH SOMERSET COINS

	17 Elm Close
	Yatton
	Avon
Telephone	Yatton [0934] 838187
Hours	09.00-17.00
	Postal only

NORTH WALES COINS LTD

	1b Penrhyn Road
	Colwyn Bay
	Clwyd
	Wales
Telephone	Colwyn Bay [0492] 533023/532129
Hours	09.30-17.30
Closed	Wed Sun
Member	BNTA

NOTABILITY

	'Mallards'
	Chirton
	Devizes
	Wiltshire
	SN10 3QX
Telephone	Chirton [038084] 593
Hours	07.30-22.00
	Postal only
Member	IBNS

THE NUMISMERY

	189b Oxford Road
	Reading
	Berkshire
	RG1 7UZ
Telephone	Reading [0734] 582145
Hours	11.00-20.30
Half-day	Sun

ONGAR COINS

	14 Longfields
	Marden Ash
	Ongar
	Essex
	IG7 6DS
Hours	Postal only
Regular ads	Coin Monthly

PANDORO'S COIN CO

	47 Downsview
	Chatham
	Kent
	ME5 0AP
Telephone	Chatham [0634] 406032
Hours	Postal only
Regular ads	Coin Monthly

PATRICK SEMMENS

	3 Hospital Road
	Half Key
	Malvern
	Worcestershire
	WR14 1UZ
Telephone	Leigh Sinton [0886] 33123
Hours	Postal only
Regular ads	Coin Monthly

PAUL DAVIES LTD

	PO Box 17
	Ilkley
	West Yorkshire
	LS29 8TZ
Telephone	Ilkley [0943] 603116
Fax	[0943] 816326
Hours	Postal only
Regular ads	Coin Monthly
Member	ANA BNTA

PENRITH COIN & STAMP CENTRE

	37 King Street
	Penrith
	Cumbria
	CA11 7AY
Telephone	Penrith [0768] 64185
Hours	09.00-17.30
Half-day	Wed
Closed	Sun

PENTLAND COINS

	Pentland House
	92 High Street
	Wick
	Caithness
	Scotland
	KW14 L5
Hours	Postal only
Member	IBNS

PETER F BROADBELT

	10 Dragon Road
	Harrogate
	North Yorkshire
	HG1 5DF
Telephone	Harrogate [0423] 562037
Hours	11.00-18.00
Closed	Sun

PETER HANCOCK

	40 West Street
	Chichester
	West Sussex
	PO19 1RP
Telephone	Chichester [0243] 786173
Closed	Sun

PETER IRELAND LTD

	31 Clifton Street
	Blackpool
	Lancashire
	FY1 1JQ
Telephone	Blackpool [0253] 21588
Fax	[0253] 300232
Hours	09.00-17.30
Closed	Sun
Member	BNTA IBNS

PETER MORRIS

	1 Station Concourse
	Bromley North Station
	Bromley
	Kent
	BR1 1NN
Telephone	081-466 1762 & 081-313 3410
Hours	Fri 16.30-20.00
	Sat 09.00-14.00
	Or by appointment
Postal	PO Box 223
	Bromley
	Kent
	BR1 4EQ

PHILCARD INTERNATIONAL

	58 Greenacres
	Hendon Lane
	London
	N3 3TD
Telephone	081-349 1610
Fax	081-346 6007
Hours	Postal only

PHIL GOODWIN

	7 Salterns Avenue
	Southsea
	Hampshire
	PO4 8QH
Telephone	Havant [0705] 871773/452001
Hours	Postal or by appointment
Regular ads	Coin Monthly
Member	ADA

PHILIP COHEN NUMISMATICS

	20 Cecil Court
	Charing Cross Road
	London
	WC2N 4HE
Telephone	071-379 0615
Hours	10.30-17.30
Half-day	Mon Sat
Closed	Sun
Regular ads	Coin Monthly
Member	ANA

PHILIP GREENE

	11a Ladybridge Road
	Cheadle Hulme
	Cheshire
	SK8 5LL
Telephone	Manchester [061] 440 0685
Regular ads	Coin Monthly

PHILLIPS OF OXFORD

	39 Park End Street
	Oxford
	Oxfordshire
	OX1 1JD
Telephone	Oxford [0865] 723524
Fax	[0865] 791064
Hours	Mon-Fri 08.30-17.00
	Sat 09.00-12.00
Half-day	Sat
Closed	Sun
Regular ads	Coin Monthly

POBJOY MINT LTD

	92 Oldfields Road
	Sutton
	Surrey
	SM1 2NW
Telephone	081-641 0370
Fax	081-644 1028
Hours	09.00-17.00
Closed	Sat Sun
Regular ads	Coin Monthly
Member	ANA BNTA

S R PORTER

	18 Trinity Road
	Headington Quarry
	Oxford
	Oxfordshire
	OX3 8LQ
Telephone	Oxford [0865] 66851
Hours	08.30-14.30
	For telephone only 17.30-18.30
	Postal only
Closed	Sat Sun
Regular ads	Coin Monthly
Member	ANA

RARE COIN INVESTMENTS PLC

	Weir Bank
	Bray on Thames
	Nr Maidenhead
	Berkshire
	SL6 2ED
Telephone	Maidenhead [0628] 776907
	[0836] 322966
	24 hour answer phone
Fax	[0628] 770701
Hours	07.30-17.00
Closed	Sat Sun
Regular ads	Coin Monthly

A E B REED, COINS OF THE WORLD

	1a Lansdowne Crescent
	Lansdowne
	Bournemouth
	Dorset
	BH1 1RU
Telephone	Bournemouth [0202] 555778
Hours	10.00-13.30
	18.00-21.00
	Postal only
Closed	Sun
Regular ads	Coin Monthly

DR P A REES (BANKNOTES)

	39 Shoreswood
	Bolton
	Lancashire
	BL1 7DD
Hours	Postal only
Member	IBNS

REGTON LTD

	82 Cleveland Street
	Birmingham
	B19 3SN
Telephone	Birmingham [021] 359 2379
Hours	09.30-17.00
Closed	Sun

RHYL COIN & STAMP CENTRE

	12 Sussex Street
	Rhyl
	Clwyd
	Wales
Telephone	Rhyl [0745] 338112
Hours	10.00-17.30
Closed	Sun

RICHARD W JEFFERY

	Trebehor
	Porthcurno
	Penzance
	Cornwall
	TR19 6LS
Telephone	Sennen [0736] 871263
Hours	Postal only

RICKY'S DISCOUNT COINS

	PO Box 112
	London
	WC1B 3LU
Fax	071-323 2860
Hours	Postal only
Member	ANA IBNS

F J RIST

	Rectory Lane
	Nailstone
	Nuneaton
	Warwickshire
	CV13 0QQ
Telephone	Ibstock [0530] 60009
Hours	Postal only
Closed	Sun

ROBERT BREND

	23 Green End
	Gamlingay
	Sandy
	Bedfordshire
	SG19 3LF
Telephone	Gamlingay [0767] 50649
Hours	08.00-21.00
	Postal only
Regular ads	Coin Monthly

ROBERT JOHNSON COIN CO

	PO Box 194
	15 Bury Place
	London
	WC1A 2JN
Telephone	071-831 0305
Hours	10.30-18.00
Half-day	Sat 10.30-15.00
Closed	Sun
Member	BNTA

ROBERT SHARMAN NUMISMATIST

	36 Dairsie Road
	Eltham
	London
	SE9 1XH
Telephone	081-850 6450
Hours	Mon-Fri 09.00-18.00
	Postal only
Member	ANA

ROBERT TYE

	Poll Toran
	Loch Eynort
	South Uist
	Western Isles
	PA81 5SJ
Hours	Postal only

ROBIN FINNEGAN STAMP SHOP

	83 Skinnergate
	Darlington
	Co Durham
	DL3 7LX
Telephone	Darlington [0325] 489820/357674
Hours	10.00-17.30
Closed	Wed

RONALD C WHITE

	21 Brookly Gardens
	Fleet
	Hampshire
	GU13 9BU
Telephone	Fleet [0252] 615536
Hours	Postal only

S J ROOD & CO LTD

	52-53 Burlington Arcade
	London
	W1V 9AE
Telephone	071-493 0739
Closed	Sun
Member	BNTA

ROWLETTS

	338 High Street
	Lincoln
	Lincolnshire
Telephone	Lincoln [0522] 24139
Hours	09.00-17.00
Half-day	Wed
Closed	Sun

SAFE ALBUMS (UK) LTD

	16 Falcon Business Park
	Ivanhoe Road
	Hogwood Lane
	Finchampstead
	Berkshire
	RG11 4QW
Telephone	Reading [0734] 328976
Fax	[0734] 328612
Hours	09.00-17.30
Closed	Sat Sun
Regular ads	Coin Monthly

SALTFORD COINS

	Boyds Paddock
	Grange Road
	Saltford
	Bristol
	Avon
	BS18 3AQ
Telephone	Saltford [0225] 873512
Hours	09.00-18.00
	Postal only
Regular ads	Coin Monthly

I S SANDIFORD & CO LTD

	3 Marriotts Court
	Brown Street
	Manchester
	M2 1EA
Telephone	Manchester [061] 834 9346
Hours	09.00-16.30
Closed	Sun

SCHWER COINS

	6 South Hill
	Felixstowe
	Suffolk
	IP11 8AA
Telephone	Felixstowe [0304] 278580
Fax	[0394] 271348
Telex	987129
Hours	09.00-18.00
	By appointment
Half-day	Sat
Closed	Sun
Regular ads	Coin Monthly
Member	ANA BNTA

STUART J TIMMINS

	Smallwood Lodge Bookshop
	Newport
	Shropshire
Telephone	Newport [0952] 813232
Closed	Sun

B A SEABY LTD
	7 Davies Street
	London
	W1Y 1LL
Telephone	071-495 2590
Fax	071-491 1595
Hours	09.30-17.00
Closed	Sat Sun
Regular ads	Coin Monthly
Member	BNTA IAPN

T SEXTON
	19 Great Western Avenue
	Bridgend
	Mid Glamorgan
	Wales
	CF31 1NN
Telephone	Bridgend [0656] 4861
Hours	Postal only
Member	IBNS

SHEPSHED COINS & JEWELLERY
	24 Charnwood Road
	Shepshed
	Leicestershire
	LE12 9QF
Telephone	Shepshed [0509] 502511
Hours	09.15-16.30
Closed	Tue Sun

SHREWSBURY COLLECTORS' GALLERY
	18 The Parade
	St Marys Place
	Shrewsbury
	Salop
	SY1 1DL
Hours	09.00-17.30

SIMMONS & SIMMONS LTD
	PO Box 104
	Leytonstone
	London
	E11 1ND
Telephone	081-989 8097
Hours	Postal only
Regular ads	Coin Monthly
Member	ANA BNTA IBNS

E SMITH
	489 Skellingthorpe Road
	Lincoln
	Lincolnshire
	LN6 0QW
Telephone	Lincoln [0522] 684681
Hours	09.00-18.00
	Postal only
Member	ANA BNTA IBNS

J SMITH
	47 The Shambles
	York
	Yorkshire
	YO1 2LX
Telephone	York [0904] 654769
Hours	09.30-17.00
Closed	Sun
Member	BNTA

SOUTH COAST COINS
	16 Fairlawn Close
	Southampton
	Hampshire
	SO1 8DT
Telephone	Southampton [0703] 738697
Hours	Postal only

SOUTHERN COINS
	51 Beach Road
	Selsey
	West Sussex
	PO20 0LT
Telephone	Chichester [0243] 606698
Hours	10.00-22.00
	Postal only
Regular ads	Coin Monthly

SPINK & SON LTD
	5-7 King Street
	St James's
	London
	SW1Y 6QS
Telephone	071-930 7888
Fax	071-839 4853
Telex	916711
Hours	09.30-17.30
Regular ads	Coin Monthly
Member	ANA BNTA IAPN IBNS

SPINK MODERN COLLECTIONS LTD
	PO Box 222
	29-35 Gladstone Road
	Croydon
	Surrey
	CR9 3RP
Telephone	081-689 5131
Fax	081-689 3397
Hours	09.00-17.00
	Postal only

THE SPINNING WHEEL
	1 Liverpool Road
	Birkdale
	Southport
	Merseyside
	PR8 4AR
Telephone	Southport [0704] 68245/67613
Closed	Tue
Member	IBNS

SQUIRREL PUBLISHING LTD
	Hobsley House
	Frodesley
	Shrewsbury
	Shropshire
	SY5 7HD
Telephone	Acton Burnell [06944] 268
Fax	[06944] 268
Hours	09.00-18.00
Half-day	Sat
Closed	Sun
Member	BNTA IBNS

292

THE STAMP & COIN SHOP

(Mahogany coin cabinets)
3 Norman Road
St Leonards-on-Sea
East Sussex
TN37 6HH

Telephone	Hastings [0424] 436682
Hours	09.00-18.00
Regular ads	Coin Monthly

STAMP & COLLECTORS CENTRE

404 York Town Road
College Town
Camberley
Surrey
GU15 4PR

Telephone	Camberley [0276] 32587
Fax	[0276] 32505
Hours	Mon Tue Thu Sat 09.00-17.00
	Wed Fri 09.00-19.00
Closed	Sun

STAMP INSURANCE SERVICES

2 Bakery Meadow
Puddington
Tiverton
Devon
EX16 8LW

Telephone	Tiverton [0884] 860061
Hours	09.00-18.00
Closed	Sun
Hours	Postal only

STANLEY GIBBONS

Parkside
Ringwood
Hampshire
BH24 3SH

Telephone	Ringwood [0425] 472363
Fax	[0425] 470247
Hours	08.30-17.00
	Postal only

STEPHEN J BETTS

4 Victoria Street
Narborough
Leicestershire
LE9 5DP

Telephone	Leicester [0533] 864434
Hours	Postal only
Regular ads	Coin Monthly

STERLING COINS & MEDALS

2 Somerset Road
Boscombe
Bournemouth
Dorset
BH7 6JH

Telephone	Bournemouth [0202] 423881
Hours	09.30-16.30
Closed	Wed

STEWART WARD

1 London Road
Westerham
Kent
TN16 1RF

Telephone	Westerham [0959] 63997

STRAWBRIDGE

Blue Hills
Blowing House Hill
Ludgvan
Penzance
Cornwall
TR20 8AW

Telephone	Penzance [0736] 740201
Hours	Postal only
Regular ads	Coin Monthly

STUDIO COINS (S MITCHELL)

16 Kilham Lane
Winchester
Hampshire
SO22 5PT

Telephone	Winchester [0962] 53156
Hours	09.00-17.00
	24 hour answer phone
	Postal only
Member	ANA BNTA

SYMES PROMOTIONS

93 Charlton Mead Drive
Westbury-on-Trym
Bristol
Avon
BS10 6LW

Telephone	Bristol [0272] 501074
Hours	09.00-18.00
Regular ads	Coin Monthly

G THORP – COINS

8 Ley Hey Avenue
Marple
Stockport
Cheshire
SK6 6PS

Telephone	Manchester [061] 427 6347
Hours	Postal only
Regular ads	Coin Monthly

TIM OWEN COINS

63 Allerton Grange Rise
Leeds 17
West Yorkshire

Telephone	Leeds [0532] 688015
Hours	Postal only

TOAD HALL MEDALS

Toad Hall
Court Road
Newton Ferrers
Plymouth
Devon
PL8 1DH

Telephone	Plymouth [0752] 872672
Fax	[0752] 872723
Hours	08.30-19.30
	Postal only
Closed	Sun

TONY RADMAN

Denver House
17 Witney Street
Burford
Oxfordshire
OX8 4RU

Telephone	Burford [099 382] 2040
Fax	[099 382] 2769
Hours	10.00-17.00
Regular ads	Coin Monthly

TRAFALGAR SQ COLLECTORS CENTRE

Trafalgar Square
7 Whitcomb Street
London
WC2H 7HA

Telephone	071-930 1979
Hours	10.00-17.30
Closed	Sat Sun
Member	ANA BNTA LM OMRS

D TRAYNOR

PO Box 1
Disley
Cheshire
SK12 2HD

Telephone	New Mills [0663] 762424
Hours	10.00-22.00
	Postal only
Regular ads	Coin Monthly

VAL SMITH

170 Derby Road
Nottingham
Nottinghamshire
NG7 1LR

Telephone	Nottingham [0602] 781194
Hours	11.00-16.30
Closed	Thu

VALE

21 Tranquil Vale
Blackheath
London
SE3 0BU

Telephone	081-852 9817
Hours	10.00-17.30
Closed	Thu Sun
Regular ads	Coin Monthly
Member	ADA

VANITY FAYRE

2 Commercial Road
Mousehole
Penzance
Cornwall

Hours	Summer 10.00-17.00
	Winter 14.00-17.00
Closed	Summer Sun
	Winter Thu Sun

VICTORY COINS

184 Chichester Road
North End
Portsmouth
Hampshire
PO2 0AX

Telephone	Portsmouth [0705] 751908/663450
Hours	09.15-17.30
Closed	Sun
Regular ads	Coin Monthly

G W WALKER

40 Saunders Road
Oxford
Oxfordshire
OX4 2EF

WALLIS & WALLIS

West Street Auction Galleries
Lewes
Sussex
BN7 2NJ

Telephone	Lewes [0273] 476562
Hours	09.00-17.30
Closed	Sat Sun

WARWICK'S & CO

81 Worchester Street
Wolverhampton
West Midlands
WV2 4LE

Telephone	Wolverhampton [0902] 21607
Hours	09.30-17.30
Half-day	Thu
Closed	Sun

WATLING & CROMEEKE

142 King Street
Ramsgate
Kent
CT11 8PJ

Telephone	Thanet [0843] 592715
Hours	09.30-12.00
	13.30-17.00
Closed	Thu Sun

B M & S A WEEKS

Unit 6
Mr Micawbers Attic
73 Fisherton Street
Salisbury
Wiltshire
SP2 7ST

Telephone	Salisbury [0722] 337822
Hours	10.00-17.00
Closed	Mon Wed Sun
Regular ads	Coin Monthly
Member	BNTA

WENTWORTH COINS

140 Higham Road
Rushden
Northamptonshire
NN10 9DT

Telephone	Rusden [0933] 55063
Hours	Postal only

WESSEX NUMISMATIC LTD
	PO Box 13
	Eastleigh
	Hampshire
Hours	Postal only
Regular ads	Coin Monthly

WEST ESSEX COIN INVESTMENTS
	176 Hoe Street
	Walthamstow
	London
	E17
Telephone	081-521 8534
Fax	081-521 8534
Hours	09.30-17.30
Closed	Sun
Member	BNTA IBNS

WHITMORE
	Teynham Lodge
	Chase Road
	Upper Colwall
	Malvern
	Worcestershire
	WR13 6DT
Telephone	Colwall [0684] 40651
Hours	Postal only
Member	BNTA

M WILKES
	Bowbridge Lane
	Cheltenham
	Gloucestershire
	GL52 3BL
Telephone	Cheltenham [0242] 574624
Fax	[0242] 227474
Hours	Postal only

J L WILLIAMS
	502 Clive Court
	Maida Vale
	London
	W9 1SG
Telephone	071-286 3461
Hours	Postal only
Regular ads	Coin Monthly

WORLD COINS
	35-36 Broad Street
	Canterbury
	Kent
	CT1 2LR
Telephone	Canterbury [0227] 68887
Hours	09.30-17.30
Half-day	Thu
Closed	Sun

B N YARWOOD
	Yarwood Hall
	Luttongate Road
	Sutton St Edmund
	Spalding
	Lincolnshire
	PE12 0LH
Hours	Postal only
Member	ANA

YESTERDAY'S NEWS
	43 Dundonald Road
	Colwyn Bay
	Clwyd
	Wales
	LL29 7RE
Telephone	Colwyn Bay [0492] 531195
Hours	09.30-21.00

Foreign Dealers

COIN INVEST TRUST
	Meierhofstrasse 17
	Vaduz
	Liechtenstein
	FL-9490
Telephone	[010 41 75] 26454 or 27411
Fax	[075 20317]
Hours	08.00-12.00 13.00-17.00

P FLANAGAN & ASSOC
	PO Box 35544
	Canton
	Ohio 44720
	USA
Telephone	[010 1 216] 494 4044
Fax	[216] 494 2636
Hours	Telephone any time
	Postal only
Member	ANA

RONALD J GILLIO INC
	1013 State Street
	Santa Barbara
	California 9310
	USA
Telephone	[010 1 805] 963 1345
Fax	[805] 962-6659
Hours	09.00-17.00
Closed	Sat Sun
Member	ANA IAPN

Dealer Directory – Specialities

The following pages indicate at a glance the various specialities of the dealers listed in the previous section. There are forty specialities in all:

Africa
Asia
Australasia
Commonwealth
Europe
Scandinavia
South America
World

Austria
Belgium
Britain
Canada
France
Germany
Islands
Netherlands
USA

Bronze
Copper
Crowns
Gold
Hammered
Minors
Modern
New Issues
Proofs
Silver
Year Type Sets

Accessories
Banknotes
Books
Byzantine
Greek
Maundy
Medallions
Medals
Roman
Tokens
Treasure Hunting
Valuations

The dealers are listed geographically by country and by county. Dealers' addresses and details of hours and telephone numbers can be found in the first section of Dealer Directory (see page 273) which is arranged alphabetically and no geographically.

	Africa	Asia	Australasia	Commonwealth	Europe	Scandinavia	South America	World	Austria	Belgium	Britain	Canada	France	Germany	Netherlands	Islands	USA	Bronze	Copper	Crowns	Gold	Hammered	Minors	Modern	New Issues	Proofs	Silver	Year Type Sets	Accessories	Banknotes	Books	Byzantine	Greek	Maundy	Medallions	Medals	Roman	Tokens	Treasure Hunting	Valuations
Channel Islands																																								
JERSEY																																								
HOMELAND HOLDING LTD																•																								
JERSEY COIN CO LTD					•																	•	•	•	•	•				•	•									
England																																								
AVON																																								
BATH STAMP & COIN SHOP																																								
NORTH SOMERSET COINS								•																		•										•	•			
SALTFORD COINS		•	•	•	•				•																		•			•						•	•			
SYMES PROMOTIONS		•	•	•				•										•	•	•	•	•	•				•									•	•			
BEDFORDSHIRE																																								
CASTLE COINS	•				•	•		•	•	•	•	•	•	•													•	•	•											
JOHN GAUNT																		•	•		•					•	•				•				•	•				
MODERN COINS & STAMPS																																								
D H MORLEY													•				•	•		•	•						•	•							•	•			
ROBERT BREND	•	•	•	•	•	•	•	•	•	•	•	•	•	•	•		•	•		•	•						•	•			•				•	•			
BERKSHIRE																																								
BERKSHIRE COIN CENTRE		•	•					•					•							•	•					•	•				•				•	•			
FRANK MILWARD								•	•	•	•		•	•						•	•					•	•				•				•	•			
LODGE COINS																																								
MARK CARTER																																								
THE NUMISMERY																																						•		
RARE COIN INVESTMENTS PLC																																								
SAFE ALBUMS (UK) LTD					•					•	•	•	•	•								•							•											
BUCKINGHAMSHIRE																																								
ELVIDGE TEAL				•																																				
EUROPA NUMISMATICS	•	•	•	•	•	•					•						•	•			•	•			•	•	•				•				•	•			•
CAMBRIDGESHIRE																																								
THE CAMBRIDGE STAMP CENTRE LTD																																								
ELY STAMP & COIN SHOP																																								
GRANTA STAMP & COIN SHOP								•																																
C MOORE LTD													•	•	•	•						•					•	•			•	•		•	•	•	•	•		
CHESHIRE																																								
A F BROCK & COMPANY	•	•	•	•	•	•	•	•	•	•	•	•	•	•	•		•	•		•	•						•	•			•				•	•		•		
B R M COINS	•	•	•	•	•	•	•	•	•	•	•	•	•	•	•	•	•	•	•	•	•	•	•	•	•	•	•	•		•	•	•	•		•	•	•	•		
JOHN OF SATIN	•	•	•	•	•	•	•	•	•	•	•	•	•	•	•		•	•	•	•	•					•	•	•			•				•	•		•		
JUMBO COINS	•	•	•	•	•	•		•	•		•						•	•	•	•	•					•	•				•				•	•			
KEITH S RYAN																		•		•	•					•	•			•					•	•			
PHILIP GREENE					•								•																											
G THORP COINS	•	•	•	•	•	•		•	•		•							•	•	•	•					•	•				•				•	•		•		
D J TRAYNOR								•												•	•						•	•											
CO DURHAM																																								
DUNELME COINS & MEDALS					•																														•	•				
ROBIN FINNEGAN					•				•		•	•	•	•				•		•	•						•								•	•	•			
CORNWALL																																								
GEORGE SOWDEN			•																																					
MICHAEL TRENERRY LTD										•	•	•	•	•	•	•		•	•	•	•						•				•				•	•		•		
RICHARD W JEFFERY	•	•	•	•	•													•		•	•						•								•	•		•		
STRAWBRIDGE	•	•	•	•	•	•	•	•	•		•	•	•	•	•		•	•	•	•	•						•	•				•				•	•			
VANITY FAYRE				•																•	•						•				•				•	•				
CUMBRIA																																								
BANKING MEMORABILIA	•	•	•	•	•	•	•	•	•	•	•	•	•	•	•		•													•	•				•	•		•		
HARRY WALKER					•																																			
PENRITH COIN & STAMP CENTRE					•													•	•	•	•						•								•	•		•		
DEVON																																								
D G BARNEY					•													•	•	•	•						•								•	•		•		
R G HOLMES				•				•										•	•	•	•						•	•			•					•				
JAK																					•						•	•							•	•				
J R KADOW					•																																			
STAMP INSURANCE SERVICES																																								
TOAD HALL MEDALS					•																															•				
DORSET																																								
CAPRICORN																																								
CHRIS BELTON																																								
COTREL MEDALS					•							•		•	•											•														
DORSET COIN CO LTD	•	•	•	•	•	•	•	•	•		•	•	•	•			•			•					•	•	•				•			•		•	•	•		
GLADSTONE					•																																			
D J JEWELLERY					•													•	•	•	•						•								•					
MICHAEL E EWINS													•																							•				
A E B REED, COINS OF THE WORLD	•	•	•	•	•	•		•			•							•	•	•	•				•	•	•				•				•	•			
STERLING COINS & MEDALS								•																			•	•							•	•			
EAST SUSSEX																																								
BRIGHTON COIN COMPANY	•	•			•	•		•	•		•	•	•	•	•		•										•	•			•					•				
DAVID R RUDLING		•			•		•					•								•	•						•				•				•	•				
JAMES & C BRETT					•													•	•	•	•						•								•	•				
McKNIGHT & CO																		•	•	•	•						•				•				•	•				
THE STAMP & COIN SHOP																		•	•	•	•						•									•				
WALLIS & WALLIS					•																						•	•							•	•	•		

DEALER SPECIALITIES

	Africa	Asia	Australasia	Commonwealth	Europe	Scandinavia	South America	World	Austria	Belgium	Britain	Canada	France	Germany	Islands	Netherlands	USA	Bronze	Copper	Crowns	Gold	Hammered	Minors	Modern	New Issues	Proofs	Silver	Year Type Sets	Accessories	Banknotes	Books	Byzantine	Greek	Maundy	Medallions	Medals	Roman	Tokens	Treasure Hunting	Valuations
EAST YORKSHIRE																																								
C J & A J DIXON LTD											●										●															●				
ESSEX																																								
ALFRED S ALLEN & CO								●			●							●	●	●	●		●	●			●	●												
ART OF ARTS LTD (UK)																																			●					
E J & C A BROOKS																		●	●	●		●	●							●										●
COIN & STAMP CENTRE								●			●							●	●	●	●	●					●		●	●				●	●	●	●	●		●
R & J COINS								●			●							●	●	●		●				●	●	●	●	●						●	●	●		●
COLLECTORS' FORUM	●	●	●	●	●	●	●	●	●	●	●	●	●	●	●	●	●	●	●	●	●	●	●	●		●	●	●	●	●	●			●	●	●	●	●		●
COLIN JAMES O'KEEFE					●						●							●	●	●	●													●						●
DRIZEN COINS								●			●							●	●	●		●																		
GEORGE & JANE WHITE																													●	●	●									
GLAZENWOOD				●	●	●		●					●	●			●		●				●	●					●											
P HANSON								●																																
HUDSON					●			●			●								●				●	●					●	●	●								●	
KENDONS								●										●	●	●	●						●		●	●						●				●
LANCE CHAPLIN											●											●										●	●				●	●	●	
ONGAR COINS								●												●				●	●															
GLOUCESTERSHIRE																																								
BUTLER & CO			●					●									●			●			●											●		●	●	●		
M WILKES											●						●			●	●	●				●	●								●	●				●
GREATER LONDON																																								
AGORA IN ASTARTE					●													●	●			●					●					●	●				●			
BAIRD & CO	●	●	●	●	●	●	●	●	●	●	●	●	●	●	●	●	●				●																			
A H BALDWIN & SONS LTD	●	●	●	●	●	●	●	●	●	●	●	●	●	●	●	●	●	●	●	●	●	●									●	●	●	●	●	●	●	●		●
BAUDEY & BRICHER																															●				●					
BIRCHIN LANE GOLD COIN COMPANY								●			●										●			●						●										●
CHELSEA COINS LTD	●	●	●	●	●	●	●	●	●	●	●		●	●	●	●		●	●	●	●	●	●											●						
CHRISTIE MANSON & WOODS LTD																																								
CHRISTOPHER EIMER																																			●					
COINCRAFT			●	●	●		●	●			●	●	●	●		●	●	●	●	●	●	●	●	●	●	●	●	●	●	●	●	●	●	●	●		●	●		●
COLIN NARBETH & SON LTD																														●	●									
DOLPHIN COINS	●	●	●	●	●	●	●	●	●	●	●	●	●	●	●	●	●	●	●	●	●	●	●	●		●	●			●		●	●	●	●	●	●	●		●
FYODOR																																								
GANCE																					●																			●
GEMINI JEWELLERY, STAMPS & COINS																																								
GEORGE RANKIN COIN CO LTD	●	●	●	●	●	●	●	●	●	●	●	●	●	●	●	●	●	●	●	●	●	●	●	●		●	●	●		●				●	●	●	●	●		●
GLENDINING'S					●			●			●						●	●	●	●	●	●	●	●		●	●	●				●	●		●	●	●	●		
GOLD INVESTMENTS LTD																					●						●													
GROVE PHIL, COINS & ANTIQUITIES								●										●	●	●	●	●	●	●	●	●	●	●	●	●	●	●	●	●	●	●	●	●	●	●
J HARDIMAN & SON	●	●	●	●	●	●	●	●	●	●	●	●	●	●	●	●	●	●	●	●	●	●	●			●	●							●	●		●	●		●
INTERCOL LONDON								●																					●	●	●					●		●		●
JAN LIS					●													●			●	●					●								●			●		●
KNIGHTSBRIDGE COINS			●								●	●					●				●																			
LUBBOCKS			●		●		●	●			●	●					●				●					●				●										
MALCOLM BORD																																								
M R GORDON MEDALS & MILITARIA																													●	●						●				●
I MARKOVITS								●																											●	●				
M MARSTON & CO (GOLD COINS)											●										●			●																
C J MARTIN (COINS) LTD																						●									●	●	●				●			
MICHAEL COINS	●	●	●	●	●	●	●	●	●	●	●	●	●	●	●	●	●	●	●	●	●	●	●	●	●	●	●		●	●	●			●		●	●	●		●
MICHAEL DICKINSON	●	●	●	●	●	●	●	●	●	●	●	●	●	●	●	●	●	●	●	●	●	●	●											●	●			●		●
MICHAEL O'GRADY																														●										
PHILCARD INTERNATIONAL																									●															
PHILIP COHEN NUMISMATICS	●	●	●	●	●	●	●	●	●	●	●	●	●	●	●	●	●	●	●	●	●	●	●	●	●	●	●	●						●				●		●
RICKY'S DISCOUNT COINS			●	●	●			●			●	●					●	●	●	●	●	●	●	●		●	●	●	●	●	●	●	●	●	●		●	●		●
ROBERT JOHNSON COIN CO			●	●	●	●		●	●	●	●		●	●	●	●	●	●	●	●	●	●	●	●		●	●		●	●	●	●	●	●	●	●	●	●		●
ROBERT SHARMAN											●											●																●		●
S J ROOD & CO LTD																					●			●																
B A SEABY LTD											●										●	●					●						●				●			●
SIMMONS & SIMMONS LTD	●	●	●	●	●	●	●	●	●	●	●	●	●	●	●	●	●	●	●	●	●	●	●				●			●	●	●	●		●		●	●		●
SPINK & SON LTD																																								
TRAFALGAR SQ COLLECTORS CENTRE																	●													●						●				●
VALE											●							●	●	●	●	●	●				●		●		●		●	●	●	●	●	●		●
WEST ESSEX COIN INVESTMENTS		●	●	●	●	●	●	●	●	●	●	●	●	●	●	●	●	●	●	●	●	●	●	●		●	●	●		●				●	●	●		●		●
J L WILLIAMS (WHOLESALERS)																								●	●					●										
GREATER MANCHESTER																																								
COLIN COOKE								●			●				●			●	●	●	●	●	●	●		●	●							●						●
MANCHESTER COIN & MEDAL CENTRE			●	●	●	●	●	●			●							●	●	●	●	●	●				●		●	●					●	●		●		
I S SANDIFORD & CO LTD																	●			●	●						●			●						●				
HAMPSHIRE																																								
COLISEUM COINS		●																															●				●	●		
JEREMY TENNISWOOD																																								
SPM JEWELLERS								●	●	●	●	●	●	●	●	●	●	●	●	●	●		●	●	●	●	●	●		●										
NEW FOREST LEAVES																															●									
PHIL GOODWIN																						●										●	●				●		●	●
RONALD C WHITE											●									●							●													
SOUTH COAST COINS											●							●	●	●				●	●	●	●	●						●						●
STANLEY GIBBONS																													●											
STUDIO COINS (S MITCHELL)																				●	●	●					●							●						●

	Africa	Asia	Australasia	Commonwealth	Europe	Scandinavia	South America	World	Austria	Belgium	Britain	Canada	France	Germany	Islands	Netherlands	USA	Bronze	Copper	Crowns	Gold	Hammered	Minors	Modern	New Issues	Proofs	Silver	Year Type Sets	Accessories	Banknotes	Books	Byzantine	Greek	Maundy	Medallions	Medals	Roman	Tokens	Treasure Hunting	Valuations
VICTORY COINS																					●																			
WESSEX NUMISMATIC LTD			●	●	●	●		●			●	●		●	●	●	●	●	●	●	●			●			●												●	●
HEREFORD & WORCESTER																																								
B B M COINS											●										●						●													●
HERTFORDSHIRE																																								
K B COINS											●						●	●	●	●	●	●		●		●	●	●							●					
COLLECTORS CORNER					●	●	●	●	●	●	●	●	●	●	●	●	●	●	●	●	●		●				●								●	●	●			
DAVID MILLER (COINS & ANTIQUITIES)											●																								●	●		●		
LIBRITZ STAMPS					●																								●	●	●									
ISLE OF MAN																																								
THE COIN MART									●		●																●													
MANNIN COLLECTIONS LTD									●		●			●																	●		●				●	●		
ISLE OF WIGHT																																								
ARNOLDS ANTIQUES																							●	●		●														
KENT																																								
COIN INVESTMENTS			●								●																													
COINS & MILITARIA			●	●							●							●	●	●					●	●														
COINS OF CANTERBURY																																								
COLLECTORS CORNER	●	●	●	●	●	●	●	●	●	●	●	●	●	●	●	●	●	●	●	●	●	●	●	●	●	●	●	●							●					
C J DENTON					●						●																												●	●
JOAN ALLEN ELECTRONICS LTD																																							●	●
CAPT L E MULCROW														●																						●				
PANDORO'S COIN CO									●																															
PETER MORRIS			●								●							●	●	●	●	●	●	●		●	●	●							●	●	●			
STEWART WARD																																								
WATLING & CROMEEKE																																								
WORLD COINS	●	●	●	●	●	●	●	●	●	●	●	●	●	●	●	●	●	●	●		●		●				●													
LANCASHIRE																																								
J BRIDGEMAN COINS	●	●	●	●	●	●	●	●	●	●	●	●	●	●	●	●	●			●	●									●					●	●	●			
BRITANNIA JEWELLERY CO																																								
R & L COINS			●	●	●						●							●	●	●	●						●													
B J DAWSON (COINS) REGD											●							●	●	●	●	●					●				●		●		●	●	●			
FARTHING SPECIALIST (REGD)	●		●								●							●	●		●						●													
LANCASHIRE COIN & MEDAL CO																																								
PETER IRELAND LTD	●	●	●	●	●	●	●	●	●	●	●	●	●	●	●	●	●										●	●							●					
DR P A REES (BANKNOTES)																											●													
LEICESTERSHIRE																																								
G BARRINGTON SMITH																													●											
M COESHAW	●	●	●	●	●			●	●	●	●	●	●	●	●	●	●	●	●	●	●								●						●					●
COINTACT SERVICES		●	●	●	●			●	●	●	●	●	●	●	●	●	●												●							●			●	●
COSMO COINS				●							●																●				●									
DAVID C PINDER																											●													
MINIATURE MEDALS																																			●					
SHEPSHED COINS & JEWELLERY					●													●	●	●	●					●	●													
STEPHEN J BETTS			●		●															●						●	●		●											
LINCOLNSHIRE																																								
GRANTHAM COINS																																								
ROWLETTS				●							●										●										●		●			●		●		
E SMITH	●	●	●	●	●			●	●	●	●	●	●	●	●	●	●	●	●		●		●				●	●		●			●			●	●	●		●
B N YARWOOD									●		●										●																		●	
MERSEYSIDE																																								
GEOFFREY WEDGWOOD LTD																																								
LES HUGHES			●	●							●						●	●			●	●					●											●		●
LIVERPOOL COIN & MEDAL CO					●						●			●	●		●		●		●	●					●			●					●		●	●		
THE SPINNING WHEEL									●									●	●	●	●	●					●				●		●		●	●				
MIDDLESEX																																								
CONSTANTIA CB														●																						●				
DAVID ALLEN	●	●	●	●	●	●	●	●	●	●	●	●	●	●	●	●	●			●			●	●		●	●							●	●		●		
DON MAC RAE COINS											●							●	●	●	●	●					●	●		●	●	●	●	●	●	●		●		●
H FINE & SON LTD																		●	●	●	●						●													
NORFOLK																																								
CLIVE DENNETT		●	●		●			●		●	●		●				●	●	●	●	●					●	●			●	●				●					●
ELM HILL STAMPS & COINS		●		●			●		●									●	●	●	●						●								●					●
JAMES OF NORWICH	●	●	●	●	●	●	●	●	●	●	●	●	●	●	●	●	●																			●		●	●	●
MALTHOUSE COINS & ANTIQUITIES									●											●		●															●	●	●	●
NORTH HUMBERSIDE																																								
BAXTERS COIN & STAMP EXCHANGE	●	●	●	●	●	●	●	●	●	●	●	●	●	●	●	●	●	●	●		●			●						●	●		●		●	●				
BYZANTIUM NUMISMATISTS																															●	●	●				●			
NORTH YORKSHIRE																																								
ANCIENT WORLD									●									●	●	●	●	●					●				●	●	●		●	●	●			
CATHEDRAL COURT									●									●	●	●	●			●		●	●								●					
PETER F BROADBELT			●	●							●																●													
J SMITH																																								
NORTHAMPTONSHIRE																																								
BARRY BOSWELL BRITISH BANKNOTES																														●	●									
COLLECTA COINS LIMITED		●	●		●	●	●	●	●	●	●	●	●	●			●	●	●	●	●		●	●		●	●						●		●	●	●	●		●
GIUSEPPE MICELI COIN & MEDAL CENTRE					●			●		●								●	●	●	●	●	●																	●
WENTWORTH COINS		●	●		●																																			●
NOTTINGHAMSHIRE																																								
ARTHUR COBWRIGHT																																					●		●	●

	Africa	Asia	Australasia	Commonwealth	Europe	Scandinavia	South America	World	Austria	Belgium	Britain	Canada	France	Germany	Islands	Netherlands	USA	Bronze	Copper	Crowns	Gold	Hammered	Minors	Modern	New Issues	Proofs	Silver	Year Type Sets	Accessories	Banknotes	Books	Byzantine	Greek	Maundy	Medallions	Medals	Roman	Tokens	Treasure Hunting	Valuations
S BURROUGHS PRECIOUS METALS																																								
COINS OF BEESTON	●	●		●	●				●									●	●			●	●						●	●	●	●	●	●	●	●				●
NOTTINGHAMSHIRE																																								
M T R COINS (M T RAY)					●			●									●	●	●	●	●	●		●		●	●	●	●	●					●			●		●
A J CONSULTANTS								●									●	●	●	●	●	●		●	●	●		●		●										
D D & A INGLE								●									●	●	●	●	●	●	●	●	●	●	●	●		●						●			●	
MICHAEL BEAUMONT	●	●	●	●	●	●	●	●	●	●	●	●	●	●	●	●	●	●	●	●	●	●	●	●	●	●	●	●		●					●	●	●			●
MULLHULLAND IGNATIOUS																		●	●	●	●		●	●		●		●		●						●	●			
NATHAN HARRIS COINS & MEDALS					●													●	●	●	●		●	●		●	●	●		●					●	●	●			
VAL SMITH																																								
OXFORDSHIRE																																								
PHILLIPS OF OXFORD				●							●									●															●	●	●			
S R PORTER								●										●	●	●	●	●		●		●	●	●		●					●	●	●			
TONY RADMAN																																								
G W WALKER																																								
SHROPSHIRE																																								
SHREWSBURY COLLECTORS																																								
SQUIRREL PUBLISHING LTD				●							●							●	●	●	●	●	●	●		●	●	●		●					●				●	●
STUART J TIMMINS																																								
SOMERSET																																								
N J AVES																		●	●	●	●		●					●							●		●		●	●
EDDIE BAXTER BOOKS																																								
FOX & CO	●	●	●	●	●	●	●	●	●	●	●	●	●	●	●	●	●	●	●	●	●	●	●	●	●	●	●	●		●										
SOUTH HUMBERSIDE																																								
BROOKLANDS COLLECTIONS	●	●	●	●	●						●				●		●	●	●	●	●	●		●		●	●	●		●					●					
CAVECELLAR LTD	●			●	●		●	●	●	●	●	●	●	●			●	●	●	●	●		●		●		●	●		●										
HUMBER COINS REGD		●	●	●	●	●	●	●	●	●																	●	●					●	●	●					
JOHN L HOMAN																																								
SOUTH YORKSHIRE																																								
CASTLE CURIOS								●																			●			●					●	●		●		
MARRON COINS								●										●	●	●	●		●				●			●					●	●		●		
STAFFORDSHIRE																																								
AURELIO TRIVELLA				●				●										●	●	●	●	●		●	●		●	●		●										
JOHN WELSH				●				●										●	●	●	●		●				●			●										
SUFFOLK																																								
JAMES IN IPSWICH LTD								●																					●	●	●					●			●	●
SCHWER COINS	●	●	●	●	●	●	●	●	●	●	●	●	●	●	●	●	●	●	●	●	●	●	●	●	●	●	●	●		●					●			●		●
SURREY																																								
DAVID KEABLE & CO																													●											
DAVIDSON MONK FAIRS																																								
FAR EAST COINS LTD	●	●		●							●		●				●	●	●	●	●	●		●		●										●				
GRAEME & LINDA MONK			●	●	●						●			●			●	●	●	●	●		●				●								●			●		
LAURIE BAMFORD											●							●	●	●	●		●				●													
LIGHTHOUSE PUBLICATIONS (UK)																													●											
MALCOLM ELLIS																																								
POBJOY MINT LTD																					●			●	●	●	●	●												
SPINK MODERN COLLECTIONS LTD								●										●	●	●	●		●	●		●									●	●				
STAMP & COLLECTORS CENTRE								●										●	●	●	●		●	●		●				●	●									
TYNE & WEAR																																								
BRITANNIA ENTERPRISES																													●											
B FRANK & SON	●	●	●	●	●	●	●	●	●	●	●	●	●	●	●	●	●	●	●	●	●		●	●		●	●	●		●	●					●			●	
WARWICKSHIRE																																								
LINDNER PUBLICATIONS LTD																							●						●		●									
F J RIST								●			●										●														●	●		●		
WEST MIDLANDS																																								
BRITISH NUMISMATIC TRADE																																								
DAVID FLETCHER LTD	●	●	●	●	●		●				●						●	●			●	●	●	●	●	●	●	●		●					●			●		
DON OLIVER GOLD COINS					●			●													●	●		●						●					●	●				
DYAS COINS & MEDALS																														●	●				●	●				
EDEN COINS																																				●				
FORMAT OF BIRMINGHAM LTD	●	●	●	●	●	●	●	●	●	●	●	●	●	●	●	●	●	●	●	●	●	●	●	●	●	●	●	●		●					●	●				
MIDLAND MEDALS																																								
REGTON LTD																																								●
WARWICK'S & CO			●	●	●					●							●	●	●	●	●		●				●	●		●	●				●	●	●			
WEST SUSSEX																																								
NIGEL A CLARK								●										●	●	●	●	●		●		●	●				●				●	●		●	●	●
PETER HANCOCK						●		●										●	●	●	●		●				●				●				●	●		●		●
SOUTHERN COINS	●		●	●	●		●										●	●	●		●						●				●				●	●				
WEST YORKSHIRE																																								
AIREDALE COINS			●	●	●						●													●	●	●	●	●		●					●	●	●	●	●	
ANTIQUE BOUTIQUE			●	●	●													●	●	●	●		●				●	●		●					●	●	●	●	●	
COIN & COLLECTORS CENTRE						●		●										●	●	●	●		●				●			●					●	●				
COINS INTERNATIONAL	●	●	●	●	●	●	●	●	●	●	●	●	●	●	●	●	●	●	●	●	●	●	●	●	●	●	●	●		●		●	●	●	●	●	●	●	●	●
COLLECTORS CORNER								●										●	●	●	●																			
K A CUDWORTH	●		●	●	●	●	●	●	●	●	●	●	●				●	●	●	●	●				●	●	●	●							●	●				
PAUL DAVIES LTD					●																●						●													
TIM OWEN COINS																																								

	Africa	Asia	Australasia	Commonwealth	Europe	Scandinavia	South America	World	Austria	Belgium	Britain	Canada	France	Germany	Islands	Netherlands	USA	Bronze	Copper	Crowns	Gold	Hammered	Minors	Modern	New Issues	Proofs	Silver	Year Type Sets	Accessories	Banknotes	Books	Byzantine	Greek	Maundy	Medallions	Medals	Roman	Tokens	Treasure Hunting	Valuations
WILTSHIRE																																								
CASTLE GALLERIES (JOHN C LODGE)											•							•	•	•	•		•	•	•	•	•	•	•	•	•				•	•	•			•
JAMES GARRIOCK											•										•												•	•				•		•
F J JEFFREY & SON LTD			•			•																		•	•				•	•						•		•	•	•
NOTABILITY					•																			•	•				•	•					•	•		•		•
B M & S A WEEKS			•	•	•			•		•	•	•	•	•	•	•	•			•	•						•		•	•					•	•	•	•		•
WORCESTERSHIRE																																								
EVESHAM STAMP & COIN CENTRE			•			•												•	•	•	•		•	•	•	•	•		•	•					•	•	•			•
PATRICK SEMMENS			•			•												•	•	•	•		•	•	•	•	•		•	•					•	•	•	•	•	•
WHITMORE	•	•	•	•	•	•		•	•		•	•			•	•			•	•			•	•		•		•							•	•	•			
Republic of Ireland																																								
CORK																																								
EAGLE COINS											•												•																	
DUBLIN																																								
COINS & MEDALS (REGD)	•	•	•	•	•	•		•	•	•	•	•	•	•	•	•	•		•	•	•	•	•	•		•	•		•	•	•	•	•	•	•	•	•	•		•
Scotland																																								
CAITHNESS																																								
PENTLAND COINS																															•									
DUMFRIES																																								
R I GROVES					•		•																																	
FIFE																																								
ALISTAIR GIBB																															•									
LOTHIAN																																								
DAVID L CAVANAGH					•																																			
EDINBURGH COIN SHOP	•	•	•	•	•	•		•	•	•	•	•	•	•	•	•	•		•	•	•	•	•	•	•	•	•		•	•						•	•	•		•
STRATHCLYDE																																								
GLASGOW STAMP SHOP																		•	•	•	•																			
A D HAMILTON & CO					•					•			•		•	•		•	•	•	•																			•
MARSH COINS					•													•	•	•	•					•	•													•
WESTERN ISLES																																								
ROBERT TYE	•		•																•																					
Wales																																								
CLWYD																																								
GOULBORN COLLECTION											•							•	•	•	•		•																	
NORTH WALES COINS LTD			•		•						•								•	•	•																			
RHYL COIN & STAMP CENTRE					•													•	•	•	•	•			•				•						•	•		•		•
YESTERDAY'S NEWS																											•								•					
GWENT																																								
A HALSE					•																																			
LLOYD BENNETT	•	•	•	•	•	•		•	•	•	•				•					•	•						•		•	•					•	•		•		•
DECUS COINS																		•	•	•	•											•	•	•	•		•			
MID-GLAMORGAN																																								
T SEXTON																																								
DYFED																																								
R P & P J BECKETT											•																													
BOOKMARK																		•	•	•	•									•										
POWYS																																								
GALATA COINS LTD	•	•		•	•	•		•	•	•	•	•						•	•	•		•	•				•		•	•	•	•	•		•	•	•	•		•
WEST GLAMORGAN																																								
GOLD SILVER SHOP																																								

Auctioneer Directory

Auctioneers not included in this directory but who wish to be in *Coin 1993 Year Book* should write to the Editor, Sovereign House, Brentwood, Essex CM14 4SE. There is no charge.

England

Avon

SOLENT PHILATELIC AUCTIONS
PO Box 11
Keynsham
Bristol
Avon
BS18 1DG
Telephone   Bristol [0272] 724049

Cheshire

A F BROCK & COMPANY
269 London Road
Hazelgrove
Stockport
Cheshire
SK7 4PL
Telephone   Manchester [061] 456 5050/5112
Auctions   Saleroom
Regular ads   Coin monthly

Cornwall

W H LANE & SON
65 Morrab Road
Penzance
Cornwall
TR18 2QT
Telephone   Penzance [0736] 61447
Fax   [0736] 50097
Auctions   Saleroom

W H LANE & SON
Trafalgar House
Malpas Road
Truro
Cornwall
TR1 1QH
Telephone   Truro [0872] 223379
Auctions   Saleroom

DAVID LAY ASVA
The Penzance Auction House
Alverton
Penzance
Cornwall
TR18 4RE
Telephone   Penzance [0736] 61414
Fax   [0736] 60035
Auctions   Saleroom

PHILLIPS CORNWALL
Cornubia Hall
Par
Cornwall
PL24 2AQ
Telephone   Par [072681] 4047
Fax   [072681] 7979
Auctions   Saleroom

AUCTIONEER DIRECTORY

Devon

MICHAEL NEWMAN IN ASSOCIATION WITH BONHAMS (WEST COUNTRY)
	Kinterbury House
	St Andrews Cross
	Plymouth
	Devon
	PL1 2DQ
Telephone	Plymouth [0752] 669298
Fax	[0752] 226124
Auctions	Saleroom

East Sussex

GRAVES, SON & PILCHER FINE ARTS
	71 Church Road
	Hove
	East Sussex
	BN3 2GL
Telephone	Brighton [0273] 735266
Fax	[0273] 723813
Auctions	Saleroom

WALLIS & WALLIS
	West Street
	Auction Galleries
	Lewes
	East Sussex
Telephone	Lewes [0273] 480208
Fax	[0273] 476562
Telex	896691 TLX 1RG
Auctions	Postal & Saleroom

Greater London

CHRISTIE, MANSON & WOOD LTD
	8 King Street
	St James's
	London
	SW1Y 6QT
Telephone	071-839 9060
Telex	London 916429
Auctions	Saleroom

GLENDINING & COMPANY
	101 New Bond Street
	London
	WIY 9LG
Telephone	071-493 2445
Fax	071-491 9181
Auctions	Postal and Saleroom
Regular ads	Coin Monthly

PHILLIPS
	101 New Bond Street
	London
	WIY 9LG
Telephone	071-629 1877
Fax	071-409 3466
Telex	29 8855 Blen G
Auctions	Saleroom
Regular ads	Coin Monthly

SOTHEBY'S
	34-35 New Bond Street
	London
	WIY 2AA
Telephone	071-408 5312/3/4
Fax	071-493 6863
Telex	London 24454 SPBLON G
Auctions	Saleroom
Regular ads	Coin Monthly

SPINK & SON LTD
	5-7 King Street
	St James's
	London
	SW1Y 6QS
Telephone	071-930 7888
Fax	071-839 4853
Telex	916711
Auctions	Saleroom
Regular ads	Coin Monthly

Hertfordshire

CROSS AUCTIONS
	34 Lea Road
	Harpenden
	Hertfordshire
	AL5 4PG
Telephone	Harpenden [0582] 715781
Auctions	Saleroom

Lancashire

KLEEFORD COIN AUCTIONS
	27 Egerton Road
	Blackpool
	Lancashire
	FY1 2NP
Telephone	Blackpool [0253] 293698
Auctions	Postal & Saleroom
Regular ads	Coin Monthly

Leicestershire

WARNER AUCTION ROOMS

16-18 Halford Street
Leicester
Leicestershire
LE1 1JB

Telephone	Leicester [0533] 519777
Fax	[0533] 510078
Auctions	Saleroom

Merseyside

NORTH WESTERN PHILATELIC AUCTIONS (1990) LTD

1st Floor
North West House
Grange Road
West Kirby
Wirral
Merseyside
Liverpool
L48 4EW

Telephone	Liverpool [051] 625 5589
Fax	[051] 625 2032
Auctions	Saleroom
Regular ads	Coin Monthly

OUTHWAITE & LITHERLAND

Kingsway Galleries
Fontenoy Street
Liverpool
Merseyside
L3 2BE

Telephone	Liverpool [051] 236 6561
Auctions	Saleroom

Norfolk

JAMES NORWICH AUCTIONS LTD

33 Timberhill
Norwich
Norfolk
NR1 3LA

Telephone	Norwich [0603] 624817
Fax	[0603] 663750
Auction	Postal & Saleroom
Regular ads	Coin Monthly

Northamptonshire

WENTWORTH COINS

140 Higham Road
Rushden
Northamptonshire
NN10 9DT

Telephone	Rushden [0933] 55063
Auctions	Postal

Nottinghamshire

COINS OF BEESTON

PO Box 19
Beeston
Nottinghamshire
NG9 2NE

Auctions	Postal
Regular ads	Coin Monthly

HENRY SPENCER & SONS

20 The Square
Retford
Nottinghamshire
DN22 6BX

Telephone	Retford [0777] 708633
Fax	[0777] 709299
Auctions	Saleroom

NEALES

192-194 Mansfield Road
Nottingham
Nottinghamshire
NG1 3HU

Telephone	Nottingham [0602] 624141
Fax	[0602] 607456
Auctions	Saleroom

Oxfordshire

R & W COIN AUCTIONS

307 Bretch Hill
Banbury
Oxfordshire
OX16 0JD

Telephone	Banbury [0295] 275128
Auctions	Saleroom

Somerset

LAWRENCE FINE ART AUCTIONEERS

South Street
Crewkerne
Somerset
TA18 8AB

Telephone	Crewkerne [0460] 73041
Hours	Mon Wed Thu 09.00-17.30
	Tue 09.00-19.00
	Fri 09.00-17.00
Closed	Sat Sun

Suffolk

DIAMOND MILLS & CO

117 Hamilton Road
Felixstowe
Suffolk
IP11 7BL

JAMES IN IPSWICH LTD

47 St Nicholas Street
Ipswich
Suffolk

Telephone	Ipswich [0473] 231095
Hours	09.00-17.00
Closed	Wed

Surrey

CROYDON COIN AUCTIONS

272 Melfort Road
Thornton Heath
Surrey
CR7 7RR

Telephone	081-656 4583 & 081-684 6515
	Bristol [0272] 520505
Fax	081-656 4583
Auctions	Postal and Saleroom
Regular ads	Coin Monthly

Tyne and Wear

B FRANK & SON

3 South Avenue
Ryton
Tyne & Wear
NE40 3LD

Telephone	Tyneside [091] 413 8749
Auctions	Postal and Saleroom

South Yorkshire

SHEFFIELD COIN AUCTIONS

c/o 7 Beacon Close
Sheffield
Yorkshire
S9 1AA .

Telephone	Sheffield [0742] 433500
Auctions	Postal and Saleroom
Regular ads	Coin Monthly

West Midlands

CARISS RESIDENTIAL

20 High Street
Kings Heath
Birmingham
West Midlands
B14 7JU

Telephone	Birmingham [021] 444 0088

FELLOWS & SONS

Augusta House
19 Augusta Street
Hockley
Birmingham
West Midlands
B18 6JA

Telephone	Birmingham [021] 212 2131
Fax	[021] 212 1249
Auctions	Saleroom

West Sussex

SOTHEBY'S

Summers Place
Billingshurst
Sussex
RH14 9AD

Telephone	Billingshurst [0403] 783933
Fax	[0403] 785153
Telex	87210 GAVEL
Auctions	Saleroom

SUSSEX AUCTION GALLERIES

59 Perrymount Road
Haywards Heath
West Sussex
RH16 3DS

Telephone	Haywards Heath [0444] 414935
Fax	[0444] 450402
Auctions	Saleroom

West Yorkshire

PHILLIPS AT HEPPER HOUSE

17a East Parade
Leeds
West Yorkshire
L51 2BU

Telephone	Leeds [0532] 448011
Fax	[0532] 429875

Wiltshire

T GILLINGHAM

42 Highbury Park
Warminster
Wiltshire
BA12 9JF

Telephone	Warminster [0985] 216486
Auctions	Saleroom
Regular ads	Coin Monthly

Scotland

Glasgow

CHRISTIE'S SCOTLAND LTD

164-166 Bath Street
Glasgow
Scotland
G2 4TG

Telephone	Glasgow [041] 332 8134
Fax	[041] 332 5759
Auctions	Saleroom

Ayrshire

HOODS POSTAL COIN AUCTIONS

23 High Street
Kilbirnie
Ayrshire
Scotland
KA25 7EX

Telephone	Kilbirnie [0505] 682157
Auctions	Postal

Orkney Isles

VIKING COIN AUCTIONS

Fairlands
Market Green
Dounby
Orkney Isles
KW17 2HU

Telephone	Kirkwall [0856] 77376
Auctions	Postal
Regular ads	Coin monthly

Foreign

NUMISMATICA ARS CLASSICA AG

Niederdorfstrasse 43
CH – 8001 Zürich

Telephone	[010 41 1] 261 1703
Fax	01 261 5324
Auctions	Saleroom

Club Directory

Secretaries whose clubs are not in this Directory but who wish them to be included in *Coin 1993 Year Book* should write to the Editor, Sovereign House, Brentwood, Essex CM14 4SE. There is no charge

England

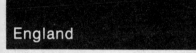

Avon

BATH & BRISTOL NUMISMATIC SOCIETY

Founded	1950
Membership	27
Subscription	£1.00 Junior
	£1.00 Student
	£4.00 Adult
	£4.00 OAP
	£6.00 Husband & wife
Meetings	Manvers Street Baptist Church
	Bath
	and
	Kingswood Community Association
	Kingswood
	Bristol
Frequency	Second and fourth Thursday
	of each month
Time	19.30
Secretary	A J Derrick
	c/o 75 North Street
	Bedminster
	Bristol
	Avon
	BS3 1ES
Telephone	Bristol [0272] 663718

Bedfordshire

BEDFORD NUMISMATIC SOCIETY

Founded	1966
Membership	20
Enrolment fee	Nil
Subscription	£3.00 Junior
	£3.00 Student
	£6.00 Adult
	£3.00 OAP
Meetings	RAF Association Club
	93 Ashburnham Road
	Bedford
	Bedfordshire
	MK40 1EA
Frequency	Third Monday of each month
Time	19.30
Secretary	N K Lutt
	47 Bower Street
	Bedford
	Bedfordshire
	MK40 3RD
Telephone	Bedford [0234] 228833 office
	358369 home

Berkshire

NEWBURY COIN & MEDAL CLUB

Founded	1971
Membership	15
Meetings	Various
Frequency	Monthly
Time	20.00
Secretary	J W Child
	97 Enborne Road
	Newbury
	Berkshire
	RG14 6AR
Telephone	Newbury [0635] 41233

READING COIN CLUB

Founded	1964
Membership	40
Subscription	£3.50 Junior
	£7.00 Adult
	£7.00 OAP
Meetings	The Abboy Gateway
	The Forbury
	Reading
	Berkshire

Frequency	Monthly
Time	19.30
Secretary	Brian Pewhirst
	4 Abbotts Road
	Newbury
	Berkshire
	RG14 7QW
Telephone	Newbury [0635] 44502

Buckinghamshire

BUCKINGHAMSHIRE NUMISMATIC SOCIETY

Founded	1961
Membership	12
Enrolment fee	Nil
Subscription	£2.00 Annual Junior
	– Student
	£4.00 Annual Adult
	– OAP
	30p meeting fee Adult
Meetings	Church of the Good Shepherd
	Churchill Avenue
	Aylesbury
	Buckinghamshire
Frequency	First Tuesday of each month except January, February, July & August
Time	19.30
Secretary	J A Wilson
	21 Finmere Crescent
	Aylesbury
	Buckinghamshire
	HP21 9DQ
Telephone	Aylesbury [0296] 22783

Cambridgeshire

CAMBRIDGESHIRE NUMISMATIC SOCIETY

Founded	1946
Membership	45
Subscription	£1.50 Junior
	£5.00 Adult
Meetings	Friends' Meeting House
	12 Jesus Lane
	Cambridge
	Cambridgeshire
	CB5 8BA
Frequency	Third Monday of each month September-June
Time	19.30
Secretary	P W Lawrence
	24 Lambourne Road
	Hardwick
	Cambridgeshire
	CB3 7XB
Telephone	Madingley [0954] 210968

PETERBOROUGH COIN & MEDAL CLUB

Founded	1967
Membership	15
Subscription	£1.00 Annual Junior
	£0.10 Meeting fee Junior
	£2.00 Annual Adult
	£0.20 Meeting fee Adult
Meetings	The Club Room
	APV-Baker Sports and Social Club
	Alma Road
	Peterborough
	Cambridgeshire
Frequency	Last Tuesday of each month except July and August
Time	19.30
Secretary	Rex Heaford
	105 Welland Road
	Peterborough
	Cambridgeshire
	PE1 3SJ

Cheshire

CREWE & DISTRICT COIN & MEDAL SOCIETY

Founded	1968
Membership	30
Subscription	£0.50 Junior (under 16)
	£3.00 Adult
	£4.50 Husband & wife
Meetings	Memorial Hall
	Church Lane
	Wistaston
	Crewe
	Cheshire
Frequency	Second Tuesday of each month excluding January and July
Time	19.30
Telephone	Crewe [0270] 69836

Co Durham

DARLINGTON & DISTRICT NUMISMATIC SOCIETY

Founded	1968
Membership	20
Subscription	£1.50 Junior
	£3.00 Adult
Meetings	Darlington Arts Centre
	Vane Terrace
	Darlington
	Durham

Frequency	Third Wednesday of each month
Time	19.30
Secretary	D Wilkin
	46 Pennine View
	Romanby
	Northallerton
	North Yorkshire
Telephone	Northallerton [0609] 772976

Cornwall

CORNWALL COLLECTORS' CLUB

Founded	1990
Membership	30
Enrolment fee	£3.00
Meetings	The Swan Inn
	40 Bosvigo Road
	Truro
	Cornwall
Frequency	First Wednesday of each month
Time	20.00
Secretary	Simon Goudge
	68 Daniell Road
	Truro
	Cornwall
	TR1 2DB
Telephone	Truro [0872] 73376

Derbyshire

DERBYSHIRE NUMISMATIC SOCIETY

Founded	1964
Membership	41
Subscription	£0.80 Junior
	£0.80 Student
	£2.00 Adult
	£0.80 OAP
Meetings	The Friends' Meeting House
	St Helens Street
	Derby
	Derbyshire
Frequency	Third Monday of each month
	except August
Time	19.45
Secretary	E W Danson
	63 Ferrers Way
	Darley Abbey
	Derby
	DE3 2DB
Telephone	Derby [0332] 552928

Devon

DEVON & EXETER NUMISMATIC SOCIETY

Founded	1965
Membership	22
Subscription	£1.00 Junior
	£6.00 Adult
Meetings	Exeter Community Centre
	17 St Davids Hill
	Exeter
	Devon
Frequency	First Wednesday of each month
Time	19.30
Secretary	T H Pullman FRGS
	15 Fox Road
	Whipton
	Exeter
	Devon
	EX4 8NB
Telephone	Exeter [0392] 67799

PLYMOUTH COIN & MEDAL CLUB

Founded	1970
Membership	18
Subscription	£0.50 Junior
	£0.50 Student
	£1.00 Adult
	£1.00 OAP
	(per meeting)
Meetings	R A F A Club
	5 Ermington Terrace
	Mutley
	Plymouth
	Devon
Frequency	Fourth Wednseday of each month
	except December
Time	19.30
Secretary	M J Westcott
	18 Goad Avenue
	Torpoint
	Cornwall
	PL11 2ND
Telephone	Plymouth [0752] 814971

TORBAY & DISTRICT COIN CLUB

Founded	1967
Membership	10
Subscription	£1.50
Meetings	British Rail Social Club
	Brunel Road
	Newton Abbot
	Devon
	TQ12 4PB
Frequency	First Tuesday of each month
Time	19.45
Secretary	J W Nicholson
	28 Seymour Drive
	Torquay
	Devon
	TQ2 8PY
Telephone	Torquay [0803] 326497

Dorset

WESSEX NUMISMATIC SOCIETY

Founded	1948
Membership	30+
Subscription	£1.00 Junior (under 18)
	£5.00 Adult
Meetings	Hotel Bristowe
	Grange Road
	Southbourne
	Bournemouth
	Dorset
Frequency	Second Thursday of each month
	except August
Time	19.45
Secretary	Mrs F R Lockyer
	24 Stourwood Road
	Southbourne
	Bournemouth
	BH6 3QP

East Sussex

BRIGHTON & HOVE COIN CLUB

Founded	1971
Membership	30
Subscription	£2.00 Junior
	£5.00 Adult
Meetings	Methodist Church Hall
	St Patrick's Road
	Hove
	East Sussex
Frequency	Last Wednesday of each month
	except December
Time	20.00
Secretary	L R Keen
	74 Hangleton Road
	Hove
	East Sussex
Telephone	Brighton [0273] 419303

RYE COIN CLUB

Founded	1955
Membership	12
Subscription	£0.50 Junior
	£0.50 Student
	£3.00 Adult
	£1.00 OAP
Meetings	Rye Further Education Centre
	Lion Street
	Rye
	East Sussex
Frequency	Second Thursday in Oct Nov Dec
	Feb Mar Apr May
Time	19.30

Secretary	C Banks
	9 Conqueror Road
	St Leonards-on-Sea
	East Sussex
	TN38 8DD
Telephone	Hastings [0424] 422974

Essex

ESSEX NUMISMATIC SOCIETY

Founded	1966
Membership	40
Subscription	£0.25 Junior
	Free Student
	£5.00 Adult
Meetings	Chelmsford & Essex Museum
	Moulsham Street
	Chelmsford
	Essex
Frequency	Fourth Friday of each month
	except December
Time	20.00
Secretary	Ivan R Buck
	2 Chestnut Grove
	Braintree
	Essex
	CM7 7LU
Telephone	Braintree [0376] 21846

HAVERING NUMISMATIC SOCIETY

Founded	1967
Membership	96
Entry fee	£1.50 Member
	£2.00 Dealer
Subscription	Free Junior
	Free Student
	£1.50 Adult
	Free OAP
	Free Overseas
	£10.00 Life Member
Meetings	Fairkytes Arts Centre
	Billet Lane
	Hornchurch
	Essex
Frequency	First and third Tuesday
	of each month
Time	19.30
Secretary	F J Bonner
	80 Painesbrook Way
	Harold Hill
	Romford
	Essex
	RM3 9LS
Telephone	Ingrebourne [04023] 45730

REDBRIDGE NUMISMATIC SOCIETY

Founded 1968
Membership 20
Enrolment fee Nil
Subscription Nil Junior
£5.00 Student
£5.00 Adult
£5.00 OAP
Meetings Gants Hill Library
Cranbrook Road
Ilford
Essex
Frequency Fourth Wednesday of each month
Time 19.30
Secretary Mrs Pam Williams
23 Airlie Gardens
Ilford
Essex
IG1 4LB
Telephone 081-554 5486

ROCHFORD HUNDRED NUMISMATIC SOCIETY

Membership 22
Enrolment fee Nil
Subscription £3.00 Junior
£3.00 Student
£6.00 Adult
£5.00 OAP
Meetings Civic Suite
Rayleigh Town Hall
Rayleigh
Essex
Frequency Second Thursday of each month
Time 20.00
Secretary J Bispham
103 Ferry Road
Hullbridge
Essex
SS5 6EL
Telephone Southend-on-Sea [0702] 230950

THURROCK NUMISMATIC SOCIETY

Founded 1970
Membership 25
Enrolment fee £4.00 per year
Subscription Free
Meetings Stanley Lazell Hall
Dell Road
Grays
Essex
Frequency Third Wednesday of each month
Time 19.00
Secretary A Chant
77 Hampden Road
Grays
Essex
RM17 5JP

Gloucestershire

CHELTENHAM NUMISMATIC SOCIETY

Secretary B M Greenaway
'Lordswood'
The Butts
Lydiard Millicent
Swindon
Wiltshire
SN5 9LR

Greater London

BRITISH NUMISMATIC SOCIETY

Founded 1903
Membership 525
Enrolment fee £1.00 (Juniors excepted)
Subscription £7.50 Junior
£18.00 Adult
Meetings Warburg Institute
Woburn Square
London
WC1H 0AB
Frequency Monthly except July,
August and December
Time 18.00
Secretary G P Dyer
c/o Royal Mint
Llantrisant
Pontyclun
Mid-Glamorgan
Wales
CF7 8YT
Telephone Llantrisant [0443] 222111

COIN CORRESPONDENCE CLUB

Founded 1988
Membership 27
Enrolment fee Nil
Subscription Free
Meetings Postal
Secretary A H Chubb
49 White Hart Lane
Barnes
London
SW13 0PP
Telephone 081-878 0472

ENFIELD & DISTRICT NUMISMATIC SOCIETY

Founded 1969
Membership 10
Subscription £1.00 Junior
£2.00 Student
£5.00 Adult
£2.00 OAP

Meetings	Millfield House Arts Centre
	Silver Street
	Edmonton
	London
	N18 1PJ
Frequency	Third Monday of each month
Time	20.00
Secretary	G Buddle
	4 Hermiston Court
	Hermiston Avenue
	Hornsey
	London
	N8
Telephone	081-340 0767

INTERNATIONAL BANK NOTE SOCIETY

Founded	1961
Membership	1600
Enrolment fee	Nil
Subscription	£5.00 Junior (11-17)
	£10.00 Adult
	£12.00 Family
Meetings	Victory Services Club
	63-79 Seymour Street
	London
	W1
Frequency	Last Thursday of each month
	except December
Time	18.00
Secretary	S K Gupta
	11 Middle Row
	North Kensington
	London
	W10 5AT
Telephone	081-969 9493

LONDON NUMISMATIC CLUB

Founded	1947
Membership	103
Subscription	£3.00 Junior
	£10.00 Adult
Meetings	Institute of Archaeology
	31-34 Gordon Square
	London
	WC1H 0PY
Frequency	Monthly
Time	18.30
Secretary	Nash Patel
	British Gas plc
	C & I Department
	326 High Holborn
	London
	WC1V 7PT
Telephone	071-242 0789 ext 3672

ORDERS & MEDALS RESEARCH SOCIETY

Founded	1942
Membership	2,700
Subscription	£6.00
Meetings	National Army Museum
	Royal Hospital Road
	Chelsea
	London
Frequency	Monthly
Time	14.30

Secretary	N G Gooding
	123 Turnpike Link
	Croydon
	CR0 5NU
Telephone	081-680 2701

ROYAL NUMISMATIC SOCIETY

Founded	1836
Membership	1000
Enrolment fee	£5.00
Subscription	£18.00
Meetings	Society of Antiquaries
	Piccadilly
	London
	W1
Frequency	Monthly October-June
Time	17.30
Secretary	J G Cribb
	c/o Dept of Coins and Medals
	British Museum
	London
	WC1B 3DG
Telephone	071-323 8585

Hampshire

ROMSEY NUMISMATIC SOCIETY

Founded	1969
Membership	12
Enrolment fee	Nil
Subscription	£8.50 Adult
	£8.50 OAP
Meetings	Romsey W M Conservative Club
	Market Place
	Romsey
	Hampshire
	SO5 8NA
Frequency	Fourth Friday of each month
	except December
Time	19.30
Secretary	Dr G T Dunger
	65 Hocombe Road
	Chandlers Ford
	Hampshire
	SO5 1QA
Telephone	Chandlers Ford [0703] 253921

Hertfordshire

ST ALBANS & HERTFORDSHIRE NUMISMATIC SOCIETY

Founded	1948
Membership	25
Subscription	Free Junior
	£10.00 Adult
	£10.00 OAP

Meetings	St Michael's Parish Church

Meetings | St Michael's Parish Church
St Michael's Village
St Albans
Hertfordshire
AL3 4SL
Frequency | Second Tuesday of each month except August
Time | 19.30
Secretary | G Sommerville CEng MIMechE
19 The Lawns
St Albans
Hertfordshire
AL3 4TB
Telephone | St Albans [0727] 862060

Humberside

HULL & DISTRICT NUMISMATIC SOCIETY
Founded | 1967
Membership | 18
Enrolment fee Nil
Subscription | £1.00 Junior
£3.00 Adult
Meetings | Hull Central Library
Albion Street
Hull
HU1 3TF
Frequency | Monthly except August and December
Time | 19.30
Secretary | G M Percival
86a Victoria Avenue
Hull
HU5 3DS
Telephone | Hull [0482] 441933

Kent

BEXLEY COIN CLUB
Founded | 1968
Membership | 18
Enrolment fee Nil
Subscription | £2.50 Junior
£2.50 Student
£10.00 Adult
£5.00 OAP
£2.50 to £5.00 Hardship/Unemployed
Meetings | St Martin's Church Hall
Erith Road
Barnehurst
Bexleyheath
Kent
Frequency | First Tuesday of each month except January and August
Time | 20.00

Secretary | A J Gilbert
76 Merlin Road
Welling
Kent
DA16 2JR

DARTFORD AREA RELIC RECOVERY CLUB
Founded | 1974
Membership | 12
Enrolment fee Nil
Subscription | £1.00 per meeting Junior
£1.00 per meeting Student
£1.00 per meeting Adult
£1.00 per meeting OAP
Meetings | Stage Door Public House
Hythe Street
Dartford 1
Kent
Frequency | Fourth Tuesday of each month
Time | 20.00
Secretary | D Parslow
49 Holmdale Road
Chislehurst
Kent
BR7 6BY

KENT & MEDWAY TOWNS NUMISMATIC SOCIETY
Founded | 1903
Membership | 30
Subscription | £5.00 Adult
Meetings | Adult Education Centre
9 Sittingbourne Road
Maidstone
and
King's School
Preparatory School
King Edward Road
Rochester
Frequency | First Friday alternate months
Time | 19.30
Secretary | Richard H Hardy
Copse End
Chart Road
Chart Sutton
Maidstone
Kent
NE17 3RB
Telephone | Maidstone [0622] 843881

TOKEN CORRESPONDING SOCIETY
Founded | 1971
Membership | 151
Subscription | UK £6.00 per 4 issues
Overseas £10.00 per 4 issues
Editor | Anthony Gilbert
76 Merlin Road
Welling
Kent
DA16 2JR

Lancashire

THE LANCASHIRE & CHESHIRE NUMISMATIC SOCIETY

Founded — 1864
Membership — 20
Enrolment fee — Nil
Subscription — £2.50 Junior
£5.00 Adult
Meetings — Manchester Central Library
St Peter's Square
Manchester
M2 5PD
Frequency — Monthly, September-June
Time — 18.30 Wednesday, 14.30 Saturday
Secretary — Michael Robinson
Telephone — Manchester [061] 973 2590

MORECAMBE & LANCASTER NUMISMATIC SOCIETY

Subscription — Free Junior
Free Student
£2.00 Adult
£2.00 OAP
Time — 19.30
Secretary — K F Brook
55 Yorkshire Street
Morecambe
Lancashire
LA3 1DF
Telephone — Morecambe [0524] 411036

PRESTON & DISTRICT NUMISMATIC SOCIETY

Founded — 1965
Membership — 33
Enrolment fee — Nil
Subscription — £3.00
Meetings — Eldon Hotel
Eldon Street
Preston
Lancashire
Frequency — First and third Tuesday
of each month
Time — 20.00
Secretary — William G Kay
1 Reigate
Great Knowley
Chorley
Lancashire
PR6 8UJ
Telephone — Chorley [02572] 66869

ORMSKIRK & WEST LANCASHIRE NUMISMATIC SOCIETY

Founded — 1970
Membership — 16
Enrolment fee — Nil
Subscription — £2.00 Annual Adult
Meetings — Greyhound Inn
Aughton Street
Ormskirk
Lancashire
Frequency — First Thursday of each month
Time — 20.15
Secretary — N Mercer
c/o 25 Hoghton Street
Southport
Lancashire
Telephone — Southport [0704] 531266

SOUTH MANCHESTER NUMISMATIC SOCIETY

Founded — 1967
Membership — 35
Enrolment fee — Nil
Subscription — £5.00 Junior
£5.00 Student
£5.00 Disabled
£10.00 Adult
£5.00 OAP
Meetings — Cheadle (Kingsway) Cricket Club
Manchester
Lancashire
Frequency — Fortnightly
Time — 20.00
Secretary — R Pearson
20 Riverton Road
East Didsbury
Manchester
Lancashire
M20 0QJ
Telephone — Manchester [061] 445 2042

Leicestershire

LOUGHBOROUGH COIN & SEARCH SOCIETY

Founded — 1964
Membership — 65
Subscription — £4.00 Junior
£4.00 Student
£5.00 Adult
£4.00 OAP
£6.50 Family
Meetings — Central Public Library
Granby Street
Loughborough
Leicestershire
Frequency — First Thursday of each month
Time — 19.30
Secretary — G C Fowler
155 Parklands Drive
Loughborough
Leicestershire
LE11 2TA
Telephone — Loughborough [0509] 261352

Lincolnshire

HORNCASTLE & DISTRICT COIN CLUB

Founded | 1963
Membership | 19
Enrolment fee | Nil
Subscription | £3.50
Meetings | Bull Hotel
 | Bull Ring
 | Horncastle
 | Lincolnshire
Frequency | Monthly except August
 | Second Thursday of each month
Time | 19.30
Secretary | F W Mason
 | 134 Wainfleet Road
 | Skegness
 | Lincolnshire
 | PE25 2EJ
Telephone | Skegness [0754] 2706

Merseyside

MERSEYSIDE NUMISMATIC SOCIETY

Founded | 1947
Membership | 18
Enrolment fee | Nil
Subscription | £0.50 Junior
 | £5.00 Adult
Meetings | The Lecture Theatre
 | Liverpool Museum
 | William Brown Street
 | Liverpool
 | Merseyside
 | L3 8EN
Frequency | Monthly excluding July & August
Time | 19.00
Secretary | W H R Cook
 | c/o The Liverpool Museum
 | William Brown Street
 | Liverpool
 | Merseyside
 | L3 8EN
Telephone | Liverpool [051] 929 2143

Middlesex

HARROW & NORTH WEST MIDDLESEX NUMISMATIC SOCIETY

Founded | 1968
Membership | 50

Subscription | £1.00 Junior
 | £5.00 Adult
Meetings | YWCA
 | 51 Sheepcote Road
 | Harrow
 | Middlesex
Frequency | Second Thursday and fourth
 | Tuesday
 | of each month
Time | 20.00
Secretary | J H Hume
 | 107 Halsbury Road East
 | Northolt
 | Middlesex
 | UB5 4PY
Telephone | 081-864 1731

HAYES (MIDDLESEX) & DISTRICT COIN CLUB

Meetings | The United Reformed Church Hall
 | Swakeleys Road
 | Ickenham
 | Middlesex
Frequency | Third Thursday of the month
Time | 19.45
Secretary | C D Haselden
Telephone | 081-422 9178

Norfolk

NORFOLK NUMISMATIC SOCIETY

Founded | 1967
Membership | 50+
Subscription | £2.00 Junior
 | £2.00 Student
 | £5.00 Adult
 | £5.00 OAP
Meetings | Assembly House
 | Theatre Street
 | Norwich
 | Norfolk
Frequency | Third Monday of each month
Time | 19.30
Secretary | C Wastell
 | 90 Oxford Road
 | Lowestoft
 | Suffolk
 | NR32 1TP
Telephone | Lowestoft [0502] 582767

Northamptonshire

NORTHAMPTON NUMISMATIC SOCIETY

Founded | 1969
Membership | 18

Subscription	£2.50 Junior
	£2.50 Student
	£4.00 Adult
	£4.00 OAP
	£5.00 Family
Meetings	Old Scouts RFC
	Rushmere Road
	Northampton
	Northamptonshire
Frequency	Third Monday of each month
Time	20.00
Secretary	P D S Waddell
	69 Marlow Road
	Towcester
	Northamptonshire
	NN12 7AR

Nottinghamshire

NUMISMATIC SOCIETY OF NOTTINGHAMSHIRE

Founded	1948
Membership	40
Enrolment fee	£2.50
Subscription	£1.25 Junior
	£2.50 Adult
Meetings	The Meeting Room
	County Library
	Angel Row
	Nottingham
	NG1 6HP
Frequency	Second Tuesday of each month
	September to April inclusive
Time	19.30
Secretary	Grenville Chamberlain
	Numismatic Society of
	Nottinghamshire
	c/o County Library
	Angel Row
	Nottingham
	NG1 6HP
Telephone	Nottingham [0602] 257674/259850

Oxfordshire

BANBURY & DISTRICT NUMISMATIC SOCIETY

Founded	1967
Membership	15
Subscription	£0.50 Junior
	£1.50 Adult
Meetings	Horse & Jockey Public House
	West Bar
	Banbury
	Oxfordshire
Frequency	Second Monday of each month
	except July and August
Time	19.45
Treasurer	W Slack
Telephone	Banbury [0295] 254451

South Humberside

LINCOLNSHIRE NUMISMATIC SOCIETY

Founded	1932
Membership	15
Subscription	Free Junior
	Free Student
	£3.00 Adult
	£3.00 OAP
Meetings	Grimsby Bridge Club
	Bargate
	Grimsby
	South Humberside
Frequency	Fourth Wednesday of each month
	except August
Time	19.30
Secretary	D Goodey
	13 Hunsley Crescent
	Grimsby
	South Humberside
	DN32 8PU

South Yorkshire

ROTHERHAM & DISTRICT COIN CLUB

Founded	1982
Membership	7
Subscription	£3.00 Adult
Meetings	Rotherham Art Centre
	Rotherham
	South Yorkshire
Frequency	First Wednesday of each month
Time	19.00
Secretary	R A Goodwin
	4 Thryberch Hall Road
	Rotherham
	South Yorkshire
	S62 5JU
Telephone	Rotherham [0709] 528179

SHEFFIELD NUMISMATIC SOCIETY

Membership	20
Subscription	Nil
Meetings	Under review
Secretary	Alan J Miller
	22 Spooner Road
	Broomhill
	Sheffield
	S10 5BN

Suffolk

IPSWICH NUMISMATIC SOCIETY
Founded | 1966
Subscription | £2.00 Junior
| £2.00 Student
| £4.00 Adult
| £2.00 OAP
Meetings | Ipswich Citizens Advice Bureau
| Tower Street
| Ipswich
| Suffolk
Frequency | Third Wednesday of each month
Time | 19.30
Secretary | S E Sewell
| 103 Penzance Road
| Kesgrave
| Ipswich
| Suffolk
| IP5 7LE
Telephone | Ipswich [0473] 623856

Surrey

KINGSTON NUMISMATIC SOCIETY
Founded | 1966
Membership | 42
Subscription | £1.50 Junior
| £1.50 Student
| £5.00 Adult
| £7.00 Husband & wife
Meetings | King Athelstan's School
| Villiers Road
| Kingston-upon-Thames
| Surrey
Frequency | Third Thursday of each month
| except January
Time | 19.30
Secretary | R N Clarkson
| FGA, D DIP, RJ DIP, FRNS
| 62 Cheshire Gardens
| Chessington
| Surrey
| KT9 2PG
Telephone | 081-397 6944

Tyne and Wear

TYNESIDE HISTORICAL & NUMISMATIC SOCIETY
Founded | 1954
Membership | 27

Subscription | £1.00 Junior
| £1.00 Student
| £2.50 Adult
| £2.50 OAP
Meetings | Magnet Club
| High Street
| Gateshead
| Tyne & Wear
Frequency | Second Tuesday of each month
Time | 19.30
Secretary | S M Spence
| 14 Edward Avenue
| Horden
| Peterlee
| Durham
| SR8 4RQ
Telephone | Tyneside [091] 586 5449

Warwickshire

NUNEATON & DISTRICT COIN CLUB
Founded 1968
Membership | 23
Subscription | £0.50 Junior
| £0.50 Student
| £1.00 Adult
| £0.50 OAP
Meetings | United Reformed Church Room
| Coton Road
| Opp Council House
| Nuneaton
| Warwickshire
Frequency | Second Tuesday of each month
Time | 19.30
Secretary | A Fergusson
| 42 Seymour Road
| Nuneaton
| Warwickshire
| CV11 4JD
Telephone | Nuneaton [0203] 371556

West Midlands

BIRMINGHAM NUMISMATIC SOCIETY
Founded | 1964
Membership | 25
Subscription | £2.00 Junior
| £2.00 Student
| £6.00 Adult
| £1.00 OAP
Meetings | Birmingham Midland Institute
| Margaret Street
| Birmingham
| West Midlands
| B3

Frequency	Second Tuesday of each month
Time	19.30
Secretary	Phil Leighton
	17 Roughley Drive
	Four Oaks
	Sutton Coldfield
	West Midlands
	B75 6PW
Telephone	Four Oaks [021] 308 1616

BRITISH CHEQUE COLLECTORS' SOCIETY

Founded	1980
Membership	80
Subscription	£5.00
Meetings	Midlands, North and
	AGM in London
Secretary	John Purser
	71 Mile Lane
	Cheylesmore
	Coventry
	West Midlands
	CV3 5GB

West Sussex

CRAWLEY COIN CLUB

Founded	1969
Membership	30
Subscription	£2.00 Junior
	£5.00 Adult
	£2.00 OAP
Meetings	Furnace Green Community Centre
	Ashburnham Road
	Furnace Green
	Crawley
	West Sussex
Frequency	First Tuesday of each month
Time	20.00
Secretary	M F Dixon
	78 St Marys Drive
	Pound Hill
	Crawley
	West Sussex
	RH10 3BH
Telephone	Crawley [0293] 548671

WORTHING & DISTRICT NUMISMATIC SOCIETY

Founded	1967
Membership	21
Enrolment fee	Nil
Subscription	£10.00 Adult
Meetings	Kingsway Hotel
	Marine Parade
	Worthing
	West Sussex
	BN11 3QQ
Frequency	Third Thursday of each month
Time	19.30

Secretary	Roger J Davies
	4 Marlborough Road
	Worthing
	West Sussex
	BN12 4EZ
Telephone	Worthing [0903] 41503

West Yorkshire

BRADFORD & DISTRICT NUMISMATIC SOCIETY

Founded	1967
Membership	25
Subscription	Free Junior
	Free Student
	£0.25 Adult
	Free OAP
Meetings	East Bowling Unity Club
	Leicester Street
	Bradford
	West Yorkshire
	BD4
Frequency	Third Monday in the month
Time	19.00
Secretary	A J Ferguson
	58 Spennithorne Avenue
	Leeds
	West Yorkshire
	LS16 6JA
Telephone	Leeds [0532] 677151

YORKSHIRE NUMISMATIC SOCIETY

Founded	1909
Membership	70 to 80
Subscription	£2.00 Junior
	£5.00 Adult
Meetings	Swarthmore Institute
	Woodhouse Square
	Leeds 1
	West Yorkshire
Frequency	Usually first Saturday of each month
Time	14.15
Secretary	Cyril Peel
	162 Acres Hall Avenue
	Pudsey
	West Yorkshire
	LS28 9EQ
Telephone	Pudsey [0532] 579834

HUDDERSFIELD NUMISMATIC SOCIETY

Founded	1947
Membership	25
Subscription	£0.20 Junior
	£3.00 Adult
	£3.00 OAP
Meetings	Tolson Memorial Museum
	Ravensknowle Park
	Huddersfield
	West Yorkshire
Frequency	First Monday of each month
	except July and August

CLUB DIRECTORY

Time	19.30
Secretary	A J Howarth
	141 Hightown Road
	Liversedge
	Yorkshire
	WF15 8DG
Telephone	Cleckheaton [0274] 876443

Scotland

Wiltshire

Glasgow

SWINDON & DISTRICT NUMISMATIC SOCIETY

Founded	1962
Membership	10
Meetings	Members' Houses
	Swindon area
	Wiltshire
Frequency	Second Monday of each month
	September to June
Time	20.00
Secretary	D E Garratt
	60 Malvern Road
	Swindon
	Wiltshire
Telephone	Swindon [0793] 526428

WILTSHIRE NUMISMATIC SOCIETY

Founded	1965
Membership	38
Subscription	£0.25 Junior
	£0.25 Student
	£2.50 Adult
	£2.50 OAP
Meetings	The Bell Inn
	Seend, near Devizes
	Wiltshire
Frequency	First Wednesday of each month
	March to December
Time	20.00
Secretary	B Weston
	220 Frome Road
	Trowbridge
	Wiltshire
	BA15 0DS
Telephone	Trowbridge [0225] 765586

A reminder to all Society and Club Secretaries and to Fair Organisers: Please send your latest programme of events to *Coin Monthly* for inclusion in Diary Notes

GLASGOW & WEST OF SCOTLAND NUMISMATIC SOCIETY

Founded	1947
Membership	55
Subscription	£2.00 Junior
	£2.00 Student
	£6.00 Adult
	£2.00 OAP
	£2.00 Non-resident
Meetings	29 Bute Gardens
	University of Glasgow
	Glasgow
	G12 8QQ
Frequency	Monthly October to May inclusive
	normally second Thursday of
	each month
Time	19.30
Secretary	Dr J P Goddard
	10 Essex Drive
	Glasgow
	G14 9NA
Telephone	Glasgow [041] 959 6247

Strathclyde

MID LANARK COIN CIRCLE

Founded	1969
Membership	22
Subscription	£0.50 Junior
	£2.00 Adult
	£0.75 OAP
Meetings	Hospitality Room
	The Civic Centre
	Motherwell
	Lanarkshire
Frequency	Fourth Thursday of each month
	September to April (not December)
Time	19.30
Secretary	J W Wright
	Flat 2/4
	Glassford Court
	83 Wilson Street
	Glasgow
	G1 1UZ
Telephone	Glasgow [041] 552 2083

Wales

South Glamorgan

SOUTH WALES & MONMOUTHSHIRE NUMISMATIC SOCIETY

Founded	1958
Membership	30
Subscription	£0.50 Junior
	£0.50 Student
	£1.00 Adult
	£0.50 OAP
Meetings	Lyceum Tavern
	Malpas Road
	Newport
	Gwent
Frequency	Second Wednesday of each month
Time	19.30
Secretary	A G Cox
	9 Maynard Court
	Fairwater Road
	Llandaff
	Cardiff
	South Glamorgan
	CF5 2LS
Telephone	Cardiff [0222] 561564

ROYAL MINT COIN CLUB

	PO Box 500
	Cardiff
	CF1 1HA
Telephone	Llantrisant [0443] 222111
Enrolment	Free
Subscription	Free